LOOSE SHOES

*To Jim —
You guys truly are incomparable
with my best wishes*
James M. Shacter

The Story of Ralph Sutton

*To Jim —
In Memory of
your Dad
Ralph Sutton*

LOOSE SHOES

The Story of Ralph Sutton
by James D. Shacter

The Updated and Expanded Edition of *Piano Man*

Jaynar Press
P.O. Box 14221
Chicago, Illinois 60614

Copyright © 1994 by James D. Shacter

All rights reserved

Jacket photograph copyright © by
Paul J. Hoeffler, Toronto

Frontispiece: Ralph Sutton at Cafe des Copains, Toronto, by Maxine Schacker, chalk pastel, 22" high x 28" wide, © 1988 (*Collection of Stephen Quinlan*)

Front endsheets design from the
collection of Ralph Sutton

Back endsheets design from the
collection of Pierre Terbois

Library of Congress Catalog Card Number 93-80452

ISBN 0-9639101-0-8

Printed in the United States of America

Acknowledgments

I am deeply grateful to many people for their assistance in the preparation of Ralph Sutton's biography. Some provided professional expertise in various aspects of book production. Others shared their thoughts about Ralph as his peers in the elite of traditional jazz, as members of his family, or as his friends. *Piano Man*, the first edition of the Sutton story, was published in 1975; and the second edition, with the new title of *Loose Shoes*, in 1994.

Sara Dreyfuss, the copy editor of *Loose Shoes*, improved the manuscript immensely with her fine changes. Bernard Arendt, who designed both books, created a jacket for *Loose Shoes* that combined Sutton's total dedication to his art with his lusty sense of humor. Sandra M. Dyrlund offered wise advice as consultant in the selection of photographs.

Excellent pictures were provided by such photographers as Lyn Alweis, Paul J. Hoeffler, Charles Peterson (through the courtesy of his son, Don), Duncan P. Schiedt, and A.P. White, Jr. Al White's cotton company has bought and sold countless bales of the fiber, but he undoubtedly has taken even a larger number of photos of jazz musicians.

Pat Hawes, an English jazz pianist, started a fruitful chain reaction when he sent me an engaging photo of Dick Wellstood, Dick Hyman, and Sutton that had appeared in *The Jazz Report*. Publisher Bill King gave me the phone number of Paul Hoeffler, who took the photo. Hoeffler not only contributed the jacket photo and several other pictures, but also told me about Maxine Schacker, an artist friend of his. Schacker had painted a number of jazz artists, and her colorful pastel of Ralph became the frontispiece of the book.

Neither edition of the Sutton biography could have been written without the help of all those who contributed their memories and impressions of Ralph. His wife, Sunnie, was an invaluable source of information.

She cheerfully tackled large or small tasks involving research, digging out old clips and photos, or doing anything else requested of her. When she talked about her feelings for Ralph, her eyes frequently filled with tears.

Barbara Sutton Curtis furnished especially valuable insight into her brother's character. Harold E. Curtis shared many thoughts as Ralph's brother-in-law. Ralph's three sons—Jeff, Pete, and Nick—revealed poignant feelings about him, first as young men and then as husbands and fathers 20 years later. Norman K. Muschany provided a tour of the area of St. Charles County, Missouri, where he and Ralph grew up together.

I would be remiss if I did not again express thanks to a number of former colleagues at *The World Book Encyclopedia* for their help with *Piano Man*: Bernard Arendt, Clare Atwood, John M. Babrick, Eleanor E. Ballwanz, Marilyn A. Boerding, Sara Dreyfuss, Joseph A. Erhardt, Ann Eriksen, Kathleen L. Florio, Philip B. Hall, Robert J. Hemsing, Lynn Iverson, Susan C. Kilburg, Henry Koval, Cecilia M. Kurtzweil, Edward C. Schulz, and Ronald A. Stachowiak. A special bow to Rex D. McNeese of Kingsport Press.

To my son, Joe, goes loving appreciation for suggestions that greatly improved the manuscript of *Loose Shoes*. I repeat the acknowledgment of his understanding for the cancellation of many of our Sunday evening gin rummy bouts years ago in favor of *Piano Man*.

Shortly after the publication of *Piano Man*, my wife, Ruth, embarked on a career as a human resources officer for a large Chicago corporation. Her job precluded any repetition of what must have seemed endless hours transcribing taped interviews and observations for the first edition. Thankfully, she had the wisdom to persuade me, with Joe's assistance, to master the intricacies of a word processor for *Loose Shoes*. Ruth offered encouragement and loving companionship throughout both Sutton Projects, as she has throughout our years together.

JDS

Undoubtedly the most important member of the rhythm section is the pianist.
-Duke Ellington

Contents

    Preface *1*
    Some Loose Thoughts About *Loose Shoes* *5*
1. A Spot on the Road *13*
2. Harlem Rhythm *19*
3. He Could Play a Hymn That Brought Tears to Your Eyes *25*
4. Everyone Knew Him Best as a Pianist *31*
5. What Ya Wanna Play, Gate? *38*
6. All I Wanted to Do Was Music *45*
7. It's Like a Priest Kneeling at the Altar *50*
8. You Sure Don't Play Like a White Boy *57*
9. A Musical Education *64*
10. Very Much a Pianist's Pianist *79*
11. I Love Humanity; It's the People I Can't Stand *86*
12. I'll Play It the Way *I* Play It *93*
13. A Bit of God on the Keyboard *101*
14. I'm a Whorehouse Piano Player *107*
15. She Saved My Life *118*
16. Ralph's Music Is Ralph *128*
17. It's Like a Locomotive Coming at You *137*
18. A Gentleness of Spirit *150*
19. He's Very Easy to Live With *159*
20. The True Giants Remain Neglected *166*

21. He Spoils Me for Everybody Else..*181*
22. The Trademark of a Truly Great Pianist *187*
23. 'Tain't Nobody's Bizness..*191*
24. My Marriage Comes First and Music Second *208*
25. You Have to Prove Yourself to Ralph..*214*
26. Words Cannot Express What Ralph Has Meant to Me......................*227*
27. It Was Inspiring to Play with Him *237*
28. A Better Trick Is Not to Be Had *250*
29. The Two Pianos Did Everything but Fly...*261*
30. Ralph Is a Living Legend, of Course *272*
31. I'll Just Have to Get Out of the Way of Ralph's Left Hand *283*
32. His Music Jumps Up and Grabs You *294*
33. What a Bargain! Three Hours of Ralph Sutton for $10 ....*306*
34. He's Never Anything but Right..*317*
35. I'm Happy Being a Hermit with *Very* Loose Shoes..........................*330*
    Discography *340*
    Index *379*

For Ruth, Joe, and Sara

Preface

Ralph Sutton and I had two things in common as college kids. We both played jazz piano, and we both sat in with Jack Teagarden.

A month after Teagarden heard Ralph play, he wired the 19-year-old college sophomore and asked him to join his band. Ralph promptly dropped out of school and took a train to New York and Teagarden—and thus began the career of one of the top jazz pianists in history. In my case, Teagarden exhibited remarkable tolerance. He played better jazz merely blowing the spit out of his trombone than I ever could at the piano. He never offered me a job, and I gave up any idea of playing jazz piano for a living.

This book really began, I suppose, when I was 12 years old. After eight years of classical piano lessons, I had started to play what in the late 1930s was called popular piano. One day, I heard Jess Stacy playing behind Nappy Lamare's vocal on "Do You Ever Think of Me?" by Bob Crosby's Bob Cats. Stacy's piano on that record thrilled me, and I have been thrilled ever since by jazz piano as played by the giants of traditional jazz—such men as Stacy, Joe Sullivan, Fats Waller, Bob Zurke, and, above all, Ralph Sutton.

Like so many of the people who helped me with this book, I first heard Ralph play about 1950, during his long stint as intermission pianist at Eddie Condon's club in New York. For the next 20 years or so, I thought little about him except when listening to him on records from time to time. Then, in May 1971, the World's Greatest Jazzband came to Chicago for two weeks. My wife and I decided to hear the band—not because Sutton was on piano, but simply because we hadn't heard any top-notch live jazz for a while. The WGJ was playing at the Happy Medium, a theater-club on Rush Street, and Ruth and I bought tickets for the first two sets on a Friday night.

Of course, we stayed for all three sets. From the opening blast of "Wolverine Blues," the first tune of the evening, we sat enchanted through the final bar of the band's theme, "My Inspiration," early the next morning.

Never had we heard such marvelous music. And never had we heard such magnificent and powerful swinging piano as that played by the tall, muscular man with short-cropped hair and horn-rimmed glasses. Ralph Sutton drove that group of superb jazzmen—Yank Lawson, Billy Butterfield, Vic Dickenson, Eddie Hubble, Bob Wilber, Bud Freeman, Bob Haggart, and Gus Johnson—as no piano man we had ever heard with any band.

He just sat there, as stiff-spined as a military cadet, playing with apparently no effort, rarely smiling or showing any expression whatsoever. The other men acknowledged with a smile and perhaps a slight bow the applause that followed their choruses during the ensemble tunes. But Ralph never even turned his face to the audience. He did stand and nod in response to the applause after his solo in each set, but he seemed uncomfortable and appeared relieved to sit down again.

After the last set, we hurried to catch Sutton before he left the building; and he listened patiently while I gushed about his playing. His only response was, "Thank you very much," repeated once or twice in a voice surprisingly soft for so large a man. He obviously wanted to get away, and so we let him go. Again, he seemed relieved.

The next day, I started to compile a discography of Ralph's work. A few months later, it became apparent that contact with the man himself might help in gaining knowledge of all the records on which he had played. I telephoned Peggy Clifford of Aspen, Colorado, a close friend of Ralph's who had written most of the liner notes for one of his records. She promised to tell Ralph of my desire to get in touch with him. I called Clifford on September 10, and a cordial note from Sutton arrived on September 18. His prompt reply must have set some kind of record for a jazz musician's writing to a stranger. Ralph was on the road with the World's Greatest Jazzband, and his wife had told him of my efforts to reach him. He wrote from a motel in Danvers, Massachusetts, and frequent correspondence followed.

A couple of weeks after his first note, Ralph sent a list of all the records he could recall playing on. He forgot a number of records, and his memory was fuzzy about several others. "I'd hate to take on your job of unraveling this mess," he wrote, "and I appreciate what you are doing."

The WGJ played in Champaign, Illinois, on November 8, 1971, four days after Ralph's 49th birthday, and Ruth and I drove downstate with the dual purpose of hearing the band again and of getting to know Sutton personally. We called him after checking into the Holiday Inn where the band was staying, and he came right over to our room.

The three of us chatted for about 45 minutes, and then Ralph had to return to his room to dress for dinner and the band's performance. I remember little of our conversation except telling him how the ideas he expressed in his playing thrilled me and how his three solos had knocked me out when we heard the band in Chicago. He had played "Viper's Drag," "Love Lies," and "California, Here I Come."

When Ralph got up to leave, he surprised Ruth and me by asking us to go along. Immediately after we entered his room, Ralph showed us pictures of his wife and their home in the Rockies, near Denver. There were several snaps of their three Saint Bernards, and he obviously missed wife, home, and dogs alike.

As we talked, Ralph took off the sport shirt and slacks he had worn around the motel. He folded them neatly and hung them on hangers. Then he put on his band uniform suit. He couldn't have given a thought to the fact that he was walking around in his powder-blue boxer shorts while chatting with a couple he had met personally only an hour before. We were charmed by the man's completely natural behavior.

Sutton couldn't join us for dinner because he had a date with friends who had driven up from St. Louis. He surprised us again by telling—not asking—us to meet him backstage after the show.

Ralph delighted me that night by choosing "Viper's Drag" and "California" as his two solos. When I thanked him backstage, he grinned broadly but said nothing. He asked us to join him and his St. Louis friends for a drink, and we said we'd try to make it. But these were obviously old and close friends, and we had to start for Chicago early the next morning. So we returned to our room.

A while later the phone rang. "This is Ralph Sutton," the caller said. "I just wanted to make sure you were all right since you didn't join us."

Sutton intrigued me for several reasons, and the idea of this book came during the drive home. He played fantastically beautiful piano so effortlessly—and so unemotionally. He was a thoughtful, considerate person, and he behaved naturally and casually—witness those powder-blue shorts. But most of all, I was curious about this man who presented such a colorless front to the world. There had to be something beneath any quiet, seemingly indifferent human being who could create such incomparable music, and I wanted to find out what it was and then share it with others.

Ralph responded in his most indifferent manner when I told him about the book idea by phone while the band was in North Carolina. He hesitated for a moment and then said, "OK"—as nonchalantly as though someone came up with the same notion every month or so.

Virtually all the material for this book came from several hundred taped interviews with—or letters from—Ralph, members of his family, fellow musicians, and friends ranging back to his boyhood days in rural Missouri. During the research that went into *Piano Man*, Ralph commented to Ruth and me and to others that he couldn't imagine anyone's being interested enough in him to (1) write a book about him or (2) read the book if it ever got written. He was wrong on the first point, and he turned out to be wrong on the second as well.

Some Loose Thoughts About *Loose Shoes*

alph Sutton has a way of doing the unexpected. It never occurred to me, after spending several years researching and writing *Piano Man*, that I would take on a second edition of the great jazz pianist's biography. Much less that this taciturn, unassuming man would give me the incentive—and give it *verbally*—to do so.

Through the years after the book was published in 1975, a number of people asked me—and Ralph—when I planned to update the Sutton story. I took none of them seriously, figuring they were just making small talk. I had the same reaction when Ralph himself, wearing his widest grin, brought up the same question more than once. He had to be kidding. Why would the normally reticent Ralph have any desire to go through all that fuss and bother a second time?

He asked me once again as we were taking a walk with our wives during the 1984 jazz party in Midland, Texas. It finally dawned on me that Ralph was completely serious. He *wanted* me to bring his story up to date.

Loose Shoes includes the text of *Piano Man*, with considerable new material added to that section. Eleven new chapters update the Sutton biography. The number of pages of photographs has been doubled.

Why the change from *Piano Man* to *Loose Shoes* as the title of Ralph's biography? I thought the story of a jazz musician as renowned and unique as Sutton deserved a title that did not also identify a rock singer-pianist, several jazz records, a novel about neither Sutton nor jazz, a neighborhood bar a few blocks from my home, and assorted other entities. The title appears as well in two fine jazz writings. It is a chapter heading in *An Autobiography of Black Jazz* by Dempsey J. Travis, referring to his father and the rent party days in Chicago; and it is the name of a series of 13 articles about Claude Hopkins by Warren W. Vaché, Sr. These articles, written for *Jersey Jazz*, grew into the biography *Crazy Fingers*.

The English cornetist Digby Fairweather influenced my decision to change the title. He threw me a curve and a compliment in the same sentence when writing the liner notes for a record that Sutton made in Copenhagen in 1977 with a Danish rhythm section. In the notes, Fairweather commented that *Piano Man*, "despite its title, is one of jazz's greatest biographies." His praise was especially gratifying because the record arrived while Ralph was staying with Ruth and me after one of his Last of the Whorehouse Piano Players gigs in Chicago with Jay McShann, Milt Hinton, and Gus Johnson.

I wrote Fairweather and thanked him for the compliment. Although puzzled by the curve regarding the book's title, I said nothing about it.

A number of years later, Fairweather contributed many entries, including the one on Sutton, for a reference book called *Jazz: The Essential Companion*. I wrote to congratulate him and his collaborators, Ian Carr and Brian Priestley. I also asked why he didn't like the title *Piano Man* for Ralph's biography.

"At the time [of writing the liner notes]," Fairweather replied, "I was having a small campaign against jazz catch phrases. Some, like 'swingin' trumpet man' or whatever, sometimes seem to belittle the awesome intent of any musician who takes upon himself the onerous life of a jazz artist. It may well be that I'm a little too serious about this—probably the scars of 15 loving years in the profession, which have persuaded me that the music could do with a bit of dignifying. This, of course, is exactly what your beautiful book on Ralph did for him, so no hard feelings, I do hope."

I assured Fairweather that I had no hard feelings, just curiosity. His explanation, I thought, made sense.

Loose Shoes became the new title because the phrase describes Sutton's personality rather well. Ralph also jokingly considers loose shoes one of the three most basic things in life.

From time to time, people ask me the name of my favorite Sutton recording. Which is like asking a person who loves chocolate chip cookies to pick one favorite cookie out of the bag. I've got a lot of favorite Sutton recordings, but one of my most cherished samples of Ralph's incomparable piano was never recorded.

On a July afternoon in 1974, the World's Greatest Jazzband was testing the sound system at the London House in Chicago prior to starting a two-week engagement. The band played the opening bars of "Love Is Just Around the Corner" at least a dozen times as the club's technicians adjusted the microphones to assure the best reception. Ralph kicked off the tune with a swinging—and completely different—eight-bar intro every time, each impeccably tasty and innovative. It was a remarkable example of jazz improvisation at its finest.

During the summer of 1988, I bought a telephone-answering machine. To give my recorded greeting a little flavor, I superimposed it over several bars of one of my favorite Sutton solos. This solo appears on the 1967 live recording at Elitch Gardens in Denver by the Ten Greats of Jazz, the group that evolved into the World's Greatest Jazzband. Ralph romps through three choruses of "Jazz Me Blues" that are vintage Sutton. Bud Freeman shows his appreciation of the solo by calling out, "Atta boy, Ralph." To me, it is the epitome of jazz piano.

Like many people in the entertainment business, Sutton spends a lot of time on the road. He usually calls from O'Hare Airport to say hello when one of his flights has a stopover in Chicago. During the months after my answering machine had been installed, Ralph called several times while I was away from my office. Each time, of course, he listened to himself playing the segment of the "Jazz Me Blues" solo. I had not told him about combining it with my greeting on the machine. Not once did he say a word about it.

Then, in January 1990, Ralph's flight to Toronto was grounded at O'Hare. The passengers were transferred to another plane, and he called during the layover. This time, Sutton ended his recorded message with what for him was a lengthy commentary: "I like that piano music in the background."

Clearly, Ralph would not qualify as a loquacious person. He prefers to remain quiet unless, in his opinion, talking would be an improvement over silence. Pete Sutton, one of Ralph's three sons, described this trait with a loving quip: "Every couple of years he completes a sentence."

If there were such a person as a typical jazz musician, it wouldn't be Ralph Sutton. Not unless a typical jazz musician and his wife lived in a home high in the Rocky Mountains of Colorado, with a sparkling river that tumbled through their property and was stocked with more brown and rainbow trout than Sutton, an avid fisherman, could ever catch. And unless they shared their home with three dogs, five cats, and three burros.

The Sutton household included three Saint Bernards and three cats when *Piano Man* was published. Long before *Loose Shoes* appeared, Ralph and Sunnie had moved about 3 miles down U.S. Highway 285 into a much larger home. They named it Morning Air Ranch. Their menagerie had also expanded considerably. The burros—a male and female and their ranch-born offspring—occupied their own domain, consisting of a pasture and barn on the opposite bank of the river. Ralph could call out any of their names from his house and get an immediate and identifiable bray in reply. He was at his happiest when his schedule permitted him to escape from the grind of the road and spend some time at home with Sunnie and their beloved animals.

For a performer who habitually presents a serious, unsmiling image to audiences, Sutton has a surprisingly puckish sense of humor. He has been a practical joker since childhood and delights in such pranks as reversing the rolls of toilet paper in the homes of friends (including Ruth and me) with whom he sometimes stays while on the road. He occasionally reverses the rolls in his own home and waits for Sunnie to react.

I should have suspected that Sutton was up to some kind of mischief when he called with a ridiculous question while Ruth and I were unpacking at home in Chicago after the 1991 Mid-America Jazz Festival. Ralph and his sister Barbara had headlined the program with their two-piano sets. We had said our farewells at the hotel in St. Louis a few hours earlier, and he was the last person I expected to be calling.

"Have you checked out yet?" Ralph wanted to know.

"Where are you?" I asked.

"I'm calling from downstairs in the lobby," he told me. For a moment, I thought he meant the lobby of our apartment building—which, needless to say, was unlikely. I asked once more where he was.

"I'm in the hotel lobby [which was equally unlikely] and just wanted to say good-bye again," Sutton said. "Have you checked out yet?"

Knowing he had thoroughly confused me, Ralph continued the banter for a few moments before laughing and letting me in on the joke. He was calling from O'Hare while waiting for a flight to Florida, where he played a private party that night.

Sutton's sense of humor has contributed a number of unique expressions to my vocabulary. One of them is based on a dandy pun. Ralph uses it when agreeing with something a person has said. He will likely reply, "The feeling is pari-mutual."

Several months after he had enthusiastically, and with great laughter, approved the new title of his biography, a story in the *Chicago Tribune* told about a high school boy who played piano for patients at the Rehabilitation Institute of Chicago. The patients called him "Piano Man." I sent a copy of the story to Ralph, noting that here was yet another reason for the change of title.

"Enjoyed the article on the young piano man," Sutton wrote back. "Piano men are getting as thick as pecker gnats."

That colorful expression came from Ralph's boyhood in a farm community near St. Louis. The insects made life miserable for dogs trying to take a nap on a summer day.

The term *stride piano* appears frequently in this book. Sutton is a stride pianist, so it might be appropriate to explain the term.

The predominant feature of stride piano is its swinging bass. The left hand plays a tenth, an octave, or a single note on the first and third beats of each measure; and a chord on the second and fourth beats. This motion makes the left hand appear to be striding up and down the keyboard. The right hand uses chords, octaves, or single notes to play the melody of the tune or to improvise on the melody ad lib. When an accomplished stride pianist is swinging away, the listener's feet may find themselves tapping along in rhythm almost automatically.

Epitaphs for traditional jazz first appeared soon after the advent of bop in the 1940s. Millions of people throughout the world, among them George Bacos, still scoff at these periodic reports. Bacos, a Chicago barber who began cutting hair in 1954, had always loved jazz and thought his customers would enjoy it, too. He was right. Bacos started playing jazz cassettes in his North Side barbershop in 1988, and the patrons found themselves getting haircuts to the tunes of Louis Armstrong, Charlie Barnet,

Loose Shoes

Duke Ellington, Ella Fitzgerald, Benny Goodman, and other top names of the Big Band Era.

Bacos' wife had urged him for years to retire, but he enjoyed working and listening to jazz too much. One customer told him he came to the barbershop to hear the jazz, not for a haircut. Another was always accompanied by his wife, who found the music relaxing. The younger patrons, most of whom had never heard that kind of music before, loved it, as did Bacos' grandchildren. No one objected to the jazz or asked him to turn down the volume. A number of customers made cassettes of their jazz records for him.

I introduced Bacos to Ralph's music, and he became an avid Sutton fan. On many of the tunes, he could not believe that only one person was playing the piano. Bacos repeatedly asked for confirmation that Ralph was improvising, not reading any music. "Impossible," he would say.

According to one review of *Piano Man**, Ralph Sutton was "at the height of his career" in 1975, when the book was published. That was still true in 1994, when *Loose Shoes* went to press.

Every year, Sutton performed at many of the growing number of jazz parties and festivals in the United States, in addition to playing concerts, nightclub engagements, jazz cruises, and private parties. He also toured annually in other countries, including Canada, the United Kingdom, France, Germany, Italy, Switzerland, Japan, Australia, and New Zealand.

Audiences gave Ralph standing ovations at one performance after another, as they had through the years. Despite being an intensely private person of extremely few words, he rarely failed to attract large numbers of admirers who wanted nothing more than to chat with him and let him know how much they enjoyed hearing him play.

Sutton has recorded prolifically since 1946, and some of his finest playing can be heard on recordings produced relatively late in his career. These include a collection of tunes that Ralph played at the Cafe des Copains in Toronto between 1983 and 1987. One highlight is the beautiful rendition of "Laugh Clown Laugh," a song that few of Sutton's fans had ever heard him play before. He came up with another surprise during a

---

*"A Book Review" by August W. Staub, Chairman of the Drama and Communications Department of the University of New Orleans, in *The Second Line* (Winter 1976), published by the New Orleans Jazz Club.

concert recorded in Woking, England, in 1990. About a third of the way through "Clothesline Ballet," one of his many Fats Waller perennials, Ralph unexpectedly switches from 4/4 to 3/4 time. He waltzes lightly through a principal section of the tune and then returns to 4/4 for the swinging final choruses.

Ralph plays solo piano on both of the above recordings. He is unsurpassed as a soloist, but his highest accolades have perhaps come for his comping—performing in a supportive (complementary) role behind a soloist. This type of piano playing is an art in itself. The pianist must provide a strong background for the soloist, enhancing the solo but not detracting from it. Sutton never demonstrated this art better than he did on a band recording made the day after the Triangle Jazz Party in Raleigh, North Carolina, in 1991. Several of the musicians who had played at the party donated their talent in making this fine recording for Friends In Need, a nonprofit charitable organization. Ralph's comping behind the two trombones of Dan Barrett and George Broussard on "Just Friends" is especially gorgeous.

Passing his 71st birthday in 1993, the one-time Missouri farm boy never sounded better and showed no sign of slowing down. He continually confirmed his rank as one of the greatest jazz pianists—and arguably the premier stride pianist—in history.

Chapter **1**

A Spot on the Road

ell, I might as well start at the beginning," Ralph Sutton said. "I was born on November 4, 1922, in Hamburg, Missouri, in a house on a hill where my dad and mother lived. When I was about 5, we moved down the road to Howell. My dad ran a construction business and he built a new house there, and that's where I grew up.

"Our place was on the edge of the town, but Howell wasn't even a town. It was just a spot on the road. When you drove through Howell—*pffffft*—you were through it. There was a blacksmith shop and a country store that had a cooler of hot pop. The gas pumps stood outside, and you had to pump the gas up by hand.

"The back door of our house led right into the woods, and I played there a lot. In the winter, I used to put out traps and catch 'possums with two brothers who were buddies of mine, Clifford and Emmett Schierbaum. In the summer, we'd go squirrel hunting. I don't go hunting any more at all because I don't care to kill anything. But in those days, a 'possum or a squirrel meant something to eat.

"My family didn't live in an actual farmhome, but it was a farming area and there were farms all around us. I pitched wheat and put up hay on many of those farms. We had a big yard and lots of trees. My mother kept a garden with fresh vegetables, and we raised hogs and chickens. In the wintertime, we'd butcher the hogs and I'd get to stay home from school because this was a big deal. All the neighbors would come around and help, and we'd have a big kettle out there with the tongue and different parts of the hogs cooking. We'd make sausage out of all that.

"All the farmers would go around and help one another in the fall at threshing time, too, and I'd always get the job of pitching wheat. I loved that! I think I got around 15 cents an hour, and I was happy to get it.

"And the food those farmers' wives put out—it was just too much. Oh, man, I'll never forget it. There'd be lots of fried chicken and country-cured ham, and all kinds of meats that you'd naturally eat on a farm. Then we'd finish up with pies, cakes, cookies—the works. All the wives cooked to help one another out, and so they all tried to outdo each other, and the table would be loaded.

"I've got a lot of love in my heart for my childhood. Remembering all the people I knew back in Howell helps me keep my balance as an adult. They had a homespun philosophy that was really great."

The towns of Hamburg and Howell no longer exist. The United States government wiped them off the map in 1940. The two towns lay near the Missouri River, about 35 miles west of St. Louis. Hamburg had existed for 100 years, and Howell was even older. Francis Howell, a merchant, established the settlement of Howell's Prairie on the site about 1800.

The Suttons, along with many others who lived in the area, never got over their bitterness at the government for uprooting about 500 families. The War Department wanted the land for a TNT plant, which it planned to build as part of the national defense program of the pre-World War II era. It paid about $2,700,000 for the 17,289 acres of rich, rolling farmland that also included the town of Toonerville. The TNT plant closed in January 1944 after operating less than 28 months. Its short life added to the anger of the uprooted families, many of whom had lived in the area for generations.

Hamburg, the largest of the three towns destroyed by the government, had a population of about 150. The towns served mainly as marketplaces for the crops and livestock from surrounding farms. The only Hamburg buildings mentioned in newspaper clippings from around 1940 were the post office, a general store, and a gas station.

Ralph Earl Sutton was the oldest of the three children born to

Earl and Edna Sutton. Both his parents had been born on farms in the area and had grown up there. They named him for his mother's brother and for his father. A half brother, Harold, 11 years older than Ralph, came to live with the family while Ralph was in diapers. Harold Sutton remembered that Ralph could hum "It Ain't Gonna Rain No Mo' " before he could talk: "Ralph heard more music during his first two years than he heard people talk. We had a phonograph that you cranked up, and records were played a lot."

When the Suttons moved from Hamburg to Howell, 4 miles away, Edna's parents, Nicholas and Barbara Zeyen, moved in with them. The Zeyens had little money, and Nicholas, whom everyone called "Uncle Nick," became the maintenance man of the Francis Howell High School, a country block up the road. Ralph went to elementary school in the town's one-room schoolhouse. David Schneider, a classmate, remembered only one thing about Ralph as a first-grader: "He had quite a temper."

Besides the Schierbaum brothers, only two or three boys of Ralph's age lived in the community. [Emmett Schierbaum contributed his first name to a humorous expletive coined and frequently used by Ralph: "Goddammit, Emmett!"] Ralph's closest friend was Norman K. Muschany, whose home was just a cow pasture away. Muschany, who was a year younger than Ralph and became a St. Louis gynecologist, recalled that Ralph always sat in the back row of the schoolroom.

"He just didn't like to be up in front," Muschany said. "As a matter of fact, I think he'd like to have been clear out of school.

"My fondest memories of Ralph are how he stuck up for a somewhat frail buddy—me—in school. He used to take the wires out of a battery and bend them and shoot 'em like paper wads. They'd feel almost like a BB when they hit you. One day, a girl in the front of the room got hit and swore it came from my direction. But Ralph said no, that he had done it. And anytime I got into trouble, I knew that Ralph could get me out of it. I wasn't real sure *I* could get out of it, but he was very loyal to me and always came to my rescue. No one really bluffed him."

Muschany described Howell as "a little bit of Dixie and a little bit of real country." Most of the people, including Edna Sutton, had German ancestry, but Earl Sutton was of Irish descent. The people raised their children in a stern Bible Belt atmosphere, though the Muschanys were stricter than the Suttons. Claude Muschany, Norman's father, taught Sunday school and banned all reading on the Sabbath except the Bible. He also prohibited drinking and card playing on Sunday.

"The children in this environment were very respectful of their elders," Norman Muschany said. "All the men were called *Mister*. Even if you knew them well enough to call them by their first name—like me with Ralph's father—it was always *Mr. Earl*, not *Mr. Sutton*. If you called him *Mr. Earl,* it meant he was a next-door neighbor. If you lived in another town, you might have called him *Mr. Sutton*. And it was *Miss Edna*, too. You never called your seniors by their first names only."

In addition to working on the farms while in elementary school, Ralph joined his father's construction gang as water boy. After a while, he graduated to digging ditches, packing shingles, and pushing a wheelbarrow of concrete.

"When I started as water boy, the carpenters were getting 25 cents an hour," Ralph said. "I think I got a nickel or a dime an hour from Dad. He remodeled two old Daniel Boone farmhouses—one in Matson and the other near Defiance. They were old rock houses. Dad knew how to build, and he remodeled those houses perfectly, along with putting up barns and sheds. I loved him so much, and I marveled at what he could do.

"I don't think Dad went past fourth grade, but he was a whiz with figures and had a lot of common sense. It always amazed me how he could work out the blueprints to build a home or remodel an old farmhouse. He tried to get me interested in that kind of work later, but I was always more interested in music."

Harold Sutton remembered his father as "a real serious person who organized his work crew well and didn't leave the job when he came home. He often thought about his work and planned it at night, and he wasn't the easiest person in the world to get along with at home. He was sort of king and master of the home situation, and people were forced to respect him because of his size and his temper. He weighed about 230 pounds and he was big all over, with an Irish temper and an Irish sense of humor.

"My father was well liked," Harold Sutton said, "and he was generally outgoing with the public—sparkling, shaking hands, and grinning. But he didn't always have that jovial outlook at home. I think this is probably reflected in what Ralph and I picked up from him because when we tackle something, we're pretty serious and dedicated to it, whether other people think it's worthwhile or not."

The old-timers of the community, including Ralph's grandfather, spent many hours at the country store in Howell. They sat around the potbellied stove during the winter, and in summer they moved out to the front porch and sat on the nail kegs. Claude Muschany owned the store, and so Norman spent much more time there than Ralph did. Most of the people in the area were Democrats, but Earl Sutton was a Republican and got into a lot of arguments with his neighbors when they encountered one another at the store.

"There'd be a fire in the stove in the back of the store where everybody loafed, and things would get pretty hot and heavy there when the men started arguing," Norman Muschany said. "Lots of family affairs and financial problems were settled around that stove. Women were never allowed back there because there was a lot of horsing around and a lot of vulgarity. If one entered the store, you'd hear 'em all say, 'Ssh, here comes a woman.' "

In 1930, about three years after the Suttons moved to Howell, Ralph's sister Barbara Louise was born. His other sister, Janice Ruth, was born in 1934. As a boy, Ralph was never particularly close to his brother or his two sisters because of the great differences in age. Harold entered the University of Missouri when Ralph was only 7, and Ralph himself started college when Barbara was just 10.

Today, Ralph is close to all three. Harold Sutton is a retired professor of art at Florida State University in Tallahassee. Barbara, who followed in Ralph's footsteps and became a top-notch jazz pianist, is the wife of a high school English teacher in Ukiah, California. She met her husband, Harold E. Curtis, while playing in a USO center in St. Louis. Hal Curtis, who had frequently heard Ralph perform at Eddie Condon's club in New York, thought he was hearing one of Ralph's records in the USO. But then he remembered that Ralph had never recorded the tune. The music turned out to be live, and the pianist a 20-year-old woman who looked like a feminine version of Ralph and played remarkably like him. Barbara Sutton Curtis still plays occasional gigs, serves as a substitute music teacher, and gives piano lessons. Jan Sutton works for an insurance company in San Francisco.

A drive through the area where Ralph grew up offers little to see today except a couple of brick building foundations, a few sets of stone steps that once led into houses, and acres of weeds. In 1967, a number of the former residents of the community held a reunion on what became the first annual TNT Homecoming Day.

ing of what he was doing. I loved his singing and his whole feeling toward life. The closest I ever got to knowing Fats was through his records, but I knew immediately that I loved him. He just knocked me out. They played some Art Tatum on that program, too, and those guys were my idols. Between the two of them, they had the whole thing covered.

"I've never heard a piano man swing any better than Fats—or swing a band better than he could. I never get tired of him. Fats has been with me from the first, and he'll be with me as long as I live."

Ralph started to improvise on the piano "almost from the beginning," though he had no idea that what he was doing was called improvisation.

"Fats's playing influenced me, of course, and I just began doing it. My interest in jazz kept growing with the records I heard on the radio and that I later bought. It had to be the records that influenced me because I had no contact with any jazz musicians at all while I was growing up. I also bought the Fats piano folios. They'd have the regular version of a tune and then Fats's arrangement of the tune on the next page."

Corinne Ebert taught Ralph for about six years. She said she "didn't especially want him to have a love of jazz until he had a good knowledge of classical music, but he much preferred jazz."

One of Ebert's sisters began calling Ralph "Cookie" because his friends so often asked him to play the tune "Lookie, Lookie, Lookie, Here Comes Cookie." The nickname stuck with him through his school days, much to his distress, and several of his former classmates still use it.

Earl Sutton played violin by ear and taught Ralph to accompany him with chords on the piano. Ralph showed so much promise that, a couple of years after he started taking piano lessons, his father organized a dance band with the 11-year-old boy at the keyboard.

"We used to play country dances," Ralph said. "In addition to Dad and me, we had a cello, a guitar, and a bass fiddle. Shortly before Dad organized the band, I played in an outfit that won second prize in an old fiddler's contest in the Woodman Hall above the IGA store in Hamburg. That group included a fiddler named Currier Fridley and my great-uncle Pete [Zeyen] on cello. I can't remember who the others were, but there was probably a banjo and a guitar. Each of us got $1.75 in the contest, and that was the first money I ever made in the music business."

Earl Sutton's band later consisted of violin, C-melody sax, piano,

Chapter **2**

Harlem Rhythm

 alph began piano lessons at the age of 9, but he didn't burn up the track. His teacher, Corinne Ebert, said he was just an average student: "He practiced 30 or 40 minutes a day and he liked music, but he often had to be reminded to practice in his earlier years."

Edna Sutton prompted Ralph occasionally to get him to the piano, but only once did she really land on him to practice.

"One day," she said, "I made him get up to the piano and practice, whether he played the right notes or not. I don't remember exactly what I told him, except to sit down and stay there. He didn't argue at all. He just turned around at the piano and practiced—or went through the motions. After that, I didn't have any more trouble with him."

The Suttons had a player piano, but Earl removed the automatic mechanism, which Ralph liked to operate. Earl wanted the boy to "knuckle down at the piano" and not be distracted by playing all the right notes the easy way.

Ralph didn't stick too long to scales and other basics. Fats Waller saw to that.

"About the time I started taking piano lessons," Ralph remembered, "I used to catch a radio program out of St. Louis on WIL. It was called 'Harlem Rhythm'—a 15-minute program, five mornings a week. They always played a record of Fats Waller's, and they'd have Duke Ellington, Fletcher Henderson, Andy Kirk and His Clouds of Joy, and all the others. It was strictly a Harlem program, and a lot of times they'd play a whole program of Fats. He really influenced me and made me so happy.

"I loved the way he covered the keyboard with both hands and the way he swung. I didn't even know the word *swing* then, but I got the feel-

guitar, banjo, and drums. He and one of his carpenters, Theodore (Tot) Mades, built a dance floor platform next to Mades' home in Hamburg. It had a roof and a small band shell, and Earl's group played for dances there.

"We played Friday and Saturday nights, four hours a night, and had maybe one 15-minute intermission," Ralph recalled. "If we were lucky, we got two intermissions. Three bucks a night each. Dad stood at the side of the piano while we played. I didn't see how he could play, with his fingers all thick and callused from work, but he'd do it.

"We used stock arrangements, or I would buy the sheet music of popular tunes of the day, like 'Goody, Goody,' 'Wahoo,' and 'Moonlight and Roses,' which was one of Dad's favorites. I'd learn the tune, and then I'd teach it to Dad, measure by measure."

The opportunity to earn money with his music gave Ralph a tremendous thrill. His mother said "he was so proud to show us the money he had made—*playing.*"

Earl's band sometimes played at a tavern and dance hall in Toonerville, midway between Hamburg and Howell. The place was owned by a close friend, Charlie Gross, who called Earl one evening when Ralph was about 14. Pepper Martin, the star third baseman of the St. Louis Cardinals, had dropped in with his girlfriend and guitar. He had broken the team's curfew by sneaking from his hotel room, and Gross thought it would be great if Earl and Ralph stopped by.

"Dad brought his violin, and he and I went down to Charlie's," Ralph said. "After a few beers at the bar, we went into the dance hall with Pepper and his guitar and played all the pop tunes. He sang some country songs, too. We were there for three or four hours, just Pepper and his girlfriend, Charlie and his wife, and Dad and I.

"Pepper amazed me by standing flat-footed and jumping up on the bar. He must have had steel legs. Being with him was a big thrill for me because I was interested in baseball at that time, especially Pepper Martin, Joe Medwick, Enos Slaughter, and the other Cardinals."

Norman Muschany also took piano lessons from Corinne Ebert, but only because his mother made him do so for six years. He spent many Saturday and Sunday afternoons with Ralph in the Muschany living room, listening raptly while his friend played piano.

"Ralph would come over and roll our piano out into the middle of the room," Muschany remembered. "He said you couldn't hear it if it was against the wall. Then he'd play for two or three hours almost without interruption. Oh, maybe we'd tell a joke or horse around a little, but we'd come right back to the piano. Just two boys sitting in a parlor, and I was fascinated. I just loved it. I couldn't believe anyone could play so long and enjoy it.

"Then, suddenly, Ralph would stop playing and say, 'C'mon, let's go up to the store and get a Pepsi.' He'd walk out and leave the piano sitting in the middle of the parlor, and my mother would get so mad. She'd holler, 'That boy's been in here again, and he won't put the piano back!' It really annoyed her. She'd give Ralph hell, but it wouldn't faze him a bit. He'd do the same thing the next week, just to spite her.

"He liked to keep everybody needled a little bit. It's like the teenaged boy who walks through the room and swats his mother on the fanny. He was needling my mother, but there was nothing mean about it. It was just his sense of humor."

For a couple of summers, Ralph and Norman also were co-leaders—and sole voting members—of a club that convened in the trash heap in the woods behind the Sutton home. The nonvoting membership consisted of J.C. (for James Claude) Muschany, Norman's younger brother; Barbara Sutton; and assorted cats, dogs, and chickens.

"I was interested in parliamentary procedure, and so I'd keep the minutes of our meetings," Muschany said. "My kid brother and Barbara couldn't write yet, and so Ralph and I felt they shouldn't vote. I'm not sure what the club's principles or achievements were, but we had lots of meetings.

"Out there in the country, no one picked up the trash and garbage. You just found a low area on your land and dumped all your junk there—not garbage so much as things like tin cans and broken appliances. They eventually rusted and wasted away. I'd make periodic checkups on the Suttons' trash and bring home anything I found that looked interesting. Miss Edna didn't particularly like this, and neither did my mother, because she thought I was hauling home all the Suttons' junk."

Barbara Curtis remembered the club with great fondness because its meetings were among the few times that Ralph let her tag along with him.

"I was the youngest member, and J.C. was just a little older," she said. "He was my boyfriend. I remember one time we went back to the dump and J.C. found a chamber pot and presented it to me. I thought it was the most marvelous gift."

By the time Ralph reached fifth grade, he had a reputation as a prankster. One of his favorite stunts, in addition to shooting battery wires at the girls, was to set up a steady vibration on the schoolroom floor by pumping up and down on the balls of his feet while sitting at his desk. Ralph's heels never touched the floor, but the vibration shook the entire building. A young teacher named C. Fred Hollenbeck came to Howell that year to start his professional career. He soon learned about the Sutton boy.

"I remember Ralph as a rather well-built, nice-looking, well-groomed, mannerly boy," Hollenbeck said. "He was not above trying out the new teacher, however. While seated behind his geography book, he could cause the whole floor to vibrate with his feet. Of course, the glances of the younger pupils at the culprit soon led the exasperated, inexperienced teacher to the source. We reached an understanding, and we couldn't have had a better teacher-student relationship—even though Ralph may not have always worked up to his mental capacity."

During Ralph's sixth-grade year, his teacher, Verna Muhm, lived with the Suttons. She described him as "studious, extremely well-behaved, very mild-mannered, and not at all a bully type like most boys that age. Ralph was on the retiring side, almost shy, and spoke softly. He was always neat, clean, and well-groomed. I can't remember that he ever came to class without his assignments up to par. But his penmanship was miserable, and I often had to guess at his answers.

"I'll always remember one thing that really touched me," Muhm said. "The day before school closed, Ralph Earl wrote on a little piece of note paper, 'I'll miss you, but don't tell or show this to anyone.' He signed his name and slipped the note under my door. I kept this secret, and also the note, for many years, and it is still dear to my memory."

While in eighth grade, Ralph competed in an amateur contest given by the school in nearby New Melle. Leonard W. Fuerman, an eighth-grader at the school, worked backstage as curtain puller.

"Just as the last act was about to be introduced, the piano seemed to explode into music," Fuerman recalled. "All the lights were out, and so my teacher grabbed me and told me to get some light out to the guy who was playing. I brought him a flashlight, but he didn't need it because he had no music. As he played a hard, fast jazz tune, the lights went on and the audience stood up to see this talented musician. Needless to say, Ralph won first place."

Fred Hollenbeck became superintendent of the local school district before Ralph started eighth grade. That year, Hollenbeck called a meeting at the Francis Howell High School of the students of all the elementary schools under his direction. He urged them to go to high school, which few children in the area did at that time. Amos E. Jose, an eighth-grader from Hamburg, first saw—and heard—Ralph at the meeting:

"Mr. Hollenbeck called on a boy to play a couple of numbers on the piano for entertainment. The boy very casually and nonchalantly seated himself on the piano stool and gave a professional performance. That performance by the boy in blue denim bib overalls was indescribable and heavenly to me and, I can imagine, to a heck of a lot of the others in the audience. It was live entertainment, and most of us didn't have a radio in our home. In fact, most of us didn't even have electricity.

"But Cookie's performance was nothing to the way he accepted the applause. He was unbelievably modest. This was—and still is—Cookie."

Chapter **3**

He Could Play a Hymn That Brought Tears to Your Eyes

uring the summer of 1937, shortly before Ralph started high school, Harold Sutton and his wife, Beth, visited Howell. Beth remembered: "Ralph kept tuning in his Fats Waller broadcasts and listening to his Fats Waller records. He was really intrigued with Fats. He read about him, listened to his music, and improvised as he thought Fats did.

"On those hot summer days, we'd smell the grapes ripening out in the arbor, and Uncle Nick always had some tomatoes getting ripe—and a little wine in a keg in the cellar. Edna would cook great big country dinners with fresh, light bread. And in would come Ralph after working with the construction gang. He'd clean up and eat that big dinner and then sit down at the piano."

When Ralph practiced piano, his sister Barbara often pulled her little chair up to the couch, which she used "as *my* piano to practice on.

"I really looked up to Ralph throughout my childhood and adolescence," Barbara said. "I wanted to do things with him, but I had few opportunities because of the age difference. He certainly didn't want a kid sister hanging around spoiling his fun.

"One thing we shared was the piano. When I was 8, Dad asked me if I wanted to take piano lessons from Mrs. Ebert, too. I recall how overjoyed I was at the prospect. Maybe I could play like Ralph!

"On still summer evenings, sounds carried so clearly from a distance. I remember one such evening when we heard Mrs. Ebert playing at her house, about half a mile away. Ralph got up and went to our piano, determined to outplay her.

"Growing up, I used to think that country boys were wilder and rougher than town boys. I didn't have much of a basis for comparison, but

I know I was right because they were always tipping over outhouses and putting farm wagons on rooftops at Halloween and teasing girls and causing trouble in school.

"Ralph seemed daring to me and seemed to have lots of freedom and fun. I adored him and imitated him. One day, Ralph had a BB gun and I had a broomstick for a gun, and we were shooting at the windshield of a car parked in our driveway. It belonged to some fellow Ralph was pissed off at. Dad gave Ralph a whipping for this, and I watched and was glad I wasn't getting whipped because Dad didn't lay back any. I liked it that Ralph had let me be his accomplice, but I felt a little guilty that I was glad not to be on the receiving end of the whipping."

Ralph recalled the incident a bit differently. "The car belonged to Mrs. Ebert's husband," he said, "and I just wanted to see if a BB would go through the windshield. It did."

The Suttons' dining room and kitchen were in the basement. At mealtime, if Ralph was upstairs playing the piano or doing something else, his mother would save steps by banging on the ceiling with the broom handle to call him to the table. Jan Sutton remembered that he pulled some of his favorite pranks during dinner, "especially on Sunday, when we usually had fried chicken. It would be cooked and on the platter, but Ralph would begin squawking like a chicken and pretend it was still alive. Mom would get after him, and then he'd start talking about bugs on the food—just to get her upset."

Norman Muschany said Ralph was mischievous "particularly around Halloween—but not necessarily just Halloween—when he would turn over outhouses. He really got a bit destructive. Ralph and some other boys would take automobiles and wagons apart and put them up on top of buildings. They'd put horses and cows on front porches, and the next day the people would find the animals and a lot of manure there. Halloween sort of served as a time when all this devilment was allowed, but it went on all year."

Ralph chuckled at the recollection of turning over the outhouses and said, "We were damn lucky we didn't fall in."

The Suttons and Muschanys were among the first Howell families to have indoor plumbing—which meant a faucet in the kitchen. Ralph was about 17 and Norman 16 before they knew the luxury of an indoor bathroom at home.

He Could Play a Hymn That Brought Tears to Your Eyes

As teenagers, Ralph and Norman worked for Norman's uncle, who was the Howell undertaker. Ralph will never forget Morris Muschany and his son, Don, who later ran a funeral home in St. Louis.

"I'd help embalm the cadavers and I'd run errands," Ralph said. "They'd send me out for sandwiches and Cokes, and they'd put them right next to the stiff on the table. I had to eat outside because I couldn't take that. It wouldn't bother me now, but it sure did then. I'd help out at funerals, too. It was quite an experience. Made me really feel pretty big."

Norman Muschany also had vivid memories of his uncle's funeral home: "Uncle Morris would call me—sometimes it would be late at night—and say, 'Norman, go up and get the fire going. I'm going out and make a pickup.' Which meant somebody had died, and he was going out in the hearse and pick up the body. Ralph and I were to go up and get the embalming room warm. As soon as we got the body in and started the embalming, Uncle Morris would say to Ralph or me, 'Now go over to the store and get us some food and some Cokes.'

"While the embalming was going on, the formaldehyde burned your eyes and nose until you couldn't breathe. We'd pump out the abdominal contents, mostly stool, which really smelled foul, and inject the formaldehyde—and Uncle Morris would be eating his sandwiches and drinking his Coke. I couldn't stand it either.

"But the one thing you could say about Uncle Morris was that he paid well. We'd each get $5 for a funeral, which meant maybe a day and a half of work. That was a lot of money back in those days."

While in high school, Ralph switched piano teachers. He felt he had learned all he could from Corinne Ebert. Earl Sutton was remodeling the home of Lillian Carpenter and her husband, who had bought a large, old farmhouse. He converted the two front rooms into one big, long one so the Carpenters would have space for their grand piano and their collection of antique furniture. Earl learned that Lillian Carpenter gave piano lessons and asked her to take Ralph as a student. Ralph made the change, and so did Barbara a short time later. Carpenter gave them both their first instruction in basic music theory.

"She used to kid me about playing dance music," Ralph recalled. "I'd ask her, 'Well, Mrs. Carpenter, how can I pay for my piano lessons unless I do it?' But she was very lenient with me. I had memorized

'Solfeggietto' by Bach and Beethoven's *Sonata Pathétique* and something by Brahms, and I'd give little solo recitals in her home or in the ladies' club or in St. Louis. I'd be nervous and sweatin', afraid I'd make a mistake with all those women listening to me."

Asked if he had been Carpenter's prize student, Ralph replied shyly, "Well, she kinda put it that way." She congratulated him by telegram after he won first place on Arthur Godfrey's "Talent Scouts" radio program on February 23, 1948. "I played 'Three Little Words' and happened to be lucky enough to win. She was so proud, and she told all her friends that I was her student."

Ralph's great-uncle Elmer Weyrauch lived in St. Louis, and he and his family often drove out to Howell. "We'd have a Sunday afternoon of relatives," Ralph remembered. "There'd be fried chicken and the whole works. In the evening, there was always a recital in the living room. Uncle Elmer had two daughters, Marguerite and Virginia, who were a little older than I. One played violin and one played piano, and they were really studious. Everyone would be sitting around the living room, and I'd duck out because I knew I'd have to perform. Someone would always ask me, 'What have you learned on the piano lately?' There was a little competition between the girls and me, and they'd perform and then I'd have to.

"Everyone would say, 'Where's Ralph? Where's Ralph Earl?' I'd be outside riding my bike, but I'd have to come in and play a couple of things that my piano teacher had given me. Oh, man, let me out of here! I'd be achin' to bust into something like 'Dinah' or 'Honeysuckle Rose.' My uncle would lecture me: 'Now you should stick with your piano pieces, you know, because that's the only way you're going to get anywhere—like Marguerite and Virginia.' And I'd say, 'Sure,' and I'd agree. But then I'd tell him, 'Uncle Elmer, I love this music, and I'm going to stick with it, no matter what you say. I'll stay with the serious music, but this is where my heart is.' "

Barbara remembered the day Ralph followed Marguerite and Virginia with a swinging version of "Flat Foot Floogie": "What a contrast to the classical music the girls had played! Their parents were justifiably proud of their musical ability. I thought Ralph was wonderful, but Uncle Elmer thought he was going to the dogs."

During Ralph's high school years, his father dropped out of the band because of the pressure of the construction business. Ralph took over as leader and added a trumpet. The band folded after he left for college because his father had little reason to continue it. Harold Sutton said Earl had organized the group "primarily for Ralph's sake."

The Suttons belonged to the Presbyterian church about a block from their home. The family, except for Uncle Nick, who said he didn't believe in religion, always arrived early at the white frame building so Ralph could play some jazz on the pump organ before anyone else showed up. His actions displeased Curtis Snyder, a deacon of the church, who lived across the road from the Suttons. Barbara and Jan stood guard outside the church in case Snyder—whom Edna Sutton described with a laugh as "so religious"—or any other disapproving person happened to come by.

The lookout system apparently broke down one Sunday because Snyder caught Ralph playing jazz on the church organ. He said nothing to the boy's parents, but he put his hand on Ralph's shoulder and told him: "Now, Ralph, I love you and your jazz music—but not in the house of God. There are some things that are permissible in my brother's blacksmith shop or in the Muschany store that are not permissible here."

Ralph did not take kindly to the criticism. Snyder recalled: "There was a small lever on our front porch that turned our electric power on and off. Ralph turned the lever and cut off the power. When his dad got home and heard about this, he gave him a good whipping and had his mother take him over to our home to apologize. I saw immediately that Ralph was in no mood to apologize, and so I said to him, 'Ralph, there is no need for an apology. I am just so sorry this happened.' Ralph's face lit up and his expression changed completely."

Norman Muschany was the church janitor and bell ringer, and he built the fire in the church stoves before services. He had a key to the church and remembered that "Ralph would talk me into going there during the week. He'd play a lot of hymns, but then he'd branch off into jazz. The sound of jazz on an organ intrigued him, particularly one that you pumped with your feet. We'd get the church going fairly good, hoping no one would catch us."

Snyder's wife, Olive, was the regular church organist, but she gradually allowed Ralph to play some of the music during services.

"Miss Olive couldn't play the organ worth a hoot," Muschany said.

"She'd lose her place, and the congregation would sort of wind down on the hymn singing until she found it again. But Ralph was really good. He could play a hymn that brought tears to your eyes—not jazzed up but just good, because he played enough and practiced enough on the organ that he became an excellent church organist. He was sincere and conscientious about it, and there was no horsing around during services.

"Ralph and Curt nipped at each other all the time. Curt just couldn't stand Ralph, and Ralph felt even more strongly about him. Ralph would try to do things that would aggravate Curt—just like a gnat flying around your head. And Curt would get mad and yell and talk to Mr. Earl. Ralph sort of went from one bit of trouble into another bit of trouble.

"There was a constant feud between the Suttons and Muschanys on one side and the Snyders and some others on the opposite side. Those adult men would sit on the highest board of the church and wrangle for hours about Ralph's playing jazz in church. Mr. Earl and my dad were in on it, and I think the Muschanys and Suttons won most of the time.

"After Ralph became eligible to be the church organist, there was the question of what he did on Saturday nights, when he played piano with the band at dances—whether he should be allowed with that alcohol breath to come in on Sunday morning and play for services. That brought on another big squabble. And there was also a great deal of wrangling about the church's buying a new organ. Ralph wanted a certain kind of organ, and the church eventually bought the one he wanted."

Claude Muschany's Sunday school class included Ralph, who Norman said was a pretty good student: "It wasn't the easiest thing in the world to play in a dance band on Saturday night and then get up and go to Sunday school, but Ralph showed up every week. I think he enjoyed my dad, and I know my dad enjoyed him. Ralph was sort of a rounder as far as country living was concerned, and it was a credit to himself and to my dad that he came to Sunday school regularly."

Chapter 4

Everyone Knew Him Best as a Pianist

red Hollenbeck recalled that from elementary school through high school, Ralph "was a favorite among his classmates. He did well in his schoolwork and took part in school activities, including sports. But everyone knew him best as a pianist. He played for school programs and assemblies, special music groups, his church, and community and special events. Our school was small enough so that the whole student body would meet for assembly. Many assemblies in which Ralph performed ran over into class time with the students calling for more. He always obliged without complaint."

One of Ralph's high-school teachers, Charles A. Kienberger, had vivid memories of the boy's musical ability—in typing class: "Typing students were allowed to practice when no teacher was in the room. Several times, when I came down the corridor to the typing room, I could hear Ralph jazzing up the typewriter. He would type in the rhythm and tone of a musical piece. I can't describe exactly how he did it, but I believe he hit the keys quickly for short, high notes and dragged his fingers over the keys for a low half note or a whole note.

"Ralph made the typewriter sound as though he were playing real jazz, and the other students would stop and listen just as they did when he was actually playing the piano. I think he added a little humming to complete the effect.

"Ralph was a rather quiet, serious-minded boy—well-mannered and with a more mature outlook on life than most boys his age. He was accepted by the students, though he didn't have an opportunity to be with them much because practically all of them lived outside Howell and rode the bus to and from home.

"Most of the students recognized Ralph as a great jazz musician and knew he played piano in a dance band. They talked about how good he was, and many looked up to him. I attended many dances at which the Sutton band played. Ralph seemed to put everything he had into his playing. On a hot summer night, the perspiration ran down his face, and by the end of the evening he looked tired.

"In passing the Sutton home, he could be heard practicing. He spent very little time on the streets, and it was unusual to see him in a store. Ralph arrived at school just before classes started and left as soon as school ended. He went home for lunch every day and returned just in time for classes. His practicing and playing seemed to take most of his time."

Amos Jose, a member of the typing class, remembered the picture of President Franklin D. Roosevelt that Ralph created on the typewriter: "He used both small and capital letters, chiefly the letter *x*. The picture was beautiful, artistic, and lifelike.

"I'm sure he never had any trouble with his grades, though he possibly could have applied himself a little more. If he had, he could have ranked first in our high school class. But what was the use? Music was his love.

"The girls all liked Cookie very much, but music occupied most of his time and thoughts. I remember going with him to a couple of dances where he played, and I don't think the subject of girls came up during the whole evening. He loved to tease the girls, though, especially Pearl Ida Rehmeier."

Pearl Rehmeier Wilmer remembered that she and Ralph "really liked each other" in high school. They played opposite each other in the sophomore, junior, and senior class plays. In their sophomore year, Pearl was the maid and Ralph the butler. The next year, they were sweethearts in the play; and in the senior play, they were a married couple.

Ralph, as a member of the basketball team, was not supposed to smoke—either at or away from school. But Pearl Wilmer told of the day he lit a cigarette in study hall and Edward Heidbreder, the basketball coach, entered the room. Ralph stuck the cigarette in his pants pocket, but he couldn't do anything about the smoke. Heidbreder, who was in charge of the study hall, questioned him, and Ralph stammered that he knew nothing about it. Wilmer thought Ralph could get away with anything because he was such an important member of the team.

Herman J. Mang, a classmate, said Ralph "was always friendly and well liked by everyone. Girls went for him real big, and I don't remember his showing any real interest in any one girl. Music came first in his life, and he would play piano anytime or anyplace. I suppose his playing sort of discouraged dates because the girls didn't want to just sit around at dances."

Another classmate, Betsy Fulkerson Combs, agreed that Ralph had little interest in girls. She described him as "quiet but quite friendly and very popular. I never dated him, and I can't remember that he had a girl in particular. He always seemed to be part of the band that the rest of us danced to."

Dave Schneider, who had noted Ralph's temper in first grade, remembered him in high school as a "very intense but very happy person who loved to kid around and joke. During assemblies in the gym before a basketball game, Ralph would play the piano while we sang the school song. He'd turn around and grin at some of us, hit a few jazz notes, and then very sedately go back to playing the song."

In the fall of 1939, when Ralph started his junior year, a young teacher of English named Gail Albright joined the faculty of the Francis Howell High School. He was only 21, not too much older than some of his students. Albright recalled: "I soon learned about young Ralph's red-hot piano. He was certainly not an outstanding student—and he didn't care to be. I believe that as far as he was concerned, school was mainly a necessary evil, and by far the best parts of it were basketball, opportunities to get to a piano during the day, and some fun times with his classmates. He had a keen wit and sense of humor—and such remarkable talent at the keyboard. He did moderately well in my classes and in all his academic work.

"My job at the school, and perhaps the greatest challenge of my life, had been prescribed by Mr. Hollenbeck. I was to build the English program, establish and teach speech, and re-establish music in the curriculum. There had been no music the preceding year. I struggled with the English and probably helped improve the program a little. The one speech course was no problem. And the music, as Hollenbeck and I had agreed, would be limited to vocal music—primarily a mixed chorus and a couple of glee clubs. He wanted a band, but I wasn't an instrumental man. I was an English and speech major with only a minor in music, and that was chiefly in vocal music.

"I couldn't play more than 'Chopsticks' on the piano, and so you can imagine the predicament I'd have been in had there been no student pianist to accompany the groups. Here's where Ralph Sutton first became significant in my life. He was the answer to more than one prayer and, with his usual good nature and willingness to cooperate, agreed to be the accompanist. Of course, it could have been with the thought that the hours spent with my vocal groups not only would give him that many more chances to play piano, but also would get him out of some study hall periods, which he abhorred.

"One day in a study hall early in the year, things were going along as smoothly and peacefully as they always should have but often didn't. I was in charge of those juniors and seniors in a room on the second floor of the old, two-story brick building. I never would have suspected that the building, sound and obviously well constructed, could have been subject to what was about to happen.

"Penetrating the quiet and calm of the group at study came the slight but increasingly noticeable tremor of the whole building. Windowpane after windowpane began to rattle, until it seemed that all were rattling. Floors and walls vibrated with increasing intensity. I slowly raised my head from the work on my desk in confused amazement, trying to assume an attitude of composure and control as I glanced about the room. Even more amazing, however, were the reactions of the students—not reactions of fear or excitement, but quite the contrary, ranging from tittering to snickering to half-hidden glances in the direction of one of their classmates.

"I followed their glances to one unassuming lad, his head down in an obviously pretentious posture of study. The lad was Ralph Sutton. But the tremors and rumblings had ceased, and I just as pretentiously resumed my work. Then slowly came another tremor, and the entire scene was repeated; except this time my attention focused more promptly on Ralph—promptly enough to detect the cause of the whole thing.

"A physicist could explain it scientifically. I can only say that a bundle of pent-up energy was being released in about the only way it could in a study hall. With toes pivoted on the floor, and legs and thighs bouncing rhythmically, Ralph set up vibrations at such a frequency as to cause waves of motion to spread throughout the building.

"I continued to stare at him until, eventually, he glanced up just enough to catch my suspicious eyes. He looked questioningly around the room; but, failing to divert me, he finally gave me a sheepish grin, tucked his chin, and there were no more tremors.

"I later learned that this was nothing new to the students. They frequently had experienced such quakes from what they called the Sutton Fault. Soon afterward, Ralph and I had a little talk. He was too respectful and understanding to cause any more disruptions by *that* means in my classroom.

"Ralph's years of piano study, working with the classical music demanded by his teacher, had well-prepared him to be accompanist for the kind of music we sang in the school groups. But it soon became obvious that he could take just so much of 'In the Gloaming' or 'O Holy Night' before the compulsion to cut loose on 'St. Louis Blues' or a bit of boogie overcame him. He'd have his fling for a moment, throw the class into gleeful chaos, and then agreeably settle back to the obviously dull task at hand. Yet I was thankful to have him. Only with Ralph's assistance did I succeed in building some fairly decent vocal groups during my two years at Francis Howell."

As a high school junior, Ralph received special recognition for his ability at the piano. He played the processional and recessional at the baccalaureate and commencement services. His father, as president of the school board, presented the diplomas to the graduating students.

Virginia Ryker, who joined the faculty at the start of Ralph's senior year, organized the school's first band. She said Gail Albright "spent every minute he had available listening to Ralph play the piano in the band room." Ryker remembered running into Lillian Carpenter one day, "and she seemed very happy. I asked her why, and she answered, 'I *am* happy. I gave Ralph Earl Sutton a piano lesson this morning, and he is such a joy. I do have a little trouble keeping him on scales though.' "

In the summer of 1940, Ed Heidbreder visited Howell to get an idea of the kind of basketball team he would be coaching that fall. He had just been hired and remembered meeting several members of the team: "Most of them were about my height—5-7 or 5-8—but presently a young fellow came along who was about 6-2. 'That's Ralph Sutton,' one man told me. 'He'll be a senior next year, and he'll be on your team.'

Then he introduced me to Ralph, and I was very happy to see a fellow of that size.

"Ralph told me his mother was concerned about his playing basketball because she was afraid he would injure a finger, which would hurt his music. But Ralph was the most valuable member of the team, partly because back in those days, a 6-2 basketball player was a fairly tall boy.

"We had another fellow who was a little shorter than Ralph but had longer arms. He could outjump Ralph at center, and so Ralph played guard. He was a good rebounder because he had plenty of weight and handled himself well. At times, when the referee wasn't looking too closely, Ralph used his weight to get some of the other team's fellows out of the way so he could get a rebound. Sometimes I played him at forward so he could be under our basket. He was a good shooter, especially in close.

"Although he was a great asset to the team, Ralph was rather modest. In most of the games, he was one of the leading scorers. But if anyone tried to say much to him about how he had played, he would turn his back and walk away. He never wanted to take any credit."

Ralph was on the starting team at Howell for three years, and Norman Muschany thought his "fiery temper" helped make him a good player. He remembered: "When the score was tied with a minute to go, Ralph was the guy who elbowed somebody and got called for a foul and cussed under his breath. You could hear the old country people twitchin' about what he had said. But then he'd knock somebody down and score the winning point and end up the hero."

Leonard Fuerman said Ralph "was known and respected for his actions with his elbows. I was on the second-string team, and so I played against Cookie quite often in practice. I still have two teeth with chips broken off as a result of not ducking his elbows."

Amos Jose recalled that during basketball practice, Ralph often "jumped up on the stage in the auditorium and hammered out some jazz for 10 to 15 minutes. It was pure delight, his playing not for anyone especially or even for himself. He'd just get carried away and let it all pour out."

The class of 1941, which included Ralph Earl Sutton, was the last to graduate from the old Francis Howell High School before the government took over the building, along with the entire community, for the TNT plant. Leonard Fuerman remembered that Ralph played a piano solo during the graduation ceremonies: "He played with such vigor that the vase of flowers on top of the upright piano almost teetered off. I don't know if the audience was more awed by Ralph's playing or by the vase sliding across the piano."

Some families in the community resisted the government takeover, and their property was condemned. Ralph said his father "kind of went along with the government because he knew what was coming." Earl Sutton's construction business was doing very well at that time, and the local Republican leaders asked him to run for clerk of the circuit court. He won election to the office and four years later was reelected. Earl later regretted his venture into politics because he could have been more successful financially by giving all his time to construction.

The summer after graduation, Ralph worked on the construction gang. So did his brother, who joined the gang every summer to earn some extra money. One day, the men put the roof on a building in a pouring rain, with Ralph carrying shingles up a ladder. He came down and told Harold, "I'm going to do something with music instead of hauling these damn shingles for the rest of my life."

Chapter **5**

What Ya Wanna Play, Gate?

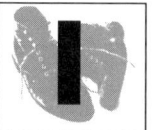
n September 1941, Ralph began what turned out to be an abbreviated college career. He enrolled as a music major at Northeast Missouri State Teachers College in Kirksville, about 200 miles from St. Charles. The Suttons had moved from Howell to St. Charles that summer as part of the mass exodus that made way for the government's TNT plant.

Barbara felt "kind of excited about moving because it was going to be something new, living in a big town." But except for a few families who had wanted to sell their land anyway, the government action left nothing but anger and sadness among the displaced people. Many of the men, including Earl Sutton, never could understand why fine farmland had to be destroyed, especially after the TNT plant closed so soon. Barbara said Ralph "was really in a rage because we weren't treated fairly."

Gail Albright had urged Ralph to go to college in Kirksville. He had graduated from the school himself and later taught speech there. Through the years, he encouraged many young people to attend the school, which became Northeast Missouri State University. "It's an exceptionally fine school and much less expensive than most," Albright said. "Then, as now, students were not just a number but were the subject of a real personal concern to most of their instructors. The school also had a great music department that offered opportunities for a student to develop artistically and professionally, whether interested in teaching or not."

During Ralph's senior year in high school, Albright took him to Kirksville and introduced him to several members of the music faculty. On the way, they stopped at Albright's home in La Plata, just south of the college town. There, he introduced Ralph to an old friend, Armon Adams, a music teacher in the La Plata public school.

"I had grown up with Armon and wanted him to hear Ralph," Albright said. "I knew how great Ralph was, and I was anxious to have Armon hear this student, who had such remarkable talent. Armon was playing sax and clarinet in a combo at the time and was quite a musician himself."

Adams was indeed impressed: "I can still see Ralph as he sat at the old upright piano in our gym to give us a 'first listen.' And what a listen it was! I was amazed to hear such a style already forming and to hear the feeling for jazz that came from this young man just finishing high school. I remember the rather large hands and the effortless ease with which they danced over the keyboard. Later that year, I was lucky enough to be in a dance band with this young fellow at the piano, though he was truly head and shoulders above the rest of us."

Ralph received top grades in his college music courses. He enjoyed such subjects as music theory, counterpoint, and harmony and had little difficulty with them. He took private piano lessons as part of his academic program, sang in the college a cappella choir, and even played some basketball. But to his great annoyance, he learned that "to get a degree in music, you had to take so many other things—liberal arts courses and other stuff that I wasn't interested in. You even had to learn to twirl a baton—for a fourth of a credit."

Ralph and his roommate, Warren (Red) Huesemann, another music major, took clarinet lessons together as part of the curriculum. They could afford to rent only one clarinet between them. On the day of a lesson, each tried to con the other into carrying the instrument to class.

"We'd leave it under a bed and be a block away or even get clear to class without it," Huesemann remembered. "Then we'd look at each other and ask, 'Where's the clarinet?' "

One of them would finally give in and run back for the clarinet. But Ralph never did learn to play it.

Kirksville was—and is—also the home of the Kirksville College of Osteopathic Medicine. The social calendar of the students at both colleges and of the town itself included enough dances and parties to keep two or three dance bands busy throughout the school year. During the summer before Ralph started college, one of the bands reorganized.

Lewis C. Baum, who played lead alto sax in the group, recalled: "We were having difficulty locating a good piano man. One Saturday afternoon in September, some of us met at the Theta Psi fraternity house on the Osteopathic College campus to audition a big, tall, gangly guy from St. Charles by the name of Ralph Sutton. I had great misgivings and felt disappointed when I first saw him because he absolutely did not look like a piano man—or even a musician.

"My feelings changed as soon as Ralph sat down and started to play. He played and played and played. And it was as though we had struck gold. We all realized that he would be the backbone of our band."

The band was a 12-piece group with a male and female vocalist, and Baum said they all "were quite happy to play a three-hour dance for $3 or $4 each." Armon Adams drove up from his teaching job in La Plata to play in the group, and he also wrote arrangements.

Every Thursday, Ralph played for the local Kiwanis Club luncheon. He became known to a number of the business and professional people and other residents of Kirksville, and many of them invited him to play for evening functions at their home.

Ralph lived in various rooming houses, including the home of Todd Kirk, whose ancestors had established the town and, later, the college. Kirk owned a saloon called the Tap Room, where Ralph liked to play the piano—and drink draft beer for a dime. The two got acquainted, and Kirk invited the boy to rent a room in his home. Ralph and Red Huesemann roomed together there.

While in college, Ralph held a variety of nonmusical jobs because his father could afford to pay only part of his tuition and other expenses. Ralph delivered clothes for a cleaner and then got a job as busboy and counter boy at a little restaurant called the Manhattan Cafe. After a while, he talked the owner into putting in a piano and letting him earn all his meals by playing every evening for the students who ate there.

"One evening, I walked in and the piano was gone," Ralph said. "The guy just didn't think it was worth it—my getting breakfast, lunch, and supper. I thought, well, I'll get my counter job back or I'll bus dishes. But, no, he wouldn't give me my job back.

"I was kind of prepared for this guy because I expected he was going to pull some shit on me, and so I swiped three or four of those little green pads that restaurants use to write the customers' checks. After he let me go, I went into the place several times and had a T-bone steak. The steak cost about $1, but I'd have written down a hamburger and a Coke on the pad, and so I'd pay only 15 or 20 cents. He caught me one day and said he was going to turn me into the school and call up my father. I was so goddamned mad, I said, 'You call them both. You screwed me when you took the piano out and didn't give me my job back, so you go ahead because it doesn't embarrass me a bit.' But he didn't do anything at all.

"Then I got a job at Troester's Clothing Company for 35 cents an hour. I worked after school and in the evening. I couldn't even wrap a parcel, but I had to wrap a lot of things up and tie them. Oh, Christ, I sweated that job. And then I worked in a drugstore for 35 cents an hour. They had me in the back room changing around the stuff on the shelves. I couldn't stand that, and I worked just one evening there."

In October 1942, at the beginning of Ralph's sophomore year in college, Jack Teagarden came to Kirksville with a big band. He played at a public dance in the Armory Building, and Ralph was determined to hear him: "I didn't have the money to get in, and so another guy and I snuck in through a basement window. Jack was one of my idols—he still is—and I just had to hear him. He was having an awful time those days, losing guys right and left to the draft and picking up other guys in various towns and taking them along with him.

"I was standing along the sidelines listening to the band and just watching Jack, and some of my friends started trying to get me to go up and sit in. I told them, 'No, I don't want to do that.' They got on Jack and told him, 'Hey, Jack, there's a guy down here plays piano.' You know how those things are. It was embarrassing to me, and I would have been too embarrassed to even go up and say hello to Jack. But he said, 'Sure, Gate,' with that big smile. Man! 'C'mon up here. What ya wanna play, Gate?'

"I'll always remember the tune. It was my dad's favorite, 'Indiana.' We went into it, and Jack got a big charge out of me. I was so thrilled to be playing with this guy that I got goosebumps. It was unbelievable. Here's my god! We played two or three other numbers, and I was anxious to get off then. I'd had it, and I was nervous. After the dance, Jack told me, 'Ralph, give me your address. You might be hearing from me.' And I thought, 'Oh, man.'

"A month went by, and a telegram came from Jack to the osteopathic school. 'I'm trying to contact a piano player by the name of Ralph Sutton. If you can locate him, have him get in touch with me at the New Yorker Hotel in New York.' They found out where I was living and called me. I phoned Jack right away. He offered me a job, and I told him, 'Yes, I can make it.' I had been planning to quit school anyway because the draft was coming, and I figured it was a wonderful opportunity. I was just thrilled."

Ralph had no hesitation about dropping out of school, "not when Jack Teagarden says 'I want you to join my band.' " Ralph's parents had no objection, and they knew he would soon be drafted anyway. Asked if any faculty member encouraged him to stay in college, Ralph said, "No, I made up my own mind."

The head of the college music department, John Biggerstaff, was one of Ralph's piano teachers in Kirksville. Lewis Baum described Biggerstaff as "an outstanding musician in every way, though he was really a longhair and didn't get a great deal of pleasure from jazz. He told Ralph that he obviously had great promise but that he should concentrate on serious music and thereby develop his skill and technique. I know that Ralph respected Biggerstaff and really admired him, but he continued right on in the same groove."

John Goetze had Ralph as a student in his music theory class. He remembered that Ralph "loved to play piano and was an excellent musician with a distinctive style all his own. Biggerstaff tried to discourage him away from jazz and into the classics, but I saw where Ralph was going and I didn't try to interfere. Ralph understood what he was doing, so why try to stop him?"

Few people know that Ralph Sutton at one time considered becoming a concert pianist. He is an outstanding classical musician and a superb sight reader. He says, "I've never gotten away from classical music, and I never will. I had thoughts of being a classical pianist, but I had jazz on my mind, too. And I knew what I'd have to go through to become a concert pianist. You have to be really dedicated to practice eight hours a day, and I had to go out and make a living. I just couldn't do it. But if I'd have been financially fixed so I didn't have to worry about money...."

Years later, during a radio interview with Bill Culter in Columbus, Ohio, Ralph was talking about some old rags he had recorded. He expressed mild displeasure that his thorough musicianship had escaped attention.

"It's a funny thing," he told Culter. "You make a record and you play the ragtime tunes, and people accuse you of being a ragtime piano player. It's amazing they don't say anything about my being able to read the music. A lot of the things I practice at home I've never recorded—things like Bach and Beethoven and Chopin and Scarlatti. I've never been accused of being a concert pianist, though I would love to be one."

Sutton calls Jack Teagarden "the greatest in my book" and refers to him as "my godfather in the music business." However, Ralph may not have had such fond feelings toward Teagarden while trying to find a comfortable position for his long legs during the overnight train trip from St. Louis to New York to join Jack's band in December 1942.

"Jack sent me a one-way ticket—chair coach, not even a sleeper," Ralph remembered. "So I got on the train with my big suitcase and rode into Penn Station in New York. I was just a farm boy, and I began looking at those buildings. I didn't know shit from apple butter. Talk about being scared! I got a cab and told the driver I wanted to go to the New Yorker Hotel. 'It's right over there,' he told me. 'You can walk.' He could see I was a rube.

"I walked over to the hotel and called Jack on the house phone. He said, 'Yeah, Gate, c'mon up.' So I went up, and he and his wife were still in bed, even though it was early afternoon. He could see that I was pretty much of a greenhorn because he'd been through the same thing. But he took me under his wing. He called the Forrest Hotel on 49th off Broadway, where all the musicians stayed, and got me a room there. He and Addie went over in a cab with me. Jack told me, 'Wear a tuxedo,' but I didn't have one. I got a tux, and he bought me a pair of Florsheim tux shoes.

"I was with Jack for about two months, and then I got my draft notice and had to leave. We were on the road playing one-nighters and college dates. I'll never forget the first job I played with Jack—in a college gym somewhere in Pennsylvania. It was colder than a son of a gun that night, but I was sweatin', trying to do my best. Jack had a piano book, but it was all messed up. The tunes had been numbered, but they weren't in numerical order. Dottie Reid was the vocalist with Jack's band then, and she sat alongside the piano and really helped me out. That piano book was so thick and fouled up. Jack would call out some tunes, and she'd try to find them for me."

Ralph returned to St. Charles after leaving Teagarden and spent a couple of weeks doing odd jobs before reporting for induction into the Army. He washed cars in a filling station and painted a shoe factory fence. "That's where I stepped off a ladder into a bucket of paint," he recalled.

In February 1943, Ralph and his high school classmate Leonard Fuerman found themselves in the same group of inductees at Jefferson Barracks in St. Louis.

"We had bunk inspection the first morning," Fuerman remembered. "The PFC in charge took one look at Ralph's bunk and ripped it apart and had him make it again and again. I was shipped to Texas that day, and that was the last time I saw Ralph while in service. I always wondered if he ever passed bunk inspection."

Chapter **6**

All I Wanted to Do Was Music

rivate Ralph Earl Sutton was sent from Jefferson Barracks to Camp Roberts in California. He found himself in the infantry: "I didn't know infantry from field artillery or anything else. I immediately tried to get into a band somewhere on the base. All the Army B.S. got me down, and I goofed off a lot. Finally, one morning I was on KP and someone told me to pack up my stuff and report to the bugle outfit. They thought any musician ought to be able to play a bugle. I figured anything would be better than the infantry because they needed cannon fodder in those days.

"I never did learn to blow a bugle, but I tried. Eventually, some friends in the field artillery headquarters battalion got me moved over there. I rode a bicycle around getting rations for the kitchens, and then I'd get in a truck with the driver and go down to the commissary to pick up what they needed. That was nice duty."

One day, Ralph wandered into the Red Cross recreation center while a soldier named Bill Reich was playing the piano. Reich had no idea of Sutton's talent at the keyboard.

"I invited him to join in, but he wouldn't," Reich remembered. "I must have been pretty bad. Even so, he told me, 'No thanks, man, you're doing fine. Keep it up!' I went back to the rec room a few days later, and hordes of GIs were standing around the piano listening to some real wild-ass playing. It turned out to be the same guy—Ralph. No wonder he didn't want to play when he heard me. He was probably ready to throw up at what he heard."

The Army chose both Ralph and Bill Reich for the ASTP (Army Specialized Training Program) and assigned them to Stanford University. Sutton balked at being picked for the college program, but he had the time of his life at Stanford: "They picked me because I had some college education. I told them I was happy in the field artillery and didn't want to be in the ASTP, but that didn't make any difference. They just put me in the engineering program up at Stanford. I was there for about six weeks, and I had a wonderful time. I kept praying that I wouldn't get sent somewhere else because Stanford was really a good deal. It was a beautiful campus, and life was very easy there. We went to class all day and actually slept on sheets.

"Bill and I used to sneak out at night after bed check and hitchhike down the road to a joint called Dinah's Shack. They had a piano there, and I'd start playing. That's where I first started drinking Scotch. Until then, it had been bourbon or beer. Man, I had a ball there in Palo Alto. The Army didn't keep too close tabs on us, and it was just great."

Bill Reich had gone to Stanford for two years before being drafted. The Army sent him there ahead of Ralph, and Reich remembered having "a welcoming committee of cute gals and a red convertible waiting when Sutton showed up. Ralph quickly became known around the Stanford campus. When he was down at Dinah's, the people couldn't line up enough drinks on his piano, getting him to play 'Honeysuckle Rose,' 'Muskrat Ramble,' and all the other good tunes. Every once in a while he would break into 'Honky Tonk Train' and bring the whole house down. Most of the people I had known during my first two years at Stanford were still there, and they were all entranced with Ralph and scooped him up as a newfound friend. He was always very shy, modest, and self-effacing.

"We used to go to my home in Berkeley on weekends," Reich said. "My Episcopalian mom made like a Jewish mother, feeding Ralph on goodies until he nearly popped. We spent hours listening to all the Art Tatum stuff that I had been collecting since 1934. Ralph fit into my civvies pretty well, though his arms stuck out about a foot past the cuffs. We'd go out with my folks to eat—and wherever we'd go, people would coax him to play. My mother was nuts about Ralph and wanted to adopt him."

After Ralph's six weeks at Stanford, the Army sent him to the University of Oregon in Eugene to continue his studies. But he had little aptitude or interest in engineering: "It was a scuffle. All I wanted to do was music, but we didn't have too much free time. They really worked us up there—five days and Saturday mornings in class. We lived in a dormitory, and the ladies of the town cooked our meals. I'll never forget the name of the head cook—Mrs. Turnipseed.

"A bunch of us got a big band together at Oregon. A guy named O. J. Bailey organized it. He played trombone and loved Jack Teagarden, and he had been in Billy Butterfield's big band."

Bailey, who later ran a music store in Chattanooga, Tennessee, recalled meeting Ralph just after being transferred to the ASTP at Oregon himself: "One Sunday morning, I was walking down the corridor and heard some cat playing some pretty fine piano. Naturally, I had to go up and say something to him. We talked about music and road gigs and so forth, and it turned out that he had been with Jack Teagarden, one of my idols. We immediately established rapport and began talking about what a dull place Eugene was. We speculated about the possibilities of changing the scene and talked about putting a combo together. But then we decided to go all out and organize a big band.

"Everyone was pessimistic and told us to forget it because it had been tried there before. But we had nothing to lose, and so we gave it a whirl and got the available guys to agree to an early Sunday morning rehearsal. They had to be desperate to agree to that. I don't remember how many men we had at first, but it was by no means a full band. We had a good lead alto player, but he had just gotten married and was thinking of giving up music. We had to tell him there was something else besides sex.

"Ralph's prestige as a pro and as a big-name musician was most helpful. Everyone soon recognized him as a real talent, and players on the campus wanted part of the action. After we began to sound like a band, the question of a name came up. There must have been a zillion suggestions, but Ralph and our drummer suggested Fathah Bailey & Crew, and so that was the name we used."

After about seven months at Oregon, Ralph "got kicked out on purpose." He explained that "I let myself get caught copying on a test because I was tired of the civilian instructors. It was too much—having to take a lot of guff from them as well as from all the Army noncoms and officers." The Army assigned him to O. J. Bailey's old outfit, the 104th Infantry, which was stationed in Yuma, Arizona, at the time.

"I got down there about 2 o'clock in the morning—a one-man troop movement," Ralph said. "The 104th was out on maneuvers in the

Mojave Desert. Oh, that desert! I wished I was back in Oregon. All the guys in the band of the 104th knew O. J. Bailey very well, and they welcomed me because they knew I was a friend. The band already had a piano player, but they took on another one. They asked, 'What other instrument can you play?' and I said, 'Glockenspiel.' I had never played one before, but it was very simple. The notes were written right on the bars of the thing. So there I was in the desert with a goddamned glockenspiel."

The 104th was eventually sent to Camp Carson, Colorado, near Colorado Springs, and Sutton frequently played piano at the Village Inn, a local bar that "looked like a little old church." The outfit went overseas from Camp Carson, but Ralph got a medical discharge in April 1945 because of his eyes. He had started to wear glasses for astigmatism at the time he entered college and has worn them ever since. Today, he always carries two pairs of glasses. He switches to bifocals to read music or anything else.

Ralph happily remembered the day he went into the Village Inn with his discharge in his pocket: "I drank all day before the train pulled out for St. Louis at 6 that night. I wasn't loaded, but I was feeling good. I was so glad to be out of the Army."

Ralph relaxed at home for a month or so and then went back to work. He got a booking in the restaurant of Roy Bowman's gambling casino in East St. Louis, Illinois.

"At that time, gambling was still legal in Illinois," Sutton recalled. "I lived in a real dump in a section of East St. Louis called the Valley. That's where all the whorehouses were. Bowman's gambling joint would close about 5 in the morning, but just long enough to sweep out. Then they'd open up again about 6. There'd always be somebody waiting to get in for his breakfast beer."

One Sunday afternoon, after Ralph had been at Bowman's about three months, Joe Schirmer, a St. Louis guitarist, came in to hear him. Schirmer was leading a quartet at the Steeplechase Bar of the Chase Hotel in St. Louis. He said, "Some guests had raved about a young piano player in East St. Louis. So many people told me about Ralph that I decided to drive over. I distinctly remember that as I walked in the door I couldn't see anything. It was a bright, sunny day, but the place was dark and full of smoke. I heard a piano and a bass playing, and I thought to myself, 'Boy, that sounds like a good Fats Waller record.' After my eyes got used to the darkness of the room, I realized there was a fellow up on the bandstand playing the piano. The bass player was a little guy named Jack Stern, who was working with Ralph.

"I had never heard anybody play a piano like Ralph could, and I never have since. I've worked with a lot of wonderful piano men, but there's something about Ralph's playing that always gets to anyone who has any kind of an ear at all for jazz piano.

"My quartet had just broken up because one of the guys had been drafted, and I asked Ralph and Jack if they'd like to form a trio with me at the Steeplechase. They said they'd love to make that kind of scene, and so we got together, had a few rehearsals, and started playing at the Chase. I think we had a five-week booking, but we worked between the Chase and the Park Plaza for about 2½ years."

Schirmer's proposition came at just the right time for Ralph, who had been anxious to get out of East St. Louis: "It wasn't a very attractive place, and Joe's offer sounded great to me. He was a fine musician. Besides the guitar, he played the electroharp, the instrument that Alvino Rey plays; and he was an excellent banjo soloist, too. We had quite a trio."

The Joe Schirmer Trio brought Ralph his first taste of public acclaim. It also led indirectly to his entrance into the big time of jazz.

Chapter **7**

It's Like a Priest Kneeling at the Altar

oe Schirmer and Ralph Sutton played together for the last time in 1947. But 26 years later, Schirmer still spoke of Ralph in words of awe: "It's an amazing thing to watch Ralph work. After you look at him for a while when he's playing, you'd swear he isn't even breathing. He reminds me of a clock. He just sits there straight up and never blinks an eye. And, boy, what he does with the keys. His execution and technique are something I've never heard from any other piano player in my whole career.

"Ralph has always had two exceptionally strong hands. When one of his fingers hits the keyboard, it's like somebody coming down with a hammer. Everything he plays is so clean. You know every note he plays. There isn't one slur. There are no mistakes. No way he'd make a mistake. He takes everything at the right tempo, regardless of how technical it is, and I've never heard him goof. Never.

"He's a stickler for the beat. If the rhythm picked up or slowed down when he and Jack and I were playing together, that really burned him. That's one thing Ralph could never take. When he or I set a tempo, that's exactly what it was supposed to be as far as Ralph was concerned. And if it wasn't that way, he'd look up over those glasses at you from the piano, and you knew something was really wrong because of the expression on his face.

"Ralph is not only a tremendous pianist, but he is also a man of very strong character. I've never heard anybody say anything bad about him. He has a heart as big as the world, and that's exactly the way he plays. He's such a sweet, warm-hearted fellow that it's almost unbelievable to me that he would even swat a fly.

"He has nothing but love for people—in his own way, of course. He does demand respect when he plays for people to listen. I know he gets perturbed when there's any noise in the audience while he's playing solo piano on something like 'Echo of Spring.' Tunes like that are absolute musical masterpieces; and when they're played the way Ralph plays them, you should really listen in order to get them all over you. He does a beautiful job with them."

In 1945, the Joe Schirmer Trio went to New York for a four-week engagement at the Village Vanguard. They played the Blue Angel on their night off. Ralph wanted to stay in New York after they closed at the Vanguard; but Schirmer and Stern voted to return to St. Louis, and so back they all went to the Chase Hotel.

During his years in St. Louis with Schirmer, Sutton also did radio studio work. He played for a while in Bobby Swain's orchestra at station KXOK and then in the studio orchestra at KWK, upstairs in the Chase. Carl Hohengarten, whom Ralph considered "a fine conductor and arranger" and who helped give Gordon Jenkins his start, led the KWK group.

One of Ralph's high school classmates, Betsy Fulkerson Combs, who had danced to his music so often in Howell, frequently went to the Steeplechase on dates. "I asked Ralph to play 'Holiday for Strings' so many times," she said, "that he finally started to play it whenever I walked in the door."

While playing at the Chase, Sutton met George Ledbetter, who became one of his closest friends. On Saturday nights, when Ledbetter usually dropped in, Ralph performed one of his lesser-known feats.

"He'd buy the early Sunday edition of the *Post-Dispatch* and spread the comics across the top of the piano," Ledbetter said. "Then he'd play the greatest jazz you ever heard—and read the funnies at the same time. It was fantastic to watch him putting out such great music while he was sitting there laughing and reading the comics."

After leaving the Chase, the trio played the Merry-Go-Round Room of the Park Plaza Hotel in St. Louis. They got a big break when CBS gave them a radio shot every night at 10.

"The people started gathering at about 8 o'clock," Schirmer said, "and there'd be a standing line waiting to get in when we began playing at 9. The room held about 200 persons; and by the time 10 o'clock came and we went on the air, you couldn't get in. On a Saturday night, a butterfly wouldn't have been able to squeeze into the place.

"I owe an awful lot to Ralph Sutton because he picked up loads of friends along the way. Every place we played, there was a never-ending line of people around the piano watching him. It seemed like everybody who heard Ralph play would tell someone else about him.

"Up on the stand, Ralph sat on my right and Jack was on my left. When one of us took a solo, we'd punch a button so that the man and his instrument would light up. Sometimes when Ralph started a solo, he'd play two or three choruses of boogie with his left hand to kind of set the mood, and then he'd get into the right hand, and then he'd get both hands going together. I'd say, 'Spread out,' and that meant for him to get down to the lowest keys with his left hand playing boogie and up to the highest keys with his right hand. When he got going on that routine, it was something else.

"He had another thing that set me on fire, too. He'd play with both hands way high up on the keyboard, with his left hand in a kind of real sharp boogie pattern and his right hand playing all the trills and licks.

"I remember when 'Bumble Boogie' came out. Ralph woodshedded it, and it didn't take him too long to add it to our book. With all respect to the man who first recorded that tune, when Ralph played it, it was nowhere close to the original.

"And when Ralph started out on 'Little Rock Getaway,' nobody could hold him. He played that baby note for note just like Joe Sullivan and Bob Zurke used to play it. Personally, I don't think there was any comparison because of Ralph's tremendous power. It's tough to play an intricate thing like 'Little Rock' with a lot of pressure and weight because you just don't play the piano or any other instrument that way. Ralph was the only exception I've ever known. He played fast and clean; and he always leaned on the 2 and 4, which is a big thing with me."

Ralph performed "Bumble Boogie" as a solo as well as with Schirmer's trio. The composer, pianist Jack Fina, had adapted the tune from Nikolai Rimsky-Korsakov's famous "Flight of the Bumblebee," and it became one of the most popular hits of the day. Fina recorded it with Freddy Martin's band and later with the rhythm section of his own group.

Drew Page, who played clarinet and sax with Martin and then Fina and in many other big bands, set forth his memoirs in a book called *Drew's Blues*, published in 1980. He remembered when Fina's band opened an engagement at the Chase Hotel:

"The first night I was there I heard a marvelous piano player named Ralph Sutton who was playing solo in the lounge. He played his own jazz versions of most things but was also doing Fina's arrangement of 'Flight of the Bumblebee' as a throwaway. He asked me whether he should go to Hollywood or New York to try to break into the big time. I recommended Hollywood, but as it turned out, he wound up in New York."

Unfortunately, the Joe Schirmer Trio made no commercial recordings. However, they did record a group of 43 tunes for Standard Radio Transcriptions. These numbers are showcases for the great individual and group talent of Schirmer, Sutton, and Stern. During the bridge of one of the tunes, "Christopher Columbus," played at a bat-out-of-hell tempo, Ralph brings "Nola" whirling onto the scene, followed by "The Sailor's Hornpipe." He kicks off another of the numbers, a Schirmer composition called "Wild Man," at an even more frantic tempo.

Schirmer enjoyed recalling the trio's trip to Chicago in the spring of 1946 to make the transcriptions: "I told Jack and Ralph, 'Now, fellows, there won't be any drinking on the train because we've got all these tunes to cut.' They were all head arrangements.

"Ralph had bought himself a brand-new white lambskin coat. I'll never forget it. It was absolutely beautiful. He got lost in the club car somewhere along the line, and I didn't see him all the way to Chicago. I went looking for him after we got there, but I couldn't find him anywhere. I guess everybody had left the train except me, and I was still looking for Ralph and all the instruments.

"Finally, I looked way up the platform to the entrance where the passengers were walking into the station, and I saw a white coat sitting there. Ralph was perched on my amplifier, and all the smoke and stuff from the trains had landed on his coat. He was really a mess.

"Ralph had a pretty nice little package made, and I was kind of afraid because you've got just so much time to turn out a great job when you're recording, along with all the pressures in making records. But there was nothing to worry about. If I've had a few drinks, I have a little problem playing. But not Ralph. I don't care how many nights he's been out or where he's been or what he's done. When he sits down at the piano, it's like a priest kneeling at the altar. It's all there."

In 1946, Ralph married a young woman he had met at the University of Oregon. Charline Pelly was a coed from Berkeley, California, and first saw Ralph while he was playing with the band at Oregon. He impressed her as "a fantastic musician and a sweet, sensitive soul." Ralph and Chuck, as she was known, had three sons—Jeff, Pete, and Nick.

The marriage began to fall apart in the late 1950s. In September 1964, Ralph met Sunnie Anderson, who owned a supper club in Aspen, Colorado. He and Chuck were divorced in June 1965. Ralph married Sunnie the same day.

When I told Ralph my idea of writing the story of his life, I mentioned that sooner or later, I would be asking him about his first marriage. His only response was, "I don't want Sunnie to be hurt." During the first of our sessions together in the preparation of this book, Ralph took me through his whole life—without mentioning Chuck or their sons. I asked him if I concluded correctly that he did not wish me to contact any of them while conducting research for the book. "That won't be necessary," he replied, and I of course followed his wishes.

Several months later, however, I pointed out to him that any account of Ralph Sutton's life and career would, at best, be incomplete without some mention of his first wife and his sons. To my surprise, after reflecting for only a few moments, Ralph wrote down the phone number and address of each. "Go ahead and call them," he said. This deeply private man had decided, not without some reluctance, to let others share at least a little of an intensely personal part of himself. Subsequently, Charline Sutton and Ralph's sons all contributed to the book.

While with the Joe Schirmer Trio, Ralph met Hubert S. Pruett, a St. Louis surgeon, jazz fan, and former major-league pitcher. Hub Pruett had put himself through medical school by pitching during the 1920s for the St. Louis Browns—he struck out Babe Ruth 10 times—and, later, for three National League teams. He became a friend of many top jazz musicians, and they often stayed at his home when performing in St. Louis or passing through the city.

Pruett's friends included Wild Bill Davison, who took a break early in 1947 from his chair in the band at Eddie Condon's club in New York. Davison brought a combo to St. Louis for an engagement at the 400 Club, an old burlesque theater that had been converted into a night spot. He lived in Pruett's home while playing there, and the physician told him about Ralph.

"I suggested to Bill that he let Ralph sit in with him," Pruett recalled. "We went down one evening, and Bill let Ralph play. He fell in love with Ralph's piano, too."

But it actually didn't happen so simply. Pruett brought Ralph into the 400 on the Schirmer trio's night off, but Davison wanted nothing to do with the young pianist at first.

"I took a look at Ralph, and he looked like a banker or a kid out of high school," Davison said. "I just dread letting guys sit in, especially someone who looks the way Ralph looked. I really didn't want him to sit in, but I finally told him he could play after we had finished the floor show.

"Well, he came up after the show and sat down—and he broke it in half. Holy mackerel! We had never heard such a piano player. I thought, 'Who *is* this guy?' I told him, 'Ralph, you've got to get out of this town. You've got to go to New York. Man, if they ever heard you play in New York!'"

After Sutton's experience with Davison, Schirmer "had a feeling that Ralph wanted to branch out a little bit and get with a bigger band." So it couldn't have been a great surprise when Ralph dropped out of the trio later that year. Jack Teagarden had come through St. Louis on a tour with a band that included Lips Page and J. C. Higginbotham.

The band played at the Tune Town Ballroom, where Charlie Wells handled public relations. One of his jobs was to set up guest appearances on radio and TV shows for bandleaders and jazz personalities. Wells, who in 1982 established the annual Mid-America Jazz Festival, took Teagarden to KWK in the Chase Hotel.

"Rush Hughes was in charge of the show," Wells recalled. "After Jack had been interviewed on the air, he told Rush, 'Please come down the hall with me. There's a young man I want you to hear play piano.' Of course the young man was Ralph Sutton. Jack told us that Ralph was going to join his band, and the rest is history.

"Ralph and I have been friends ever since we met that day. He is a warm, congenial artist and a gentleman in every sense of the word, a great pianist and a super performer."

Sutton fondly remembered an evening spent with Teagarden during the Tune Town gig. He picked up the great trombonist at his hotel, and they had dinner together and then went to Ralph's apartment.

"Jack brought his horn with him and we played together, just the two of us," Ralph said. "He was working out an arrangement of 'Lover' that he recorded. He showed it to me and we played it. Later I drove him down to the Tune Town.

"Jack told me he was leaving the tour and was going to open at the Famous Door on 52nd Street in New York. He asked me to join him, and I told him I'd love to. So I gave my notice to Joe and to KWK, and a bit later I drove back to New York—and back to the Forrest Hotel. We opened at the Famous Door with Max Kaminsky, Peanuts Hucko, Jack Lesberg, Eddie Shaughnessy, and Jack and myself. It was really exciting to play with those guys. They knocked me out."

Hucko remembered that Teagarden "was just crazy about Ralph's playing, and so were we all." Lesberg said the older musicians got "quite a thrill hearing this young guy come up and carry on with the piano the way he did. It probably was one of the very first times that Ralph actually played with a band like that on a regular basis, and I must admit he was a little overpowering. We'd never had a piano player who could charge in with both hands the way Ralph did. His playing is so full, and he really took over."

Wild Bill Davison had raved to Eddie Condon about Ralph after returning to New York from St. Louis. One night, Sutton went down to Condon's club in Greenwich Village and sat in with the band there. Condon was so impressed that he made the following observation in his book *We Called It Music*, published in 1947: "Jazz players remain a small group; only occasionally does a youngster appear who is capable of joining them; there is a bare trickle of new names—Ralph Sutton, Johnny Blowers, Peanuts Hucko, Johnny Windhurst."

Chapter **8**

You Sure Don't Play Like a White Boy

alph played at the Famous Door for about a month and a half, after which Teagarden joined Louis Armstrong's newly formed All Stars. Sutton then worked "one night here, one night there," including an engagement as intermission pianist at Jimmy Ryan's, another top jazz spot on 52nd Street. Jack Palmer, the lyricist of "I Found a New Baby," "Everybody Loves My Baby," and several other jazz standards, went to Ryan's one Saturday night to hear the newcomer.

"As I went in," Palmer recalled, "I saw a good friend of mine, Dorothy Kilgallen, who was a great jazz buff. She had come to Ryan's for the same purpose as I had—to catch a new pianist, Ralph Sutton, whom neither of us had ever heard of before. I invited her to join me at a table near the bandstand, and I also called over Red McKenzie, who was standing nearby.

"I thought there was a mistake when a big, athletic, good-looking fellow sat down at the piano. There had been an important football game in New York that afternoon, and I thought he might have been one of the players. But after he played about 16 bars of 'Honeysuckle Rose,' Dorothy, Red, and I looked at one another without a word and just nodded.

"Ralph finished up with 'Carolina Shout,' and if I had closed my eyes, I could have been listening to James P. Johnson or Fats Waller, who were themselves such great stylists and piano players. Ralph had no intention of copying either of them; but his style, feeling, and execution were astounding. I had always been a follower of Fats's and James P.'s because their style and drive were right in the idiom I wrote in, and so hearing Ralph was an added incentive in my work.

"After Ralph left the stand, I called him over for a taste so I could meet him. His handshake could have been that of a football player, and he warmly acknowledged our praise with his sheepish grin and his kind, soft voice. He and I seemed to dig each other pretty well, and I dropped in at Ryan's quite often from then on."

On June 28, 1947, Ralph made the first of 12 appearances on the weekly "This Is Jazz" radio show. Rudi Blesh, the m.c., introduced him as "the phenomenal young St. Louis pianist." The next week, Blesh declared that "the playing of this young but accomplished pianist has already brought in a heavy response.... It's heartening to find so young a man—he's only 24—thoroughly alive to the real artistic merit of ragtime." On the September 20 show, Blesh again praised "our sensational young pianist... from St. Louis, which was originally the ragtime capital of the world. To say that he carries on that sort of tradition ably is really to put it mildly because he adds a lot of modern touches of his own...."

Blesh had a deep interest in ragtime, and so his comments associating Ralph with this piano style came as no surprise. He and Harriet Janis were writing their book *They All Played Ragtime*, which was published three years later, in 1950. The authors gave Ralph a deep bow of acknowledgment for his help: "Ralph Sutton, brilliant ragtime pianist, earned our gratitude by devoting many a Sunday to playing by sight scores of difficult rags. His skill and sympathy brought to life for us over a hundred numbers unheard for a generation or more."

In their postlude, Blesh and Janis commented that "Sutton's playing, like that of the Negro ragtimers, supplements the sheet music with brilliant added variations of his own, which re-emphasize the fact that ragtime has always been a music primarily of playing, rather than composing. Sutton and [Wally] Rose are the leaders of a whole generation of white ragtimers...."

The band on the "This Is Jazz" show consisted of Wild Bill Davison, Jimmy Archey, Albert Nicholas, Sutton, Danny Barker, Pops Foster, and Baby Dodds. Sidney Bechet, Edmond Hall, and Johnny Blowers also played on some of the programs on which Ralph performed. The notes for an album of "This Is Jazz" records, which were made during the broadcasts, describe Ralph as "bespectacled, young, a phenomenon in the jazz world. A big, two-fisted guy who beat on the piano as though he really meant it and enjoyed it, too." During the broadcasts, the engineering booth in the studio was crowded with radio people who "would jam up against the thick glass, fascinated by Sutton's big, active hands."

In September 1947, Ralph made his first commercial records—four sides with the Milt Herth Trio. He then accepted Herth's invitation to play a two-month tour with the organist and drummer Gary Chester.

"We traveled in a station wagon, which I drove," Ralph said, "and Milt had his organ and his speakers and the drums in a little trailer. The tour started in Chicago at the Oriental Theater. We were on the bill with Wee Bonnie Baker, and it was the first time I ever had to wear pancake makeup.

"I could see immediately that I wasn't going to like this tour because Milt held me down. All he wanted me to do was oom-cha, oom-cha and smile at the people. Well, I knew this wasn't going to work, but I said I would make the tour. Between shows at the Oriental, I ducked down the alley to Pete's Steak House and drank martinis.

"I began getting calluses from unloading Milt's organ and speakers, and I was putting away quite a bit of juice to put up with this shit. We hit Springfield, Illinois, and he was going to give me my notice unless I straightened up and flew right. He said he'd get a piano player from Chicago, and I'd have to pay my way back to New York.

"We got down to Collinsville, near East St. Louis. I said something one night over the mike that wasn't too bad, but Milt was very insulted. The next night, we were playing Brahms's 'Lullaby,' and I said something like, 'What the hell do you want me to play anyway?' It went out over the room, and the next night he wouldn't speak to me. So after the first set, I said, 'Milt, if you can get that piano player from Chicago, I'd just as soon go home.' He told me I owed him an apology for what I had said over the mike, but I told him it wasn't so bad. I said, 'I've had it. You're not doing me any good, and I'm not doing you any good.' But then he cooled down and said, 'It's about the end of the tour.' So we went back to New York, and I was still driving the station wagon."

At one spot on the tour, George Ledbetter showed up with a portable tape recorder—as he did whenever possible at the places Ralph played. Herth refused to let Ledbetter record the trio, but Ralph's friend went ahead anyway.

"Old Miltie used to grind that organ up until you couldn't hear Ralph," Ledbetter remembered, "and so I sneaked up and unplugged one of his speakers. Ralph saw me do it and busted out laughing, but he kept on playing. Since Milt wouldn't let me bring the recorder in, I lifted it through the window of the men's room and slipped the microphone cord under the door. I put the mike in the piano and got a recording with Ralph in the foreground and Milt in the background. Miltie never knew we had made it."

In 1948, Ralph formed a trio with Albert Nicholas and Arthur Trappier. Nicholas praised Sutton as being not only "a perfect accompanist who could play *anything*," but also "so inventive as a soloist. He always wanted to play, and I never got tired of listening to him. What's more, he's a friendly, kind, and reliable person."

The trio played at Jimmy Ryan's, and then Ralph and Trappier joined a band headed by Max Kaminsky at the Village Vanguard. The band often accompanied Maxine Sullivan, Lee Wiley, and other singers. Sullivan recalled: "I was amazed that Ralph and I had so much in common. He was a young boy, and here I was from the old school, doing things like 'If I Had a Ribbon Bow' and 'Molly Malone.' I was mired in the folk groove, which was a hangover from 'Loch Lomond'—and I was really stuck with that tune. I like to sing jazz, and I had sort of a souped-up repertoire going for me. It was supposed to be avant-garde at the time.

"We did the 'Loch Lomond' bit, but after that we started doing some real music. I didn't even realize there was anyone around who could play that kind of music like Ralph could. We found each other immediately and did quite a few things together. I think I had more fun listening than I did working with Ralph. We became each other's fans, and it really enhanced the engagement.

"In 1948, piano styles had gone in all directions. I even heard some piano players who probably had something going for them originally—like playing with two hands. But they were changing their style to mostly right hand with a few little movements in the left hand. I was terrifically impressed because Ralph had everything going for him—real stride—and it really took me back.

"I had worked with quite a few pianists at the time; and besides his being able to do solo work, he was a great accompanist. We heard the same things. We heard the same changes. We didn't get in each other's way. I sing a melody; but I also improvise, and his piano fit in just perfectly."

Ralph returned the praise, calling Sullivan "a wonderful girl who really can sing. I don't like most singers. They're pretty tough to work with a lot of the time. They think they know more about the music than the musicians do, and they're always giving the musicians the devil. If something goes wrong, it's the musicians' fault. But Maxine—that little girl is so easy to work with, and she swings beautifully."

At the Village Vanguard, Ralph met a man who became one of his dearest friends. He named his first son after this man, John Theobold, a black physician.

"One night," Ralph said, "I happened to look up from the piano, and there was a dignified-looking man standing there. I didn't know him, but I immediately had a feeling for the guy. John must have been 20 or 25 years older than I. He had been born in Jamaica and was a ship's cabin boy when he was about 8. He studied medicine in Paris and became a gynecologist and surgeon. He also served with the French intelligence. I found all this out later.

"Anyway, he looked over at me and he said, 'You sure don't play like a white boy.' That is one of the highest compliments, of course. We shook hands and he invited me over to the bar with him. We struck it off right away, and after I finished work that night we went up to Harlem. We hit the after-hours spots up there and had a ball. We became so close that when my first son was born, I asked John to be his godfather."

After leaving the Vanguard, Ralph got his trio together again. He, Nicholas, and Trappier opened at the Barrel Bar in St. Louis in July.

"We played there for six weeks and broke it up," Ralph said. "But before we even opened, I almost got into a scuffle. The union had a white local and a Negro local in St. Louis at that time. I belonged to Local 2, the white local, and so I filed the contract for the job there. St. Louis was on the border between the North and the South, and we had a few assholes around. One musician told me, 'If you're going to open tonight with these niggers, some of us boys are comin' out there.' I said, 'Listen, you son of a bitch...' and I let him have it real good. I didn't hit him, but he was awful lucky."

The racial incident that preceded the Sutton trio's engagement at the Barrel was not the first occasion when Ralph had expressed his views on black and white musicians' performing together. About three years earlier, Jimmy Forrest was playing in George Hudson's band at the Plantation Club in St. Louis. He had tried but failed to get a job in another St. Louis club where Sutton was performing. That club, according to Al Grey, who later toured frequently with Forrest, "was on the other side of the fence." Forrest told Grey that Sutton persuaded the club to let down its color bar.

"Ralph loved black people," Grey said, "and he couldn't see why they couldn't work in the club where he worked. He tried for a period of time to bring Jimmy into that club, and through pure heart he eventually got him in for a one-nighter. Jimmy was the first black artist to work there. It came off so well that the people at the club started saying, 'These guys aren't so bad. They can play.' After Jimmy told me that, I found myself falling in love with Ralph."

Grey began his interview for this book by spontaneously relating the Forrest-Sutton story. Ralph could not recall the incident but said it must have happened if Grey said it had. Sutton's opinions about racial equality went back to childhood, and he obviously did not regard helping Forrest as a big deal.

"There was never any feeling in my family or myself about race," Ralph said. "People were people—pink or green or black or whatever."

Sutton did remember—with great pleasure—the night he and Jack Teagarden, who had a gig in town, sat in with Hudson's band at the Plantation after the club closed at 4 or 5 in the morning. Clark Terry, who came from St. Louis and played with Hudson, also took part in that memorable session.

Charlie Menees, St. Louis' first jazz disk jockey, met Ralph around this time after giving the young pianist's career a big boost. Menees, a reporter for the *St. Louis Post-Dispatch*, had started to moonlight in 1945 at an East St. Louis radio station. He then moved to station WIL in St. Louis and remained active in jazz broadcasting until his death in 1993.

Menees recalled that the Gaiman Appliance Company "was the best jazz store in town." The owner, Hymie Gaiman, "sold a few percolators and posters, but his principal interest was in jazz records." Menees knew of Ralph only by reputation when Gaiman called one day and told him about a "This Is Jazz" album with Sutton on piano.

"I put that record on the next night I was on the air, and it took off," Menees said. "It was somewhat amazing that Hymie had to order several dozen copies, because he was accustomed to buying only half a dozen of something like that. It was the first big hit that I had as a disk jockey. It's indelible in my mind because the impetus was the fact that Ralph was on piano.

"I got a note from Ralph thanking me for what I had done for that record. 'Big Butter and Egg Man' was one of the tunes on it. That was my first experience with Ralph Sutton's piano playing. It was also my first exposure to how many friends and supporters he had around St. Louis. People came from St. Charles to buy that record.

"I can't remember where and when I met Ralph for the first time, but it might have been at the Barrel Bar when he played there with Albert Nicholas and Art Trappier. We've been close friends ever since."

During an intermission at the Barrel one night, Ralph joined some friends at their table. The group included Wilbur G. Payne, who recalled a momentous event in Sutton's career: "Ralph was called to the phone and returned a few minutes later somewhat in a daze. He told us the phone call had been from Eddie Condon in New York, inviting him to play solo piano at his place. This was an unforgettable moment for all of us, and we were so pleased to have shared it with Ralph."

Condon had invited Ralph to replace Joe Sullivan as intermission pianist because Sullivan was moving to San Francisco. Ralph immediately accepted the offer to play during the "lull," Condon's term for the band's break between sets. Dick Cary filled in on piano at Condon's until Sutton finished the Barrel engagement. In August 1948, Ralph opened at Condon's. Except for brief appearances elsewhere, he played intermission piano there for eight years.

Chapter **9**

A Musical Education

alph calls Condon's "the best saloon I ever played." He sat down at the keyboard at 9 o'clock every night except Sunday, and he and the band played alternate 30-minute sets until 4 the next morning. When Georg Brunis was in the band, he introduced Ralph as the group left the stand: "Now, ladies and gentlemen, I'd like you to meet Ralph Sutton, the piano player. He looks like the late Glenn Miller, and he's got a profile like a Yale key. C'mon up here, Ralph."

On Tuesday nights, Condon brought in two or three extra musicians. Ralph always looked forward to these jam session nights, when he played with such luminaries as Billy Butterfield, Lee Castle, Bobby Hackett, Jimmy McPartland, Lips Page, Johnny Windhurst, Tommy Dorsey, Brad Gowans, Bennie Morton, Freddy Ohms, Bob Wilber, Jimmy Dorsey, Bud Freeman, and Gene Krupa.

"Musicians would also drop in on their own and play with me," Ralph said. "Just piano and another instrument. The highlight for me would be when Jack Teagarden and I would play duets. We'd do the Bix Beiderbecke piano pieces and some of Willie the Lion Smith's tunes. Working at Condon's was really a musical education for me."

When Ralph began his long stay at the club, he and Chuck lived in a one-bedroom apartment near Columbia University. Their first son, John Jeffrey, was born in 1948. The apartment became rather crowded because the family also included Bad Sam, a scrubby alley cat; and Chamois, a blond cocker spaniel that Ralph often called Chamois-She-Wabble. Three years after Jeff was born, the Suttons bought a home in Hastings-on-Hudson—which Ralph refers to as Hasty-on-the-Pudding—about 30 miles north of Greenwich Village. Pete Pesci, Condon's partner, lent

Ralph $1,000 to help him make a down payment on the large Victorian house, and Sutton paid it back at the rate of $20 a week from his salary.

Ralph earned $140 a week when he started at Condon's. "I finally got a raise three or four years later," he said. To meet his various expenses, Sutton worked extra jobs on Sundays. He played at Yale and at other universities in the New York area, at jam sessions at Jimmy Ryan's and other clubs, and at private parties. He also performed frequently on the "Piano Playhouse" radio show and on many of the Condon jazz shows on radio and television. The additional income came in especially handy after the birth of his other sons, Peter Gardiner in 1952 and Nicholas Richard in 1954.

During his years at Condon's, Ralph became known as one of the top jazz pianists of all time. Unfortunately, he also gained a reputation for having an extremely short fuse when dealing with the public. He began to drink heavily, chiefly because the liquor helped him become immune to the many patrons who got under his skin night after night.

These people annoyed Sutton by requesting—or demanding—that he play certain tunes, or by talking or otherwise making noise while he was at the keyboard. He explained his irritation at taking requests: "Since I'm playing the piano, leave it up to me what to play. It's as simple as that. If I'm at a friend's home and I'm playing, that's different." Ralph's resentment of those who refused to keep quiet while he played was, of course, common among entertainers. He had a lower boiling point than most of them, however.

Every day, the booze changed Ralph from a quiet, mild-mannered man into a testy, bad-tempered performer who told off anyone who annoyed him. Whether this image hurt his career is anybody's guess. He mellowed somewhat through the years but still refuses to take any guff from anyone. Sutton views himself as a man who minds his own business and bothers no one—and he expects others to do the same.

Ralph especially detested people he called "coattail pullers." These characters touched off a number of incidents at Condon's, and Ralph's eyes gleamed angrily even years later when he related such episodes:

"One night when I started playing, there were only two guys and a gal in the place. I was playing around with some of the Beiderbecke numbers, and one of the guys came up and pulled on my coattail while I was in the middle of a tune. I didn't pay any attention until I finished the number, and then I turned around and asked what I could do for him. He told me to quit playing that kind of stuff and to play something like 'Sweet Leilani' instead. My blood pressure went up, and I asked him what he did for a living. He said he sold apartment buildings in the Village. 'Well, listen, you son of a bitch,' I told him, 'you sell your fucking apartment buildings and go back and sit down and leave me alone.' He walked straight back to his table and didn't bother me anymore.

"Norman McLeod, the movie director, was another coat puller. He was sitting at the front table one evening, and there were some Southerners with him. John Theobold was standing next to the piano, and I was playing for him. McLeod didn't pull my coattail that night, like he had done a few times before, but he and the guys at his table said some things and I blew my stack at him—again. I read him off, and he was ready to go for me; and I was ready for him. It ended when he reported the incident to the cashier, Bill Funaro, who was also the bouncer. I finished my set, and McLeod was still talking to Bill. We just glared at each other when I went by on my way to the end of the bar, where I always sat between sets. Condon called me aside and asked me if I knew who I had been tangling with. I told him I didn't give a shit who it was.

"One Friday night, the place was packed and there were two guys and two gals sitting to the right of the stand. People always seem to try to get as close as they can to me—I don't know why. Anyway, I was playing and I heard something hit the curtain at the back of the stand. I didn't know what the hell it was, but I wasn't about to turn around and pay any attention to the people or find out what they were trying to do. I was just trying to stay by myself. The waiters were watching the whole thing though. They told me later that these jerks were throwing swizzle sticks at me—probably trying to get my attention so they could make some silly-assed request.

"Finally, a swizzle stick hit my glasses, and I stopped playing and turned around. I told them, 'All right, let's cut this shit out.' One of the guys said, 'What'd you say?' So I repeated it, and he said, 'You can't talk like that. We have two ladies here at the table.' I told him I couldn't see any.

"I was trying to keep my temper, and I was telling myself, 'Ralph, settle down.' Then the two guys got up and one of them grabbed my right wrist. I yanked it free, and then I got up and grabbed my chair and held it over my shoulder. I told them, 'All right, you cocksuckers, c'mon.' By that time, Bill Funaro had come up. He called their waiter over and told him to give the people their check. As they went out, one of the women told Bill, 'Don't blame the piano player. He was doing the best he could, but we were throwing swizzle sticks at him and we hit him in the face.' "

Funaro remembered Ralph as "a great guy who rates with the best as a jazzman. He stayed by himself most of the time and never really got involved in anything. I liked him very much and had no trouble with him at all. He was the least likely of the musicians to do anything crazy, like Davison and Brunis did from time to time.

"Ralph did have a temper though, and it came out every once in a while," Funaro said. "If a patron asked to hear a number he had already played, Ralph would tell him to play it himself. He walked off the stand one night, and when Pete asked him why, Ralph told him to look around—that everyone was so loud and drunk they didn't even know he wasn't up there playing. And he was so right."

One of the customers at whom Ralph exploded was his future brother-in-law, Hal Curtis. Hal had grown up in Englewood, New Jersey, just 45 minutes from Condon's. He had loved jazz for as long as he could remember and frequently dropped in to hear Ralph.

"One summer night in 1950," Curtis recalled, "a woman at the table next to me was getting drunked up. She kept hollering at Ralph to play 'Honeysuckle Rose,' and Ralph was trying to ignore her. As I got up to leave, this broad grabbed my arm and told me to ask him to play it.

"I thought she'd shut up if I did, and so I went over to Ralph and told him a woman wanted him to play 'Honeysuckle Rose.' 'Goddammit, I *heard* her,' Ralph yelled at me, his eyes blazing with fury. I walked out of Condon's rather bewildered at his anger toward *me*. After all, I had been listening to him for about two years, and *I* hadn't been bugging him. What neither of us could possibly have known was that we would be brothers-in-law within another two years—and had just had the first of many conversations."

By the spring of 1951, Curtis was in uniform at Scott Air Force Base. One day he went to the USO center in nearby St. Louis: "I was just sitting there listening to what I thought was Ralph's record of 'Muskrat

Ramble' from his *Piano Moods* album. I heard several other tunes that sounded so much like Ralph, but then I remember thinking, 'My God, he never recorded *that* one.' I finally realized I was hearing live music.

"I walked into the next room, and there was a girl playing the piano. After she finished the tune, I said to a lady standing next to me, 'You know, she sounds like somebody I've heard.' The woman smiled and asked, 'You mean Ralph Sutton?' I nodded, and she laughed and told me, 'That's Ralph's sister.' Then Barb and I began talking, and that's how we got together."

Barbara visited Hal in New York that fall to meet his parents, and Ralph arranged for her to sit in with the band at Condon's. She was only 20 and remembered being "really nervous about playing with all those guys I admired so much—Wild Bill, Cutty Cutshall, Ed Hall, Jack Lesberg, Morey Feld, and Eddie himself. Condon announced me by saying, 'Ralph Sutton, our intermission piano player, has been complaining that he needs a vacation. If he doesn't watch out, this may be it!'"

Ralph also got his sister a gig with Pee Wee Russell and at the Central Plaza, where she played with Red Allen, Georg Brunis, and Conrad Janis. Hal said the scene at the Central Plaza, a huge hall where jam sessions featuring top jazz musicians were held on Friday and Saturday nights, was "like the rape of Rome. Everyone yelled and stomped, and nobody listened.

"After Barb finished playing," Curtis recalled, "we went over to Condon's because Ralph wanted to know how it had gone. 'God, it was just awful,' she told him. 'Nobody listened to me. Everybody was screaming, and no one appreciated what I was doing.' Ralph just smiled and asked her, 'Why are you complaining? What the hell do you think this business is all about? You made money, didn't you? You got heard and you played with some good musicians, didn't you?' Barb agreed with all that, and then Ralph told her, 'Well, what the hell. Why are you so sensitive? You did fine. That's what it's like—and if that's what you want to put up with, you stay in the business. And if you don't want to put up with it, you don't.'

"Barbara had played a lot in St. Louis, where people listened to what she was doing, but this was her first experience with the big time. She thought it would be a lot more glamorous than it actually was. But it wasn't so good as St. Louis in some respects, though the musicians were better.

"Ralph was very nice to her. He and Barb had a real brother-sister scene as he reassured her, and he impressed me deeply. It was so typical of Ralph because she needed reassurance. He revealed himself, too. He let Barb know it isn't very glamorous in the big time—nothing like working in a concert hall. Ralph told her what he's been saying for years: 'I play for those few people out there who are listening, and the hell with the rest of them.'"

Wild Bill Davison remembered Ralph's hostility toward patrons who annoyed him: "I felt sorry for Ralph playing by himself with all those noisy bastards out in front. Sometimes I'd grab my horn, get my mute, and go up with him and we'd play. Once we were playing some soft little things, just for the two of us. A girl came up and asked Ralph to play some song, and he said, 'Why don't you get the fuck out of here?' That's the way he felt about it, and so he said it. The poor little broad started crying and went tearing over to her boyfriend. He began talking about beating Ralph up—but it would have taken something to have done that."

Sympathy for Sutton did not motivate Davison when he joined Ralph on the stand one evening in the spring of 1954. Anne Stewart, who had been a movie actress, singer, and painter but knew nothing about jazz, had come to Condon's with a friend. Her escort had suggested that they have a nightcap there, and she recalled being "horrified at the idea of even going to such a dump." Stewart's companion, who knew Condon, introduced her to him and to Davison.

Davison spent the rest of the evening at their table except when he was on the stand playing with the band. During one intermission, in reply to his question, Stewart told him that her favorite song was "Georgia on My Mind." Davison promptly returned to the stand and played the tune with Ralph accompanying him and with his cornet pointed at her. They were married in December.

The Davisons had one of the happiest marriages in jazz for just short of 35 years until Wild Bill died in 1989 at the age of 83. "When I think of Bill," Ralph wrote in a letter of condolence to Anne Davison, "it puts a smile on my face."

Dick Cary subbed for Gene Schroeder, the band pianist, one night and ended up playing intermission piano as well. "A woman yelled up some inane request while Ralph was on alone," Cary remembered. "He replied, 'Fuck you, lady,' and kept on playing. But several seconds later his curiosity must have made him turn back to see how the woman had taken this. She was very irate and yelling at her companion to retaliate. Whereupon Ralph continued the little scene by asking her, 'What's the matter, lady, don't you like fucking?' Bill Funaro soon escorted Ralph off the stand, and I had to do both jobs the rest of the night."

Cliff Leeman also described how Ralph reacted to people he considered pests—but Leeman added a significant observation: "As with most of us musicians, Ralph didn't have too much tolerance for the squares. He used to perform Bix's piano solos and the Lion's tunes, like 'Echo of Spring,' which call for a quiet, listening audience. But the joint would be mobbed, with lots of noise and excitement, and Ralph would stop playing and tell the crowd, 'For Christ's sake, shut up!' A belligerent retort from a customer would get a blunt 'Fuck you!' This was the Ralph that such people knew. But anyone who knows him well realizes that, above all, Ralph is the epitome of the word 'gentleman.' "

Charlie Baron, a close friend of Sutton's, confirmed that "the atmosphere at Condon's was quite often not conducive to the performance of a fine musician like Ralph. He'd come on alone after the band had been blaring, and all the people in the place would be half loaded. He'd go through this night after night, and he'd constantly be at war with a lot of the customers.

"Ralph had some pet peeves and great resentments regarding some of the patrons," Baron said. "He didn't care for the society people, and he particularly disliked Jackie Gleason—and the feeling was mutual. Gleason would come in and act like he owned the place. He'd ask Ralph to play something, and Ralph, of course, would refuse. They got into some pretty heated arguments.

"One Friday night, a gang of college kids from some Southern school came up for a football game and took over Condon's. Ralph was playing 'In a Mist,' a very sensitive, beautiful thing; but he wasn't getting anywhere because the audience was so busy talking and waving their Confederate flags. In the middle of the tune, the kids started singing, 'Oh, I wish I was in Dixie.' Ralph stood up and told them, 'I wish the hell you were, too'—and walked off the stand.

"Another time, a guy came up to him while he was playing and started to bug him with questions and 'Will you play this or play that?' Ralph turned around and asked him, 'How would you feel if I came into your office and interrupted you while you were working?' The guy was taken aback, of course, and Ralph proceeded to tell him how he was doing the same thing to him at the piano."

Al Greenspan, another friend of Ralph's, made a mistake the first time he spoke to the pianist: "I dared to try to talk to him while he was playing. Ralph was concentrating intensely, as he always does from the moment he sits down until the last phrase. He tolerates no interference from anyone. He spent his entire 30 minutes between sets telling me off—even though I was a paying customer—and my ears still get red when I think about it. But, being the kind of man he is, he came over to my table at his next break and insisted on washing down his bitterness and my shame."

During his years at Condon's, Ralph continued to keep a protective eye on Norman Muschany. His boyhood pal occasionally came to the club from Philadelphia, where he was attending medical school. Muschany had "fond memories of a humble med student finding himself in the midst of night life and famous people. Ralph was very kind to me every time I went in to hear him play. When he finished a set, it was always, 'Where's Norm? Where's Norm?' I was sort of his charge, and he felt that he had to take care of me."

Shortly after Ralph opened at Condon's, Mischa and Genevieve Reznikoff dropped into the club. They had known Condon for years, and Genevieve Reznikoff remembered seeing "a new man playing piano while the band was off. The minute we heard Ralph play, we knew he was 'somebody in charge,' as Eddie used to say. He had just come in from St. Louis, and we had never even heard of him. Mischa introduced himself to Ralph at the bar after he finished playing and brought him over to our table. It was one of those times when you meet someone and things click immediately."

The Suttons and Reznikoffs became friends, and the two families rented next-door houses in Hastings-on-Hudson for the summer of 1949, two years before the Suttons bought a home there. Ralph and Mischa often sat together on the Suttons' patio, and Genevieve Reznikoff related an incident that revealed much about Ralph: "One afternoon they were sitting out there, and Mischa was naturally doing most of the talking because Ralph is not a great talker. Suddenly, Ralph just got up without a word and walked into the living room and started to play the piano. 'That's the way he wanted to talk to me,' Mischa said later. Sometimes Ralph could be insensitive, but this was very sensitive. It was his way of communicating with someone he loved, and he really loved Mischa." The Reznikoffs later bought a home in Dobbs Ferry, a few miles from Hastings-on-Hudson.

The kitchen in the Victorian house of the Suttons had every modern convenience, including a gas stove—but Ralph also bought a huge old-fashioned wood-burning stove for $30. "Food tastes better when it's cooked on a wood stove," he said. "My mother had one, and I had always wanted one for my own home. When you make things like biscuits and soup on a wood stove, they're really something else. We cooked on it every once in a while, and it gave us extra warmth during the winter." Ralph enjoyed walking to the nearby forest to chop wood for the stove, which Cliff Leeman remembered was "his pride and joy."

Ralph commuted to Condon's in a Hillman Minx convertible. He recalled that several other jazzmen also liked foreign sports cars: "Johnny Windhurst had an MG, Edmond Hall drove a Jaguar XK120, and Wild Bill had a Riley. It was an interesting sight to see the fleet parked out in front of the club."

Three-year-old Jeff Sutton occasionally sat on the floor next to the piano at Condon's while his father played. At home, he said, "Dad liked to throw parties and invite all his musician friends. They drank wine, ate, and jammed together until the wee hours."

By the early 1950s, the spaniel Chamois had been succeeded by Thurber, a large female basset hound that sometimes got drunk by lapping the wine out of Ralph's glass. Sutton enjoyed the work of the famous humorist James Thurber and named the dog for him. "That dog was too much," he said. "She was kind of hard to get along with because her previous owner had mistreated her. We showed her so much love and kindness that she started to ease up a bit, but she didn't like kids and always snapped at them. She never took any crap from anyone, including other dogs. If another dog came into our yard, Thurber chased it out—even if it was bigger than she was."

During Ralph's first winter at Condon's, one of the top Hollywood motion-picture companies sent a crew to the club to make a short film featuring the band. The producer, Ralph remembered, told Condon that Edmond Hall would have to be replaced in the picture because "we couldn't show it in the South with him playing with a bunch of white guys."

"If I'd have been Condon, I'd have told them to get their goddamn ass out of there," Ralph said. "But they went ahead and made the picture, and someone filled in on clarinet. I can't remember who.

"The whole thing really made my blood boil, and I think the *New York Star* commented about the incident. Anyway, I wrote 'em a letter—the only time I've ever written to a newspaper. I'm just as strong in my opinions now as I was then, but I don't care about expressing them anymore. I know the way I feel, and that's good enough for me."

In his letter, which was published in the Letters to the Editor column of the *Star*, Ralph did not mention the episode at Condon's. He praised the newspaper's "democratic type of writing and thinking" and criticized "flag wavers [who] overlook a host of indecencies." Then he commented: "My skin happens to be white, and I was born to a Protestant family, neither of which was my fault, neither of which am I particularly proud. Neither is it the other fellow's fault how he happens to be born. There is one rule to live by, and that is the Golden Rule. Why can't everyone wise up to the fact that that rule includes us all, regardless of race, color, or religion?..."

On a summer day in 1949, Charles Peterson, one of the first outstanding jazz photographers, brought a number of musicians, including Ralph and other members of the Condon gang, to his farm home in Easton, Pennsylvania. The occasion was the wedding of Helen O'Brian, Peterson's agent and photo editor of *Cosmopolitan* magazine, and Duane Decker, a sports novelist. Jazz reigned as the couple's main interest in life, and they spent as much time as possible at Condon's and the other New York jazz clubs.

The musicians, many of whom were Peterson's close friends, played for the wedding. The photographer hoped to produce a picture story of the event for publication in *Life* or some other top magazine. That project fell through, however, according to his son, Don, administrator of the Charles Peterson photo archive.

"As a sidebar to the wedding," Don Peterson recalled, "my father arranged to have Ralph, Jonah Jones, and Willie the Lion Smith run over to Nazareth, Pennsylvania, a few miles from our home, to jam at the Whitfield House. Since he hoped to get this picture story published in one of the slicks, he thought it would be a good twist: New York jazz musicians invade the Whitfield House, which is held in reverence by the descendants of the early Moravian settlers and is about as far removed from the jazz world as you can get."

The Whitfield House, built in 1742, served as a Moravian meeting place. Local Indian tribes left their weapons there while visiting the town. The building later became a museum that housed one of Pennsylvania's oldest and most famous organs. Ralph and Willie the Lion tried out the organ, and Charles Peterson took a photo of Sutton wearing an amused expression at the keyboard while watching Jonah Jones play his trumpet. The Lion and Rudi Blesh are also in the picture.

Peterson took one of his most poignant photos on February 27, 1951. That morning, Ralph and several of the other Condon musicians got to bed much later than usual. So did their friend Josh Billings, a lithographer who had played drums—actually, suitcase—with Red McKenzie's Mound City Blue Blowers in the late 1920s. After closing the club at 4 A.M., the group killed some time at Billings' apartment near La Guardia Airport and then went to the terminal at 6 o'clock to meet Pee Wee Russell's plane.

Russell was returning from San Francisco, where he had been recuperating from surgery after collapsing with a liver ailment. Peterson's photo at the airport shows the terribly emaciated patient telling Gene Schroeder, Bob Casey, Buzzy Drootin, Condon, Sutton, and Peterson himself about his near-fatal experience.

Shortly before Russell's collapse, he had played in a combo led by Ralph at the Say When Club in San Francisco. This club was down the street from the Hangover Club, where Sutton frequently played after moving to the West Coast a few years later.

Ralph recorded under his own name for the first time in January 1949, when he made four 78 sides for Rudi Blesh's Circle label. He played four piano solos—"St. Louis Blues," "Carolina in the Morning," and two rags, "Whitewash Man" and "Dill Pickles." They were issued in an album called *St. Louis Piano*, for which Blesh and writer Bob Aurthur each contributed notes. Blesh wrote that "Sutton is an inward man, and all the color, force, and imagination of his rich personality—belied by his impassive face—are poured forth in his music...."

Aurthur wrote that "Ralph Earl Sutton is everyone's idea of the Jack Armstrong type—slightly on the studious side. Serious, contemplative, strictly nonbarrelhouse in appearance, he expresses himself best through his music.... It is to be safely predicted that Ralph Sutton is destined for solid jazz fame.... [He plays piano] better than damn near anyone around...."

Aurthur also wrote the first of many articles about Ralph that have been published through the years. In the April 1949 issue of *Playback*, he declared:

> [Sutton] plays the damndest piano heard in the jazz world for the past decade....This man Sutton, working with only his two hands and nothing up his sleeves, is probably the most dynamic force on the piano today.... You're liable to forget that Sutton is only 26 years old. That's because he sneaked on the scene with little or no excitement, and before you knew what was happening, there he was—mixing it up with the greatest of them, giving way to no one....
>
> Listening to Ralph Sutton, you hear a jazz miracle—a young player with a phenomenal wealth of talent who has absorbed all the great playing of several generations and who has emerged with a definite, powerful style of his own. He can play anything from cocktail music to barrelhouse and play it in an exciting, moving manner....

In April, Ralph played in a ragtime concert that Blesh, the m.c., called "the first ever given in New York history." The musicians were a trio known as the Ragpickers—Tony Parenti, Sutton, and Tony Spargo, who, as Tony Sbarbaro, had been the drummer in the Original Dixieland Jazz Band. Virgil Thomson, the renowned music critic of the *New York Herald Tribune*, singled out Ralph for special praise. Thomson's comments were republished in a 1951 book, *Music Right and Left*, a collection of his reviews and essays.

"... The artists were impeccable; the program was distinguished," Thomson wrote. "... All three are technical masters and musicians of refined style, as becomes the exponents of a classical repertory. If any of them seemed to this listener more remarkable than the others, it was the pianist. Perhaps we are more used to fine clarinet and drum playing than to pianism of Mr. Sutton's solid standards. In any case, I found the latter most satisfying...."

Ralph first recorded with the Condon band in the spring of 1950. His piano is featured on "Maple Leaf Rag," "Yellow Dog Blues," and "Dill Pickles." That summer, Ralph contributed eight tunes to the Columbia series called *Piano Moods*. Early the next year, he recorded eight Fats Waller numbers that Columbia issued under the title *Salute to Fats*.

In July 1951, Ralph received acclaim from *Time*, which declared that he "delivers some of the solidest gutbucket piano being pounded out today.... [He is] the new leading exponent of old-time jazz piano...." The magazine went on to say that Sutton played Fats's tunes "as they had not been played since the late great Negro pianist bubbled through them himself."

The Condon band played on a number of "Dr. Jazz" radio programs, with Ralph appearing as solo pianist and occasionally subbing for Gene Schroeder with the group. Announcer Aime Gauvin, in the role of Dr. Jazz, made some comments to the studio audience during the program of December 10, 1951:

"No evening at Eddie Condon's is complete until you've heard Ralph Sutton at the piano. We're going to do that now. But before Ralph plays, I want to scotch a rumor that's been going around to the effect that Ralph has 10 fingers on each hand. That is not true. Ralph, hold up your hands. You see? The normal complement of fingers. What Ralph does possess to an incredible degree is the ability to make them *sound* like 20 fingers. Ralph, will you demonstrate, please?"

Sutton followed by playing "Morning Air." Later in the program, before Ralph played "'A Flat' Dream" as his second solo, Dr. Jazz offered some additional observations:

"About this Ralph Sutton kid, what can you say after you say he's wonderful? Well, you can say that Fats would have liked him. Jelly Roll [Morton] would have liked him. I think if Jelly Roll were around today, he would probably call Ralph a dispenser. Jelly Roll, as I remember, was not a man overgiven to praising the opposition. A 'dispenser,' in his language, was a man who took a piece of music and made something out of it. I think Ralph's a dispenser. Ralph, will you dispense?"

Eighteen-year-old Barbara Coe of Santa Ana, California, was working in a record store during the summer of 1950 when one of Ralph's albums arrived. She listened to it because the liner notes told of his love for Fats Waller. Coe got hooked for life.

"I started buying all of Ralph's records I could find," she said. "About a year later I found out he was playing at Condon's, so I dropped a letter off to him. I can't remember all the details, but I mentioned how much I loved his music. I asked him if there were any other records that were available that I might not know about, expecting I probably wouldn't hear from him.

"Within three weeks I got the nicest postcard. It kind of floored me. Very friendly and warm and nice, and telling me about additional records that he had made. About a month later, I decided to write another letter. I got a beautiful letter back from him. It was like somebody I had known for 20 years, it was so nice. Those were the only fan letters I've ever written.

"I didn't write after that, simply because I'm not a very good correspondent, plus the fact that I moved away, got married, and raised a family. I've been a fan of Ralph Sutton's all these years but got away from being so involved in music."

Neither Barbara Coe Alderson nor Ralph could remember what she said in her first letter, but it obviously had impressed him. Sutton wrote on his postcard: "Your letter was the first fan letter I have received that agrees with my thoughts on music. So many people really go out on a limb with their ideas in letters. When you mentioned the sound of a piano, I understood you immediately." He closed by saying, "Please write again soon."

In his letter, sent in December 1951, Sutton noted that "my correspondence is slipping of late." He wrote about being in the process of buying a home and hoping to move during Christmas week: "It's a nine-room house with basement and garage in a quiet wooded section. Keep your fingers crossed.

"I'm still working at Condon's and enjoying it. The 20th [of December], Eddie celebrates his 6th year, which is very good for a jazz club. The place is an institution now, so I guess Eddie's worries are over. I've been there 3 years this past August, which seems hard to realize."

Following their brief correspondence, Ralph and Barbara Alderson lost touch. They eventually met in 1989, when she heard him in a live performance for the first time and introduced herself. Alderson also showed Sutton his postcard and letter, which she had saved for 38 years. It was a day she would never forget.

Chapter **10**

Very Much a Pianist's Pianist

alph flew to London in June 1952 and performed in a concert presented by the National Federation of Jazz Organisations. Sinclair Traill, the editor of *Jazz Journal*, had heard some of Sutton's records and urged the English jazz association to bring him across the Atlantic. Ed Kirkeby, who had been Fats Waller's manager, arranged the trip.

"Ralph is without a doubt the nearest to Fats of all jazz pianists, living or dead," Kirkeby said. "When I hear Ralph play, I close my eyes and see Fats. I have quite a time realizing it isn't Fats playing. Ralph is just the greatest. Nobody can touch him when it comes to a left hand. He loves Fats so much, and he talked about him all the time we were in England. Ralph was a sensational hit from the time he got there."

Writing in *Jazz Journal* prior to Ralph's appearance in London, Traill informed English jazz fans "that they are going to hear a pianist who in everything he does shows an impeccable taste, allied to a technique of impressive proportions." In his review of Ralph's performance at the Royal Festival Hall on June 28, Traill called Sutton "superb." But he regretted that the program, which included other soloists and several bands, did not provide more time for Ralph:

> The wonderful talents of Ralph Sutton were frittered away in an appalling manner. He played five solo numbers, which merely left the audience yelling for more....
>
> All those who met him were as charmed by his personality as they were staggered by his playing. I was pleased to see that he paid us the compliment of appearing in tails—complete with white waistcoat hurriedly borrowed from the Hon. Gerald Lascelles. It was a nice gesture from a delightful American gentleman....

Lascelles, a cousin of Queen Elizabeth's—and a jazz fan since boyhood—got married during Ralph's stay in London. Traill and his wife, Mips, took Ralph to the wedding and then to the reception at St. James's Palace.

"Ralph was knocked out by the church organist, took his champagne like a gentleman, and looked great in the conventional morning coat and top hat," Traill remembered. "Then we went back to our house, where Ralph was a guest. The press descended, and, despite requests to leave us alone, one reporter broke into the house via the back garden. The question all the newspapers wanted answered was whether Ralph had played at the wedding reception. Actually, of course, he hadn't, but that wasn't the answer they wanted. Jazz and the Royal Family were news.

"We couldn't get the interloper out of the house until Ralph, now clad only in his underpants, offered to throw him through a convenient window. Ralph looks formidable when stripped—and the fellow went."

The reporter was probably intimidated by the sight of Sutton, who stands 6 feet 2 inches tall, weighs just under 200 pounds, and has little fat on his body. Ralph wears size 13 AA shoes, recalling Fats Waller's famous record of "Your Feet's Too Big."

Other English reviews echoed Traill's praise. Ernest Anderson wrote in *Melody Maker* that Sutton "is beginning to be recognized for what he is: the undisputed champion of the piano jazz classics and one of the cleverest professors that ever stroked a keyboard. . . ." Steve Race, writing in *Jazz Journal*, lauded Ralph as "very much a pianist's pianist. . . . [His playing] can be summed up as perhaps the most exciting swing in white solo piano history."

In an article on Ralph that appeared in *Jazz News* 10 years later, Barry McRae recalled:

> The sight of Ralph Sutton walking onto the stage of the Royal Festival Hall in 1952 was something of a shock to me. I was convinced that the immaculate gentleman in tails could not be the great barrelhouse pianist that I knew from records. Twenty minutes later, the erudite man in horn-rimmed spectacles had allayed my fears by generating the atmosphere of a Harlem rent party in the clinical atmosphere of Britain's new concert hall. . . .

Very Much a Pianist's Pianist

About a year before Ralph went to England, he received a letter from Arthur Goepfert, a Swiss jazz fan. They exchanged a number of letters, and, upon learning that Sutton planned a trip to London, Goepfert arranged a series of concerts for him in several Swiss cities after the London performance. "Arthur and I were like old friends when he met me in Zurich," Ralph said.

Another Swiss jazz enthusiast, Giovanni Pozzi, quoted Goepfert's widow as recalling that Ralph lost his wallet while traveling in Switzerland. Goepfert lined up a recording session for him in Basel so he would have some money, and Ralph recorded two 78s for the Elite Special label. In London, he had made an LP of eight tunes for Lyragon.

While in Basel, Sutton met a friend of Goepfert's, Hans Philippi, who said, "Ralph's open and happy nature was fascinating from the beginning. We had dinner together, and Ralph had a ball with an amusing and attractive waitress. Then we went to a coffee bar, the Atlantis, where solo pianists usually appeared.

"Joe Turner, who was living in Switzerland at that time, played a couple of sets," Philippi remembered. "Then he introduced Ralph to the crowd and asked him to play. I shall never forget that happy hour when Ralph played his favorite tunes by Willie the Lion and Bix, and also some ragtime classics."

The next night, Ralph played a concert in a Zurich cafe. The audience included Johnny Simmen, who has written many articles for jazz publications through the years. He and his wife, Liza, met Sutton and heard him play live for the first time, starting a close friendship. According to Simmen, "Ralph was still grinning about his session with Joe Turner the night before.

"Joe later told me, 'That boy is really great,' " Simmen wrote in the September 1963 issue of *Dig It*. "Everybody got knocked out by Ralph's tremendously exciting playing. Unfortunately, the guy who had organized the soiree in Zurich had not asked the authorities for permission to present it. So, to everybody's regret, the law stepped in; and what had looked like a romping all-night session came to an abrupt halt."

Sutton returned to his intermission spot at Condon's after the European trip. Bud Freeman remembered "dropping in quite often just to hear Ralph because he had so much warmth and so much power and drive in his playing." Billy Butterfield described how "Ralph used to gas everybody all by himself. He'd take over after Davison and the thundering herd left the stand, and the room would remain at the same pitch—which is pretty hard to do. But Ralph did it for a long time. He's a giant music-wise and a real landmark in jazz."

Davison recalled that "Ralph used to pound away at the Fats Waller tunes, getting everything exactly right. He could play Fats better than Fats himself could. The things he could do! He played such wonderful stuff, but he never put himself in the spotlight. He was always so withdrawn. I always thought he should have been further out in front than he was, but he never tried to put himself there."

"It was a marvelous contrast in piano styles when Condon substituted Ralph for Gene Schroeder on record dates," Davison said. "They were both so great. Ralph is a real band player. He's got that big fat left hand, and he's a whole rhythm section by himself. With him in a band, you could get away without a bass."

Tommy Reynolds chose Ralph for some combo recordings because "I wanted the best there was, and he was it. He had tremendous feel and rhythm, and the ideas just flowed. I've always thought—and still think—that Ralph is the greatest."

Jack Lesberg said Ralph "surprised everyone at Condon's with the background of material that he played—the Scott Joplin rags and all the Fats Waller and James P. Johnson things. And his touch on the Bix Beiderbecke pieces was unsurpassed. Nobody plays them more beautifully or so perfectly. He obviously made a real study of those things and practiced them very thoroughly in order to have that kind of feeling for them."

Cliff Leeman related that after first hearing Ralph play, "I was drawn to the wonderful skill and style of his musicianship; then, as time passed, to the guy himself. I found him to be a warm, sensitive man—and humorous to a great extent.

"Ralph's sense of humor predominates in his Fats Waller characterizations," Leeman said. "He isn't a copy of Fats, but he represents the continuance of a lost art and a great artist; and he perpetuates a phase of music that isn't around anymore. I've always maintained that Ralph plays Willie the Lion Smith's tunes the way the Lion would have liked to have played them if he had had Ralph's facility and technique—and also his keen interpretation. That's a pretty broad statement, but I'll stand by it."

Dick Cary told how, while playing piano with the Condon band, "I'd sometimes see Ralph at a nearby table and catch his eye and get a small grin of appreciation. Ralph never has talked much, but that grin was a lot more meaningful than any words. I recall it with pleasure. Of course, if you think you're playing badly, you avoid those glances. But if you think you might have done something that Condon would have called 'fairly respectable,' you may look about to see if one of your peers will offer some small confirmation.

"I sat in a lot with the band when I wasn't actually working at the club," Cary said, "and sometimes I sat in on trumpet with Ralph. So did Johnny Windhurst, and we used to comment that very few pianists could provide such a fine rhythmic accompaniment without bass and drums.

"Playing intermission piano anywhere is a terribly hard job. I think it takes a certain type of thick-skinned person to play in piano bars, too. I gave up trying years ago. If you're a man and you don't sing, it's no use—even if you're a Tatum. Most of the patrons want stuff like 'I'm Looking Over a Four-Leaf Clover.' And they seem to think a piano player's no good unless he smiles all the time. Ralph and I have one thing in common—we don't grin unless there's a damn good reason. Do we go into a businessman's office and demand that he smile during dictation?"

Buzzy Drootin, while playing at Condon's, spent many intermissions "listening to Ralph walk on the piano. He'd sound so good that I'd run up to the stand and play with him. Edmond Hall used to love to sit in with him, too. Ralph and I became pretty good friends.

"After leaving the club, I lived in Boston for a couple of years," Drootin recalled. "Then Ralph called and asked me to work with him as an intermission duo at Condon's. Just he and I—and it was quite an experience. He came up to Boston with his Jeep station wagon and moved my wife and me and our infant son and all our furniture to his house in Hastings-on-Hudson.

"I think I got to know him there. He loved to go for walks in the woods, away from everything. Especially when there was chaos in the house, with the kids of two families screaming. He'd just leave and go for a walk. As nice a guy as he was, he could be that selfish."

Drootin remembered a gig with Hall and Sutton at the Encore Lounge in St. Louis: "Every once in a while when Ralph got loaded, he'd sing to me away from the mike. One night I insisted that he sing to the public, and, just as I thought he would, he broke up the club. The people loved the way he sang all the Fats Waller tunes—and in the same style that Fats did. He's so talented, and it's all being wasted.

"When Ralph realized that he was a hit, he refused to sing anymore. His excuse was that he hates people. But I couldn't understand that because he had so many friends. I tried to convince him that it was just as artistic to sing as to play the piano—especially the way he sings. No one sings that way anymore.

"I got him to sing again another night, but he got loaded and started to tell the audience that 'the people in St. Louis have no imagination'—and other insults. The boss, who loved us, called me the next day and told me there'd be no more singing by Ralph."

Johnny Vine liked to recount a Sunday evening session at Matarese's Restaurant, a roadhouse in Berlin, Connecticut: "I was the house drummer at the weekly jazz concerts that were held there for about eight years. All the great musicians you could name performed at those sessions. One night we had Lips Page, Munn Ware, Omer Simeon, Ralph, and myself. No bass. We were cookin' real good. It was just marvelous. Whenever Ralph and I got together, we never fail to talk about that night.

"Being a drummer," Vine added, "I know how wonderful it is to have a bass in the section. But with Ralph on piano, you can make it without one. He's a complete jazz piano player and makes it so easy for a drummer. He's a very warm and humorous guy, too. A prince."

That Sunday session also left a deep impression on Ralph, who said that "from beginning to end, it sounded like Fats's little band. Everybody was *on*. Man, it was the most jumpin'est thing!" Munn Ware wrote a friend: "I'm very fond of Sutton because he keeps telling people I was part of one of the greatest sessions he ever played."

Ralph left Condon's in July 1956, and the Suttons moved to San Francisco. He had grown weary of New York after eight years and looked forward to living on the West Coast: "I liked the cleanliness and the cosmopolitan atmosphere of San Francisco—and lots of jazz fans lived there." Ralph had built a following in the city during the summer of 1954, when he led a quartet—which included Edmond Hall, Walter Page, and Charlie Lodice—at the Hangover Club.

A few months before Ralph and his family moved, the Condon band recorded an album called *Eddie Condon's Treasury of Jazz*. Ralph played on four of the tunes, including the rousing "Duff Campbell's Revenge," but Condon's liner notes identify the pianist as John Jeffrey, the name of the oldest Sutton son. Musicians sometimes recorded under pseudonyms to avoid conflicts with different companies with which they had contracts.

Chuck drove from New York to San Francisco with Jeff and Thurber, and Ralph flew out with Pete and Nick. The two younger boys, who were 4 and 1½, respectively, both threw up on their father en route. As a result, he enjoyed the flight even less than they did.

Chapter **11**

I Love Humanity; It's the People I Can't Stand

harlie Baron grew up during the Big Band Era and, like so many of his peers, was surrounded by swing music and jazz throughout his high school and college years. His account of his close friendship with Sutton reveals much about Ralph—and the dilemma of many top-ranking jazz musicians and other artists.

Here is Baron's story, as he told it:

I started taking piano lessons at about 9 and was considered a pretty good classical pianist for a kid. But by the time I entered college, I realized that I wasn't much of a piano player and would never be a really great one; and so I just quit then and there.

A lot of people say it's too bad I don't play anymore. But I think you can learn to appreciate something only by attempting it yourself; and even if you fail, you at least have a guideline to judge others by. I believe that's why I developed a keen interest in music, particularly jazz. I had been exposed to jazz during the '30s; and, of course, much of it came from the big bands. I had a lot of records and went to many college dances, especially when someone like Goodman or one of the Dorseys or Teagarden came to town. I loved to get practically inside the band. I'd stand in front and move from section to section, listening to the various parts.

I don't think I really began to appreciate true musicianship until I started college. I had worked as an iceman during the summers and saved my money; and just before I entered Trinity College, I bought a big console Silvertone radio-phonograph at Sears and had it sent up to the dorm in Hartford. This was a pretty big deal in 1942, and it made me a big man on campus. A lot of guys brought their records to my room, and we'd play all kinds of music.

One day while I was shaving, there was a knock at the door. It was a guy I hardly knew, but I'll never forget him—Ken Wynn. He had a record with him that he wanted to play, and I asked him who it was. "Art Tatum," he said. And I said, "Oh"—like "So what?" Believe it or not, I had never heard of Art Tatum. I went back into the bathroom and continued shaving, and Ken put the record on. It was "Humoresque," which has a break where Tatum swings from the regular version into the jazz version. When he went into that thing, it was like pulling up a shade to let the sunlight in. A real awakening.

I became fascinated with Tatum and Teddy Wilson and many other piano players of that period, and I bought all their records. Later, I met Tatum and became quite friendly with him. It was a privilege to know him; and, of course, the experience heightened my interest in jazz, particularly jazz piano.

I joined the merchant marine in 1943. My ship frequently docked in New York, and I'd go to various jazz places in the Village and on 52nd Street. I'd also stop in at the Commodore Music Shop on 42nd Street and pick up some records to take to sea. The Commodore was run by two wonderful guys, Lou Blum and Jack Crystal [the father of comedian Billy Crystal], who put on the jazz sessions at the Central Plaza on Friday and Saturday nights.

Whenever I dropped into the Commodore, I'd always ask for a Tatum record. The shop had some little cubicles in the back where you could sit down and listen to records you might want to buy. I came in off the ship one day in 1952 and asked Lou if he had any new Tatum. He said he didn't; and I was in a hurry and started to leave. "Wait a minute," Lou said. "I got a record I want you to hear." I asked him who it was, and he said, "Oh, a guy by the name of Ralph Sutton." I told him, "Forget it. I gotta get out of here. I'm in a hurry."

Well, Lou had this record in his hand, and he jammed it into my stomach and pushed me back toward the cubicles. It was Ralph's *Piano Moods* album, and hearing it was the second awakening. I had never heard him play before, either recorded or live, and he really turned me on. I bought the record, of course, and Lou told me that Ralph was playing at Condon's.

I had a date that night, and we went down to hear Ralph. Condon's was jammed, and Ralph was playing intermission piano. He was just too much. When he walked by our table on his way back to the bar, I saw those two goddamn hands; and I couldn't believe a guy with hands that size could have such dexterity.

I went back to hear Ralph whenever I was in New York. But I had a feeling that he was reserved and shy, and so I stayed away from him. When strangers spoke to him, there was a sort of—I wouldn't call it unfriendliness, but maybe impatience on his part. I stopped in over a period of three or four months—a night or two at a time and then out to sea again—and never said a word to Ralph.

I happened to know Gene Schroeder, and he and I were sitting together one night while Ralph was on the stand. We started talking about how great Ralph was, and I mentioned that I had never met him. So Gene introduced us. It was love at first sight for me. We hit it off just great. Ralph asked me to come up to his place on Sunday for dinner, and I was thrilled to death. Doc Theobold and his wife were at the house, too, and we all had a wonderful afternoon. Ralph played a few tunes on the piano, and everyone just sat around having a very relaxed time. That was the beginning of a friendship that has lasted all these years. I consider Ralph about my best friend.

After I left the merchant marine in 1953, I lived in Brooklyn and went to Condon's almost every night. I sat behind the piano, away from the audience, while Ralph played; and between tunes we'd chat a little bit. It was a great close-up of this fantastic artist.

I had received about $2,000 in severance pay from the merchant marine, and I suggested to Ralph that we use the money to put on a concert or two—and maybe make enough for a concert tour in Europe. He thought this was a fine idea, and so we decided to do a concert in Symphony Hall in Boston and then do one in Town Hall in New York.

Ralph got a group together—the Ralph Sutton Quartet. They were all from Condon's: Edmond Hall on clarinet, Walter Page on bass, Buzzy Drootin on drums, and Ralph on piano. We also lined up other musicians for the program—Vic Dickenson, Lips Page, Wild Bill Davison, Bud Freeman, Doc Cheatham, Cutty Cutshall, Cozy Cole, and two or three others.

Ralph and I called our program For Listeners Only, and we went up to Boston one day to promote it. Ralph did a 15- or 20-minute shot on the piano at Harvard, Brandeis, Boston University, and some other schools;

and I gave a pep talk to get the college students interested in the concert. Ralph also played on a Boston disk jockey show.

We did the concert in Symphony Hall on the Tuesday or Wednesday night before Easter in 1954, and it was a success. We made a few bucks, and I was rather encouraged. I thought we'd knock 'em dead a couple of weeks later in New York because accolades would precede us from Boston. We scheduled the Town Hall concert for a Saturday afternoon, April 17, and we had pretty much the same lineup as in Boston.

I'll never forget that Saturday as long as I live. It rained. I went over to the Commodore Music Shop around noon to wait for the hall to open and stood at the window watching the rain pour down. Lou Blum and Jack Crystal tried to console me. "Don't worry, Charlie," they said, "it's going to let up." But the rain just came down harder and harder and harder.

We assembled backstage for the program—and no Vic Dickenson or Buzzy Drootin. They were playing in Boston and were going to fly down and then fly back. But their plane got hung up over La Guardia Airport because of the storm and couldn't land.

No more than a couple of hundred people showed up in a house that could seat about 1,500. So the thing was a disaster—whereupon I formally got out of the jazz business. I learned later that the rainfall had set the 1954 record for New York.

That summer, I moved to Dobbs Ferry, a couple of miles from where Ralph lived. He and I spent a great deal of time together until he moved to California in 1956, and it was one of the greatest periods of my life. But both Ralph and I were hitting the bottle pretty heavily, and I think this drinking was probably the beginning of the end of his marriage to Chuck. Things started to kind of deteriorate toward the latter part of their years in Hastings-on-Hudson. However, before they moved to the West Coast, I had the honor to become the godfather of their youngest boy, Nicky.

I'd drive down to Condon's with Ralph in the early evening and come back with him after the place closed. I began to get inside this guy somewhat and find out what made him tick.

I think Ralph's hostility toward so many patrons was—and still is—a resentment of not being listened to. And I think he and many other jazz musicians also resent America's worship of performers with mediocre talent who are promoted by gimmickry. The big money-makers in music are people like Liberace, Elvis Presley, and Alice Cooper. They make it big, and an awful lot of truly talented artists resent the fact that talent doesn't pay off. Unfortunately, this is the way it is in America. The situation bugs Ralph—probably more than it does many other musicians.

A hell of a lot of fine jazz musicians have always walked the streets without any money while others—far less talented but more commercial—were making the bucks. I think Ralph's bitterness led to his asking himself, "Do I really have any friends, or are the people around me interested in me because I amuse them? Do they really like me because I have something to offer them as a friend or as a human being; or am I just a guy up there playing the piano better than the average person—and this is why they like me?" I think Ralph distrusts the so-called average American, and the distrust is a permanent part of his makeup.

At the same time, there's another side to this man. If he's your friend, you won't have a better friend because you can't do anything wrong in his eyes. If you do, he'll tell you about it, but that's as far as it goes. Ralph's a very perceptive fellow. He can meet someone right out of the cold, and if the person is with it and is a good person, Ralph will smell this out. He has the quality of instantly liking what I would call the real people of this world.

I don't know anyone who has more friends—and I mean real friends who are fine people—than Ralph Sutton. Everywhere he goes, people know him and love him. And he keeps up with his friendships. He writes to people and stays in contact with them. So his resentment isn't universal, but it is deep-rooted. Ralph doesn't have a resentment against humanity. He says, "I love humanity; it's the people I can't stand."

Another thing that turns Ralph off is a lot of mugging by a musician. He's straightforward and honest, and he has nothing but contempt for anything that detracts from the music that's being played. A lot of people say he's shy. Well, he might be shy, but I think he just doesn't want to encumber the musical experience with any extraneous nonsense. He's got the attitude, "If you're there to hear the music, listen to it, for God's sake; and to hell with the theatrics."

Ralph came back to New York from the coast for a few gigs, and one time he made a record that got titled *Ragtime U.S.A.* Only one of the tunes was a rag, and so the title of the album was a misnomer if there ever was one. That title was a constant source of irritation to Ralph. He can't seem to shake the "ragtime pianist" label for some reason, and if there ever was a guy who hates labels—even good labels—it's Ralph. Unfortunately, jazz critics and jazz writers are very strong with labels. They call it modern or progressive or Dixieland or ragtime, and I guess most of us know what they're talking about when they use those terms. But do we really know?

The only label that means anything to Ralph is *swing*. As he says, "If it doesn't swing, it's nowhere."

It's always interesting when Ralph is sitting at your table in a club where he's playing, and a label character invites himself along. The character will go into one of three or four things like, "What's your definition of jazz, Ralph, baby?" Or "Do you like Dave Brubeck or Burt Bacharach?" Or "What do you think of Joe Blow's style?" If Ralph is in a quiet mood, he'll just look at the guy and say, "Whatever's right." But if he's a little more vociferous, he'll tell him, "I hate music!" Which, of course, always shocks people.

That reminds me of the night a guy came into Condon's and sat down at the table where Eddie and I were talking. He went into the "What do you think?" routine and asked, "Mr. Condon, what's the difference between a trumpet and a cornet?" Eddie told him, "Well, you can put more dirty laundry in a cornet case."

Ralph is very cynical and believes the public doesn't know anything—that people will take anything that's jammed down their throat and adopt it as a vogue. I think he believes this because we're a nation of statisticians. Everybody knows baseball players' averages and who gained the most yards in a football game. People are always talking about who's best and who's worst and who's the most popular and who's the richest and what's the best seller and who's the best dressed and who's the best piano player. It's a meaningless exercise as far as the arts are concerned, and yet artists—whether they're painters or sculptors or classical musicians or jazz musicians—are somehow caught up in this popularity contest.

If you listen to the radio today, you hear ear-splitting rock 99 percent of the time. The other 1 percent, you hear some good classical music or some good jazz or something worthwhile that somebody is saying. How can anyone growing up today form any ideas relative to taste or true values, particularly in the arts, when nobody is really saying anything? At least you can't hear it if they're saying something.

All this is a fundamental thing in Ralph's character—his cynicism with our way of life and our values and the fact that the public is being led down the road with a ring through its nose.

It's very interesting that a fellow can have such bitterness and animosity toward public attitudes and still play the spontaneous, happy, grabbing music that he does. You'd think Ralph would be a depressed person, but he isn't at all. This dichotomy is a basic part of his personality.

To sum up, Ralph is a typical example of a great talent in a native art form. He's as talented as Rubinstein was in his field or as Picasso was in his. But Ralph's talent has gone virtually unrecognized except by a small percentage of jazz fans. That is the tragedy.

I can't say that Ralph isn't recognized because he hasn't had opportunities. Ralph has probably done as much against the promotion of Ralph Sutton as he's done for it. He has resisted any form of commercialism, and I don't agree with all his decisions in that area. He could have done a little more to promote himself.

One of my great hopes is that someday his remarkable talents will gain the attention they deserve. I don't think it's beyond the scope of imagination to create a situation—an environment within this commercial world we live in—where Ralph could become far better known to the general public and become recognized for what he is—a superb musician.

Chapter **12**

I'll Play It the Way I Play It

pon moving to San Francisco in August 1956, the Suttons rented a home in Belvedere, an island suburb in San Francisco Bay. Ralph went to work as intermission pianist at Bob Scobey's new club, Storyville. Scobey had offered him the job in January while Ralph was playing at the London House in Chicago.

"I thought I'd be working in San Francisco full-time," Ralph said, "but Scobey talked me into going on the road with his band. His piano player, Tiny Crump, didn't want to go. I didn't either, but Bob was paying good money. I stayed with his band a year to the day. I call that year 'the year of the vest' because we wore vests and sleeve garters.

"I had some good moments with Scobey, but I didn't like the way his band swung. It sat too far back in the saddle. I loved Scobey and all the guys, but he'd even hold down the drummer, Dave Black. Dave's a fine drummer who played with Duke Ellington, and he could swing—but he did what Scobey told him to do. One night at the Flamingo in Las Vegas, I said to Dave, 'Let's take the tempo when Scobey kicks the beat off, and let's hold it.' It was work, but we did it. Bob kept looking around like he was wondering what was wrong with me."

Hal Curtis remembered Clancy Hayes's crying with laughter while telling about the night that the Scobey band played a private party in the home of a wealthy family. Ralph sat down at the old spinet piano and discovered that it was several steps out of tune. Throughout the evening, while occasionally smiling at the host in an effort to appear pleasant, he kept muttering under his breath, "Goddamn fuckin' box."

Ralph played on four LPs with Scobey, including a fine swinging record featuring Bing Crosby, who recalled: "I was much impressed with

Ralph not only as a pianist and accompanist and a great jazz artist, but also with his personality. He doesn't have much to say, and he's very reticent about discussing his exploits. You have to kind of drag things like that out of him.

"Ralph is a rare talent—a very sensitive accompanist. He plays all kinds of piano. He can play Fats Waller just like Fats Waller and also do the Lion or Tatum or anybody else that you want to hear. But he has a style of his own that's individual and distinctive."

During the session at which Crosby made his *Bing with a Beat* record with the Scobey band, Jack Teagarden dropped by to pick up Ralph and take him to his home for dinner. Nick Fatool, who had played drums for the session, remembered that "Jack raved about Ralph's great left hand. He thought Sutton was one of the best, and I sure agreed. Ralph's feeling and rhythm on the piano make it a pleasure to work with him."

Ralph had a harrowing experience one Saturday afternoon while walking to a San Francisco television studio to play a show with Scobey. He had just passed the Pickwick Hotel when he heard a crashing noise right behind him. He turned around and saw the remains of a woman who had committed suicide by jumping out of a hotel window. She narrowly missed Ralph when she hit the pavement. Sutton didn't look back again. He crossed the street and hurried into the first bar he saw—and then went on to the TV studio.

Shortly after Ralph settled on the West Coast, three local businessmen came up with the idea of converting a large boat into a jazz club and using a combo including him as the house band. One of the men was a fan of Ralph's and of Dick Cary's. Cary, who at the time was playing with Bobby Hackett in New York, recalled: "Ralph and I wrote back and forth and made plans. We were going to have two grands. I'd play trumpet and alto horn mostly, but I also loved the idea of playing duo piano with Ralph. We talked about doing a two-piano album, too. Those wonderful plans with the boat never worked out, and I was very disappointed."

After leaving Scobey in 1957, Ralph played solo piano at the Hangover Club. Then he played there in Earl Hines's band while Hines was touring Europe. Muggsy Spanier took over as leader of the group, which also included Jimmy Archey, Darnell Howard, Pops Foster, and Earl Watkins. Ralph J. Gleason, the jazz critic of the *San Francisco Chronicle,* wrote of Sutton:

> His ability is so great that, even though he chooses to play in the style of Fats Waller..., Sutton does it so well he makes the modernists stop and listen.
>
> Pianists who wouldn't spend 10 minutes listening to Fats Waller records, have never bothered to hear Jelly Roll Morton, and probably don't even know about James P. Johnson are aware of Sutton and admire him.
>
> There are several reasons for this. In the first place, he swings. Sutton has a tremendous personal beat and drive.... Andre Previn once referred to Sutton as one of the few jazz pianists who had complete mastery of his instrument. Sutton plays with both hands and 10 fingers, a full harmonic sense, and a delightful wit in his solos. He can swing a band, too.
>
> ... Modern pianists pay no attention whatsoever to such great jazzmen as Jess Stacy or Bob Zurke, which is a shame. One of the weaknesses of modern jazz, incidentally, is this disdain for tradition.
>
> Ralph Sutton may do a good deal to straighten this out. By listening to him, modern jazz pianists may discover the great background of jazz piano, stretching all the way to the early '20s....

Sutton was also featured as intermission pianist at Turk Murphy's club, Easy Street. "Those were very enjoyable times," Ralph said. "When Turk went out on the road, he'd bring in Louis Armstrong—Peanuts Hucko was with him them—and Red Norvo's quintet and Louis Jordan and his Tympany Five. It was a real ball. Later, I had a solo job in white tie and tails at the Mark Hopkins Hotel, led a quartet at the Canterbury Hotel, and played a lot of other spots in the area when I wasn't on the road."

Larry Conger, who played trumpet with Murphy, had met Ralph at Condon's several years earlier while a student at Cornell University. He played in a band at Cornell and remembered that "sometimes we'd be lucky enough to be at Condon's on Tuesday night, when the visiting firemen sat in.

"The top-notchers sat in with the regular band, but all the rinky-dinks and second-class musicians—including me—played with Ralph during the intermissions," Conger said. "It must have been a big drag to him, and I don't know how he put up with it. In 1954, when Ralph was at the Hangover, I dropped in one night to hear him. He was kind enough to say he remembered me from Condon's, whether he really did or not. We got to talking and began to know each other, and I'd go up to the Hangover from time to time to catch him.

"Easy Street opened in 1957, with Harry Brooks playing intermission piano. But he got homesick for New Jersey and left after a few weeks, and Ralph happened to be available just at that time. We jumped on him like a duck on a June bug. It was great having him play solo piano in the club. He's such a nice guy and such a great pianist. Normally, after the band finished a set, we wanted to get out of the place during intermission. We didn't want to stick around every time and talk to people. But with Ralph playing, we wanted to stay and listen.

"My brother Al played bass in the band, and he'd occasionally play the entire intermission with Ralph. Sometimes I'd get up there and play with them, and others in the band did the same thing. It was a real pleasure.

"Ralph has no peer at the piano. He can do it all—and I mean *all*. He's not only great playing by himself or with a rhythm section, but he's great with a band, too. He does a tremendous job filling in behind the horns. I never heard him goof. He could be drinking a little or drinking a lot, but he'd never goof.

"As a person, Ralph is a humanitarian. He feels for people and is genuinely concerned about them. If something happens to a friend, he really cares."

In 1957, the Suttons bought a home in Forest Knolls, another San Francisco suburb. The rent was too high in Belvedere, and Ralph liked the woody, countrylike environment of Forest Knolls, which lay about 30 miles from the city. His sister Barbara lived in nearby Mill Valley and was delighted that they could see each other frequently.

Ralph enjoyed taking long walks, especially through the woods. He usually hiked along various fire trails, which fire department vehicles used in case of a forest fire.

"The trails were completely isolated, and I'd just start walking," Ralph said. "I even got myself a pedometer and tied it to my belt so I'd know how many miles I had walked. It was good exercise, and I could get away from other two-legged animals. Every once in a while a few deer would jump out across the trail. I was with nature, and it was just great."

One or more of the Sutton boys sometimes went hiking with their father. But Ralph's working hours prevented him from being with his sons as much as he would have liked. "Dad slept late because he'd get home at 2 or 3 in the morning," Pete remembered. "After he got up, we usually had work to do around the house. Dad didn't like to stop until he had finished whatever job we were working on. He wouldn't work at a fast pace, but it would take all my energy to keep up with him. He has a temper, too, and if one of us did something he didn't dig, he'd let us know right away.

"My brothers and I used to laugh when Mom tried to give us a spanking. She would send us out to get a switch, and we'd come back with the smallest one we could find and try not to crack up when she hit us with it. But there was no fooling around when Dad lit into us."

Nick said there were days when he hardly saw his father, but he recalled other times with delight: "When I wasn't looking, he'd grab me by the knees where it really tickled, and that would drive me up the wall. Or we'd jive around the house chattering, 'Eef, Ife,' like Fats Waller used to do. Sometimes when Dad played at home, his right foot would be stomping away and he'd jabber along with the music.

"Occasionally, Mom took us to hear him play in San Francisco. I loved every minute of it. After he finished a song, he'd look over at me and wink and smile. Once I played a song that I had made up, and all the people clapped. I felt embarrassed but proud."

Jeff remembered "the sound of Fats, Bix, Art Tatum, Count Basie, and all the greats—but especially Fats—coming out of Dad's record player every day." Jeff summed up the feelings that all three of Ralph's sons have for him: "I respect him very deeply, and I would have no one else for a father. Dad taught me to stand on my own two feet and not follow the sheep. He put me on the right track."

One day, Ralph was visiting at the home of his next-door neighbors, the Zettls. Herbert L. Zettl at that time was a young doctoral candidate with a family to support. Ralph went to the refrigerator to get some ice for a glass of water and saw that it was almost empty. Saying nothing, he walked out of the house, drove to the grocery, and bought milk, eggs, meat, and other food for the struggling family. The

Zettls had no idea what he was up to until he started filling their refrigerator—still without a word about what he was doing.

Ralph also liked to visit the family of Bill Reich, his Army buddy, who lived nearby. Reich's two oldest children, Tom and Marilyn, then 6 and 5 years old, became extremely fond of Sutton.

"A typical happy day for Ralph would be to just be left alone and hike around in boxer shorts," Reich said. "It was hotter than hell there. He loved to cook, and he made some of the wildest lasagna I've ever had anywhere. The kids would sit on both sides of him when he did the cooking.

"We had an upright piano that was outstanding for an upright, and we kept it in tune. When Ralph played, the kids would sometimes climb up on his lap. In their 40s, they still remember those days with great pleasure and a couple of tears in their eyes. They just loved that man."

One night the Reichs and a group of friends played a game in which they told what they would want to be if they arrived on the earth in another lifetime. When Ralph's turn came, he declared, "I'd like to be an elephant." When the others asked why, he told them, "He's got a thick hide and nobody can hurt him."

"I think this kind of reflects a part of his personality," Reich said. "He's such a rugged guy. He's built like the proverbial brick house, and yet I think he simply doesn't want to be hurt."

Reich told about a night at the Hangover when the usual crowd of drunks held forth while Sutton was at the keyboard. One of them slammed a dollar bill down on the piano and ordered him to play "Some Enchanted Evening." Ralph looked at him politely and replied, "Jeez, man, I'd love to, but it would fuck up my income tax."

"A lot of people have a real proprietary interest in Ralph," Reich said. "He is 'My man, my pianist. I want you to meet my man.' This is one thing that drives Sutton nuts. So many of the people who cozy up to him don't know diddly about music in general, and least of all about jazz piano. And they so frequently are the ones with a bunch of bucks."

Two Denver jazz enthusiasts, John Heinz and Harney Peterson, heard Ralph at the Hangover late in 1957 and invited him to play for the Denver Jazz Club. The three agreed on a night during the week between Christmas and New Year's Day, when Ralph would be en route to Chicago for a return engagement at the London House. Christmas week is traditionally slow, and Heinz predicted a small turnout: "Our club didn't expect to make any money out of Ralph's appearance, but we hoped for the best. We advertised it and, surprisingly, we got calls from all over town and from Fort Collins and other places in the Denver area.

"People wanted to know if this was the Sutton who used to play at Condon's and had made those fine records. More than 200 persons showed up at the restaurant where we held the concert, and that was all the place would hold.

"I met Ralph's plane, which was late, and I hardly recognized him because he had a beard about half an inch long. He came in on a champagne flight that had been delayed several times and then had been detoured. Ralph was feeling fine by the time he got to Denver. We brought him to our house for some coffee and a shower. He played a tremendous concert that night—just buoyant. It was the best I've ever heard him play."

Peterson, who recalled that the restaurant owner couldn't understand why anyone would pay just to listen to a piano player, had checked the piano before Ralph's arrival: "It wasn't the greatest in the world, and there were a couple of notes that I thought would annoy Ralph. But he plunked them and they didn't bother him. He took off on 'Honky Tonk Train' without any warm-up at all. That shook a lot of people because 'Honky Tonk' is a powerhouse thing, and many piano players would warm up for a while before doing it. But Ralph just lit into it and played as beautifully and powerfully as he always does."

Several weeks before playing in Denver, Ralph had been in the woods near his home when some poison ivy brushed against a cut on his left arm. The resulting infection made his arm swell up and prevented him from closing his hand. It then spread to his face, and he grew a beard because shaving was impossible. "It was a good beard, too," he said proudly. "A real Hemingway beard. I wore it for more than a year."

Norman Muschany heard Ralph at the London House in January 1958 and saw his friend blow up at a patron: "I was always sort of frightened by the way Ralph's temper would flare at someone in an audience who would mock him or tease him or request a number that he had just played or show their ignorance about what he was doing. He would get violently angry and cuss and mumble if they got him upset enough.

"Someone at the London House asked Ralph to play 'Misty' like Erroll Garner played it. He went into a rage, and the air was blue with his swearing. He told the audience, 'I'll play it the way *I* play it—not like anybody else plays it.' That part of the evening was ruined by the person's request and Ralph's reaction to the idea that he should play anything like Erroll Garner played it. He couldn't have cared less.

"I believe that what made him a good basketball player—and what makes him an excellent entertainer—has something to do with his temper and intolerance of people who don't behave the way he thinks they should. But I've never talked to him about his temper. As a kid, I'd have been afraid to!"

Wild Bill Davison told about the time he brought a band to San Francisco to play a club where Ralph was the intermission pianist: "One night, a party of about 30 doctors and their wives took over the place. Our band was through playing for the night, but Ralph still had a set to go. Everybody was making too much noise, and it finally got to Ralph. He stopped playing, and, of course, he stopped right in the middle of a song. He got up and told the crowd, 'How would you all like to go fuck yourselves.' The boss grabbed him and said, 'What the hell are you doing?' Ralph told him, 'Fuck you, too!' And he walked out. The next night, he came back to work as though nothing had happened."

Chapter **13**

A Bit of God on the Keyboard

ne night in 1958, while Ralph was playing at the Hangover, Alex Cushing came into the club. Cushing owned Squaw Valley Lodge high in the California Sierras, about 200 miles northeast of San Francisco. At that time, workers were building the facilities needed to accommodate the athletes and spectators who would pack Squaw Valley for the Winter Olympics during the winter of 1959-1960. Ralph had played at Cushing's lodge with the Scobey band, and he recalled: "Alex really dug the way I played. He invited me to come up and play at Squaw Valley and bring my family. I told him I'd love to, and he said he'd get a new piano for me.

"Alex and I went to a music store to check a 9-foot Steinway concert grand that had been rebuilt. Then we drove to Sacramento and looked at another 9-foot Steinway. I told Alex I preferred the one in San Francisco, and so he bought it especially for me. He paid around $3,500 for it, and he got a bargain. Jesus, what a great piano it was!

"I played at Squaw Valley for four winters, from December to April, and I worked there a couple of summers, too. The whole family moved up to the mountains. Alex provided a house for us, and all our groceries; and the boys went to school there. I got a very small fee for playing, of course, but everything was covered.

"I'd start playing about 5 o'clock, when the skiers began coming off the slopes, and then I'd be off until later in the evening. I put a lock on the piano to keep everybody's clumsy hands off it, and the skiers piled all their parkas and other stuff on top. So I'd just take all their things and throw 'em under the piano and open it up and start to play."

Nick Sutton, who was only 4 when the family first went to Squaw Valley, had happy memories of those winters: "Every once in a while I would sit right behind Dad at the lodge and watch him play. I can still remember his left hand striding back and forth. Man, those were the days. Skiing, hiking, and running around like I owned the place because *my* father was the piano player there."

Alex Grossmann, a friend of Ralph's, spent several days at Squaw Valley with his wife in December 1958: "One evening I asked the bartender for a moo highball, and he questioned me as to its contents. I told him it was half orange juice and half milk—for the piano player. The bartender said Ralph would never drink it, but I told him I'd pay for it—even if Ralph broke the glass.

"Ralph didn't like the idea of my taking his drink from the piano and replacing it with the moo highball, but after a bit of discussion he accepted it. He laid off the liquor for at least six months after that. Every note, card, and letter I received from him during that time was signed 'El Sobre.' When he began signing them 'Ralph' again, I knew he had fallen off the wagon.

"Ralph and I went back to the lounge one night about an hour after it had closed, and he played a batch of numbers for my old tape recorder. That tape became one of my most cherished possessions. A few years later, Jack Teagarden asked me for a copy of it. I don't know where he had heard about the tape, but I gave him one."

In June 1959, Ralph played the Boulevard Room of the Sheraton-Jefferson Hotel in St. Louis. Another pianist, Mary Pearl, was appearing in one of the hotel's lounges at the same time. She had never met Ralph nor heard him play, and so she walked over to the Boulevard Room on his opening night: "As I neared the door and heard Ralph playing, I said to myself, 'This is not just a talent; this is a genius. This is Fats Waller, Art Tatum, Willie the Lion, and Teddy Wilson all rolled into one.' The word *genius* has long been overworked, and one almost hesitates to use it. But that still is my opinion of Ralph, and I'm more convinced of it now than ever.

"As I sat there listening, I knew I was hearing a bit of God on the keyboard. Ralph brings heaven right down to the piano. I still get the same feeling every time I hear him play, even after all these years. When Ralph plays, he touches all the centers of the emotions. He can make you laugh or cry, and he plays so clearly. He picks up where the others leave off, and his great gift is a definite contribution to the musical world. He deserves to go down in history.

"Through the years, we've played gigs at the same hotels at the same time, and it's always my pleasure and thrill to see and hear him, again and again. My respect for Ralph continues to grow because his qualities as a person match his great musical genius. He's a beautiful person, both musically and personally. If I seem to go overboard in my opinion of Ralph, it's only because I believe every word. He is a monument to the jazz world."

Ralph also played at Squaw Valley during the summer of 1959 and invited Barbara and Hal Curtis and their young daughter, Terry, to spend some time with him there in July. The lodge had a small grand piano as well as the 9-foot Steinway, and Ralph and his sister pushed them next to each other one day during the cocktail hour. Ralph gave Barb the larger instrument and sat down at the other piano himself. That afternoon, and for the next several days, they treated the lodge audience to the unique experience of hearing a top-notch brother-and-sister jazz piano team perform.

Alex Cushing heard them one evening and was so impressed that he invited Barb to join Ralph in playing at the lodge during the Olympics that coming winter. Barb accepted immediately. In December, she and Ralph shared the rental of a spinet that they somehow managed to squeeze next to her own grand piano in the Curtis' living room.

"The two of them rehearsed frequently," Hal remembered. "They wanted to have a few things worked out by the time they got up to Squaw Valley. Ralph would come over in the middle of the morning, and they'd sit down at the pianos and go to work."

Hal stayed home from school one day to recuperate after having two wisdom teeth extracted, and he recorded Barb and Ralph as they practiced. The two had appeared together on a television show in St. Louis several years earlier, and their performance received great acclaim. Except for that occasion, they had played together through the years only for their own amusement, usually at one piano. Barbara generally played the bass and Ralph the treble, though they sometimes switched parts. Listening to these two artists perform together is an exciting experience, and Hal hopes to record them someday in a three-record album for limited distribution to a select audience. He plans to have each make a solo record and have them play on two pianos for the third record.

"Ralph and I always have a ball when we play together," Barb said. "He's stronger than I am, of course, and I'm willing to quit after three or four choruses of something like 'Runnin' Wild.' Ralph always pushes for one more chorus."

Unfortunately, the plans for Barbara to play at Squaw Valley fell through because of a shortage of accommodations. The Olympic athletes and thousands of other guests had reserved all the rooms in the lodge.

One of the lodge guests before the Olympics began was Hugh A. Cregg, Jr., a radiologist from Mill Valley, California. Cregg had been a swing drummer before studying medicine and had often heard Ralph at Condon's. "I walked through the lobby at Squaw Valley one day and heard some piano that stopped me in my tracks," Cregg recalled. "I took a look and saw a bearded guy playing wonderful stride. We began chatting and wound up talking through the night. Ralph invited me to get a set of drums and join him, and I played with him a few nights while I was up there skiing. Later, we played some private jobs around San Francisco when our paths crossed."

Al Conger, who had left Turk Murphy's band, sometimes lugged his bass up to Squaw Valley on weekends or went there for three or four days just to sit in with Ralph. His brother Larry said Al "might have gotten paid a little bit, or maybe he just got his room and meals out of it."

Ralph brought three San Francisco musicians—Ernie Figueroa, Vernon Alley, and Joe Dodge, on trumpet, bass, and drums—up to Squaw Valley to play with him for the Olympics. The quartet made a record that winter, and Cushing wrote the liner notes:

> There are several good reasons why Ralph Sutton is a regular attraction both winter and summer at the Squaw Valley Lodge. But I suppose the best reason is that I happen to run the lodge, and I think Ralph Sutton is the best traditional swing pianist playing today. Even if none of the skiers at the lodge agreed with me (this is highly unlikely), I would still be president of the Ralph Sutton Fan Club, and he could plan on spending his winters and summers here for as long as he likes. . . .
>
> Ralph has a driving beat that makes for both good listening and good dancing (as the crowd up here will tell you). I can't get technical about it and describe the wonderful chords Ralph plays, or the inven-

tive right hand figures he comes up with—not to mention his having the strongest left hand in the business.... All I can tell you is that Ralph Sutton's playing has the bounce and the honest, undeniable humor of the old Fats Waller records I still enjoy. He has a way of playing just a few notes that somehow add up to a tremendous driving beat. He swings. I have a bad disposition—but not when I am listening to Ralph...."

During the Olympics, Bing Crosby was making a movie, *High Time*, on location at Stockton, California. He made several excursions to Squaw Valley to get together with Ralph at the piano.

"It's only about an hour and a half run from Stockton up to Squaw Valley, so I didn't do much work for Twentieth Century-Fox during that period," Crosby said. "They were looking for me most of the time, and after they found out where I'd been going, there were frantic calls between the Stockton location and Squaw Valley for me to please come down and complete some of the scenes. I think I added about two weeks to the schedule that they had set up for the production of the picture.

"Ralph and I just ad-libbed together at the piano. It was a rare treat for me to sing with him because he's such a sensitive accompanist. He knows every tune, and he knows every nuance and every variation that I'm likely to take. It was a great pleasure and joy to work with him. He's tremendously competent, and he's a marvelous guy to be around. He has a sly sense of humor—very wry and very amusing.

"We got to be pretty good friends, and we discussed doing a record together. I thought that would be wonderful. We'd have a small combo, and we'd feature the piano just as much as the voice and do different songs in the various styles that Ralph plays. We never got around to making that record, which I've always regretted. Possibly an opportunity will arise when we can remedy that and get it done. I hope so.

"I can't think of anybody who's better than Ralph Sutton. I've worked with a lot of great pianists and a lot of great groups—jazz groups and others—but I don't know of anything that would give me more pleasure than doing something with Ralph."

Crosby had first proposed making a record with Ralph during their recording date with the Scobey band in 1957. He pointed out that he couldn't record anything he had done for Decca and asked Sutton to come up with some songs they could do together.

"Bing had recorded hardly any of Fats Waller's tunes," Ralph said, "so I got a lot of Fats's music together and a lot of Willie the Lion's, too. I had all this music at Squaw Valley, and we ran over the tunes at Alex Cushing's house. Bing loved them. We corresponded about making a record together, but it never came off. It would have been great. It's so easy to play behind that guy. He's such a natural—so relaxed and such a fine singer. And he swings. Maybe someday we'll get around to doing that record."

Regrettably, they didn't.

Chapter **14**

I'm a Whorehouse Piano Player

wo legendary jazz singers, Ella Fitzgerald and Jimmy Rushing, had gigs in San Francisco at the same time in 1960. Gus Johnson, the drummer in the combo backing Fitzgerald at the Fairmont Hotel, went over to Sugar Hill one night to say hello to Rushing, a fellow former member of the Count Basie band. Sutton, Wellman Braud, and Herb Barman formed the trio behind Rushing.

Johnson arrived while Rushing was on stage. He laughed while recalling how he concentrated on listening to Sutton's piano rather than Mr. Five by Five's incomparable singing:

"I didn't know Ralph at the time. I listened to him that night because I had heard Jimmy while we both were with Basie. Ralph didn't sound like Basie and he didn't sound like Earl Hines or anybody else, but he could do things like Hines and Basie and Duke, too. He sounded like Ralph Sutton and he sounded great. He has his own style and he knocked me out. If I played drums like that, I'd be fine.

"When Jimmy came off after the set, I asked him who the piano player was. He called Ralph over and introduced us, and we've been friends ever since."

That was an understatement. Johnson and Sutton soon became, as Al Grey noted, as close as peas in a pod.

Rushing, quoted in Stanley Dance's 1980 book *The World of Count Basie*, was "so well pleased" with Sutton:

"Ralph carried such a heavy left hand, it sounded like a bass. We broke the show up for two weeks and I didn't feel tired once. I've seen the time when I've had five or six pieces in there, but they wouldn't carry the time the way he did playing stride piano. . . . In a way, Ralph doesn't even need drums, but he can be more relaxed when he can hear that beat all the time and he doesn't have to play so hard."

Prior to Sutton's gig with Rushing, the two had performed at the Monterey Jazz Festival with a group from Duke Ellington's band—Ray Nance, Lawrence Brown, Johnny Hodges, Aaron Bell, and Sam Woodyard, plus Ben Webster, a former Ellington sideman. Ralph ranked their set among the highlights of his career.

In November 1960, NBC presented a television show called *Those Ragtime Years*. The network had flown Ralph to New York in August for the taping of the show. Through the years, much to his annoyance, he had become known to the public as primarily a ragtime pianist. This probably occurred because he had recorded many rags and because Rudi Blesh had so frequently linked him with ragtime on the "This Is Jazz" radio program and in his book, *They All Played Ragtime*.

"I never have liked rags or enjoyed playing them," Ralph said. "They don't swing. Whenever I play rags, I try to make 'em swing. But a lot of people think a rag should be played exactly as the composer wrote it.

"Anyway, NBC brought me to New York to tape the TV show. Hoagy Carmichael was the m.c., and they had Eubie Blake and Dick Wellstood and the Wilbur De Paris band. I stood around waiting in the studio for a week like you always have to do, and then they had me play 'The Cascades.' I played it my way, and there was a consultation between the director and the assistant director. They decided it wasn't exactly what they wanted. They told me, 'Play it straight.' I said, 'What the hell did you want me to come here for? You could get any piano player in New York to come in and play this thing. It's wasting my time if I can't do it my way.' So we did it my way.

"We finished the show playing 'Maple Leaf Rag' on four upright pianos. I was on the first piano, Dick was on the next one, and then Eubie, and Hoagy was on the end. I set the tempo for 'Maple Leaf'—and it was quite a brisk tempo, which didn't make the director too happy. I played the first two choruses alone. The De Paris band and the NBC studio band joined in for the last two choruses—and if that wasn't a mess!"

A couple of years later, Ralph made the record whose title has angered him ever since. This album on the Roulette label not only is called *Ragtime U.S.A.,* but its subtitle is *Famous Themes of the Great Ragtime*

Pianists. Yet, of the 12 tunes that Ralph plays on the record, only one, "Maple Leaf Rag," is a rag, and none could be called the "theme" of any "ragtime pianist." According to Hal Curtis, Ralph was "absolutely infuriated" by the title of the record: "He wanted to have some of the top jazz pianists represented by their own tunes, but instead, the title kept alive his image as a ragtime pianist."

Jack Lesberg, who with Buzzy Drootin accompanied Ralph on the record, said it's one of his favorites: "Ralph really shows on this record his great feeling for people like Bix and Fats and James P. and Willie the Lion. 'In a Mist' came off especially beautifully. We just read it off the sheet, and so it's really as Bix wrote it. But Ralph made it sound much better than it was written, I think."

The resurgence of ragtime during the 1970s had no effect on Ralph's feelings toward the music: "So now ragtime is back again. That movie *The Sting* came out, and everybody started playing 'The Entertainer' and thinking it's so beautiful. Like they had just discovered it. Well, it *is* a beautiful thing, and I appreciate what all the ragtime composers did. But I'm no ragtime player. I'm a whorehouse piano player. Whorehouse piano swings."

An editorial in the May 1974 issue of *Jazz Journal and Jazz & Blues* praised Sutton as one of the few pianists who have "done their best to keep ragtime alive." In the same issue, an article told how "the classic ragtime piano style was kept alive over two decades ago by Wally Rose of the Yerba Buena band, and the brilliant Ralph Sutton playing solo and also in the Tony Parenti Trio." Ralph, who thought the records he made with Parenti were lousy, laughed when he read those accounts: "The only ragtime tunes I know are 'Dill Pickles' and 'Maple Leaf.' That's enough."

Eddie Condon brought Ralph back to his club twice, in 1960 and 1961, to play gigs. Condon had moved the club from Greenwich Village to 56th Street in 1957, and Sutton played there the first time with a quartet that included Peanuts Hucko, Dante Martucci, and Buzzy Drootin. Ralph didn't care much for the new place: "When I say that Condon's club was the best saloon I ever played, I don't mean the one uptown. That place didn't have it as far as I was concerned, and I think a lot of people would agree. Pete Pesci put in a dance floor after people started dancing the twist, and who needed that?

"I played 'Honky Tonk Train' one night and wore the twisters out.

They yelled for me to stop because they were so whipped, but I thought, 'Fuck 'em.' I cleared the dance floor. They were a bunch of tired, sweaty bastards."

One night during the month-long 1960 gig, a friend of Ralph's taped the quartet and made copies for the musicians and Condon. Seventeen years later, the tape became a record called *Live at Eddie Condon's*. Unfortunately, the liner notes identify the drummer as George Wettling, not Drootin, and the bassist as Montucci, not Martucci. The notes also list one of the tunes as "I Guess I'll Have to Change My Plan" instead of "Lazy Mood."

Ralph pays little attention to anything that critics, reviewers, or other commentators say about him or his playing. But he stepped out of character briefly following the release of the record in 1977. Sutton pointed out the errors in a letter to the recording company. He also wrote to a reviewer who had caught the second two mistakes but had highly praised the drummer, who he thought was Wettling. Ralph mentioned at the end of his letter that the group had been billed as the Ralph Sutton Quartet. This information does not appear on the record or in the liner notes. Neither, characteristically, did Ralph mention it when he told me about the gig for the first edition of his biography.

The reviewer quoted part of Sutton's letter for his readers and explained that the record producer had identified the drummer as Wettling on the basis of information supplied by Condon. I twitted Ralph about writing to the reviewer and suggested that perhaps he had mellowed a little. He set me straight: "No, I haven't mellowed a bit concerning critics, the public, or two-legged animals in general."

John McGill, the sports editor of the *Lexington Herald*, was driving up to Cincinnati to cover a football game one fall day in 1961. A radio commercial took his mind off his assignment with the news that Ralph Sutton was playing in the Gibson Girl Lounge of the Sheraton-Gibson Hotel there. Several months earlier, McGill had been puzzled by some jazz piano he heard on a broadcast: "At first, I thought I was listening to a Fats Waller record. But after another tune, I realized that it was a live network program.

"I couldn't understand it. I had never heard a piano played just like that, except by Fats. Then the announcer identified the pianist as Ralph

Sutton. I knew I would never be satisfied until I saw him play and met him.

"Needless to say, I went to the Gibson Girl Lounge in the hotel to hear Ralph. He sat stiffly at the piano, his hands touching the keys lightly. He seemed somewhat aloof, immersed in his music. But his smile hinted of his sense of humor and of a warmness that was deep inside, waiting for the right people. He played all the Waller tunes—'Honeysuckle Rose,' 'Alligator Crawl,' 'Ain't Misbehavin',' 'Squeeze Me,' and 'Handful of Keys.' It took me back to Huntington, West Virginia, where I had heard Fats himself play many years before.

"During an intermission, I caught Ralph as he strolled across the hotel lobby. 'Mr. Sutton,' I said, 'I believe we have a mutual friend—Fats.' He smiled broadly, obviously pleased, and we began talking.

"One night he got furious because a drunk had been calling out requests for numbers that Ralph didn't want to play. And then, when Ralph played 'African Ripples' at my request, the drunk yelled out, 'That's pretty, but what is it?' A lot of people wanted to talk to Ralph right in the middle of a number, too. He felt he had something to offer and was wasting his time unless people listened. He indicated once that he played to please himself. And if he played Bix Beiderbecke and people thought it was just dinner music—well, that was the way it would have to be.

"Ralph was booked for a return engagement at the Gibson Girl the next year, and then he played in Columbus. There, he announced to the crowd one night that he was playing a Waller medley for me. It was one of the nicest moments of my life."

Dan Havens, a professor of English at Southern Illinois University when not playing trumpet with and leading the Mason-Dixie Line, checked in at the Cincinnati hotel with his wife late one afternoon while Ralph was playing there in 1961. Their room had not been made up, and so they went into the lounge to wait. Ernie Figueroa and Dee Felice, on bass and drums, were in the trio led by Sutton. Havens had no idea who was at the piano, but he knew immediately that it was an exceptional musician. He had never met Ralph nor heard him play except on several records that he owned.

After listening to a few tunes, Havens wrote "Sugar" on a napkin and asked the waitress to give his request to the pianist. Sutton promptly played the number. Havens asked for "Sweet Lorraine," and Ralph again obliged. Thinking he would request a more challenging tune, Havens wrote

"Honky Tonk Train" on a third napkin. As Ralph powered his way through it, Havens turned to his wife.

"This guy's terrific," he said. "He plays it better than Meade Lux Lewis himself."

Havens asked the waitress for the name of the piano player.

"He just started this week," she said. "His name is Ralph Mutton."

After the set, Havens went up to Sutton and introduced himself. Ralph had a big laugh when he heard about the waitress's misnomer.

Ever since his first engagement in Cincinnati, Ralph has had a strong preference for Steinway pianos. He insists on a clause in all his own contracts specifying that a Steinway will be provided for his use. Sutton dislikes a certain make of piano in particular: "The Sheraton-Gibson had several of those pianos. I went around the hotel trying to find one that felt good, but none of them did. I played there for four weeks, and I really suffered. But I got to know the manager very well, and before I went back for the return engagement, I asked him if it would be possible to get a Steinway.

"I went to Cincinnati a couple of days ahead of time for the second gig, and I got together with the hotel's public relations man. We went to a place that handled Steinways, and I picked a 9-foot grand, the kind I had at Squaw Valley. Man, it was a beauty. I was booked at the hotel for 4 weeks, and I stayed 16. I just couldn't leave that piano!"

Ralph wasn't so lucky in Columbus, where he played a restaurant that had just opened. Tommy Henrich, the former New York Yankee outfielder, owned the spot in partnership with another man. (In 1969, Dave Thomas opened the first of his chain of Wendy's fast-food restaurants on the site.) Much to Ralph's annoyance, the restaurant had a piano of the make he dislikes instead of the stipulated Steinway—and three of its keys didn't work.

"Night after night, those damn keys would stick and not play," he recalled. "I reported it to the piano company and they sent a guy over, but nothing was really done about it. So one night I just lost my temper. I tore off the keyboard cover and ripped a few pieces of wood out of that piano. They canned me and didn't pay me for the rest of my contract. I tried to fight the thing through the union, but they wouldn't help me. I had no hard feelings toward Tommy Henrich, who's a very nice guy. But I didn't like his partner."

Charlie Baron believed the Columbus incident temporarily hurt Ralph's reputation: "It created an image of a temperamental, obnoxious individual, and I think it took three or four years for Ralph to really weather the storm. Today, of course, it's forgotten. But Ralph was having a particularly rough time because he was going through the breakup with Chuck. The Columbus blowup typified that difficult period in his life."

In the fall of 1961, Barbara Curtis was playing in a trio at the Colonel's Ranchwagon in Mill Valley. The owner of the spot, Max Horowitz, had a certificate from Governor Happy Chandler of Kentucky making him an honorary Southern colonel. The trio played Friday and Saturday nights; and Gene Burns, the drummer and leader, persuaded Horowitz to hire Ralph for the other nights. The Suttons had the Colonel's Ranchwagon tied up between them for several months, with Ralph playing piano there on Sunday through Thursday, and Barbara taking over on Friday and Saturday. Hugh Cregg frequently accompanied Ralph on drums.

Cregg remembered that Ben Webster was playing in San Francisco at the time Ralph was appearing at the Mark Hopkins Hotel. Webster asked Sutton to drop by some night, and Ralph invited Cregg to go along.

"Ralph was in the audience when I arrived," Cregg said. "Ben had Buddy Montgomery on piano. When they finished the tune they were playing, Ben spotted Ralph and asked him to sit in. After Ralph had played one number, Ben went to the mike and told the audience: 'Ladies and gentlemen, I want you to know that Buddy Montgomery is a great piano player. But tonight, Ralph Sutton is here. He is one of the last of the piano players with the paw. James P. Johnson, Fats Waller, and Willie the Lion Smith were others. I would like Ralph to play a few of the Lion's tunes.'

"Ralph started to play, and Ben walked out into the audience and sat there listening with them. Later, he explained to the people how that form of piano playing with the powerful left hand was almost extinct. As Ralph left the stand, Ben said, 'Thank God for you, Ralph Sutton.' "

One summer day, the Suttons had Webster and Jimmy Rushing over for dinner. Pete Sutton remembered that Rushing sang "Tricks Ain't Walkin' No More" for him. On Pops Foster's birthday one year, the Suttons and the Curtises, along with Earl Hines and his family, enjoyed a feast of fried chicken and homemade ice cream at the old bass player's home. "I was very young," Nick Sutton said, "but I remember Pops and his smile and how he liked to slap me on the knee."

Nick was also especially fond of Muggsy Spanier, with whom Ralph played a number of gigs. The Suttons and the Spaniers became good friends, and Nick said Muggsy regarded him almost as a son: "Whenever we'd go over to the Spaniers', I'd sit on his lap and he'd tell me jokes and tickle me. Muggsy was one of the sweetest men I've ever known."

In 1939, Muggsy Spanier and His Ragtimers had shared the billing with Fats Waller and His Rhythm at the Regal Theater in Chicago. A photograph shows Waller clowning and Spanier blowing his cornet as three members of Spanier's band—Rod Cless, Bob Casey, and Joe Bushkin, his 23-year-old pianist—watch with obvious enjoyment. Years later, Spanier inscribed a copy of the photo for Ralph: "To Ralph Sutton who brings alive the great Fats Waller magic. Always, Muggsy Spanier."

Many people have speculated, perhaps only partly in jest, that Ralph's playing sometimes sounds as though two pianists are performing. This theory took a slightly different twist in February 1963, when Ralph played on a radio broadcast by a combo led by Red Allen.

"I know that you are called a two-handed piano player," the announcer, Bob Landers, told Sutton. "That is supposed to be something of a joke, but I don't quite understand what they mean. I thought all piano players play with two hands."

"I don't know exactly what they mean either, except I have two hands and I use 'em," Sutton replied patiently.

"We'd get a big kick out of hearing you play something here," Landers said. "I have a request. Am I allowed to make requests?"

"Certainly," Ralph responded. Landers requested "Honky Tonk Train," and Ralph played it.

"Ralph Sutton, I know why they call you a two-handed piano player," the announcer declared.

Through the years, many of Ralph's friends have echoed Charlie Baron's hope that someday Sutton will achieve the fame and the material rewards they feel should be his. In 1963, one of those friends came up with the idea of joining with others and forming a corporation to promote Ralph. Sutton gave his approval, and the friend, a St. Louis businessman, asked for his reaction to a letter to be sent to the group. Ralph displayed considerable business savvy in his reply:

> This first letter is a feeler to see what results we get, so it must be a real hard-sell opener. Most people like the music I play but don't know the business end of it, so instead of thinking of me as an artist, think of me as a product. I have been in business for quite a few years and have proven my ability and drawing power, so this is not a new product. In order to do what the big companies do for cigarettes, soap, etc., the investment has to pay off if the product is properly exploited.
>
> When this first letter is sent out to the individuals, there is to be no mention made of others who are to receive this letter. Let's wait and see what the interest and expression on their part is. . . .
>
> Forty guys are too many. The less people, the less hassle. Ten guys with $5,000 each is better, and five guys with $10,000 is still better. Unless this is sent out in businesslike fashion, it won't get off the ground. I'm putting myself in the position of the investor receiving the letter, so it has to be a damn good selling letter to begin with. This is to promote Ralph Sutton and his music, and the letter should not be emotional.
>
> After we have received a response from this first letter, here are some things we have to work on before the second letter is sent. First, we have to get a sharp promoter to really present this venture to the investors—a complete outline of what is going to happen in this business, and all the ideas put together so the investors can have a clear picture of the thing. . . . These investors may be my friends and like my music, but they aren't going to part with that money on friendship and music. There is a possibility if I was on relief, they would come to my rescue, but then again I can only vouch for myself. When it comes to business, these men are successful in their individual way, and so this whole setup should be strictly hard business. (As much as it disgusts me.)
>
> It will cost a minimum of $25,000 or $30,000 to launch this thing properly, with a backlog that can be relied on. . . . Don't mention money at all in this first letter. A mention can be made stating that this is an investment of X dollars, for which they would receive shares and a return for their investment.

Ralph made a number of changes in the letter and approved the following version to be sent to prospective investors in the proposed corporation:

Dear _____:

As I understand it, we have something in common—a mutual like and admiration for Ralph Sutton, not only as a fine pianist, but as an individual as well.

I am sure you, too, on occasion have remarked to Ralph something similar to the effect, "It's a damn shame somebody doesn't get behind you, promote your talent, and help you *really make it big.*"

It occurs to me that in launching what we will temporarily refer to as Ralph Sutton, Inc. (which can always be changed), we have a product which has tremendous selling power and appeal. This product can be exploited in much the same fashion as cigarette, soap, and dairy companies exploit their products. Properly handled, the return on an investment would be unlimited.

I am sure you are as interested as I in the possibilities presented by such an endeavor. It is much like being a patron of the arts, but also getting a return on an investment.

Let me assure you first of all, my interest is a sincere belief in the talent, the man, and the fact that this can be successfully accomplished.

TO MEMBERS OF THE RALPH SUTTON CORPORATION:

We each invest X dollars for shares in the corporation, the amount to be settled upon at a later date.

The corporation is to use the capital to hire a good promoter and/or publicity man plus an able business manager. Their job is to get Ralph guest shots on the top TV shows; recording dates; bookings in the top nightclubs; concert tours, American and foreign; advertising in the proper media; and publicity, such as feature stories (free) as a follow-up on paid promotion.

Ralph Sutton is to receive a guaranteed salary.

The corporation will not only be self-satisfying, but profitable. . . .

Ralph, of course, knows of this letter, for it was from him I secured your name.

I shall look forward to hearing from you at your earliest convenience on this venture and will appreciate any comments.

The above letter was sent to about 40 people, along with an explanatory letter from Ralph. But lack of financial support prevented the venture from getting off the ground.

In January 1964, Ralph and Muggsy Spanier went to Los Angeles for Jack Teagarden's funeral. Teagarden's death devastated Sutton, who wept uncontrollably and clung to Spanier like a little boy hanging on to his father. The copy of the tape that Ralph had made for Alex Grossmann lay in Teagarden's trombone case when his body was found in a New Orleans hotel room.

Chapter **15**

She Saved My Life

ichard D. Gibson, a wealthy Denver businessman, loves jazz and enjoys being around jazz musicians. In September 1963, he and his wife, Maddie, gave the first of what became a series of annual private jazz parties, each featuring about 40 top musicians and lasting three days. The Gibsons had moved from New York to Denver in 1960 and soon found that they missed two things—the ocean and jazz. Dick Gibson couldn't do much about bringing the ocean to Colorado, but he could—and did—bring jazz there.

"Ralph was the first musician we invited to our first jazz party in Colorado—which shows what we think of him," Gibson said. "I had heard him play at Condon's many times, but I hardly knew him at all.

"The first time I heard Ralph play, I was as fascinated by his enormous hands as I was by his music. The size and dexterity of his fingers amazed me. Even his little fingers are larger than my forefingers. He became a great favorite of mine, but I don't think I ever did more than say hello to him at Condon's. I left him alone.

"I doubt that any public figure is besieged by more drunks and jerks than a jazz musician is. I felt the thing to do was to listen to Ralph play and not bother him with a lot of banalities. He was working at a job that involved tremendous virtuosity, and so I always stayed away from him. I didn't meet Ralph personally until 1963, when he came to our party."

Sutton was not only the first musician whom Gibson invited to his first jazz party, but also the first to hear about it. He played a leading, though characteristically behind-the-scenes, role in helping stage the event.

Gibson described his plan in a letter to Sutton and asked for suggestions. Ralph thought it was a wonderful idea and recommended that

Gibson request Jack Lesberg to contact the musicians and invite them to play at the party. Sutton also told Gibson to count him in on piano.

"Dick was a little worried and shy about contacting musicians himself," Lesberg said. "He called me to help him organize the first party as a result of Ralph's suggestion. It required some talking to guys, and Dick didn't know any musicians personally at that time. It was to be a musicians' party, and that was the selling point of it. Ralph suggested that I could probably call the guys and put it over because I would know who would like to come.

"Dick asked me to make the contacts for him. It was easy for me to do because I had telephone numbers and knew where everybody was, and I could talk to them easily. I was very much involved with all the guys. I had been in New York since about 1944 and was doing studio work with a lot of jazz players as a result of my association with Eddie Condon's club. I had known Ralph since 1947, when Jack Teagarden brought him in to play with us at the Famous Door. We got along very well. He and I played together a lot and had lots of fun with each other.

"The idea of Gibson's party was to provide an opportunity to reunite a lot of guys who hadn't played together for a long time—the East Coast and the West Coast musicians. These were guys who were working the studios in California and those who were doing studio work in New York. Most of the accomplished jazz musicians wound up doing studio work. It was more than a sideline. It was a good business, and we were in the studios for years.

"All the musicians at the party got the same money, which at that time was $300, and all our expenses. We could sign for anything and we could do anything we wanted. We had a free rein. It was off and running very quickly.

"Ralph had a good deal to do with putting the first party together. There are so many people who love the piano and his kind of playing. He's such a great musician, and he had quite an audience all around the country. Ralph knew these people and they really liked him, besides liking the way he plays. You go into a lot of clubs, and there are people who like the music, and people who have no place else to go, and people who just get drunk and make noise while the band is playing. Our idea was to put a party guest list together of those who like the music.

"We made a list of people across the country whom Ralph knew and had played for. A lot of them would have him come to their homes and play. Tom Morley did this often at his home on Long Island. He'd have people come in and spend an afternoon listening to Ralph play. So Ralph had a lot to do with the start of the party. But he didn't like organizing things and calling people, and he is quiet and reticent about coming forward.

"He does it great now. He certainly speaks well and has no problem with it. I think he does himself a lot of good by getting up and saying a few words here and there."

The Gibsons gave their jazz party at the Hotel Jerome in the ski resort town of Aspen. It was such a success that they held another affair there in September 1964. The guests at the second party included Sunnie Anderson, an attractive blonde who owned an Aspen supper club called Sunnie's Rendezvous. Maddie Gibson introduced Sunnie and Ralph one day during lunch at a restaurant across the street from the hotel.

After the party ended on Sunday night, most of the musicians and guests drove to Denver and kept things going at Gibson's home. Ralph, who had been drinking even more heavily than usual because of his collapsing marriage, went along; and so did Sunnie. She took some people in her car, but her group did not include Ralph. The two had exchanged hardly a word since meeting.

The second leg of the Sunday session lasted all night. Sunnie had no idea what happened to Monday; but before she knew it, Tuesday morning had arrived: "I got a few hours' sleep, and then I decided I should get back to Aspen and start running the club again. There were a few bodies scattered around the Gibsons' living room, and one of them was Ralph. He was sitting in a big chair, and he'd already had a couple of screwdrivers. I didn't know if he was still loaded from the night before or whether he was starting on a new buzz.

"At about 11 o'clock that morning, I announced that I was heading up the hill, and if anyone wanted a ride to Aspen, they were welcome to come along. Ralph piped up and said, 'Well, I have nothing to do until Saturday. I think I might ride back to Aspen with you.' I said, 'Fine.'

"He went upstairs to shower and shave and pack. An hour went by, and I started to get restless. But he finally made it down and we got into the car. I thought we'd better have something to eat to sober him up a bit, and so we went to a Chinese restaurant. I ordered a giant bowl of won ton soup for him—and that's been one of our favorite dishes ever since.

"We started for Aspen, and Ralph was feeling fine by the time we got to Fairplay. We stopped and had a drink and talked a little, and I kept wondering what in the world I was going to do with this man after I got him to Aspen. I didn't even know him, and I was getting more nervous as time went on.

"We stopped in another town, Granite, just before going through Independence Pass, which leads into Aspen. We went into the Placer Inn, which is a little bar and motel on the highway between nowhere and nowhere. A woman named Irene ran it, and she told us that a lot of people from the Gibson group had stopped there for a drink on their way to Denver Sunday night. 'It must have been a marvelous party,' she said. 'I wish some of those musicians would come here and play.' I told her, 'Well, here's a piano player right here. If you talk nice, maybe he'll play for you.' Irene asked Ralph if he would, and he said, 'Sure.' There was only one trouble—she didn't have a piano. She said she'd rent one, and I told her I'd call her on Thursday and we'd plan to be there Saturday.

"Well, Ralph had said he was leaving on Saturday, but now we had him booked at the Placer that night. We arrived in Aspen, and I took him home with me. What else could I do? He didn't have much money. The next day he had an awful hangover, but he came out of it in good shape.

"I called Irene on Thursday, and she said she couldn't get a piano. I told her it was too late to cancel the date, and that I had put an ad in the *Aspen Times* announcing that Ralph would be playing there on Saturday. I said I'd supply the piano. So Railway Express picked up the piano from the Rendezvous, and back we went to Granite on Saturday. A lot of people came over from Aspen to hear Ralph, and Dick Gibson brought a bunch up from Denver.

"Ralph wore his tux that night, and I put on one of my beaded dresses that I had worn when I worked at the Gaslight Club in New York. Our gang from Aspen and Denver took over the place, and we had a ball. Ralph started playing, and the regular customers who were sitting at the bar didn't know what to make of it. They couldn't wait for him to finish each set so they could get over to the jukebox and play 'Good Night, Irene' again. Everybody had a marvelous time. We took all the motel rooms and stayed all night.

"Ralph was supposed to get $100 for playing; but when we went to pick up his money the next morning, Irene was in the hospital. I never did find out what had happened to her, but we had to stay until Tuesday to get Ralph's money. We finally drove back to Aspen that day.

"Ralph stayed in Aspen for a week, and he played at the Rendezvous while he was there. We did a lot of talking, and he told me about his home life and the situation there. When he went back to San Francisco, I drove him to Grand Junction and put him on a plane. I knew I was madly in love with him, but I also knew he was married and had three children. I certainly didn't want any responsibility for breaking up anybody's marriage. He told me, 'I'll be back,' but I really didn't believe him. I didn't know what was going to happen. He got on the plane, and I figured, 'Well, that's that.'"

Allene (Sunnie) Anderson, the daughter of Arthur and Irene Anderson, was born in Denver on July 25, 1925. Her father, an artist and interior decorator, moved his family to the North Side of Chicago in 1933. Allene and her younger sister, Shirley, who became a nurse in Syracuse, New York, grew up in the area around Senn High School. As a child, Allene enjoyed singing, and she and several of her girlfriends liked to pretend they were in show business. She was known for her singing voice while a student at Senn. She also picked up the nickname Sunnie in high school but doesn't remember who gave it to her or why.

Sunnie's class had a graduation luncheon at the Edgewater Beach Hotel, and her classmates called on her to sing for them. A local bandleader named Carl Schreiber heard Sunnie perform. He offered her a job with his band on the condition that she study voice after leaving school.

"I took vocal lessons for about six months, and I sang with Carl's band for a year or so," Sunnie recalled. "Then I auditioned for Eddie Oliver, whose band was playing at the Edgewater Beach, and I got the job. His wife was singing with him, but she planned to retire. I sat on the bandstand for about a month and learned all her songs, but I didn't get to sing anything except a tune in a medley every once in a while. Finally, Eddie told me his wife wasn't going to retire after all.

"I sang with Ted Weems for a few months until his band went on a theater tour. I had always sung professionally under the name of Sunnie Anderson, but Ted billed me as Sunnie Day. Later, I sang for Louis Prima, and he called me Sandy Bishop—I have no idea why. Maybe he was just looking for a Sandy Bishop at the time, and I was it. Anyway, before the Weems band left Chicago on tour, Ted hired a little girl who was about 14 years old and could sing and dance and whistle and all that stuff. She ended up in the movies. Ted let me go, but he gave me several months' pay at about $50 a week. My dad used to kid me and say I was the only singer he knew who got paid for not singing. Ted was a great guy, and we remained friends until he died."

After leaving Weems, Sunnie sang with a band in Detroit and then with one in Toledo. She wound up in New York, where she joined the band of Jimmy (Dancin' Shoes) Palmer: "I sang with him on and off from December 1946 until 1953. Jimmy and I got married in 1951 and were divorced after about a year. We remarried, but I divorced him a month later. I stayed single until Ralph and I were married."

Sunnie returned to Chicago after leaving the Palmer band and worked as a fashion and photographer's model until 1958, when she went back to New York. She spent about a year as a fashion model there and then got a job as hostess and night manager of a restaurant on Sixth Avenue. The restaurant work appealed to her, and she took a course in restaurant management at Cornell University. Next, Sunnie ran the Speakeasy Room of the Gaslight Club in New York. But she still wasn't content.

"I had always wanted to come back to Colorado and have a saloon in the mountains," Sunnie said. "I kept a long black sock as a coin purse, with a sign over it that said, 'For Sunnie's Tav.' I collected about $3 in that sock once, but then I needed the money and I spent it.

"I got fed up with New York after about a year at the Gaslight, and I took a trip to Colorado in July 1962 with a girlfriend, Evelyn Duggan. We ended up in an Aspen motel called the Villa, which used to be owned by Hedy Lamarr. One of the guys who ran the Villa at that time was from New York. When he saw we lived there, he suggested that we all have dinner at a place called the Rendezvous.

"The Rendezvous turned out to be for sale, and the owner and I talked about my buying it. I was fascinated by the place. I had never tended bar before or run a restaurant completely by myself, but I thought I could do it. So I borrowed some money and sold a little stock that I owned and jumped in—all by myself.

"A few years before in Denver, I had heard a wonderful pianist named Louise Duncan. I remembered how well she played, and so I looked her up. I told her I was buying a club in Aspen and didn't know how it would work out, but I'd love to have her with me. Louise came along, and she stuck with me through thick and thin.

"I had to pay off $1,000 a month in winter and $500 a month in summer—plus the rent for my apartment. Believe me, I *really* worked to keep that club going.

Ralph said Sunnie and he clicked right away on their 150-mile drive from Denver to Aspen: "I think we fell in love immediately. She took my eye when I first saw her. I guess it was just instinct—something between the two of us—that made me go back to Aspen with her from Gibson's. I had been going through a real scene at home in California, and I was in bad shape. She saved my life. A whole new life was settled in a week. We've been a great combination ever since."

When Ralph got home to Forest Knolls after his week with Sunnie in Aspen, he found his sleeping bag in the kitchen with a note telling him to sleep in the guest house. Chuck had said several times that she wanted a divorce, but he had always talked her out of it. This time, however, Ralph decided there must be more to life than that, and so he resolved to let her go through with it.

Ralph called Sunnie and told her, "Well, everything does work out for the best." He had a booking in Odessa, Texas, in October and asked her to meet him there. The Odessa date had been planned during Ralph's week in Aspen. Two old friends from Texas, O.A. (Jim) Fulcher, an Odessa physician, and C.W. (Chili) Waller of Breckenridge, came into the Rendezvous one night. They had been at Gibson's party and had heard Ralph play at Condon's many times. Waller recalled: "Doc Fulcher hit on the idea of trying to get musicians like Ralph to come to Odessa and let West Texans not only discover the great music, which they probably had never heard, but also meet the nice guys who made the music. He contacted his friend Tom Roden, who owns the Inn of the Golden West in Odessa, and convinced him that a quartet of top jazz musicians would be a real attraction.

"Ralph rounded up the first quartet that played in Odessa. He had Edmond Hall, Major Holley, and Morey Feld. They played a short but highly successful engagement, and that was the beginning of the annual Odessa Jazz Festival."

The Odessa gig was highly successful in more ways than one. Sunnie hitched a ride to Lubbock, Texas, with a friend, a construction man who flew his own Piper Cub. Then she rented a car and drove the rest of the way to Odessa. She and Ralph both stayed in Fulcher's home.

"Ralph said his marriage had ended," Sunnie remembered. "One night after the job, he and I were eating in Doc's kitchen and he told me: 'I've always sworn that if I ever got out of this one, I'd never sign my name again. But I think maybe I'd make an exception.' I said, 'I accept.' It was kind of a half-assed proposal, but I didn't let him get out of it."

Ralph and Chuck had been like two trains traveling on different tracks but headed nevertheless for a collision. Ralph's heavy drinking and his long periods away from home unquestionably played important roles in the collapse of their marriage. Chuck attributed the breakup partly to "a difference in life styles" that developed between them and contributed to their divorce after 18 years together.

"I began to grow away from that world of boozing and going out to clubs at all hours of the night," Chuck said. "I loved the jazz people. They were so much freer than the conventional people I had grown up with. But when you are the mother of three small boys, one has to give up something. I did grow away from the jazz world. Ralph's being on the road so much was very difficult, and I am sure it had a lot to do with our breakup. It was hard on all of us.

"I have only the fondest feelings for Ralph. I think he is a sweet, sensitive man—*all inside*—which most people cannot see. The one thing I remember most vividly, as a clue to this 'seemingly indifferent human being,' was Ralph's telling me once, 'I have never known if people liked me or my music—whether they liked me because I could play the piano.'

"I guess a lot of us wonder about things like that. Sometimes it is difficult to separate our true self from our public image."

After Ralph left home, Chuck started divorce proceedings in California, where the law required a one-year waiting period before a final decree could be granted. Their divorce agreement was remarkably easy on Ralph. It required him only to pay Chuck $100 a month for the support of each of their sons until the boy reached the age of 21. Chuck, who came from a well-to-do family, asked for no alimony. "She was very generous," Ralph said. "She knew I was making hardly any money, and that agreement was her idea. She came up with it out of the goodness of her heart." Jeff was 16, Pete 12, and Nick 9 when their parents separated.

Sutton's niece, Terry Curtis, now Terry Manning, had bittersweet memories of the years Ralph lived nearby in California: "When I think of Uncle Ralph, one of the first things that comes to mind is going to his house in Forest Knolls. It was always lots of fun. Aside from the usual barbecue and games, you could always count on him to play those old-time piano songs that I remember so well—'Maple Leaf Rag,' 'Echo of Spring,' 'African Ripples,' 'Honky Tonk Train,' 'Viper's Drag,' 'Honeysuckle Rose,' 'Snowy Mornin' Blues,' and all the rest. Sometimes I even sat next to him when he played.

"One day, Uncle Ralph and a friend came over to see my mother. I was in the fourth grade and was taking piano lessons, and he asked me to play something for his friend. I didn't want to because I got embarrassed easily and knew it wouldn't sound very good. I thought he would be annoyed, and so I wished he hadn't asked me in the first place. But he understood and didn't push.

"I had washed my hair just before he came, and I was wearing a yellow bathrobe and had a towel wrapped around my head. When Uncle Ralph started to leave, he reached down and gave me a big bear hug. My robe and towel began to come loose, and it irritated me and I tried to get away. He didn't realize that I was mad because all my wraps were coming apart.

"After he left, Mom told me he was going to Colorado to live because he and Auntie Chuck were getting a divorce. It made me feel so awful and sad because if I had known that, I would have given him a bigger hug and not worried so much that my robe and towel were coming off. I felt so bad."

Ralph worked at Sunnie's Rendezvous with Edmond Hall, Clancy Hayes, and Deane Billings during the winter after his marriage broke up. Wild Bill Davison was playing across the street at the Red Onion, and he recalled: "I often grabbed my horn and went over and played with them between sets. One night, Sunnie asked me, 'Do you think I should marry Ralph?' I said, 'C'mon, what do you mean! Do you think I should tell you to marry Ralph?' 'Well,' she said, 'he's so moody. Sometimes he's so great, but the next day I can't make it with him.' I told her she had to work it out by herself. She's a fantastic girl, and I'm glad he's got her."

In April 1965, Ralph and Sunnie closed the Rendezvous for a while after Easter and drove to Las Vegas. He called Chuck from there and said that instead of her divorcing him in California, he would divorce her in Nevada—and have the whole thing over in six weeks. Ralph got his divorce on June 11, 1965, and he and Sunnie were married the same day.

Chapter **16**

Ralph's Music Is Ralph

eff, Pete, and Nick Sutton visited their father in Aspen shortly after his marriage to Sunnie. The boys knew he was playing at the Rendezvous, but he had not told them that he had remarried. Ralph tends to avoid unpleasant situations and confrontations whenever possible. He is the kind of person who often wishes that such circumstances would simply go away and leave him alone. "It was easier to let the boys find out for themselves when they got to Aspen," Ralph said. "Of course, the situation was very uncomfortable at first."

Pete remembered "prime times" with his father in the Rockies during several summer vacations. Ralph and his sons went fishing and hiking, and he took them on long drives through the mountains. "Pete and I even taught Dad how to cast lures in the Roaring Fork River," Nick said. "Man, that was outasight. Once we borrowed a friend's jeep and went way up into the mountains. We had lunch and just talked about things in general and how everybody at home was doing. I got to know my father so much better, and that made me feel good.

"At the club in Aspen, I liked to sit on the back steps listening intently to every chord and note he played. Just like Satchmo when he was young and listening to King Oliver. The feeling was really something. How can I explain it? I felt so good all over when I heard him play that I just couldn't get enough of it. I could sit there all night long. I had such a good time visiting him that when it was time to go, we didn't know what to say except I love you and we'd better start seeing more of each other."

In 1967, Jeff planned to visit his father, whom he had not seen since his first trip to Aspen: "I told him I really wanted to see him and talk to him about a lot of things. I let him know I had long hair and was freaking out, and he said, 'Well, if you're coming to Aspen, you'd better get your hair cut off.' I think he wanted to see a clean-cut kid. He had ideas of self-esteem and self-respect, and he probably figured that a freaked-out kid wasn't on the right track. But I felt that his telling me to get my hair cut off didn't get me on the right track. I thought I was there already.

"I told him I wouldn't get my hair cut, and I didn't go to Aspen. I felt pretty bad about it, but then I remembered what he had told me about standing on my own two feet and not following the sheep. I felt I was right, and I stuck to my ground."

Ralph also felt bad about Jeff's calling off his trip to Colorado. But today he says proudly that the boy did the right thing.

At the time of Ralph and Sunnie's marriage, Peggy Clifford owned a bookstore directly above the Rendezvous. She had been a fan of Sutton's for several years, ever since hearing his *Salute to Fats* record at the home of a friend who had moved to Aspen from San Francisco: "I straightaway bought *Salute* and every other available Sutton record and turned my house into Sutton Place, which it remains to this day. I already had a large record collection, but it paled next to Ralph's piano.

"My friend knew Ralph and gave me his San Francisco address, and I began to correspond with him. I wanted to get him to Aspen to perform, and he said he'd love to come. But Aspen's saloonkeepers were extraordinarily foolish. Several wanted him after hearing his records, but they were unwilling to offer enough money. Their idea of a big price was $125 a week with meals. My efforts as Ralph's agent were futile, but the correspondence was enjoyable because he writes almost as stylishly as he plays piano.

"I finally met Ralph in 1963 at the first Gibson jazz party. I found—and find—him a most attractive, amusing, unencumbered man. He's one of my favorite people and would be even if he were a plumber. The fact that he happens to be a consummate jazzman is kind of a bonus. It was the best of all possible worlds to have him not only performing in Aspen but living here, too. He was one of the town's greatest assets.

"If I had to describe Ralph in one word, that word would be *free*. I don't believe I know anyone so free as Ralph. Naturally, he's had bad times and has suffered the blues—what he calls 'the whips and jangles.' But by and large, he does what he wants to do and has a very good time. He's his own man, in other words; and, for the most part, he has lived his life his way. His freedom has allowed him to be generous, too. Generous in the broadest, deepest sense. And his freedom and generosity are naturally reflected in his music. Ralph's music is—besides being brilliant—generous and free, strong and delicate, robust and melancholy, stylish and sassy. In a word, Ralph's music is Ralph.

"I think playing with musicians he likes and respects has always been more important to Ralph than either fame or fortune. He once told me that he could be happy with just three things: a piano, a good trout stream, and a good lady."

In December 1965, six months after their marriage, Ralph and Sunnie moved the Rendezvous into a building that had just been completed. They added a second piano, and Louise Duncan and Ralph often performed together.

"Ralph is a giant at the piano," Duncan said. "He's a perfectionist, and you get his message because he projects. When he plays alone, especially, it's the moment of truth. The music comes out Ralph. It's sure and steady, with all of his own personal pretties—patterns, color, blending, expression, and strength. He's the only one of his kind."

The Suttons also brought a number of star jazzmen to their club. William A. MacPherson, an obstetrician who delivered fine jazz as well as babies, made two records at the Rendezvous for his Blue Angel label. They feature some of the musicians who played there with Ralph—Ruby Braff, Bob Wilber, Al Hall, Milt Hinton, Mousie Alexander, and Cliff Leeman. MacPherson affectionately described the scene at the Rendezvous in the liner notes for one of the records:

> It was one of those places built below street level, and it was easy to miss if you weren't in the know. There wasn't a big neon sign; just a fragrant, crackling fire of piñon pine burning in a pit in the courtyard which led you along by the nose and defrosted you when you arrived.
>
> Sunnie herself was always somewhere inside, carrying a long cigarette holder and surveying the scene with a level, cool-eyed gaze which almost concealed a heart of pure marshmallow. She had poise and dignity, and hers was a dignified establishment. Except in back, on the bandstand.
>
> There, past the dinner tables and beyond a beaded screen, a big-

shouldered man with a Princeton haircut and glasses sat rocking a grand piano like a hobbyhorse. This was Ralph Sutton, Sunnie's husband, and there is no adequate way to describe his music except to say that it affected people the way catnip affected cats. And, of course, it has not changed since then.

Ralph sits ramrod-straight at the piano, rarely smiling. And what comes out is so unabashed and uninhibited in its simple pagan joy that the net effect is somewhat unnerving. For Sutton is not an innovator; nor is he an imitator. He is simply a kindred spirit who lends himself as a meeting place for the happy ghosts of all the great Harlem pianists in whose styles he has submerged his own. . . .

MacPherson and Sutton first met at Dick Gibson's 1967 jazz party. That party honored Willard Robison, who is one of Ralph's favorite composers, and lyricist Jack Palmer. "Ralph played a medley of the real Robison grabbers like 'Cottage for Sale' and 'Think Well of Me,'" MacPherson remembered. "I asked him if he had ever recorded any of Willard's songs, and he said he hadn't, but he'd like to. We haven't made that record yet because things haven't ever been really right for it in Ralph's mind, even though Willard himself warmly approved of the idea shortly before he died."

Sutton spoke reverently of his close friendship with Robison: "Willard was a gentle, soft-spoken man and was kind to everybody. I just love his music and lyrics. He and I once wrote a tune together called 'You're So Good to Me and I'm So Tired of It All.' We had it copyrighted, but nothing ever came of it." Today, Ralph sometimes breaks into tears when he hears or plays one of Robison's songs.

"I never fail to ask Ralph to do a tune of Willard's," MacPherson said, "but it's extremely difficult to get him to play one. The vibrations have to be exactly right. The best sessions were always those at the Rendezvous after all the talkers had gone, or at Doc Fulcher's home when no one was supposed to be listening. Ralph is deeply sentimental about things that are his articles of faith, and he is quite reluctant to expose himself or his feelings in an alien atmosphere.

"My first reaction upon hearing about this book was one of disbelief that such a private person would approve of having himself dissected publicly. But I have some guesses regarding the answer. First, Ralph would do anything for a friend; and when he elects someone to friendship, it's a pretty permanent thing. Second, the most intimate thing he does is play the piano. Other forms of public exposure probably seem less indecent to him than, let's say, playing with the Milt Herth Trio out where someone might hear him. As a corollary to the first point, I believe he feels secure at the hands of those who love him."

In the fall of 1966, Ralph played with the then-current version of Bob Crosby's Bob Cats at the Rainbow Grill in New York. Condon's was only a few blocks away, and Sutton strolled over between sets late one night. Mat Geiger, an exchange student from Switzerland, watched him chat with the musicians during an intermission. The band at that time consisted of Buck Clayton, Cutty Cutshall, Herb Hall, Eddie Condon, Cliff Leeman, and a piano player whose name Geiger could not recall. There was no intermission pianist. After conversing with the musicians for a while, Sutton surprised them and everyone else in the club who knew him. He walked over to the piano, sat down, and played "Indiana" and another tune solo.

"I had never heard him play before," Geiger said. "He got up after the two tunes and left to go back to work with Crosby. It was brief but one of the most memorable jazz piano concerts I have ever heard. He got a lot of applause, especially considering the place was half empty. The reason I don't recall the name of the band pianist is probably because Ralph was so good."

Geiger and Sutton met nine years later. They became friends, and one day Geiger asked Ralph what had induced him to give that impromptu performance at Condon's, an unusual thing—especially for him—to do. Sutton shrugged and said he couldn't remember, but he agreed that it had been uncharacteristic of him.

The Bob Cats appeared on "The Tonight Show" one night during their gig at the Rainbow Grill. Larry Conger and his wife, Mary, happened to be watching at home in Camden, South Carolina. Conger called Ralph, whom he hadn't seen since their days in San Francisco together, and invited Sutton to make a record for his Solo label. Ralph accepted and flew down on his day off.

"We met him at the airport and drove right to the studio," Conger remembered. "He sat down at the piano and warmed up a little with Johnny Haynes on bass and Jim Lackey on drums, whom he had just met.

After they recorded the first tune, the engineer asked if he wanted to hear a playback. 'Hell, no,' Ralph said, 'Just turn it on and let it run. We'll go.' And that's just what they did.

"I sure would love to get him back down to do another record for Solo. There just aren't any superlatives to describe Ralph. He's the greatest piano player and a fine human being—the kind of person you like being around. He's honest. We've never had a misunderstanding. He's not the kind of person you'd normally have misunderstandings with because he'll meet you halfway on anything."

Ralph sang on a commercial recording for the first time on the record he made for Conger. His vocal on "'Tain't Nobody's Bizness" reminds the listener of Fats Waller. Sutton previously had sung the tune only for selected friends on selected occasions. Peggy Clifford wrote most of the liner notes for the Solo record.

After the gig at the Rainbow Grill, Ralph drove back to Aspen with George Barnes, whom he had booked to play at the Rendezvous. They went via St. Louis so Ralph could visit his parents in St. Charles. It was the last time Ralph saw his father, who died in May 1967. Four years later, his mother moved into a nursing home in Ukiah, California, where Ralph's sister Barbara lives.

Sutton called some St. Louis friends, Virgil and Marie Pinkstaff, and told them that he and Barnes would be going through the city. The Pinkstaffs invited the two musicians to stay at their home, and then they asked the "Sutton gang" over for an evening of music. Through the years, this group of jazz fans had gathered at parties that featured Ralph's music—live. A strict standard determined who was invited. "They had to be friends who would *listen* and not talk all evening," Marie Pinkstaff said. "In other words, music lovers. Some of Ralph's musician friends came over after their job that night just to have the pleasure of hearing him and playing with him again. Joe Schirmer called it one of the greatest parties he ever attended because it was so unusual for 70 people to listen quietly, even sitting on the floor. It was a treat for the musicians, too, in these days of so much conversation during entertainment."

When Schirmer arrived at the Pinkstaffs' home, Sutton and Barnes were playing. "It was just something unbelievable between those two fellows," he recalled. "George is one of the most talented guitar players I've ever heard. I don't think anybody else can play like he can. He gets a tone that nobody else can quite get.

"George and Ralph played a couple of things that I had never heard before. I asked them where the tunes came from, and they said, 'Oh, we rehearsed those driving down here from New York.' One of them would get an idea and start whistling and humming a passage, and then he'd tell the other to come in with his part. By the time they got to St. Louis, they could sit down and play both parts of those things just as though they had been playing them for years."

Norman Muschany tries never to miss a session when Ralph is in the St. Louis area. He and his wife, Barbara, are always invited when Sutton plays at a private party there. "I admire Ralph and am very proud to know him," Muschany said. "And, of course, I enjoy taking close friends up and saying, 'Ralph Sutton, I want you to meet so-and-so.'

"I know only one or two other people who have the ability to make friends who are not only loyal, but also terribly dedicated, and will go out of their way to do anything for them. Anyone who can attract that kind of deep friendship has something that I admire and don't have. Once Ralph makes a friend, they're locked in for life. I've been most happy to contribute any information I can about his background because I love him that much."

Ralph also got together one night with a large group of old friends at the country club in St. Charles. His sixth-grade teacher, Verna Muhm, remembered that evening as her first meeting with Ralph as an adult: "I could hardly believe that he had matured into the really big man I now saw. In spite of his fame, I was happy to see the same humility and sweetness so characteristic of the Sutton family."

Ralph likewise maintained his close friendship with Hub Pruett, the St. Louis physician whom he called "my second father." Pruett said Sutton sometimes thought he might have made a mistake by becoming a professional musician: "He wondered if he ought to get out of music and go into something else. I'd ask him, 'What else can you do? What do you know how to do, and what do you like to do?'

"The thing that bugged Ralph was that he had to travel and be away from his family so much. He just wanted to be anchored down somewhere. It wasn't because he didn't enjoy music. He undoubtedly enjoyed it, or he wouldn't have stayed with it all those years. I understood his problem because I had been a professional ballplayer and knew what it was like to be away from home so much of the time. But again, it was a question of earning dollars for the bacon for his family. If he could do it better playing the piano than doing something else, then that's the way he should have been doing it."

Ralph, like many other jazzmen, spent a great deal of time in Pruett's basement den whenever he was in St. Louis. The den featured a piano, a tape recorder, a mammoth collection of tapes and records, and even a record press.

Also in the den was a battered old sofa that had a unique name. Pruett had brought Pee Wee Russell home with him early one morning after hearing his old friend play in a local club. "We went downstairs and started winging the music around," Pruett said. "About 10 or 11 o'clock, I remembered that my son was playing in a football game that day. I told Pee Wee I was going over to the high school. I got a blanket for him and laid him on the sofa.

"I hadn't seen my wife all that time. She had been asleep when we got home, and I never even let her know that Pee Wee was there. I went to the football game, and during the first quarter I got a call over the P.A. system to phone my home. Emergency. I called, and my wife told me, 'For goodness sake, come home right away. There's a dead man in the basement. He's lying there with his hands folded, and I'm scared to death.' I told her she was wrong, but I said I'd come anyhow. I knew it was Pee Wee, of course; but knowing Pee Wee, he could have kicked off. He looked half dead most of the time anyway.

"I rushed home and ran downstairs, and there he lay. I shook him a little, and Pee Wee mumbled, 'Mmmmm, bourbon and seltzer.' From then on, all the boys called the sofa 'Pee Wee's coffin.'"

Sunnie and Ralph share a great fondness for dogs—especially Saint Bernards. The Suttons owned three of the huge dogs—plus two cats—at the time the first edition of this book was written, and they once had four Saints. When Sunnie moved to Aspen in 1962, she brought along her two Kerry blue terriers, a mother and a puppy: "The mother got killed by a car, and the pup would never stay home. I finally gave her to a family in Silt, and she's never left their front yard—which must mean something, I guess.

"A fellow who ran a sportswear shop in Aspen owned a beautiful male Saint Bernard named Tascha, and he asked me to take care of the dog for three weeks while he made a trip to Chicago. Well, Tascha and I fell in love. He wouldn't leave my side, and so the man gave him to me. There was a Saint Bernard kennel outside Aspen, and I bought a little puppy to go with Tascha. I named her Amy. Tascha died, but Ralph and I bred Amy. She had three pups—Ella, Mahalia, and Bessie. Ralph built a playpen for them. We gave Bessie to Lou McGarity and gave Ella to the Gibsons. But about six months later, Dick said, 'That's too much dog for Denver,' and so we took her back.

"One day, Ralph saw a big Saint Bernard sitting in a pickup truck in front of the club. The kid who owned the dog knew we had three Saint Bernards. He was about to go to college and was looking for a good home for his dog. Ralph thought the dog was nifty. He told me, 'Well, as long as we've got three girls, we might as well have a fella in the family.' So that's how Boozer joined us.

"We entered Mahalia and Boozer in a few dog shows. Boozer won a second-place ribbon once, and I think we could have gone on with him in other shows if we'd had the time and didn't have to run the club. Mahalia got up to 13 points in a show—it takes 15 to be a champion—but she developed arthritis in a foot, and so we had to forget about exhibiting her."

At the Rendezvous, Ralph did much more than play the piano. "Nothing was beneath him," Sunnie said. "He cleaned the johns and behind the bar, and he vacuumed the floor and hauled out the trash. I'd ask myself, 'How can you let the world's greatest jazz pianist take care of the garbage?' But he did it all every day and finished up by making the popcorn. Then he'd sit down and play.

"We concentrated all our efforts at the club and kept it cleaner than we ever kept our house. We spent almost all our time there and were hardly ever home."

Chapter **17**

It's Like a Locomotive Coming at You

unnie tried to keep the customers quiet while Ralph was playing at the Rendezvous. But she disagreed with people who thought she ran the club like a concert hall: "I'd tell some customers to shut up; but it was all in fun, and they laughed and got a kick out of it. If you let people come in and walk on you, they'll just take over. Sometimes you've got to set them straight and tell them to go somewhere else if they don't want to listen to the music.

"We used to get many people into the club just because the music was so great, and they appreciated our efforts. It's tough on Ralph to work if people sit right under his nose and talk about skiing or what they had for dinner or what they're going to do tomorrow. It's awful hard to concentrate. If he were just a barroom piano player who didn't have to think about what he's doing, that would be something else. But I have respect for what he does, and I think other people should, too. True, when Ralph's had a few too many drinks, he tells people to shut up and get lost. But I think he's really calmed down tremendously during the last few years.

"I never sat people right up in front of the bandstand if I didn't know 'em or if I didn't think they were there to appreciate what we were trying to do. If they wanted to talk, they could sit in the back of the room somewhere. But the ones that I sat right under Ralph's nose were people who were there to enjoy the music. That way, you make everybody happy. But if you've got some bad apple sitting up there yelling out requests and singing and whistling and that kind of thing, it's such a distraction that it makes things uncomfortable for everyone."

Ralph saw no reason to change his attitude toward people he considered pests just because he and his wife owned the Rendezvous. "I wouldn't take a lot of crap from anybody—even in my own place of business," he said. "I can take just so much, and then I gotta let 'em have it.

"On New Year's Eve in 1967, Louise Duncan and I were playing two-piano duets. All the idiots were out that night, of course, and we had the noisemakers and the funny hats on the tables.

"About 10 minutes before midnight, I told Louise that it would be a great idea to play straight through and forget about 'Auld Lang Syne.' That song is cornball stuff to me. We went into a romping number and finished it at about 10 minutes after 12. I knew the people were getting anxious to do their bit as midnight came along, but we just kept going. Then we left the stand after the tune.

"There was a party of 8 or 10 people in front next to the stand, and one guy in the group let me know that we hadn't played 'Auld Lang Syne.' I told him, 'Gee, I'm sorry. I didn't even know what time it was. I'm very sorry.' I had put my watch in my pocket. I went to the bar, and the guy and his wife walked over to Sunnie, who was at the door as hostess. He asked her, 'Don't you have any control over your musicians?' She told him, 'Speak to my husband. He's over at the bar.'

"So they came over and started giving me the business again about 'Auld Lang Syne.' I was very nice to them. I apologized again and said I hadn't known it was midnight. Then they started coming on stronger, and I stood there trying to keep my temper down and not say anything more. But finally I just got fed up with it. The guy said, 'Well, if that's the way it is, we'll never come back here.' I told him, 'Why don't you pay your fuckin' bill and get out and don't *ever* come back. And that goes for your friends, too.' "

The next New Year's Eve, Jack Lesberg and Jake Hanna played with Ralph. Sunnie cornered Lesberg and asked him to con Ralph into playing "Auld Lang Syne." Lesberg agreed to try: "I told Ralph we really should play it for the crowd, but he said, 'Fuck 'em. I hate to play for all those rituals.' I reminded him that it was the big night for the people—that they had paid their money to come in, and maybe we should do it anyway. He finally said, 'OK, we'll see about it.'

"A few seconds before midnight, I said, 'This'd be a good time to do it, Ralph.' Well, wouldn't you know. He broke into 'The Star-Spangled Banner,' and Jake jumped up behind the drums and started saluting and shouting at the top of his voice, 'Fuck Communism! Fuck Communism!'

The whole place broke up. Those people just roared with laughter, and I think they enjoyed it more than 'Auld Lang Syne.' They must have because they drank their champagne and wished each other Happy New Year anyway."

Hanna's trip to Aspen began on a sour note. He and Lesberg flew together from New York, and Hanna looked out as the plane started to roll away from the gate.

"What's that funny round thing on the ground?" he asked Lesberg.

"I don't know," Lesberg said. "It looks like a wheel. I hope the plane's OK."

It was. They landed in Aspen and waited for their suitcases and instruments to join them. No bass drum.

"I think I know what that funny round thing was," Lesberg said.

Sure enough, Hanna's bass drum had been left behind at JFK Airport. He borrowed one from Bert Dahlander, an Aspen drummer, for the Rendezvous gig and eventually retrieved his own. Hanna enjoyed reminiscing about the Suttons' Saint Bernards and playing with Ralph:

"Ralph and Sunnie had those enormous dogs the size of [the famous racehorse] Seabiscuit. And not too friendly either. If one of them put its head on your foot when you were sitting around the fireplace, you were stuck there until that dog wanted to move. Its head must have weighed 400 pounds.

"Ralph's a lousy guy and he plays rotten. That's what Al Cohn used to say about Bobby Hackett. Ralph is a purist. He doesn't fart around. He never shows off. Never plays any superfluous notes. Nothing to display technical facility, though he has a fantastic technique. Ralph's probably the strongest swinging piano player there is. He's the only guy I know who can sit at the piano and swing an entire band.

"We were playing over in Switzerland at a big shopping center. They had so many people that we had to move outdoors to a larger place. Danny Moss and I were standing behind the stage. Gus Johnson was playing and either Milt Hinton or Jack. The band went into an extra tune after everybody got through. Ralph started swinging and that band started roaring. Danny looked at me and said, 'That guy swings a whole band by himself.'

"Ralph wasn't stepping on anybody or knocking anyone over. He just gets infectious. It starts swinging so hard when he's playing that he makes it easy for everyone else. There's absolutely nothing to playing drums with him. Not just his solos, but behind guys, too. He gets that left hand romping and he's sensational. One of the best that ever lived.

"He's a great human being, a warmhearted guy. He'd do anything for anybody. When you work for him, you get good money, too. Ralph *always* makes sure you're taken care of when he books the job. He may not even be the leader, but he'll get the guys and you're taken care of very nicely.

"Ralph is a very tame guy, very mild mannered. But I'd hate to be someone requesting the wrong tune. He can put a dumb customer away real good. I saw him escort a guy out of the club in Aspen. Ralph looked over his shoulder, got up, took the guy by the arm—he's very strong—lifted him out of his chair, and deposited him outside. The guy kept asking, 'What's the matter? What's the matter?' Ralph didn't say a word. He just came back and started the next tune.

Cliff Leeman replaced Hanna in the trio at the Rendezvous a few nights after New Year's Eve. He had been seriously ill for several months when the Suttons invited him to play at the club: "When they called, I had been walking for only three weeks and hadn't been playing at all. But Sunnie said, 'Get your ass up here, and we'll make you well.' I did and they did. I was never treated so beautifully in all my career. Ralph and Sunnie took me into their home and fed me, and they filled me with carrot juice four times a day. The carrot juice was Sunnie's fetish. I also had the extreme pleasure of hearing Ralph play every night while working a pleasant job at the club. To top it all, they paid me too much.

"I've worked with some great pianists—Teddy Wilson, Dave McKenna, Gene Schroeder, Lou Stein, Joe Sullivan, Ralph Burns, and Billy Kyle, to name a few. But I have the greatest rapport with Ralph. He's got such sensitivity and precise execution—and good time and taste above all.

"He couldn't stand even an occasional square in front of the bandstand. One night, a customer asked him to play 'Whispering.' Ralph told him, 'Why don't you go fuck off. Take your money and go somewhere else.' Sunnie came over to see what was wrong and said to the guy, 'For Christ's sake, leave Ralph alone.' She was like a mother sticking up for a little boy who was being picked on.

"The Suttons had a huge urn in the courtyard outside. They kept it filled with logs, and Ralph lit it every night before we started playing. The flames were an eye-catcher and sort of a trademark for the club. One night after we finished a set, Ralph took off for the courtyard with a funny look on his face. I figured there was some emergency. He came back breathing a little hard and muttering, 'If I ever catch those motherfuckers. . . .' He explained that some local hippie kids liked to toss snowballs into the urn to try to put the fire out. But the Aspen Fire Department couldn't have put out the fire that Ralph built in that urn every night.

"Al Hall came to the Rendezvous a few weeks after I did, and Bob Wilber joined us later. I can still see Ralph putting on his galoshes and ski jacket in the afternoon and walking the five miles to the club through the snow to help Sunnie clean up the place and order supplies and get ready for the next night. Then he'd walk home again. We'd sit around the fireplace eating and listening to a Waller or Teagarden tape and watching the sun go down over those beautiful Rockies. Nobody would say a word. And all the time, that broad grin would be on Ralph's kisser in appreciation of the food, the music, and the company."

Al Hall also remembered the domestic scene in Aspen: "We all lived together making like housewives—cooking, cleaning, feeding the dogs, and doing other work around the house. Ralph always had a hell of a lot to do. He had to shop for food for the club, for us, and for the dogs; and he did most of the cooking, too. He'd drive us to the club, play the job, and then drive us back home again. But all that didn't stop him from being his cool self.

"Ralph Sutton is one great guy. We all know he's a great musician, but not all great musicians are good guys. What can one say after 'great'? And you can't leave Sunnie out. She is a very clever businesswoman, and they make a wonderful pair."

Sutton, Hall, and Leeman played as a trio until Bob Wilber arrived and made it a quartet. While they were waiting for Wilber to make his escape from snowbound New York, Sunnie got a phone call from Jim Cullum, Jr., in Denver. The Happy Jazz Band, led by Cullum and his father, had come up from San Antonio, Texas, to play for the Denver Jazz Club; and Jim, Jr., wanted to do some skiing. The band had performed in both Aspen and Denver the preceding two winters, and Cullum had learned to ski. He also had done some jamming at the Rendezvous while in Aspen.

"I called Sunnie to ask if there was a rhythm section in Aspen I could work with so I could go up there and ski and play and have some fun," Cullum recalled. "I thought Ralph was playing solo piano at their club, but she told me that Al and Cliff were there with him. She said, 'Why don't you come up and play with *our* rhythm section?' So I went to Aspen and stayed at the Suttons' home for several days. They are fine, charming people—warm and genuine and very hospitable.

"Sunnie impressed me because she worked awfully hard running the club. She and Ralph would go down there during the day while I went skiing. If we didn't eat at home, we'd all go to the club before the action started and have a big dinner. Sunnie put on a really good spread. Sometimes she'd get very busy if a lot of people came in at the same time and wanted to eat.

"One time, about 12 people came in and ordered roast beef. Some of them wanted it rare. Sunnie began carving the prime rib in the kitchen, and it wasn't rare at all. It was well done. But she wasn't too concerned because she had seen that the people were pretty tight. She just took a red cinnamon apple ring and rubbed it on the roast beef to make it look rare, which I thought was pretty resourceful.

"Ralph would get bugged by people who were noisy and boisterous and not completely attentive. He had a rubber hand with a suction cup on the bottom that he kept inside the piano. If somebody bugged him or requested certain tunes, he'd take out the hand. It was shooting the finger, and he'd stick it on the side of the piano and go right on playing.

"He also had a toy gun inside the piano. If someone kept bugging him to play some tune that he didn't want to play, he'd pull the gun out and point it at him with a fiendish snarl. Frankly, it kind of scared me. I didn't think it was a very good idea. But that was Ralph's style. He is truly a great pianist—and certainly the king of stride piano.

"Dick Gibson came in the last night I was there. He had formed the World's Greatest Jazzband in November 1968, and they had made their first record in December. Dick brought the record with him, and we listened to it after the job. I was very impressed with the whole project."

Milt Hinton echoed the impressions of his fellow bass man, Al Hall, about life with the Suttons in Aspen: "They're both wonderful human beings, so warm and friendly. They made all of us so welcome. We ate together and played together, both on and off the job. We couldn't wait to close the club each night, so that Ralph, Sunnie, and all the rest of us could go back to their home and sit down and reminisce about the times we've had together and the people we've known through the years. We often spent most of the night doing this.

"It was such a pleasure to live with them and to work in their club. Their dominion was ours. We were just family. And you can hear the warmth and the feeling of the guys on the records that were made at the Rendezvous. I think Ruby Braff was playing at his very best at that time, and Ralph is always 100 percent. I know I just felt happy. I was supposed to play two weeks at the Rendezvous, but Jack Lesberg broke his leg and I had to go up a week earlier. I was very glad about that—not about Jack's leg, of course, but to spend an extra week playing with Ralph. On the job, he steam-rolls things and sets fire to the whole program the moment it starts.

"Ralph is a very special human being, and he's a very special musician because of his tremendous talents. His type of piano playing is an almost lost art, and Ralph has no peer at it. He's without a doubt the greatest, and he's just about alone with it now because he's one of the few left from one of our finest and most creative piano eras.

"I'm glad to have passed through this life—just to have met Ralph Sutton. He is a beautiful, plain, salt-of-the-earth man. I've got beautiful memories of Aspen because of his kindness and humanitarianism. The way he lives—the way he respects other human beings and his whole attitude about music—is pure and wholesome. Words really can't express the joy I feel when I'm with him."

Mousie Alexander, who played with Hinton at the Rendezvous, called Ralph "one of the most beautiful people I've ever met. He's such a gracious, warm person that it comes through the moment you shake hands with him.

"As soon as Ralph sits down at the piano, it's like a locomotive coming at you," Alexander said. "Ralph's beauty comes out in his playing immediately. It's so positive. You can feel the warmth of the man as a great human being. There should be many more people like Ralph in jazz to open it up to the world and let people know there is such a thing.

"It was a great kick to live with the Suttons out in Aspen. Their home was right alongside a gorgeous trout stream, and I'd go absolutely crazy every morning just looking out and seeing the Rockies all around and that stream running through their property. Everything was so relaxed and so far removed from what we're involved with every day. And then at night, to go to the club and play with Ralph was like a bonus."

Barbara and Hal Curtis spent part of three summers with Ralph and Sunnie in Aspen. Hal recalled one special evening at the Rendezvous in August 1968: "Ralph played his usual fine piano all evening until around midnight. Then he asked Barb to take over. She played four or five tunes, and somewhere along the way they decided they'd both play. Ralph sat down with her at the same piano, and the audience absolutely flipped. The music really went wild after they got it rolling and decided whose hands were going where. It's fun to listen to on tape, and Barb and Ralph had a wonderful time doing it."

For as long as she can remember, Barb has wanted to be as good as—or better than—Ralph at the piano. She graduated with distinction in music education from Lindenwood College, where she had received a partial scholarship, but felt great frustration for years: "I really wanted to beat the socks off Ralph, though logically I should have known better. He had bigger hands than I and was stronger, and he had all those years on me of playing every night. I really wanted to cut him. It was impossible, but I lived with that feeling for a long time.

"When we were little, he'd tease me and I'd want to tease him back; but he'd sort of hold his hand out and keep me at a distance, and I never could get at him. That's kind of the feeling I always had about him with the piano. The feeling reached its peak when we lived near each other in California. It wasn't until a couple of years after he had left that I began to realize, 'Gee, I've got something of my own.' I started to feel more pride in myself, and I saw that it was ridiculous to try to compete with him.

"You almost want to cut your wrists because you can't play like he can. It's like wishing on a star. He's way up there someplace, and you'll never make it."

Barb recalled that Sunnie kept a close watch on Ralph's drinking and policed him at the club. "I wished he'd had the guts not to drink so much," she said, "but Sunnie paced him on the drinks. When she sent a drink up to him from the bar, the Scotch was really watered down. Ralph realized it, of course, and would joke to the crowd, 'God, you can hardly see it in there.' Once he sent me to the bar to get a drink from Sunnie, and she wouldn't give it to me. I had to go back and tell him that she refused to let him have the drink, and he seemed to blame me. It was as if he didn't know me—that I was his sister—and that I was withholding something from him. I was a little scared because I fear his anger."

Other guests at the Suttons' home in Aspen included Harry and Charlotte Rubin, who owned a Denver jewelry store. They had known Sunnie before she met Ralph. Charlotte Rubin remembered a phone call from Sunnie one Sunday: "She told us, 'I want you to meet the man I'm going to marry.' Ralph was somewhat shy—almost withdrawn—and not too easy to reach. But because we had been friends of Sunnie's for several years, he seemed willing to accept our friendship, too.

"We and our two teenaged daughters spent a few days with Sunnie and Ralph in Aspen. Their house stood on top of a hill and had a fantastic panoramic view of the mountains and a valley. It was a wonderful place, and Ralph made us feel so glad to be in his home. He was very warm, and he was always asking what he could do for us.

"Ralph is a great husband. He was not above vacuuming the house or performing any other task to help make things easier for Sunnie. He also kept busy as janitor at their club, scrubbing everything in sight.

"Although he is a very sweet man, he could turn into a tiger at the drop of a hat. If someone in the audience provoked him by pestering him to play a specific number, Ralph sometimes became sarcastic and maybe a bit nasty. You don't see this in him at first because he always appears shy and quiet."

At the time that Ralph and Sunnie were running the Rendezvous, Peanuts Hucko was co-owner of—and leader of the jazz combo at—the Navarre, a restaurant in downtown Denver. The Navarre had been built in 1879 as the Brinker Institute, a private school for girls. The school closed less than 10 years later, after the death of its owner, and two gamblers bought the building and turned it into a hotel. They soon lost it to two other gamblers who converted it into an elegant combination of restaurant, gambling casino, and brothel.

The Brown Palace, a now-famous hotel, was going up across the street, and the owners of the Navarre had an idea that met with the enthusiastic approval of the hotel owner. They built a tunnel with trolley tracks under Tremont Place between the two buildings. Upon the completion of the tunnel, male guests of the hotel could ride to and from the assorted pleasures of the Navarre aboard trolley cars.

By the 1920s, the Navarre had become solely a restaurant. Ralph played several gigs there during the late 1960s with Hucko, Bill Bastien, and Morey Feld. Bastien, who taught music in a Denver high school, had not met Ralph until they worked together at the Navarre. He knew of Sutton only through the comments of various people: "Those comments ranged from the highest compliments to, 'He's OK if you like stride piano.' But the first time I played with Ralph was a musical delight, and it was obvious that his musical insight and ability were of such a high quality that he was above being called 'just a stylist.' It is this rare musical ability that stands out when I think of Ralph.

"Whatever type of tune we played, he made something musical of it that was a rewarding experience to hear. A ballad could express beauty through lyrical phrasing and flowing use of harmony. On the up tunes, Ralph's drive was generated through strong rhythmic phrases and melodic lines—all within the framework of a marvelous sense of time. His playing created an excitement that drove and inspired the other musicians as well as the audience.

"When I first met Ralph, he impressed me as being not overly talkative but, nonetheless, a cordial, straightforward, no-baloney person. As time went on, my impression proved to be right. My wife took one look at the size of the man and said, 'My God, he looks like he's going to pick up the piano with his fingers.'

"When the spirit moved him, Ralph had a habit of scrunching up his face and singing—or grunting—along with the music as he played. It was humorous to watch when things got swinging. He really wailed. He's a pacifistic person and happy to please customers. But when an obnoxious person pushed him too hard for a request and wouldn't get off his back, Ralph stood up, looked the customer in the eye, and stated his position on the matter—and there was no doubt that the episode had ended."

Hucko, who regarded Sutton as a brother, thoroughly enjoyed having Ralph at the Navarre: "He plays magnificently. He's got such beautiful time, and he knows how to complement me. He always plays the right thing behind me, and he's just sensational as a soloist.

"Ralph's not a very social guy, of course. He's very quiet and reserved, and if he ever loses his cool, it comes down on you like a hammer on an anvil—and then it's over. He doesn't carry on, and in no way is he a prima donna. He's just a beautiful, easygoing guy with very simple tastes in life. He likes to live out in the country. He likes his dogs and, above all, he loves his wife. And he loves music—and shows it when he plays."

It's Like a Locomotive Coming at You

Ralph and Sunnie sold the Rendezvous in October 1969 for several reasons. Business at the club had fallen off greatly because more and more patrons wanted to hear rock rather than jazz. And Ralph rarely played there anymore because by then he was on the road almost full-time with the World's Greatest Jazzband. In addition, the Suttons were having problems with their landlord.

"We got into a big hassle with the landlord about painting and things like that," Sunnie said. "He made our life miserable. We just decided that life was too short to go on under those conditions, especially when we were working so hard. People think that clubs like ours, being in a resort area, make money eight months of the year. But it's really a tough situation. So we started looking for a buyer and found one."

On the last two nights at Sunnie's Rendezvous, the customers included Mitchell and Barbara Brown of Victoria, British Columbia. They had first heard Ralph play at Earthquake McGoon's in San Francisco eight years before. "Barb was probably responsible for our meeting Ralph," Brown said. "She kept sending requests to the bandstand for 'Alligator Crawl' or 'Clothesline Ballet.' This must have either irritated Ralph or piqued his curiosity. At any rate, he came over and had drinks with us. Since that night, we've seen him whenever we could. A couple of years later, it was quite a thrill to walk to Barney Gould's Gold Rush Steak House and hear 'Echo of Spring' wafting out into the evening fog over San Francisco Bay."

Barbara Brown will always remember the final night at the Rendezvous: "The music and the cozy atmosphere of 'just friends,' with a Saint Bernard or two thrown in for good measure, provided the kind of background that is made to order for Ralph. Sunnie sang a song to wind things up, and then she announced that the entire evening was on the house."

Peggy Clifford, in addition to running her bookstore, wrote a column called "Talk of the Times" for the *Aspen Times*. She had written several times about what she called the "musical miracle" at the Rendezvous. Shortly before the Suttons sold their club, Clifford eloquently portrayed Ralph's work in her column:

> Piano man Ralph Sutton may be Aspen's only authentic philosopher and one of the few philosophers in the world (Duke Ellington is

another) to send his message up on 88 keys. . . . He's been hanging around those 88 keys for a long time and, almost always, in very good company. He, as they say, knows where it's at.

Where it's at is a two-handed statement that is sometimes joyful, sometimes melancholy, sometimes tender, sometimes boisterous, but always original. Oh, his technique derives from Fats Waller and Art Tatum, but his style is all his own and immediately identifiable. And it is full of surprises. I have heard Ralph play "Ain't Misbehavin'" an uncountable number of times, and he's never done it the same way twice. If you don't think that's a feat, try reciting a Shakespeare sonnet 100 times and doing it differently every time. And this man is not without humor. Indeed, he is quite capable of slipping a bar or two of "Nola" into the middle of "Sunny Side of the Street" without losing either his cool or his place.

Improvisation is very important in jazz, and whether he's driving underneath the horns of the World's Greatest Jazzband or out in front taking a solo run, Ralph is consistently inventive. Like a bird, soaring and plunging, Ralph is on very good terms with his environment. The fact that many of the tunes he plays are old standards is irrelevant. The fact that he can make them sound new and fresh and vital every time he has at them is what counts. . . .

America is a country of fads and faddists, and, musically, almost everyone is provincial. On one side, we have the people who will listen to nothing but Beethoven and Schubert, and, on the other, we have the people who believe that anything that's older than yesterday is square and fatally dated. Ralph Sutton goes on pursuing the sounds of life. He is, in his pursuit, by turns elegant and stylish, rosy and bawdy, joyful and carefree, thoughtful and blue, and, always, the greatest two-handed jazz pianist playing today. . . .

Clifford was angry and disillusioned when the Suttons sold the Rendezvous. A couple of months later she wrote:

About 12 years ago, I heard a record that boggled my mind, electrified my heart, and enchanted my soul. The record was *Salute to Fats*, and the man on piano was Ralph Sutton. . . .

There is no one else around today with his style, his sass, his superb taste, and his skill at turning the piano into a one-man band. His great left hand is a five-finger rhythm section. His right hand is supple, sensitive, and capable of doing incredible and lovely things with an old standard tune.

Basically, what he does is called stride piano, and it is a jazz form that goes back many years. But there is nothing dated about Ralph's music. It is as fresh as tomorrow, as relevant as tonight's news, and as valuable and important as anything that's happening musically today.

Indeed, Ralph Sutton has been called "the best." And it's true. He is the best.

...You couldn't hear better jazz anywhere in the world than you could at Sunnie's during those halcyon days. Edmond Hall. Cutty Cutshall. Wild Bill Davison. Clancy Hayes. Peanuts Hucko. Jack Lesberg. Morey Feld. Lou McGarity. Ruby Braff. The top men in traditional jazz were coming to Aspen to play with Ralph at Sunnie's.

It was the real thing. Light-years removed from the sleazy Las Vegas comedians and obscure pop singers and background tinkly-winkly piano music that comprised most of the entertainment at most of the nightclubs. And it was great. Having Ralph in year-round residence was an amazing stroke of good fortune. Our own resident jazz genius.

But something was wrong. Ralph and Morey and Jack and Ruby would find themselves playing to a half-empty room. In the middle of a set, someone would demand "The Yellow Rose of Texas." A table of over-sauced skiers would commence yodeling or singing.... Where were all the serious aficionados of jazz? Where was that much-vaunted Aspen sophistication?

Ralph had many fans here, to be sure, but they were outnumbered by the shouters and screamers. Like any artist, he needs an intelligent, interested, hip audience. And he didn't find it here.... All he really wanted was to play good jazz every night and spend his days fishing and walking with his dogs.

Ralph Sutton's departure saddens me. I miss him, and I miss his music. But it also angers me. How did this sophisticated, cosmopolitan, hip town let a jazzman of Sutton's stature and talent slip through its fingers? By not paying attention, that's how. Maybe, just maybe, it's time that we stopped counting our money and started counting our resources—human as well as natural.

Chapter **18**

A Gentleness of Spirit

mong the guests at Dick Gibson's 1964 jazz party was Jack Gurtler, whose family for three generations had owned Elitch Gardens, a famous amusement park in Denver. Elitch's offered visitors much more than the usual roller coasters, Ferris wheel, and other rides. Many of its 36 acres, for example, displayed the beauty of the more than 2 million flowers planted in the park every spring. Elitch's also was the home of the oldest summer theater in the United States. And a few steps from the theater was the Trocadero ballroom, which played host to most of the biggest names of the Big Band Era.

Gurtler liked what he heard at Gibson's party and began thinking about bringing a jazz band composed of some of those top musicians to the Troc. But he realized that jazz might antagonize many of the dancers who for years had enjoyed the cool summer evenings there. The guests at the party also included the entertainment chairman of the Debutante Ball, held annually at the Brown Palace during the Christmas season to raise funds for the Denver Symphony Orchestra. She thought a jazz band would be great for the ball and asked Gibson to assemble a group for her.

The music at the Debutante Ball that December was furnished by Yank Lawson, Cutty Cutshall, Lou McGarity, Peanuts Hucko, Ralph Sutton, Clancy Hayes, Bob Haggart, and Cliff Leeman. During the evening, Gurtler made up his mind to take a chance. He went up to Gibson and told him, "I want those musicians for the Troc, and I want just those men who are up here."

Gurtler decided to call the band the Eight Greats of Jazz. But the Eight Greats who played at the Troc in June 1965 weren't the exact eight he had envisioned. Haggart recalled: "When Morey Feld showed up, Jack said, 'That's not Morey Feld.' He had mistaken Cliff Leeman for Morey at the

Debutante Ball. He thought he was going to get Cliff, and in walked Morey."

The band's opening night at the Troc was a disaster, thanks to a flood that ravaged Denver, causing more then $250 million in damage. After the first set, Gibson counted the house: "Huddled forlornly out on the 1-acre ballroom floor were 37 people, 14 of whom were in our party and 12 in Gurtler's. We have always regretted that we did not speak to the other 11 wet and jazz-devoted souls, if only to find out where they came from. Cutty always maintained that they must have lived directly across the street from the park."

All went well for the remainder of the band's engagement. The size of the crowds that turned out to hear the Eight Greats of Jazz induced Gurtler to bring them back to the Troc during the summer of 1966. But they were now the Nine Greats because Bud Freeman had joined the group. Freeman impishly recommended almost immediately that the name be changed to the Eight Greats of Jazz and One Really Great. Billy Butterfield came aboard for the band's 1967 appearance at the Troc, and the Nine Greats became the Ten Greats of Jazz.

The Ten Greats of Jazz played the Troc again in 1968. That fall, the Longchamps restaurant organization in New York invited them to perform in the Riverboat Room of the Empire State Building. Gibson offered to bankroll the band as an ongoing organization headed by Lawson and Haggart, and the group made its first appearance outside Denver when it opened at the Riverboat in November 1968. Carl Fontana replaced Cutty Cutshall, who had died in August, shortly after playing at the Troc; and Bob Wilber succeeded Peanuts Hucko, who remained with his combo at the Navarre in Denver. Wilber, playing soprano sax as well as clarinet, added a new dimension to the sound of the band.

Gibson not only provided financial backing but also gave the band a new name—the World's Greatest Jazzband. None of the musicians was enchanted by this name, which Gibson chose simply because he felt it described the group perfectly. The men learned to live with it, though they would have preferred something a bit more modest.

For four years, beginning in 1966, Gibson and Gurtler issued *Jazz in the Troc* albums, recorded live by the group that evolved into the World's Greatest Jazzband. The profits from these superb records went to the musicians. John S. Wilson, the jazz critic of *The New York Times*, reviewed the 1966 record in the magazine *High Fidelity*. He declared that the band "... projects a vitality and joyous urgency that almost never comes through on contemporary commercial recordings of this type of music.... Building on a magnificent rhythm section firmly anchored to Bob Haggart's buoyant bass and driven by Sutton's strong piano, the front line, both individually in solo and together as ensemble, plays brilliantly."

The 1969 album consisted of two LPs. Gibson commented in his liner notes: "How satisfying it is to make a point by stating a simple fact. For example, one does not need hyperbole to tell how high Colorado is. One fact says it all. There are 60 mountain peaks in North America more than 14,000 feet tall. Fifty-four of them are in Colorado. All right. There are 48 tunes in the *Jazz in the Troc* series. Only one of them is repeated—'Viper's Drag,' by Ralph Sutton."

Yank Lawson and Bob Haggart had frequently worked together for almost 35 years when Dick Gibson formed the World's Greatest Jazzband. Their association started in 1935 as founder-members of a cooperative band fronted by Bob Crosby. The Crosby band, one of the top outfits of the period before World War II, broke up late in 1942 after many of the men had been drafted. Lawson and Haggart spent most of the next 26 years as staff musicians at NBC in New York. They also played numerous gigs, which offered some relief from the nonjazz atmosphere of studio work. During the 1950s, they fronted the Lawson-Haggart Jazz Band, a recording group that at various sessions included Billy Butterfield, Cutty Cutshall, Lou McGarity, Peanuts Hucko, Bill Stegmeyer, Bud Freeman, Lou Stein, George Barnes, and Cliff Leeman. Haggart, in addition to being one of the foremost bass men in jazz history, has been known as a great arranger and composer since his early days with the Crosby band.

Ken Gallacher, in an article on the World's Greatest Jazzband in *Jazz & Blues* in December 1971, quoted both men as being delighted with their escape from the studios:

> ... Said Haggart: "It has been such a tremendous relief to get out of the studios. You used to walk into work every day and you simply had no idea what you might be walking into. It was hard work, and there was a lot of tension around the job. We did so many shows. I

had 'The Tonight Show' and 'The Perry Como Show' and then record dates, too. Getting a break from that routine was important for us. The [Lawson-Haggart] Decca albums were kind of a therapy."

Lawson explained these years like this: "Basically, we stayed in the studios because we wanted security and the chance for a family life. We had to consider the schooling of our children and that kind of thing, and the studio work gave us that type of stability. It was hard—just like going into an office every day, I guess—and you could get into a rut. Jazz dates helped keep us fresh. You know, I used to do eight or nine shows a week, with guys like Sid Caesar, and up to three recording dates a day for people like Sinatra or Crosby or Como. It was a period in which we made lots of money and played just about everything *except* jazz.

"Then, at one stage, I was doing all the studio work and working down at Condon's, too. First of all with Peanuts and then with Bob Wilber and Cutty Cutshall. I did that for five years. It was tiring, but I enjoyed the chance to blow at Condon's.

"It isn't that guys lose their enthusiasm, it's just that there are so few opportunities for jazz dates for them around New York. Where do they play there? There aren't too many clubs left, and there aren't too many jazz record dates either. We were lucky that there were outlets for us."

During the early days of the World's Greatest Jazzband, Gibson and Sutton often roomed together on the road. "Ralph is a great piano player and a great guy," Gibson said. "As human beings go, he's tops. He's loyal and truthful, and he has extraordinary integrity. There's absolutely no persiflage in Ralph. He has reduced things to, 'This is what I am, and I don't want to have anything to do with all the rest of it. Let me play the piano and let me walk in the woods, and don't get me involved in all that other crap.'

"He is very dependable—extremely conscientious in both big and little things. If Ralph says, 'I'll call you at 10,' you know he'll call you at 10. There's never anything like, 'I forgot' or 'The phone didn't work.' He's orderly and very neat in his personal habits. He always wears fresh clothes, and he hangs up his suits and puts his shoes away.

"But Ralph is probably the most internal individual I have ever known. He is so inert—almost sluggish in certain ways. He is an extreme example of a passive person. He has been in our home for hours and hardly opened his mouth. Not one question. No apparent interest in anything. If other people speak to him, he'll give them a pleasant, very short answer. But they will be people who don't turn him off.

"Ralph is an excellent friend. And whereas he's not an aggressive enemy, if he doesn't like you, he's rather an implacable disliker of you. I would guess he doesn't have an awful lot of close friends. But to those people who somehow have gotten inside him, or whom he has opted to like or who have qualities that he admires, he's the staunchest possible friend."

Gurtler likewise regarded Sutton as somewhat of an enigma: "I don't think anybody really knows what goes on in that fantastic head on his shoulders except himself and probably Sunnie. He's quiet and reserved, but he's very personable. He seems to have tremendous feeling for people who enjoy music. I believe Ralph is more than just a jazz piano player. He is probably a very emotional, very artistic, very inwardly feeling, thoughtful musician. I'd guess that he takes a lot of his anger and worries out on the piano and also puts lots of his love and happiness into the piano.

"It is beyond my ability to express the feeling I get when I watch Ralph play. It's something so great and so sensational. He plays not only with those big fingers, but also with the expression on his face and with his eyes, his nose—everything. He looks like an Ivy League professor at the piano because he plays with such sincerity and such poise. So many piano players bend over the keyboard, bounce around on their rumps, sway their shoulders, and swing their heads. But Ralph doesn't have to do any of that. He just sits up there—stern and erect—and creates something that is unbelievable and unequaled."

Shortly after the World's Greatest Jazzband opened at the Riverboat in New York, Peggy Clifford reported on an interesting sidelight of the gig. In her column in the *Aspen Times*, she wrote:

> A phenomenon that was born in the Hotel Jerome on a September afternoon in 1963 exploded last week on the national consciousness during an otherwise ponderous and sober Huntley-Brinkley report.
>
> The phenomenon, ironically, had nothing to do with those events which usually bring the national news spotlight in close on Aspen. It had nothing to do with ski races or think tanks or famous

visitors or classical music. It had to do with jazz—hot jazz—which, as everyone knows, has been declared officially dead more than once.

But anyone who was in the Jerome on that spirited afternoon five years ago will testify that hot jazz is not only alive, but thriving. And now, thanks to Huntley-Brinkley, the world knows of its robust health, too.

Not content to send a roving reporter to cover the story, Chet Huntley took himself to the Riverboat in New York last Thursday to listen to the World's Greatest Jazzband and talk to Dick Gibson, who oversaw the revival of hot jazz at the Jerome and subsequently gave it a major transfusion of support....

In this era of rock, pop, folk, and cool jazz, this talk about hot jazz may seem as pertinent to you as a discussion of the merits of the steam engine. But there is a joy, a mastery, a fusion of men and music in the World's Greatest Jazzband that defies time and trends....

In March 1969, in a review of the band's first record, Clifford recalled:

...When the World's Greatest Jazzband opened in New York several months ago, such stalwarts of understatement as *The New York Times* and *The New Yorker* questioned the flagrant hyperbole of the band's name. But, after hearing them, both publications agreed that the name was in fact suitable and fitting....

The thing that makes this jazzband and its record special and unique is, of course, its special and unique musicians. There's about 300 years of musicianship on this record, and you can hear it....

The members of the band are all essentially soloists. They have been soloists for years—heading their own groups. They are used to the spotlight. But, because they obviously like playing with each other, because they respect each other, they are able here to participate in a rare and positive kind of group-thing. Unlike some groups, they listen to each other and are thus able to whirl in and out of the forefront with complete musical rapport, achieving that spontaneity that is pleasing in all the arts, but essential in jazz....

While playing at Elitch Gardens in 1967, Ralph saw an old friend, Ed Heidbreder. The two had lost all track of each other since 1941, when

Heidbreder coached the Francis Howell High School basketball team during Ralph's senior year. Heidbreder and his wife, Marie, had lived in Denver for some time, and he spotted an item in *The Denver Post* about the Ten Greats of Jazz.

"We went out to Elitch's and were sitting back quite a ways when the members of the band started coming in," Heidbreder remembered. "We spotted Ralph, of course, but we wondered whether he would recognize me after 26 years. I walked up, and before I even got to the bandstand, Ralph turned around and said, 'There's my old basketball coach—Mr. Heidbreder.' It was quite a thrill to have him recognize me so quickly. I was really elated. Ralph brought Sunnie over to meet us, and they invited us to come to Aspen; but we never did get up there.

"Ralph hadn't changed from the time we knew him as a young man of 18. He was the same unassuming, modest Ralph. I was impressed by his manliness and his build and stature. He's a person you'd take a second look at. He distinguishes himself by his mannerisms and the way he acts—the way he carries himself and the way he dresses and the appearance he makes. He looks like a real man—a real gentleman."

The audience at Elitch Gardens one Friday night in 1967 included John Buchanan of the *Post* and his wife, Doris. They planned to stay only briefly before driving to their summer cabin in Nederland for the weekend. Buchanan recalled: "We got there earlier than anybody else, and I noticed a guy go out on the stage and look at the microphones and then run his fingers up and down the piano. I thought he must be the pianist, but I didn't even know Ralph was in the band.

"Almost immediately after they began playing, I told Doris, 'Listen to that pianist drive that band.' I was familiar with guys like Yank Lawson, Bud Freeman, and Bob Haggart from my records, and there they were being driven by the piano player. We stayed for the entire concert, and Ralph Sutton was the whole evening as far as I was concerned.

"We knew he and his wife ran a place up in Aspen, and we decided to go there to celebrate our 25th anniversary in October. One of the girls at my office had been at Sunnie's Rendezvous several times and had met Ralph. I wanted to be certain he would be there and not on the road, and so I asked her if it would be all right to call him. She said he hadn't been very communicative the time or two she had talked to him. But I took a chance.

"I told Ralph that my wife and I could think of no better way to celebrate our anniversary than by going up to hear him play. He seemed awfully gracious and said he'd be there and would be looking for us.

"We got to the Rendezvous and introduced ourselves to Sunnie. She told us, 'Ralph's in back if you want to go say hello to him. He's in the men's can.' So I went back, and there was Ralph Sutton. It was like meeting God. I felt overwhelmed to meet this guy—and there he was, cleaning the men's room. It's hard to describe the feelings I had that first evening—seeing and hearing Ralph play while sitting within 6 or 8 feet of him.

"We became very friendly, but I found right away that I had made one of the greatest mistakes you can make with Ralph. The subject of Fats Waller came up, and I told Ralph, 'I think you play a lot better than Fats.' He just nodded and said, 'Thank you.' But I had made a faux pas because nothing pleases Ralph more than to have someone say that Fats is the greatest. Ralph and I have spent many evenings together, and we nearly always just sit quietly—almost without saying anything—and listen to Fats.

"Ralph and Sunnie spent several weeks with us during his gigs with Peanuts Hucko at the Navarre, and I began to know him much more as a person. Ralph is quite a cook, and he often made dinner for the four of us. He used Ben Webster's recipe for pork chops Creole, which were just great. Much of our conversation centered around jazz, but many times we reminisced about his boyhood and mine, which were similar. We both came from small towns.

"One thing paramount with Ralph is his absolute integrity. He's a totally honest person. He is quick to spot a phony and will have nothing to do with him. Many times he knows that in a roomful of so-called jazz lovers, he's actually getting through to only a few. But that's enough for him. If he communicates with just one person, he can forget the rest.

"Ralph is a very warm-hearted person who has genuine regard for any friend. In 1969, I faced cataract surgery and was dreading it. Everywhere Ralph went, he gathered information from people who had undergone this operation. He was tremendously concerned about *my* surgery. Cliff Leeman, who had been through cataract surgery, came to town that year on his way to Dick Gibson's jazz party, and Ralph brought him to our place so I could talk to him. Clancy Hayes had also had cataract surgery, and Ralph made certain that he talked to me about it, too.

"After the surgery, I got a long-distance call in the hospital from Ralph. The operation on the first eye hadn't gone well, and it appeared for a while that I might have only partial vision. Everything turned out perfectly in the end, but Ralph was terribly concerned. He made inquiries of other people who had been cataract patients, and then he called me again to let me know what they told him.

"That's the way with Ralph. He has real concern and warmth for his friends. Being a friend of his is almost like being in a private club. And it's an exclusive club, believe me. Ralph called me to let me know about Clancy's death, but I wasn't home. He talked to Doris, and she told me her first reaction was, 'We've lost such a great person in music.' But Ralph's immediate reply was, 'We've lost a friend.' That was more important to him.

"Ralph might give the impression to someone who's just met him that he's a little blunt. He speaks rather bluntly at times. But as an entertainer, Ralph has so many, many people come up to him and say essentially the same thing: 'You're a wonderful piano player.' What else do you say? He has the ability to sort out those who are sincere about it and those who are just trying to make conversation.

"I think you can judge a man by some of the people he himself admires, and Ralph has great admiration for Willard Robison. After Willard's death, Dick Gibson asked Ralph to play a final set at a jazz party. Instead of winding up with some hard-driving stride piano, Ralph wound up with Willard. It was quite touching. Ralph admires a gentleness of spirit in other people, such as Willard, and he has it in himself. He may seem a little brusque to some people because he's so outspoken, but Ralph is actually an extremely gentle man."

Ralph's honesty impressed his fellow musicians as well. Dick Cary recalled a night when Sutton became annoyed by the comments of some jazz fans at one of Gibson's parties: "Ralph just grumbled, 'Bullshit,' when he heard those overly vocal fans who like to analyze jazz and take apart everything they hear. They sound so ridiculous to the musicians.

"Ralph has the quality that some people call 'down home' or 'country' or just plain 'honest.' Jazz musicians who are any good are very honest people because they know goddamn well they aren't fooling any of the guys they're working with on the stand. The public is easily fooled by mannerisms and posturings, but the men on the stand aren't; and they're the ones you're ashamed to let down.

"On the final day of that Aspen weekend, I heard Ralph dig in more than at any other time I've ever heard him play. He really stretched out on 'I Got Rhythm,' and I could swear I saw the grand piano actually quivering."

Chapter **19**

He's Very Easy to Live With

alph and Sunnie—and Amy, Ella, Mahalia, and Boozer—moved from Aspen to Pine, Colorado, in February 1970. The Suttons had spotted an ad in the *Rocky Mountain News* offering for sale a log house on 11 acres of land in the Rockies, about 45 miles southwest of downtown Denver. "We fell in love with the place as soon as we saw it," Sunnie said. "Once you've lived in the mountains, it's hard to be confined on a city block. We also wanted to be within commuting distance of a major airport so Ralph could get back and forth easily when he went on the road or came home from a tour. And, of course, it's kind of hard to live in a city with four Saint Bernards."

As though four Saint Bernards weren't enough, Boozer and Ella got together that summer, and the household grew by eight puppies in September. The pups were eventually sold, two of them to Hugh and Dorothy McCorriston, who lived nearby. "Early that year," McCorriston recalled, "we had heard that a musician—nobody seemed to know who he was—had bought a house down the hill, which in that part of the country made us close neighbors. Then we heard they had four Saint Bernards. One of our five daughters, Sheila, loves Saint Bernards, and so we stopped to meet the dogs the first time we saw them out walking with Sunnie. Ralph was on the road at the time, but we met him later. By then, of course, we had learned who he was and that he played with the World's Greatest Jazzband.

"The Suttons became good friends of ours. Sheila was a cheerleader in school that winter, and Dorothy and I both work in Denver. So Sunnie—or Ralph if he was home—drove to school to pick Sheila up after cheerleading practice. Nothing would do but that we had to have one of Ella's pups. We picked a male from the litter. One of the female puppies had been born blind in one eye, and Sunnie couldn't bear to have her destroyed. She asked if we would take her along with the male we were buying for Sheila. Our youngest daughter, Dottie Gale, was happy because that meant a dog for her, too.

"We wanted to name the dogs for people connected with music. Sheila said the only musical celebrity she knew was Mr. Sutton, and she wanted to name the male Ralph. I wasn't too sure that Ralph would appreciate having a Saint Bernard named for him, but he was delighted. We named the female Tallulah because my wife thought she looked sexy. Sunnie or Ralph came up to our house every noon and fed the pups because we were working and the girls were in school.

"Our friendship with the Suttons includes wood gathering as well as caring for Saint Bernards. When you live in the mountains, wood for fireplaces becomes an important matter during the winter. Ralph and I have spent many days with my chain saw and truck, collecting wood to keep the fires burning. I always handle the saw because I'm not a pianist and my hands are expendable. Besides, Sunnie won't let Ralph operate it, even though he's used a chain saw before.

"Ralph is just as fine a person as he is a musician. Once I got sick before I could begin splitting a big load of wood that was sitting in our driveway. When I arrived home the first day after going back to work, all the wood had been split and neatly stacked—courtesy of Ralph Sutton. Our daughter Mary was married in 1971, and Ralph offered to play the piano at her reception. It was a great honor for us, and the guests enjoyed it tremendously. Not everyone can have the world's greatest jazz pianist play at their daughter's wedding reception!"

Ralph also enjoyed helping another neighbor, J.C. Dozier, harvest hay on his ranch. Dozier took along a "field shortener"—a bottle of bourbon—when working in his hayfield, but one day he forgot it: "Ralph wanted some field shortener, and so I told him to drive the Bronco up to the house and get it. Later, I saw him walking—and it's a very long distance. When I asked him why he hadn't driven, he said he didn't know how to shift the gears. He hadn't noticed the stickshift on the driving column, and he had never seen such a thing before. We've laughed about that many times."

Harry Rubin described Ralph as "a true nature boy who likes nothing better than to plant his feet in the mountains with Sunnie and their Saint Bernards. Charlotte and I have spent some wonderful times with the Suttons at their home and at ours. One evening in Pine, while a Fats Waller tape was spinning away, Ralph and Sunnie got up and danced. Boozer seemed amazed. I guess he had never seen them dance before.

"Ralph always greets us and both our daughters with a hug and a kiss," Rubin said. "He is a genuine person—honest and real—and he knows the meaning of thoughtfulness and love. I would go so far as to say that if Ralph had to lay down his life for those he cares for, he would do it. But he isn't too trusting, and he doesn't care for everyone. He is very selective in his choice of friends.

"Whenever a birthday or an anniversary comes along, Ralph stops at our jewelry store to pick out something for his Sunnie. He doesn't have a lot of money to spend—the music business will never make him a millionaire—but if he could buy out the store for Sunnie, I'm sure he would."

The Suttons' two cats, Ralphina and P.C., got along beautifully with the Saint Bernards. Ralphina joined the family one night when Sunnie stopped at a bar about 20 miles from Pine while driving home: "The cat jumped up on my lap, and the fellow who owned the place told me he was closing for the season and didn't know where she would go. He said I could have her if I wanted her. So I took her home and named her Ralph because she was such a swinging cat. But then she had kittens, and so we had to change her name to Ralphina." P.C. (for Pussy Cat, of course) became a member of the household shortly after her birth a few months later, courtesy of a neighbor of Sunnie's mother.

When Ralph goes on the road to perform for a week or two at one club, Sunnie occasionally goes with him—especially if the club happens to be in Acapulco, Honolulu, or a similar vacation spot. Unfortunately, the Suttons cannot afford to travel together nearly as often as they would like. According to Sunnie, "We're both going to have to work until we drop." When the Suttons lived in Pine and Sunnie did manage to get away, Florence Cole moved in and tended the menagerie. Cole, a Denver widow, gave the Saint Bernards and the cats the attention to which they were accustomed, including long walks through the woods. She also was devoted to Sunnie's plants, which she sometimes nourished with coffee, tea, and beer. "I'm teaching those plants to be boozers," she explained.

A person meeting Sunnie Sutton for the first time could easily get the impression that she is strong, tough, and hard-boiled—and she is when she wants to be. But, as Bill MacPherson commented in his liner notes, she has a heart of pure marshmallow—especially when talking about Ralph, whom she fondly calls "Raliff."

"I never thought I would be able to spend 24 hours of any given day with one person," Sunnie said in Pine, "but Ralph and I have spent many 24-hour days together. He's very easy to live with and isn't demanding at all. I'm probably like a sergeant who takes advantage of his good nature most of the time, but he puts up with it. If I'm feeling poorly, he's considerate and gentle. He's just great. What else can I say? I love him, that's all.

"I'm sure most men aren't as easy to live with as Ralph. Friends have said to me, 'God, ever since Charlie retired, he's been underfoot day and night. I can't stand it. I wish he'd go out of town for a few days.' I think that's why every minute is so precious when Ralph *is* home. At the club in Aspen and sometimes now in Denver, we'll each do our own thing and then meet at the end of the day and hold hands all the way home in the car. It's been a beautiful romance from the start. When Ralph and I are together, we don't need anyone else around. That's the whole ball game."

Actually, Sunnie moved into the house in Pine alone because Ralph was on the road with the WGJ at the time. The life of a jazz musician being what it is, she found herself alone most of the time after the band was organized until Ralph left the group in 1974: "I sat in the house all that winter after we moved, all the next summer, and all the following winter. Finally, in the fall of 1971, I called Bill Winter, the owner of the Navarre, and asked him to find something for me to do there. Bill's a friend of ours, and I told him I had to get out of Pine. I didn't want to work just anywhere, but I was familiar with the Navarre. Ralph had played solo piano there, and he'd played there with Peanuts Hucko when Peanuts owned the club, and the band had played there, too.

"I went to work at the Navarre as dining room coordinator, which meant I seated people. I also tended bar and did about everything else in the place. Finally, I settled behind the bar five days a week as bartender. I've always liked the restaurant business, and at the Navarre I could work days and be home at night. We had a nice clientele, and I enjoy seeing people happy. I'll probably have a club again someday—we'll own the building the next time instead of paying rent!—and I didn't want to lose my touch.

"It's very difficult to be separated from Ralph when he's on the road a lot. My parents live in Denver now, but they didn't move out from Chicago until after I had started at the Navarre. I had a couple of aunts and an uncle in Denver, and I used to see one of the aunts quite often. But I'm just not the kind of woman who likes to play cards and gossip with the ladies five days a week, and so my life was very limited. The job provided an outlet for me because I could be around people and also get the male attention at the bar that I need as a woman.

"Naturally, there's no substitute for Ralph. He thought it was good that I keep busy because he knows how slowly the time goes when you're alone. The Navarre got to be kind of a home for me. I had hardly any trouble with men who might have had ideas after seeing a woman behind the bar. I talked a lot about Ralph from the beginning, and many of the guys who came in knew him or knew about him because he had played at the club. They knew I was working to pass the time while he was on the road. If you conduct yourself in an orderly fashion with nothing in mind, they know how to react to you. I get a bigger kick out of people telling me I'm the best-dressed bartender they've ever seen—and that I don't look like a bartender—than if I were trying to look like a little dolly to attract the guys. I'm a lady, I want to look like a lady, and I act like a lady behind the bar.

"When Ralph was on the road with the band and had a day or two off, he flew home if at all possible, depending on the season. We couldn't trust the winter weather, and so we didn't take a chance if he had to fly a long distance during those months. But in summer, he few home just for a day. That gave us a little stimulant to keep going. We got awfully tired writing letters, and our phone bills were astronomical until I told him we just had to stop all the calling. So we limited ourselves to letters and maybe one call a week when he was away. It was hard, of course, when he was moving around on one-nighters because you can't count on the U.S. Post Office.

"If Ralph could get home for only a couple of days, I took that time off from work so we could tootle around together. Of course, if he was home for two or three weeks, we couldn't afford that luxury. He was terrific in helping me around the house, especially when he was home off the road and I was working. He knew I'd be tired after work, and so he'd wash the dishes and do the laundry and vacuuming and then cook dinner and have it ready for me."

Ralph rarely sits down at the piano when he and Sunnie are home alone, chiefly because so much work always seems to be waiting for them—burros, dogs, and cats to be fed and otherwise cared for; grass to be mowed;

and timber to be cut, hauled home, and stored in the woodshed. He has no set schedule for practicing, and many days go by with no playing at all when he is home from the road and has no local gig.

"When I do practice," Ralph said, "I like to play Hanon and Czerny exercises for about 45 minutes and then go into some Bach fugues and preludes. All that helps get my fingers in shape. Then maybe I'll swing into a few things."

Ralph never plays his own records or tapes when he and Sunnie are by themselves, and only rarely when they have guests. He would rather hear Waller or Tatum. When the Suttons are in the home of a friend and Ralph is asked to play, Sunnie generally requests "I Found a New Baby," "I Got Rhythm," or some other warhorse. She said, "I'm probably one of his biggest bores because no matter where we go, I want him to play the piano—and I keep asking him to do the same things. But he won't play one of my favorites, 'Keep Your Temper,' even though I've been after him for years to brush up on it. I used to play Ralph's record of that tune all the time at the club in Aspen. He finally dug up the music and went over it a few times, but he just hasn't had a chance to woodshed it. It's been years since he made the record, and he won't play anything in public unless he's got it down perfectly."

In his effort to achieve perfection, Ralph used to practice with a tape recorder so he could immediately hear how he had played a tune. He no longer does that, but he refuses to play any tune in public that he has not played perfectly for himself at least 40 times. "That's just the way I feel about it," he said. "I'd rather have a tune under my fingers before I play it for people. If somebody asks me for a tune that I don't know and I tell them so, they always say, 'Oh, sure you know that.' But who am I kidding? I just won't do it. I'd rather know what I'm doing before I reveal myself out there."

Ralph is a perfectionist in anything he does, not just his playing. "He tries to do everything exactly right from the very beginning," Sunnie said. "When he built the playpen for the pups, he had never done such a thing before. But he did it perfectly. He's also very precise if he has a date with a person or if he says he's going to call someone. He's always on time. If he can't be somewhere at a given time, you'll get a call from him. He's very considerate of people, and he thinks of the trouble they might have gone to when arranging a date with him. He'll always be there if at all possible. He also answers people's letters promptly. Around the house, he's very neat and always hangs up his clothes. And he's always immaculate on the stand, too.

"As far as his playing is concerned, he feels free to improvise on a tune even more than usual after he has it down perfectly. I've heard him play 'Honky Tonk Train' and 'Keepin' Out of Mischief' and 'Honeysuckle Rose' so many times, but there's something new and delightful about every tune he plays each time he plays it."

Some of Ralph's fans complain that he plays too many tunes over and over again, both in person and on records. Ralph's reaction to such criticism is what might be expected: "It doesn't bother me at all. I get a bit tired of the tunes myself. I'm a little lazy, I guess, and I haven't worked up anything else. But people who say things like that don't have the musical ear to hear the different things in each version. I might even get around to 'Keep Your Temper' one of these days."

Sutton did just that, and he recorded it in a 1979 album. Ralph said he included the tune, one of Willie the Lion Smith's liveliest compositions, "as the result of some urging from the one I love." He also added it to his performance repertoire.

According to Sunnie, Ralph has never expressed any thought about perhaps being by-passed by life and not receiving the recognition that so many people think he should have had through the years. "I feel that way about him myself," she said. "Sometimes Ralph would tell me, 'I hate to leave you home alone. Maybe I should quit music and get a job working on the highway or just doing anything so we can be together.' That's when I had to forget about all my wishes and make him feel secure enough that he could go out on the road if he had to and do his thing.

"I don't know whether he just hasn't been at the right place at the right time or known the right people, or what. Ralph and so many other musicians who weren't well known before the youngsters took over with rock have stayed in the background ever since. Maybe the recognition will still come. Maybe it's not too late. Let's hope."

Chapter **20**

The True Giants Remain Neglected

ll the men in the World's Greatest Jazzband got weary of the long weeks away from home and family—of living out of a suitcase in one motel room after another, of eating in restaurants whose food fell far short of home cooking, of finding ways to meet such simple requirements as getting a haircut and having laundry cared for, and of the endless boredom and weariness that fill so many hours on the move, whether by bus or plane. Ralph, like any pianist, had an extra and unique headache—the piano itself. He was the only member of the band who had little control over the quality of his instrument, particularly when the group came to a community for only one performance and then moved on to the next stop on a tour.

The contracts of the WGJ called for a grand piano, with the A above middle C tuned to 440 vibrations per second. But Ralph played many engagements on an instrument that hardly met that provision. Once he encountered what he charitably described as "a kind of over-large spinet" at a club in Omaha. The next morning, he looked up the owner of the spot: "I asked him if he had read the contract. He said he had, but that he couldn't get a grand in Omaha. I told him that the next time he booked the band—*if* he booked us again—he'd better have a grand, or I wouldn't play. He looked very surprised and said nobody had ever talked to him like that."

A beat-up spinet awaited Ralph in Kingsville, Texas, during one tour. The man in charge explained that the owner of the place had locked up the concert grand and allowed no one to play it without his permission—and he was out of town. Somehow, the grand materialized after the band threatened to cancel the evening's program.

In Ukiah, California, the high school band director had a chat with

Ralph during the intermission of the WGJ's concert in the school auditorium. Later, the director told Hal Curtis, a fellow faculty member: "Your brother-in-law is one big guy. He sort of hulked up to me and growled, 'Did you tune that piano?' I began to quake a bit and told him I hadn't. 'Well,' he said, 'whoever did sure fucked it up.' "

Piano foul-ups can occur even at presidential inaugural balls. The band played at the ball following both the election and the reelection of Richard M. Nixon. When the men arrived at the Kennedy Center for the Performing Arts in Washington in January 1973, no piano was in sight. "Somebody sent out the word," Ralph recalled, "and pretty soon some maintenance men brought in a harpsichord. They didn't even know the difference. They finally took the harpsichord back to wherever they got it and brought in a little spinet. All I could think was, there should have been a 9-foot Steinway on that stand for an inaugural ball. I was disgusted with the whole half-assed scene."

Washington also was the home of what Sutton called the worst club he ever played. "It was the filthiest joint I've seen in my life," he said. "Cockroaches were waltzing across the floor—and I'm not kidding. The glasses were so dirty that I didn't have a drink in the place. It was a hippie rock 'n' roll joint, and we had a fag hippie announcer. He'd tell the crowd, 'And now, ladies and gentlemen, tsch, we're *so* proud to present, tsch, the World's Greatest Jazzband.' Then he'd wave at me, and I'd wave at him."

When the band traveled by bus, Ralph spent most of the long hours reading. His favorite authors include Jack London, Mark Twain, and Philip Wylie, and he has gone through innumerable paperbacks by a wide variety of other writers. He also has read assorted nonfiction, including some of Sigmund Freud's works. Four members of the band—Yank Lawson, Bob Haggart, Bud Freemen, and Gus Johnson—killed a lot of time on the bus playing five-card stud poker. Ralph doesn't play poker, but he and Johnson occasionally tried to take quarters from each other in tonk, a card game that originated in Harlem. Bob Wilber, like Ralph, read a lot on the road. Bennie Morton almost always slept most of the miles away.

The WGJ stayed at a Holiday Inn whenever possible because of a special rate given the group. On the road, where there was no wood to chop, Ralph got all his exercise by walking. He also engaged in what he jokingly calls his two favorite road activities: "kicking tires and spitting." Haggart sometimes walked with him, as did Wilber, Johnson, and Lawson.

The time passed especially slowly on rainy days when he couldn't get out of the motel for a stroll. Ralph rarely watches television, chiefly because he can't stand the commercials. Crossword puzzles are the closest thing to a hobby that he has besides walking: "I've been doing them ever since my college days. They're very relaxing, and they put my mind to work; it's usually idle."

Each member of the band was responsible for his own living expenses on the road. World Jazz, Inc., the corporation that owned the band, paid all travel costs, including a round-trip ticket to go home if the men had as little as one day off. All the musicians received a straight salary, and all except Lawson and Haggart also got 7 percent of the profits. The two co-leaders got a larger slice. The corporation absorbed any financial losses of the band.

Ralph was closer to Bob Wilber on a personal level than to any other member of the group. The two men often roomed together on the road, and they lived at each other's home when performing in or near Denver or New York. "Ralph's a marvelous roommate because he's very clean and orderly in his personal habits." Wilber said. "He's always considerate of anyone he's associated with. I like to play a lot of music in the room, and Ralph enjoys all kinds of music. And yet, if I didn't put a tape on, he would never turn on the radio or have any music at all. He enjoys silence, and sometimes I thought I was imposing on him. But he was too polite to say anything about it even if the music did bother him." Ralph, though characteristically expressing himself in few words, felt the same about Wilber as a roommate: "We stayed out of each other's way and got along fine."

Ralph believes the general public attitude toward jazz is far more favorable in other countries where he has performed—particularly the United Kingdom and Canada—than in the United States. "The way we're treated in England is unbelievable—like the difference between night and day," he said. "The people there roll out the red carpet, and they know things about my musical background that surprise me. They're sincere, and they have a real understanding and knowledgeable appreciation of jazz. The English make you feel that it's an honor for them to have you come to their country.

"I didn't want to come back to the States after the band played in England and Scotland in 1971. Sure enough, we had a real letdown on the first job we played after flying home. We took another plane right from

New York to Oklahoma City for a concert at a swanky country club. Man, that was a beautiful place. The high society of Oklahoma City. But what a difference in the people and the way they listened to music. They didn't pay any attention at all. They didn't even know who was playing for them.

"Toronto is the best town of all. It's always good to go up there and play a club like the Colonial Tavern. The people love the music; and when you're playing for a crowd that really enjoys what you're doing, you get a boost and put a little more into it. Everybody has a ball."

During the 1971 tour in England, Sinclair and Mips Traill took Ralph to a local pub that had an ancient, out-of-tune piano with many missing keys. A blind pianist named Fred played there on weekends. Traill recalled: "Ralph settled himself at the keyboard and knocked the hell out of that battered old upright. All activity in the pub came to a halt. Dart games stopped, and drinks stood untouched.

"Ralph played on, smiling when he hit a note that didn't respond. Fred came in, and the owner of the place asked him if he thought the man playing was good enough to work there whenever Fred couldn't make it. 'Good?' Fred exploded. 'He's bloody marvelous. Where did you find him? He can't be Fats, he can't be Sullivan, and he can't be Stacy. There's another man who's as good as they are, and I heard a record of his once. I can't remember his name, but that sounds like him right there.'

"Fred then sat down near Ralph and listened. He still talks about that night. He says Ralph played so wonderfully and so powerfully that he somehow managed to bang even that awful piano into tune. Ralph told us later it was the first time he had ever played a piano with 66 keys."

Ken Gallacher traveled with the band a bit in England and Scotland. "I found Ralph great company," the Scottish journalist said. "He's quiet, but he has a tremendous sense of humor and is always ready to go out of his way to talk to fans. There's never any 'big time' crap from Ralph. One of his top fans over here is Gerald Lascelles, a cousin of the queen's. Lascelles came around to see Ralph after the band opened in London, but Ralph didn't give him any special treatment—just the same kindness and courtesy that he gives any fan. There is a warmth about Ralph as a person that comes through in his playing. Ralph cares—about jazz, about people, and about playing piano the way he likes to play piano."

Derek Coller, an English jazz enthusiast, visited Ralph in his hotel room in London. The wives of three members of the band had gone on the trip, and Coller recalled that Sutton told him how much he would like to be able to afford to bring Sunnie along on future tours: "Ralph showed me some photographs of his wife and their beautiful home and Saint Bernards. He must have been wondering what he was doing in a small hotel room in London talking to a complete stranger. I had heard that all members of the WGJ were disarming and approachable, and Ralph certainly confirmed this."

A lengthy review of two of Sutton's records appeared in *Jazz & Blues* several months after the band returned to the United States. The writer, Eddie Lambert, declared that Ralph's playing on the tour had been "a particular delight." Then he commented enthusiastically about *Suttonly*, the LP that Ralph had made for Larry Conger, and *Knocked-Out Nocturne* (reissued under the title *Ralph Sutton Plays Great Jazz Piano*), on which Haggart and Johnson accompany Sutton, with Lawson and Wilber appearing sketchily in a background role on some of the tunes:

> Ralph is a player who thoroughly merits the description "two-handed pianist." Not only does his left hand stride away with great punch, swing, and presence, but it also fills out the sound of the keyboard most excellently, thereby enriching the harmonic texture.... Echoes of Fats Waller and James P. Johnson are heard, but this is clearly Ralph Sutton's music....
>
> It would be hard to imagine a contemporary pianist who more deserves the kind of exposure that solo concert tours would offer. But as is usual in jazz, it is the inferior talents who receive the critic's accolades and win the polls, while the true giants remain neglected. These two admirable LPs indicate without doubt that Ralph Sutton is indeed a giant of contemporary jazz piano.

For a man who supposedly dislikes most people and wants to be left alone, Ralph has a surprisingly large number of friends throughout the United States and in other countries. Many people think nothing of traveling several hundred miles to see him. No matter where he plays when on the road, someone is likely to show up to renew their friendship. He stays in the home of some of these friends. Bob Haggart scoffed at the idea that Ralph doesn't like people: "That's not true at all. He doesn't like certain *things* about people—certain types of people who do this or don't do that—but he sure has a lot of friends. It's ridiculous for him to say he doesn't like people. He's gotta like them. In just about every town we played, people called him up and came in to see him. Whenever we played in a club, there were always four or five tables of people whom he'd known for years.

"When you play as a solo pianist in clubs, as Ralph has, people come up and talk. Ralph detests this and tells them to get away from him. He hates to take requests. He likes to play what he feels like playing, and all his friends know this. They don't bug him by asking him to play certain tunes. They know he'll get around to all the things they want to hear."

Bob Wilber knows Ralph as well as anyone, but he can't figure out what he calls Sutton's contradictory character. "Ralph likes to live out in the country, be by himself, and not have too many people around," Wilber said. "He's always saying that nature is much better than people, and he continually talks about how so many people are assholes. And yet, of all the guys in the band, he had more friends—*close* friends—than any of the rest of us. He's a very diligent correspondent and kept in touch with them regularly. Everywhere we went, people made it a point to call him and were genuinely glad to see him. I've never known a guy who has so many friends. And yet he doesn't seem to like people in general.

"His character comes out in his music, too. He's a tremendously accomplished pianist—marvelous technique and control of his instrument. When he's on the job, playing is obviously such a great part of his life. But he'll spend a whole week at my home with nothing to do except enjoy himself—and never go near the piano. We have a beautiful Steinway grand that he didn't touch for years. He never practices. Once in a while I've seen him sit down at a piano somewhere and rattle off some Bach. Beautiful technique. But he never sits down and really practices—and yet he loves to play. I can't reconcile these contradictory things in his nature. They make him a very unusual person."

Wilber saw amusing evidence in Sutton's own home that Ralph spent little time at the keyboard. He told about it in *Music Was Not Enough*, his book written with Derek Webster and published in 1987:

("Ralph is) a natural talent and doesn't need constant practice to stay consistently brilliant. For many years he never even owned a piano. Jack Lesberg gave him his when he was moving to Australia. I was visiting Ralph about six months after he'd acquired the instrument, and when I asked him how he liked it he took me into the living room. There was the piano and bench in the corner of the room covered with plants and flowers. His wife, Sunnie, had decided that the piano was the ideal setting to display her greenery. Ralph didn't mind—he never practiced anyway. He didn't need to."

No one could have been more surprised than Wilber and his first wife, Rickie, during Ralph's stay at their home in New City, about 40 miles from New York, in 1973. The band was playing a two-week engagement in New York, and Sutton arrived with a stack of Bach scores and gave the Wilbers' Steinway a thorough workout. "Whenever Ralph had stayed with us before," Rickie Wilber said, "he sat around and wrote letters and read and took walks, but he never played the piano. This time he sat down every day and played Bach for hours. The incredible thing is that he plays it so brilliantly. It's not a jazz musician saying, 'I will play the classics.' Ralph *plays* the classics—and he plays them gorgeously. We had paid a lot of money for our Steinway about six years before, and we were worried that maybe we had a lemon on our hands. But Ralph just didn't feel like playing before. He felt like it this time, and it was wonderful to hear.

"Ralph is a great houseguest. He's no trouble at all because he takes care of himself and doesn't demand anything. We have three dogs, too, and he loves to play with them. He also likes to walk and just look at the trees and breathe the country air. He likes to be alone; but he really loves and appreciates his friends, and he's one of the most loyal people I've ever known. If you and he are on the same wavelength, there's nothing he won't do for you. If I ever got into deep trouble, I know he'd drop everything and come running. He'd even stop playing to come!

"He thinks the world is pretty full of baloney; but he sees the world as he thinks it should be, and every once in a while he gets very impatient with it. He understands what the true values of the world ought to be, and so he'll sometimes sit around and grumble about his dissatisfaction with things.

"Ralph is a great cook. He'll say, 'OK, Rickie, what do you want me to make?' or 'Let's go to the store and I'll buy.' And we'll go and get what he wants to cook for dinner. His pork chops Creole are wonderful, and he makes a jalapeño pepper sauce that he should sell commercially. It's delicious and it cures hangovers. He could make a fortune with it. Ralph has some close friends in Denver, Rich and Sylvia Priest, and we once stayed in their apartment building. The Priests invited us up to breakfast one morning, and I had a terrible hangover. Rich was cooking, and before he served the scrambled eggs he put a bowl of something lovely and red in front of me. He said it was Ralph's hot sauce. I wanted to be polite, and so I put it on my eggs and ate a big dollop of it. My head blew off—and with it went the hangover. I felt marvelous!"

Ralph got the recipe for the hot sauce from Ernie Figueroa. The trumpet and bass player told him it was "good for whatever's right," and so Sutton named it "whatever's right sauce." Ralph and Sunnie both make the concoction. It became a big favorite among Sunnie's lunch customers at the Navarre and later at another club, the Pump and Derrick. Ralph always packs a large jar of the hot sauce when he goes on the road, unless he knows he will be able to whip up a supply wherever he'll be staying.

Pork Chops Creole

Ben Webster's pork chops Creole became a favorite with Ruth and me soon after Ralph gave us the recipe. It would be inexcusable not to include it in his biography. However, Ralph and Sunnie have thoughts of marketing his hot sauce, so its secret stays at Morning Air Ranch.

8 pork chops
2 onions
2 green peppers
1 can of stewed tomatoes

Flour
Olive oil
Garlic powder and pepper
Worcestershire sauce

Dust the pork chops with flour and brown them in olive oil in a pan. Slice the onions and peppers and combine them with the tomatoes in a large pot. Add garlic powder and pepper and put the chops into the pot. Pour Worcestershire sauce into the pan and bring the liquid to a boil. Pour it over the chops in the pot. Serves four.

Ralph and the Wilbers' teenaged daughter, Beth, gave each other a lot of laughs by imitating the rural Southern drawl of Maudie Frickert, the old-lady character created by Jonathan Winters. Beth loved Ralph's cooking and was just as enthusiastic about his playing: "I've heard Ralph play ragtime, jazz, boogie—the whole spectrum of jazz piano. His playing is something else. Most of my contemporaries are rock-oriented, and I listen to rock as well as jazz. But a lot of the kids are becoming interested in jazz and are really digging it—especially jazz piano.

"It's really something to hear Ralph play Bach Inventions. They swing! His fingers work so intricately and quickly, and he never misses a beat. I asked him once which Bach Invention was his favorite, and he grinned and said, 'I don't know. I haven't played them all.' "

After the WGJ's New York gig in 1973, Ralph spent a night with Milt and Mona Hinton at their home in St. Albans, a community in Queens. The Hintons lived about 10 minutes from Kennedy Airport, and the great bassist drove Sutton there the next day after giving him a tour of the neighborhood.

Fats Waller had lived one block from Hinton's house, and Hinton took pictures of Ralph in front of his idol's home. Count Basie's house stood across from Waller's. Hinton was taking pictures of Sutton there when Basie opened the door and laughingly demanded to know what they were doing. He invited them in, and the three men chatted until Ralph had to leave for the airport.

Waller broke the color barrier in St. Albans when he and his family moved into the community in 1939. Hinton heard the story from a close friend named Anderson, who lived across the street from him until his death in the mid-1980s. Anderson and his wife were the last whites to live in the neighborhood. He told Hinton that Waller moved in as the result of the enmity between two men who lived next door to each other.

"These guys had a big fight about something," Hinton related, "and one of them said, 'I'll fix you. I'll sell my house to a nigger.' The other guy told him, 'There ain't no nigger that's got enough money to buy a house in this neighborhood.' At the time, Hinton noted, Waller "was perhaps at his height, making piano rolls and writing songs. He was doing very well. The guy sold the house to him."

A hostile crowd burned a cross on the Waller lawn shortly after the family moved into St. Albans, according to Fats's son Maurice. He said in his book *Fats Waller,* written with Anthony Calabrese and published in 1977, that the cross burners never returned. But Maurice Waller added that he and his younger brother, Ronald, "had no friends because the white children in the neighborhood were forbidden to play with us."

On the other hand, many of the white residents accepted Fats Waller's presence. Hinton said Anderson told him "it didn't disturb the neighbors so much because of the kind of human being Fats was—very sociable and congenial." St. Albans was described by Hinton as "a white sportsmen's neighborhood, a very nice, beautiful place." Babe Ruth lived there and so did Earl Sande, the famous jockey. Ruth, Sande, and Waller enjoyed one another's company in Saturday night poker games.

During the 1940s, Hinton went on, "the neighborhood changed its complexion. The white people began to move out and black people started to buy in. But they had to be black people who had a very decent income—schoolteachers, sportsmen, civil service workers."

Two black baseball stars, Jackie Robinson and Roy Campanella, moved into St. Albans. Heavyweight champion Joe Louis bought Babe Ruth's house. Mercer Ellington, Duke's son, built a house across the street from it. James P. Johnson, Fats Waller's mentor, lived in the neighborhood before Count Basie did. Waller's home was flanked by those of Johnson and Clarence Williams. Hank Duncan lived nearby. Ella Fitzgerald and Lena Horne moved in, as did Illinois Jacquet. Milt and Mona Hinton bought their home in 1949, moving from another section of Queens.

"St. Albans became 99 and 44/100ths percent black," Hinton said. "We call ourselves black bourgeois because we're schoolteachers, civil service people, doctors, and others who can afford to keep their property up. The property in our community has escalated. Nobody's moving, so nobody can buy any of it."

Basie's wife, Catherine, was Mona Hinton's closest friend. She belonged to several organizations that put on fashion shows and other affairs at her home.

"Count Basie was very uneasy around a lot of people up close," Milt Hinton said. "If he was home when she had a crowd over, Mona would be there and he'd come to our house. Basie loved silent movies. He had played background music for silent films in his early days, and I owned a lot of Charlie Chaplin movies. We would put a movie on and Basie couldn't contain himself. He'd sit there for a minute and then go over to the piano and start playing sound effects and music for the film.

"He came over one day when there was a big fashion show in their backyard for the National Conference of Christians and Jews. Catherine had hired a band but it didn't show up. She came dashing over to my house. 'Bill, you and Milt come over. We don't have any music.' They had a little piano in their yard, and I grabbed my bass and there we were. I sang 'A Pretty Girl Is Like a Melody.' The things I have to do on my day off."

In 1976, the Waller and Basie homes were designated with plaques of the Black American Heritage Trail of Landmarks.

J. Lee Hopper, who owned a piano store in Garner, North Carolina, and played jazz piano himself, knew nothing about Sutton until 1970. He happened to hear one of Ralph's records through a piano teacher named Charles Davis, whom Hopper described as "a walking history book on stride and ragtime piano players." After hearing the record, Hopper wasted little time putting his wife, Kate, his 10-year-old son, Tex, and himself on a plane for New York, where the World's Greatest Jazzband was playing at the Roosevelt Grill. He not only met Ralph but also arranged a gig for the band at a Raleigh club, the Frog & Nightgown. The intriguing name of this club popped up later as the name of a Bob Haggart tune on one of the band's records. When the WGJ played a return engagement at the Frog & Nightgown, Ralph stayed at Hopper's home.

"Ralph and Tex went fishing together almost every day," Hopper remembered. "My son always caught more fish than Ralph did, but Ralph was quite content just to be in the woods and away from crowds. He loves nature. We have a small stream and a lake and some beautiful woods behind our home, and Ralph walks for hours in those woods whenever he's with us. I thought when we first met that he was a little shy, but that isn't the case at all. He's just a quiet, reserved fellow."

Marvin Ash, who played piano for Walt Disney Productions, was a good friend of Hopper's and sent him several tapes of his playing. In 1972, Ash broke his left arm and shoulder. He wrote Hopper that the era of stride piano had thereby ended. Hopper responded by threatening to tape a few tunes himself.

"Ralph came to town the next week," Hopper said, "and I got him and our piano tuner, Doodles Minton, together at the store. Doodles used to play trumpet in an all-star Army orchestra, and he and Ralph taped some numbers. I sent the tape to Marvin and told him I was the piano player. Marvin called me and asked if I had really played on the tape. I kept him guessing, and he finally exploded: 'You s.o.b., I've done tapes for you all these years, and now I learn that you play better piano than anyone else in the world!' Ralph loved the story and told me to keep Marvin guessing a while longer."

A Chicago area disk jockey, Mike Schwimmer, credited Ralph with helping him get started with his own radio show. In 1962, Schwimmer frequently listened to a d.j. who played a lot of Sutton's recordings but kept repeating the same tunes over and over again. "One night," Schwimmer remembered, "he apologized for playing the same numbers all the time. He explained that Ralph had made only one record, and so those tunes were all that could be played. I called him up and told him I owned six or seven Sutton records, and he asked me to bring them to the station so he could play them on the air. I brought him the records, and it was a big thrill to have him talk about me on the program. Then he asked me to bring some other records down, and he began to chat with me on the show. It got to the point where I was a regular guest every Tuesday night. I ended up doing the show, and all he did was read the commercials. Eventually the bug bit me and I asked myself why I was doing that and not making any money for it when I could be doing my own program."

In 1963, Schwimmer began his own show on a new station in Highland Park, a Chicago suburb. He later became known for his "Yesterday Shop" program on station WLTD in Evanston, another suburb. The program featured jazz and music of the Big Band Era. "If it weren't for my bristling at the idea that Sutton had made only one record, I might never have gotten into radio at all," he said. Schwimmer also ran a store called the Yesterday Shop in Long Grove. There, he sold reconditioned player pianos, old 78 records, and other miscellaneous items from the past. In addition, he played washboard in the Al Capone Memorial Jazz Band, led by pianist Don Gibson.

On Gibson's birthday in May 1971, the members of his band gathered at his home in Highland Park for a party. Bob Ballenger, a friend of Ralph's, was going to hear the World's Greatest Jazzband at the Happy Medium in Chicago that night and told Gibson he would bring Sutton to the party if he could. At about 2:30 the next morning, while the Al Capone band was in the middle of a jam session, Ballenger arrived with Sutton.

"Ralph told us to keep playing," Schwimmer recalled. "He sat down and listened, and we all met him and hoped against hope that he might want to sit in. About an hour later, we took a break and Ralph asked if anybody minded if he played a bit. He went through a couple of numbers, and then he motioned to Wayne Jones, our drummer, and said one word: 'Brushes.' Wayne jumped up and grabbed his brushes, and Ralph played until after 6 that morning.

"You get the feeling just being around Ralph that he is a major talent. You have somewhat of a sense of awe—and I think you should—because he's that good."

James M. Heyn of Chicago had never heard Ralph play until Schwimmer included one of his recordings on the "Yesterday Shop" program in April 1974. Heyn wrote Ralph and asked about his records, and Sutton replied with the desired information. A couple of months later, Ralph played at the Big Horn Jazz Festival in Ivanhoe, Illinois, and Heyn and his wife went to hear him. Heyn recalled: "A big man with a Princeton haircut who looked like a bank vice president walked in, and somebody said it was Ralph Sutton. He was immediately surrounded by people who greeted him with bear hugs rather than handshakes. As soon as he left one group, another surrounded him. It was as if Arnold Palmer had shown up at the Masters after a 10-year absence.

"Ralph sat in with some of the boys from the WGJ, and then he played several solos. He received a standing ovation after each number. We had told the management that, if possible, we would like to meet Ralph. With the crowds around him, we had given up that idea until a voice behind me said, 'Are you Jim Heyn? I'm Ralph Sutton, and I'm glad you came.' This was no condescending big shot who talked to us. He turned out to be a charming, natural, almost shy man. Ralph stopped at our table several times to talk. Everybody must have wondered who the celebrities were who could command such attention from the star of the show."

When appearing in Chicago, Ralph usually got together with Bill and Crick Priestley. "At our home, he'll sometimes head straight for the piano and play a lot," Priestley said. "Other times he won't go near it, and at those times I'm sure he appreciates not being asked to play. He can be moody and want privacy. He wants to choose his time to play—which is when he feels like it. Sometimes he'll listen to records, but other times he'd rather not even talk about music. He'll go for a stroll alone or with our dog."

Another Chicago friend, Ed Levine, once planned what he was sure would be several musical hours with Ralph on the WGJ's day off: "He came up to my apartment, and I thought, 'Oh, man, what an afternoon and evening this is going to be.' I've got 3,600 feet of Fats on tape, and I figured that we'd sit down and have a couple of tastes and listen to music. But he said, 'C'mon, let's get the hell out of here and take a walk along the lake.' "

One of Ralph's friends, Connie Roscoe, then of Orange, Texas, didn't like to wait for the annual jazz party in Odessa to hear Sutton play. Beginning in 1969, he often drove hundreds of miles to enjoy Ralph's music—and Ralph. That year, Roscoe traveled to New Orleans, where the World's Greatest Jazzband was playing, and heard Ralph live for the first time. Lou McGarity told him the band would be playing at Dick Gibson's jazz party in Aspen the next month. The Gibsons, who happened to be present, invited Roscoe to the affair.

"I got to Aspen a day early," Roscoe remembered, "and so I wandered around that night hoping to run into an informal jam session before the party started. I passed a small restaurant-lounge combination below street level, but the first time I circled the block I didn't hear anything. As I went around the second time, I was about to give up and go back to my motel when I heard music coming from the place. I ran down the steps and looked in, and there were Sutton, McGarity, and Cliff Leeman! Of all the music I've listened to, that was probably the best I've ever heard. The tall, attractive blonde who ran the place turned out to be Sunnie Sutton.

"For some reason or other, people seem to think it rather amazing that I go to such lengths to hear Ralph play. But it's simple, really. We're good friends, and I'm a jazz fan—particularly a Sutton fan. Ralph and Sunnie are such nice people, and so much fun to be around. When Rich Priest, who owns a tavern in Central City, Colorado, calls and tells me Ralph will be playing there on a weekend, I drive up if I can possibly make it."

Another Texan, Bill Bacin of Kerrville, witnessed an encounter between Ralph and a member of Stevie Wonder's entourage at a private party at Disneyland in California: "At one point, none of the musicians seemed to feel like doing much. There was a beautiful piano in the place, and so Ralph started playing some Bix and some of his regular specials. A couple of Stevie Wonder's group made a few minor attempts to eject him, but he just ignored them and kept playing for about an hour and a half. Finally, a character came up and more or less ordered Ralph to get off the stand because Stevie was about to entertain. Ralph stood up, looked the guy in the eye, and told him in no uncertain terms what he and Stevie and their whole group could go do for themselves. He must have made a pretty good impression on the guy because the entire bunch left."

Bacin, who was the one-man staff of *The Jazzologist*, once asked Sutton in a radio interview what he thought of having a book written about him. "It leaves me speechless," Ralph answered. "I don't know why a guy would like to do anything like that."

Sutton took part in another interview during the summer of 1972, when the WGJ played a series of one-nighters in the Pacific Northwest. Ralph disliked the grind even more than usual because the audiences were small and the people who did show up displayed little knowledge of the music. After the concert in Pocatello, Idaho, a local disk jockey came backstage with a tape recorder to interview the musicians. Ralph said the man turned out to be a know-it-all and asked the usual questions, such as, "How old were you when you started piano lessons?" The conversation then went something like this:

"You call yourselves the World's Greatest Jazzband?"

"Yes," Ralph replied.

"Isn't that a bit pretentious?" the d.j. asked.

"Oh, I don't know," said Ralph. "After all, a name is meant to describe something that a group does or can do. In our case, we do it better than anyone else in the world."

"I see," said the d.j.

"Now we *did* have another name for the band," Ralph went on, "but we decided not to use it."

"What was that?" asked the d.j.

"Well," Sutton said, "we *were* going to call ourselves the Sheep Fuckers, but we decided not to."

Ralph never saw a tape recorder turned off so quickly.

The main street of Howell, Missouri, looked like this when Ralph Sutton was growing up in the little town during the 1930s. (*Collection of Barbara Sutton Curtis*)

Howell's general store, owned by the father of Norman Muschany, Ralph's best friend, was a favorite meeting place of the men of the town. They often argued about politics there. (*Collection of Barbara Sutton Curtis*)

Loose Shoes

Ralph was 8 years old when he posed with a protective arm around the newest member of the family, his sister Barbara. (*Collection of Barbara Sutton Curtis*)

Ralph stood in front of his sixth-grade teacher, Verna Muhm, in this photo. Norman Muschany was behind Ralph. Two other friends, the Schierbaum brothers, Emmett and Clifford, stood to Ralph's right. (*Collection of Norman Muschany*)

Loose Shoes

```
           MR. RALPH SUTTON
              pupil of
           Mrs. E.C.Carpenter

        in a short piano recital
                ********
                  **

   Prelude. . . . . . . . . . . Rachmaninoff
   Waltz . . . . . . . . . . . . . . .Chopin
   Solfeggietto . . . . . . . . . . . . Bach
   First Movement, Sonata Pathetic
                              Beethoven
   Whims . . . . . . . . . . . . Schumann
```

Ralph's piano teacher, Lillian Carpenter, sometimes typed a program when her star student gave a solo recital in Howell or St. Louis. (*Collection of Ralph Sutton*)

Earl Sutton organized a band with his 11-year-old son on piano. The group, which played country dances, later consisted of, *left to right*, the Suttons, Everett Cowgill, Ed Hollander, and the Schappe brothers, Mike and Bud. (*Collection of Harold Sutton*)

MASQUERADE BALL

AT

The Y Dance Hall

1½ Mile North of Hamburg, St. Charles Co.

FRANK MOZGVA, Proprietor

Sat. Feb. 9

8:30 P. M. to 1:30 A. M.

Modern and Old Time Music by

E. R. Sutton and his Band

6 Prizes will be Given for the Best and most Comic Costumes **6**

Each Attendant will receive FREE Admission Ticket to Dance Saturday, Feb. 16th

Refreshments of All Kinds   Everybody Welcome

B. Blackburn, Print, Paxonville

This poster advertised a dance in the 1930s at which Earl Sutton's band provided the music. Each of the musicians earned $3 for an evening's work. (*Collection of Harold Sutton*)

Ralph starred on his high school basketball team. In this photo, taken during his senior year, he stood third from the left in the rear row. Emmett Schierbaum stood to Ralph's right, and Leonard Fuerman was next to Coach Ed Heidbreder. Herman Mang was second from the right in the middle row, and Betsy Fulkerson Combs sat at the far right of the front row. (*Collection of Edward Heidbreder*)

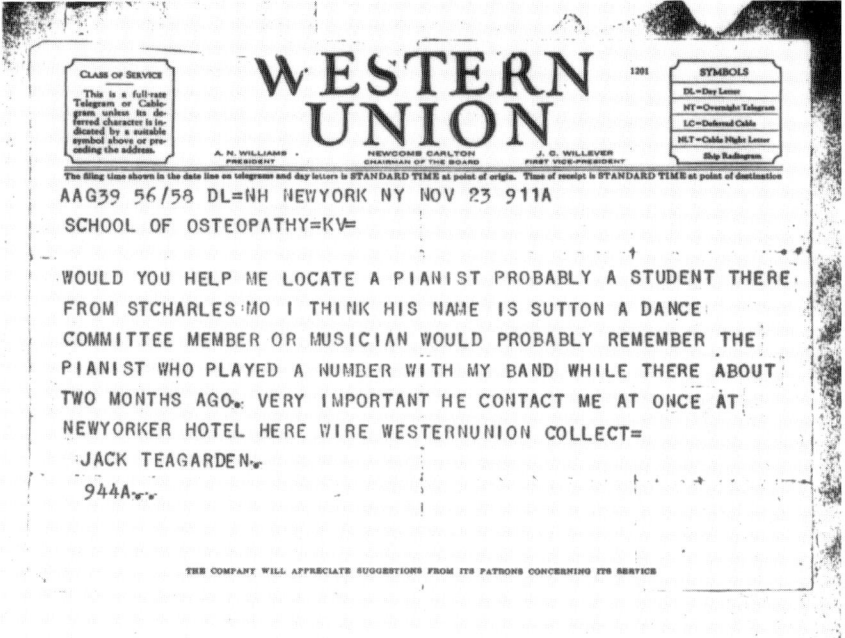

Jack Teagarden sent this telegram shortly after Ralph sat in with his band in 1942. Sutton, a sophomore music major, promptly dropped out of college when the great trombonist invited him to join the band. However, the Army drafted the 20-year-old pianist about two months later. (*Collection of Ralph Sutton*)

Loose Shoes

After his discharge from the Army, Ralph played at a gambling casino and then joined the Joe Schirmer Trio. The combo, with Schirmer on guitar and Jack Stern on bass, drew huge crowds in St. Louis hotels from 1945 to 1947 and also played at the Village Vanguard in New York. (*Collection of Ralph Sutton*)

Here are three of the reasons that St. Louis has been a jazz center for so long: Clark Terry, who was born there and won fame as a triple threat on trumpet, flugelhorn, and scat vocals; Charlie Menees, who in 1945 became the city's first jazz disk jockey; and Ralph Sutton. (*Charlie Menees Collection*)

Wide-eyed Pete Sutton and his older brother, Jeff, enjoyed sitting at the piano with their father as often as possible. (*Collection of Ralph Sutton*)

Loose Shoes

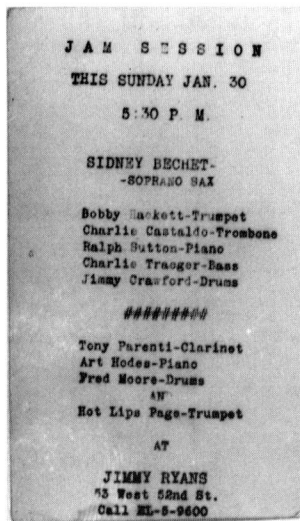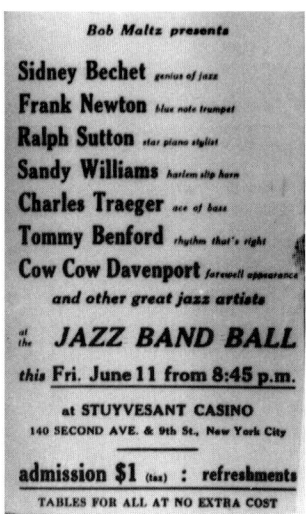

These postcards advertised two of the many jam sessions in New York that featured top jazz musicians of the late 1940s and early 1950s. (*Courtesy of Len Kunstadt*)

Arthur Trappier, *left*, and Albert Nicholas, *center*, appeared with Ralph as a trio at Jimmy Ryan's famous club on 52nd Street in New York. They were playing at the Barrel Bar in St. Louis in 1948 when Eddie Condon invited Sutton to be intermission pianist at his club. (*Collection of Ralph Sutton*)

Jeff Sutton liked to sit in with the band at Eddie Condon's club, to the amusement of, *left to right*, Cutty Cutshall, Wild Bill Davison, Condon, Edmond Hall, Buzzy Drootin, and Bob Casey. Ralph played intermission piano at Condon's from 1948 to 1956, when he and his family moved to California. (*Collection of Ralph Sutton*)

Ralph and Willie the Lion Smith, *fourth from left,* tried out the organ at the Whitfield House, a historic building in Nazareth, Pennsylvania, on a summer day in 1949. Sutton seemed amused as Jonah Jones blew his trumpet while the Lion and Rudi Blesh looked on. Charles Peterson, one of the first great jazz photographers, had brought a number of musicians from New York to play for a wedding at his nearby farm home. (*Photo by Charles Peterson; Courtesy of Don Peterson*)

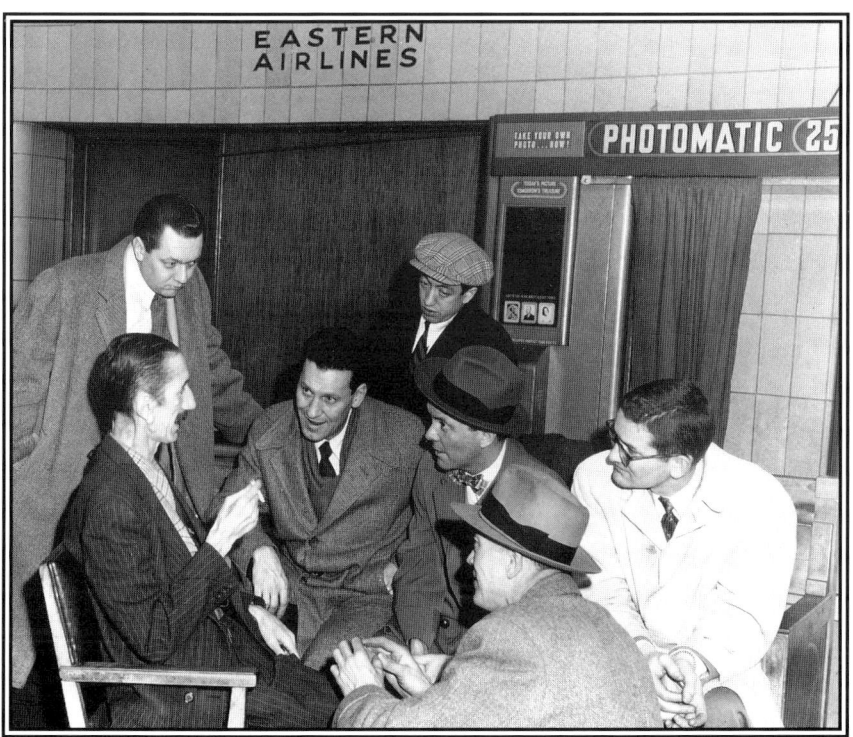

Several members of the Condon gang went to La Guardia Airport to meet Pee Wee Russell's plane early one February morning in 1951. Russell had recently undergone surgery after collapsing with a liver ailment in San Francisco. Looking terribly emaciated, he described his experience to, *left to right,* Gene Schroeder, Bob Casey, Buzzy Drootin, Eddie Condon, Charles Peterson, and Ralph Sutton. (*Photo by Charles Peterson; Courtesy of Don Peterson*)

Loose Shoes

Ralph's parents, Edna and Earl Sutton, posed outside their home in St. Charles, Missouri, in the early 1950s. (*Collection of Barbara Sutton Curtis*)

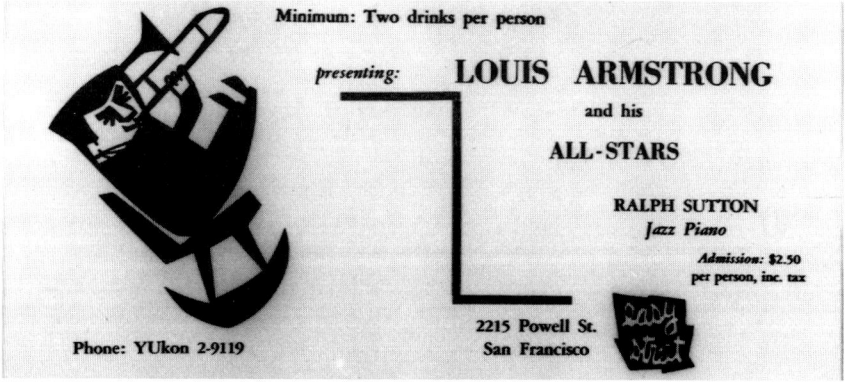

While living near San Francisco during the late 1950s and early 1960s, Ralph played at Turk Murphy's Easy Street and also at Storyville, the Hangover, and a number of other clubs in the area. (*Collection of Ralph Sutton*)

Sutton played many gigs on the West Coast with Muggsy Spanier, who inscribed this 1939 photo. It shows Spanier and Fats Waller, who had shared the billing at the Regal Theater in Chicago. Their clowning tickled Spanier's band, including Rod Cless and Bob Casey, *left,* and Joe Bushkin, who is barely visible at the piano in front of Waller. Spanier wrote, "To Ralph Sutton, who brings alive the great Fats Waller magic." (*Collection of Ralph Sutton*)

Loose Shoes

Ralph joined Bob Scobey's band in 1956 after a stint as intermission pianist at his San Francisco club, Storyville. He replaced Tiny Crump, *center*, who didn't want to go on the road. Sutton played on the record that Scobey made with vocalist Lizzie Miles, *right*. He called this period "the year of the vest" because the musicians wore vests and sleeve garters. (*Courtesy of Moss Photography and Jan Scobey*)

Ralph appears here between Bing Crosby and Bob Scobey during the recording session that produced a swinging LP called *Bing with a Beat*. Sutton's piano is heard throughout behind Crosby, who praised him as "a very sensitive accompanist" and said he couldn't think of anyone better. (*Courtesy of Jan Scobey*)

Clancy Hayes, *second from left,* played on all the records that Ralph made with Scobey. Red Callender was on bass for the session shown here. Sutton starred behind Hayes on the latter's record *Swingin' Minstrel.* (*Courtesy of Shortie Short*)

Ralph tangled with poison ivy in 1957 and lost. It produced an infection that spread to his face and prevented him from shaving. Sutton grew what he called "a real Hemingway beard" and wore it for more than a year. (*Collection of Ralph Sutton*)

Loose Shoes

Earl and Edna Sutton visited their children—Janice, Barbara, and Ralph—in California during the summer of 1963. (*Harold E. Curtis*)

This photo of Sunnie Sutton was taken in 1961, when she ran the Speakeasy Room of the Gaslight Club in New York. Sunnie and Ralph met three years later. (*Collection of Ralph Sutton*)

Loose Shoes

During the winter of 1964, after the breakup of his first marriage, Ralph played at Sunnie's Rendezvous in Aspen, Colorado. He performed with, *left to right,* Edmond Hall, Deane Billings, and Clancy Hayes. (*Collection of Ralph Sutton*)

Ralph and his sister Barbara gave the audience at the Rendezvous a special treat—and had a wonderful time themselves—when they swung through several numbers together at the same piano one night in August 1968. (*Harold E. Curtis*)

Loose Shoes

In 1971, when Ralph's biography was conceived, the World's Greatest Jazzband consisted of, *standing left to right,* Eddie Hubble, Gus Johnson, Yank Lawson, Bob Haggart, and Ralph Sutton; and, *sitting,* Billy Butterfield, Vic Dickenson, Bud Freeman, and Bob Wilber. (*Copyright © by Hickox Productions, Phoenix*)

Ralph picked some juniper berries for Ruth Shacter to sample during a long walk through the woods near his home in 1974.

Boozer, *left,* and Bogart wanted to resume the walk, but Ralph sat contentedly on his "thinking rock" for a while longer.

Loose Shoes

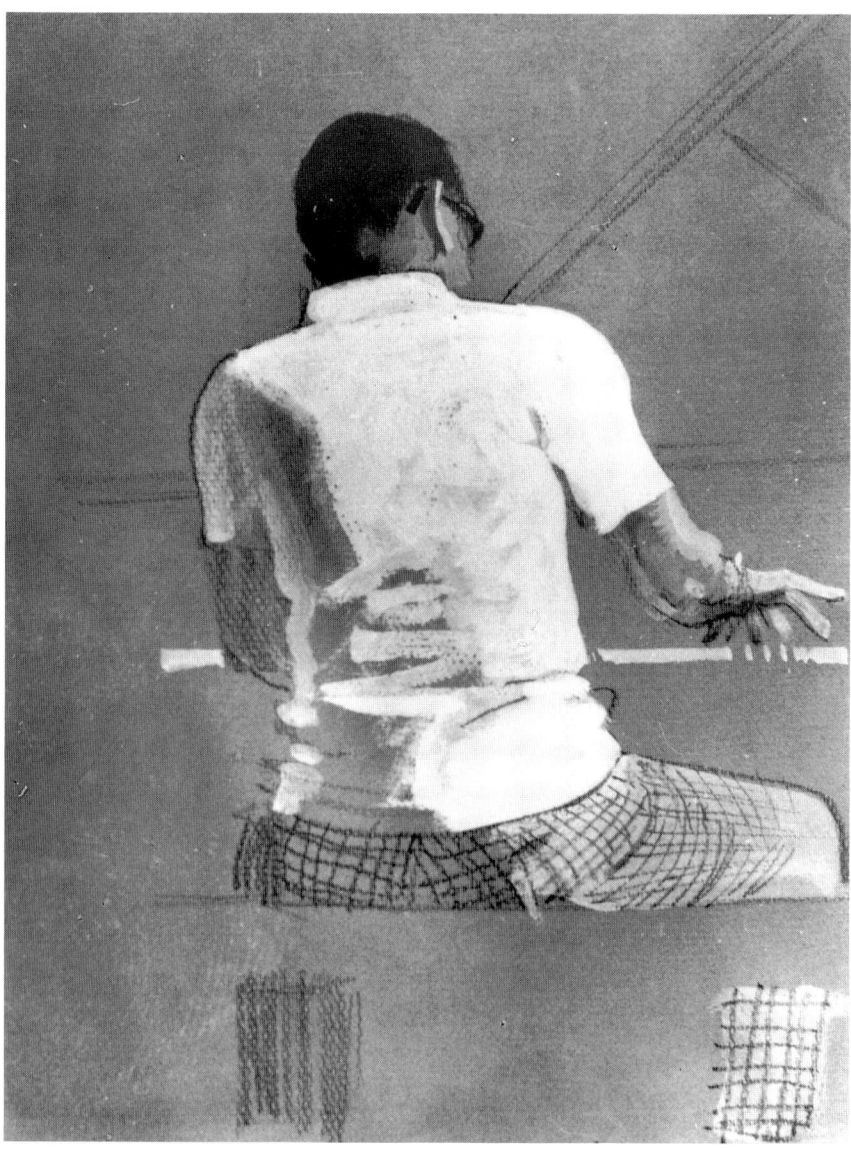

Artist John Falter, a close friend of Ralph's, drew these sketches of Sutton in 1973. He made the above drawing at the Odessa Jazz Festival and later showed the pianist stomping away at Dick Gibson's jazz party in Colorado Springs. (*By John Falter*)

Loose Shoes

Ralph didn't bother to put on his shoes or even tuck in his shirt much of the time while staying with the author and his wife during a gig in Chicago in 1973.

Sutton intrigued Joe Shacter with his habit of grunting or muttering along with the music as he played.

In 1974, a road-weary Ralph left the World's Greatest Jazzband. At the time he dropped out after almost six years, the WGJ consisted of, *left to right in rear,* Yank Lawson, Bob Haggart, and Gus Johnson; and, *in front,* Sutton, Bob Wilber, Bud Freeman, and Bennie Morton. (*Copyright © by Hickox Productions, Phoenix*)

Loose Shoes

Milt Hinton took this photo of Ralph in front of Fats Waller's former home in St. Albans, New York. Sutton holds a plaque that reads: "Residence/ Thomas 'Fats' Waller/Black American Heritage/Trail of Landmarks/In Southeast Queens/Jamaica, New York/A Bicentennial Project/1976." (© *Milt Hinton*)

Chapter **21**

He Spoils Me for Everybody Else

n 1971, Dick Gibson sold his share of the World's Greatest Jazzband to Barker Hickox of Phoenix. Under the direction of Hickox, who had been a partner in the enterprise since 1969, the band's parent corporation, World Jazz, Inc., started producing the WGJ's records itself. Before that time, the band had made four records—two on the Project 3 label and two for Atlantic. World Jazz also began selling the group's records—including the ones on Project 3 and Atlantic—by mail for people who could not find them in a local store.

The band made its first record on the World Jazz label in January 1972. This record, called *Century Plaza*, won the 1973 Jazz Record of the Year award given by *Jazz Journal*. Later in 1972, the band made a Christmas album for which Ralph provided the title—*Hark, the Herald Angels Swing*. Sutton also contributed some beautiful piano on "White Christmas" and sang a rollicking version of "I'll Be Home for Christmas," in which his affinity and affection for Fats Waller are obvious. The other men in the band persuaded Ralph to sing the tune, knowing how enjoyable he can be as a vocalist after being fortified by a few drinks. Sutton agreed—but he refused to sing with the others present. So the band recorded the number minus the vocal; and later, with only a bottle of gin in the studio with him, Ralph added 1½ choruses of the lyrics. At the end of the tune he threw in an ad lib that somehow got excised: "Open up the woodshed, baby. Daddy's comin' home with a load."

Vic Dickenson sings "Jingle Bells" on the record, and Gus Johnson and Dickenson furnish the vocal on "Rudolph, the Red-Nosed Reindeer." Yank Lawson adds the "ho, ho, ho's" at the end of "Rudolph."

The convivial atmosphere of the Christmas album reflects the camaraderie among the members of the band. The fondness of these veteran musicians for one another came not only from their feelings on a personal level, but also from each man's deep respect and admiration for the outstanding talent of all the others in the group.

The depth of the esteem that Ralph's fellow musicians have for his playing can be seen in the following remarks by members of the WGJ and other jazz greats.

Bob Haggart: He spoils me for everybody else. I hated to have another piano player sit in when he was with the band. It really was a big drag. After all those years, Ralph and I thought alike and just sort of followed each other through all the tunes. We played the same bass lines, and we were locked right into each other. The rhythm section played by itself with him in there.

It's a great feeling to play with the guy. He's such a natural, and he plays all the right harmony. Most piano players today want to change the harmony of practically every song. They invert all the chords, and it's a guessing game to try to know what harmony the piano player's going to choose. They're all trying to outdo George Shearing. He was the first to put all the alternate changes in—the bebop harmony that all the New York piano players went through. It's so refreshing to play with Ralph because he puts that stuff down—and rightly so because it's nothing like the original harmony. Those other piano players are like a bunch of parrots, but Ralph is strictly himself.

Bob Wilber: Ralph makes me play better than I do with most pianists. It's a pleasure to have him playing behind you. I think most of the players feel that way, but I know for myself that there's never any feeling of his being in the way of whatever you want to do. Ralph is always there, and yet he always defers to the soloist. He knows where to put the fills and when to be quiet and when to come up behind you.

I did quite a lot of arranging and composing for the band, and at first I'd just write out the chord symbols for Ralph, which is what you do with most piano players. But I found this wasn't the way to do things with Ralph because a chord symbol doesn't really mean that much to him. It doesn't give him a feeling of what I want. So I wrote out a complete piano part—melody and harmony. We'd play it for a few weeks, and I could see him working at it. Ralph is not a quick study musically. It takes him time;

but after he worked the thing out in his mind and really got into the piece, I knew he would play it better than any other piano player in the world because he brought out things in it that I wouldn't have conceived myself. He gets the profundity of whatever he's playing. He reaches the depths of it.

Ralph enjoys a challenge. A fast tempo is meat to him. He loves to play fast, and he does it superbly—the faster the better. We've played a lot of quartet jobs, and we have a wonderful time working together. We like the opportunity when we work just with bass and drums of really challenging ourselves—stretching out and being able to play a lot of things we didn't do with the band.

Gus Johnson: We work together like brothers. In the band, Ralph knew just how to feed the horns to make 'em sound good. We needled each other all the time. If he was right about something, he was wrong with me; and if I was right, I was wrong with him. We had a ball doing a little thing between us with a Charleston beat. I'd put the Charleston in while he was playing along real smoothly, and he'd pretend it made him angry. Then he'd do the same thing later on and I'd raise Cain with him.

He's one of the reasons I moved my family out near Denver. Ralph had urged me to move to Colorado, but I told him I didn't want to because he lived there. I didn't have any trees on my property, and so he gave me some from that beautiful place of his.

Yank Lawson: Ralph plays magnificently. I've played with almost all the great jazz pianists—Joe Sullivan, Bob Zurke, Jess Stacy. God, just name them. I think Ralph holds up with the very best and maybe surpasses most of them. He's probably the strongest two-handed pianist I've ever heard. He also knows how to keep out of the way when he's playing behind a soloist. A lot of people don't understand that it's not always what you play but what you *don't* play that makes you good.

Ralph is a strong, stubborn character, and he's stubborn mostly about the right things. It's good to be stubborn about principles, and Ralph is a principled person. I've never known him to say one thing and do another. He'll tell you the truth—sometimes painfully, but the truth, nevertheless, as he sees it.

Bennie Morton: Have you ever met Ralph Sutton? I say first thing—he's a man. When I say a man, I mean he'll speak his opinion or he might keep his mouth shut; but you believe what he says when he does open his mouth. I respect him for that, whether he plays piano or if he doesn't. But he does play a lot of piano. The piano he plays sounds like a lot of piano players because Ralph Sutton is many people in one.

Many great pianists establish themselves with some of their own numbers that will live as long as there is a Ralph Sutton or someone like him. He plays James P., Joe Sullivan, Bob Zurke, Willie the Lion, Bix Beiderbecke—all those and more with such authority. So when you hear Ralph, his playing of those people sounds just like the original thing.

He can do a show by himself. He makes the audience listen and he makes the musicians listen, even though we've been listening to him all night while we play. He's a fine musician with a classical background, but you don't hear any stiffness in his playing. He has melted classical and jazz together. He has taken advantage of the technique and skill that were given to him first and applied them to his jazz.

Keep your eye on Ralph Sutton and your ears open. You'll certainly hear something.

Bud Freeman: Ralph is a very creative player. There were nights when he knocked us all out with things we'd never heard him play before. He's one of the finest pianists in the world. There isn't anyone who can touch him in the style he plays. His playing shows the influence, of course, of Fats Waller and James P. Johnson, but I think Ralph overcomes that influence because he has such a strong feeling for this style of playing. When I hear him play, I think of Fats and I hear the real thing.

Maxine Sullivan: He sends me. He brings out more of what I have to offer than anyone else I know. Some musicians can be pretty stiff, but working with Ralph is like rolling off a log. I don't think he realizes his own strength.

As a singer, I need all the support I can get. I need somebody behind me. At the same time, I don't need anybody who's going to cut my throat. I look forward to working with Ralph every chance I get. I wish I could hire him, but he's out of my reach. I don't have enough work to offer him, and so I just have to take him whenever I can get him.

He Spoils Me for Everybody Else

Bobby Rosengarden: If you're a drummer, you know within four bars when you play with a piano player, a guitar player, or a bass player whether you're going to be compatible. I played two bars with Ralph and I knew immediately that ours was a marriage made in heaven. Strangely enough, I've never had much interest in the kind of piano he plays. I've always liked the more modern styles. But I've never played with anyone who's got better time. My God, he's got a swinging metronome built into his head. I marvel at it because it never varies or wavers. It's always in good taste, and it always swings. He communicates with me in his playing, and I feel the emotion in it. Gee, I love the way he plays. He amuses me and pleases me.

When I play with the band, we play pretty much the same numbers every night, but Ralph played new solos all the time. He kept me interested and made me want to play. I played softly—not only because I knew it was the smart thing to do, but also so I could hear him. He's a very good accompanist because he knows when to play and when not to play. He leaves holes. When I started at NBC years ago, someone told me, "It ain't the notes you play; it's the rests." Ralph knows that better than anybody.

As a person, Ralph is a pussycat. He's a gentleman in the real sense of the word. A gentle man.

Jess Stacy: He is a superb piano player and a great guy. There's nothing upstage about him. I really admire the way he plays. He's one of the few piano players who uses both hands, and it's sure nice to know that a player like Ralph is still around. I can't say enough good things about him. He's one of the greats, and I hope he gets the recognition he deserves.

Bobby Hackett: There are, sadly, very few two-handed pianists in the jazz world these days, and I, among many others, consider Ralph the current heavyweight champ. He's the first and foremost interpreter of the pianistic genius of Bix Beiderbecke, and he also has plenty going of his own.

Teddy Wilson: He's the only jazz pianist I know who plays the whole history of jazz—ragtime, Bix, Fats, Willie the Lion, James P., and on up to the present. He's a complete musician—even plays Chopin, Brahms, and Bach beautifully.

Jack Lesberg: He certainly sounded beautiful with the World's Greatest Jazzband. He made that band sound so rich and big. He's so rhythmical, and he fed the various players all the time. He accompanied the others when he should, and he was out in front when he should have been. For all his apparent shyness and quietness, it's a whole new ball game when he gets to the piano.

Billy Maxted: He is my favorite pianist. Ralph to me is Fats Waller reincarnated. Come to think of it, he's also Willie the Lion, Meade Lux Lewis, Pete Johnson, and a few others.

Nappy Lamare: I've played with a lot of piano players, but I think I like Ralph better than any of them. It's a pleasure to work with him. His rhythm is up there all the time, and he stays on top of the beat.

Matty Matlock: What a big, marvelous sound he gets out of a piano. He's got wonderfully big hands and plays beautiful stride. One of the finest pianists around.

Willie the Lion Smith (from a 1961 interview with Johnny Simmen and an article in *Jazz Journal*): I saw Ralph on TV a few weeks ago, and he was just fantastic. For many years, the Lion hasn't heard a young man play such great piano. Sutton has completely mastered the idiom.

Ralph is an exceptionally good reader and a real good two-handed pianist. He can read and play all those tough compositions at sight—the really tough ones, I mean. To be truthful, I don't know of anyone who can play "Morning Air" as well as he can—except the composer, of course. But no joking, he is a sweet man and a fine pianist. One of the greatest compliments an artist can get is when another artist writes to him, and I have received long, lovely letters from Sutton.

Chapter **22**

The Trademark of a Truly Great Pianist

he appreciation of the work of a Ralph Sutton is greatly enhanced for those who have the ear to concentrate on one voice of a musical ensemble while absorbing the total sound of all the voices. Such a person was James L. Gordon, chairman of the music department of East Waterloo High School in Waterloo, Iowa. In 1973, Gordon was a member of the Waterloo Teachers Community Concert Association, which brought the World's Greatest Jazzband to the city during a long fall tour. He had no knowledge of Ralph's playing until a memorable November evening when he and his wife, Helen, heard the band.

"Ralph's piano work was the foundation for the whole group," Gordon said. "His firm and full chord progressions led the band and soloists smoothly and surely from one chorus to the next and enabled each individual member to be creative in his own style. His fill-in playing with the ensemble added that certain style and taste that are the trademark of a truly great pianist. And what a left hand! We marveled at his fluid, deft touch that beat out the rhythm so steadily while producing so much beautiful melody. I can't understand why I hadn't heard about this man. We were all surprised by his talent."

Helen Gordon was likewise impressed by Ralph's playing: "Everybody marveled at his seemingly effortless touch, his driving rhythm, and the extra sound he created at the piano. Some friends of ours insisted that he must have had an invisible counterpart because it sounded like a piano duo was performing."

The Gordons gave a reception for the band at their home after the concert, and Helen Gordon found herself with a companion in the kitchen. "Ralph quietly picked up a bar stool," she recalled, "parked himself out of the way across from my workbench, and visited and sampled as I busied about preparing the food. He got a few first nibbles of meats and breads and relishes and seemed quite happy to do just that.

"I was enthralled by this guy who sat on the stool right smack in the kitchen hallway and leaned across my counter top to exchange little pleasantries, accept an occasional tidbit, and try to help me find my drinks or mix me another when thirsty guests walked off with them—or perhaps he or I unconsciously downed them during our conversation."

If the WGJ's performance in Waterloo was memorable for the Gordons, the concert in nearby Marshalltown the next night was even more so for two old friends of Ralph's, Armon Adams and Gail Albright. Adams had succeeded Jim Gordon in 1950 as director of the instrumental music program of the Marshalltown schools. He had lost contact with Ralph after their dance band days in Kirksville, Missouri. Albright, a member of the speech faculty at Northeast Missouri State University in Kirksville, had heard Ralph at Condon's and stayed at his home in Hastings-on-Hudson during a January weekend in 1952. He had not seen his former high school English student since then.

In October 1973, Adams wrote Ralph and expressed the hope that they would be able to get together during the band's stay in Marshalltown. Albright drove up for the concert from his home in La Plata, Missouri. He planned to have dinner at Adams' home, a couple of blocks from the high school auditorium where the band would be performing. Late that afternoon, upon hearing that the band's bus had arrived in town, Adams and Albright hurried over to the school to invite Ralph to join them for dinner and a reunion.

"It was an intensely exciting moment just to see and be with the man who had grown out of that strapping high school kid I had known and enjoyed so much," Albright said. "We found him freshening up backstage, and I couldn't help feeling a surge of relief at Ralph's appearance—clean-shaven and close-cropped hair—just as he had so immaculately kept himself groomed in high school. He accepted Armon's invitation for dinner, which especially pleased us because we had learned that the band would be leaving town immediately after the concert. We had a wonderful reunion; but the time arrived when we had to share Ralph with the rest of Marshalltown, and so we took him back to the auditorium.

The Trademark of a Truly Great Pianist

"One by one, the truly greats of the World's Greatest Jazzband strolled onto the stage—Yank Lawson, Bob Haggart, Bud Freeman, Bob Wilber, Gus Johnson, Bennie Morton, and Ralph Sutton. They were a refreshing sight in their navy blazers, gray slacks, white shirts, and dark ties. I hadn't seen such a well-groomed bunch since too far back to remember.

"Then came the music. And what music it was! I had never before experienced quite the thrill that I did upon hearing that band for the first time. Put such greats together, and what could one expect but the greatest? We were suddenly swept back into the fabulous era of jazz. But the thrill that night came not so much from the great musicianship of the WGJ as from the fact that the man at the piano was my friend and former student.

"After the concert, amidst the backstage hustle of the band to change clothes, pack, accommodate the autograph seekers, and get on the road, our little group got in our last bit of visiting with Ralph as we saw him out the door and onto the bus. Seeing that all were not yet aboard, Ralph got off, again expressed his appreciation to the Adamses for their gracious hospitality, and then grabbed me in the embrace of long-lost buddies. I couldn't help choking up a bit. For, more than anything else, it showed that the great quality of humanism and affection in the heart of that country boy from Howell, Missouri, had been unchanged by the years or by his success. It tore me up and made parting even harder."

Adams was far too excited to sleep that night, and so he wrote down his thoughts of the evening:

"Tonight, the World's Greatest Jazzband came to town to play a concert, and with it came a friend of long ago and now a piano great, Ralph Sutton.

"Just an hour ago, I was sitting in the fourth row center listening to this renowned group of all-time jazz all stars. Somehow, funny as it seems, I think it has left me with a sort of nostalgic sadness. Thirty-two years ago, I played in a college dance band with Ralph. A few years later, circumstances dictated that I choose between a life with the big bands and teaching, and I settled for the home life and the teaching profession. Although I've never felt it was a wrong decision, tonight I find myself reflecting on what might have been. Maybe I've missed it all more than I care to admit—perhaps not the bus rides and one-night stands; but there's nothing that can compare with the close professional ties, the applause, and, above all, the thrill of the sound of fine solo and ensemble work.

"Tonight, for an hour or so before the concert, Ralph and I found time to dig up a few old memories. Although I had trouble recalling the names of the musicians in that college band of ours, Ralph remembered almost all of them. We both got a chuckle recalling that we played three-hour dances for $3 apiece—and at times had to drive several miles to play.

"I lost contact with Ralph except for reading of his success. Then, about a year ago, while I was watching the World's Greatest Jazzband on TV, there he was—the same familiar figure and style that I remembered from so many years ago. I could hardly believe it when I learned a few days later that this group had been booked into our town for a concert the following year.

"Tonight, they were here. They played, and now they are gone again. Each one a top-notch musician and one of the greats. And there, in the middle of it all, whether as soloist or supplying background for someone else, sat Ralph, with hardly a body movement perceptible, but with hands moving as effortlessly as ever and with a discerning taste that left nothing to be desired. Whether on an up-tempo tune or a ballad, he always played just right, with the other musicians seemingly taking for granted that he always would.

"Ralph is much as I remember him. He was always quiet and unassuming, just as he is now; but underneath it all is a deep emotional quality that very few can detect. It was there tonight when we had to leave him on the steps of the bus. There just aren't 32 years left to wait to see him again.

"Yes, tonight I renewed an old acquaintance—or maybe two: jazz, and the guy who plays it like he owns it, Ralph Sutton."

Chapter **23**

'Tain't Nobody's Bizness

hortly after Ralph and Sunnie moved from Aspen to Pine, Ralph posted two signs on the narrow dirt road that led to their home. The log house in the Rockies was not easy to find, and Ralph wanted to discourage unwanted callers even further with the signs. The house could not be seen from the point where the signs warned, *Private Drive* and *No Trespassing*. But anyone who ignored them was soon confronted by four barking Saint Bernards that moved surprisingly fast for their size. Unless Ralph or Sunnie called them off, a friendly welcome was unlikely; though Ralph liked to joke that none of the dogs had actually attacked anyone—yet.

One June morning in 1972, Ralph waited in his front yard for my wife and me to arrive. He was deeply tanned, unshaven, and wearing only a pair of khaki shorts. Seven months earlier, I had come up with the notion of writing a book about him, and Sutton had said fine, go ahead. But Ralph had been—and still was—more than a little skeptical about the whole idea. The thought that anyone would seek him out with the objective of writing such a book amazed him. He doubted that his life had been interesting enough to warrant a biography, and he was even more dubious that anybody would ever get around to writing it. Being basically a somewhat shy man, he was a bit embarrassed by the prospect of a book about Ralph Sutton's life. But he was also rather pleased.

So now Ruth and I were driving up to get together with him and start gathering material to be used in the preparation of the biography. Ralph had given us detailed directions on how to reach his home, but he was pretty sure we would drive right by. Sure enough, an unfamiliar car moved slowly past about a quarter of a mile away. Ralph waved wildly, and the car turned toward the house. A couple of minutes later, he was greeting his guests with a wide grin while assuring Boozer, Ella, and Mahalia (Amy had died) that the visitors were relatively harmless. The Saint Bernards, after extensive precautionary sniffing, finally lumbered off into the shade and resumed their midmorning nap.

Pine, an unincorporated area with a population of about 250, lies almost 1,500 feet higher above sea level than does Denver, the Mile High City. The community has received scant attention through the years except for the time that President Dwight D. Eisenhower did some fishing there. When Ruth and I arrived, we had little idea of how the Sutton Project, as it came to be called, would pretty much dominate our lives for the next three years.

After welcoming Ruth and me, Ralph showed us around his place—the house; the woodshed; the dogs' shed with its thick carpet of hay and the adjacent fenced play area; and, finally, Sutton's pride and joy, a one-hole outhouse. "It comes in quite handy when the electricity goes off during a storm," he explained. Every year, the one-holer cost him an extra $15 in property tax because the county considered it a taxable building. Trees surrounded the Sutton property, and the snow-capped mountains provided an impressive backdrop in the distance.

The taped interviewing for the book began after Ralph had cooked mammoth hamburgers for lunch, serving them with his hot sauce on the side. Ruth swears she can still taste the large forkful of the stuff that she unsuspectingly swallowed—to her immediate regret and her host's considerable amusement. She and I had thought that lunch would come from the huge pot of stew that was simmering on the stove and filling the kitchen with its delicious aroma. The stew, however, was for the Saint Bernards. Ralph and Sunnie kept a pot of it brewing almost continuously.

Ralph and I spent the afternoon sitting in the sun as he took me through his life and answered what seemed to be endless questions and silly requests for details and amplification. Toward the end of the third cassette, Ralph tangled with Ruth after saying that he loved Bach "because he swung." Ruth had just joined us, and Ralph was replying to her question about whether he had any interest in classical music. She was a fine classical pianist who had earned a master's degree in music on a scholarship by serving as accompanist for all student vocal groups at Northwestern University.

"How can you say Bach swings?" Ruth asked. "I play him, but he doesn't swing for me."

"You're a music major and you're asking me that?" Ralph kidded. "You can make his music swing. Some fugues and preludes of his. . ."

"Do you really make the music swing?" Ruth interrupted. "You play around with it, don't you?"

"No," Ralph replied. "I try to play it as he wrote it. Bach had a sense of rhythm in what he did. Take 'Solfeggietto,' for example."

Ruth began singing the theme of the famous piano solo, and Ralph joined in by snapping his fingers on the offbeat.

"You're right!" she laughed. "He *does* swing."

"You could have a drummer with you playing the brushes," Ralph suggested—and he began to sing "Solfeggietto" himself, supplying the beat of the brushes with his hands. The effect was terrific, especially with Boozer panting in rhythm.

"That's beautiful," Ruth exclaimed. "I never would have thought of it."

Sunnie had left for the Navarre before Ruth and I arrived. That evening, she drove up and met Ralph and us at a rustic restaurant overlooking a sparkling mountain lake. During dinner, Sutton was obviously not too pleased when we told how a blooper of his had given us many chuckles. On the 1968 *Jazz in the Troc* record, Peanuts Hucko changes key on "Just a Closer Walk with Thee," but Ralph doesn't get around to changing until a couple of bars later. The effect is something less than melodious, especially when one reads Dick Gibson's comment in the album notes that "the song gradually builds to its powerful climax through a series of exciting key changes."

"I remember when I played that clunker," Ralph said. "I didn't know it was going to be on a record; and when I heard it, all I could think was, 'Oh, shit, they could have done better than to include that one.' I think I've learned to laugh at my mistakes by now, and they don't bother me as much as they used to. I've forgotten about that 'Closer Walk' thing—but I *haven't* forgotten."

At first, I could not understand how such a superlative artist as Sutton could be so bothered by the clunker's providing some laughs. After all, I thought, even the best of us foul up once in a while. But then I realized that I, a perfectionist in my own work as a copy editor, also felt like a fool when I committed an inexcusable error that provided a few laughs at the office. Playing jazz piano is a hobby for most people, but it is Sutton's *work*.

Ralph excused himself from the table immediately after I asked the waitress for the check. He returned a few moments later without a word, and the four of us continued to chat. After a while, when the waitress failed to bring the check, I repeated my request. She replied that the other gentleman had taken care of the matter, including her tip. Sutton just smiled at my protest, took Ruth and Sunnie by the arm, and escorted them from the restaurant.

That afternoon and evening were the first of many such sessions in Pine, in Chicago, and at several spots where the World's Greatest Jazzband was performing on the road. "Now how in hell do you expect me to remember something like *that*?" Ralph would ask in frustration when requested to recall a detail long buried beyond accurate memory. But then he would chuckle and do his best to supply at least an approximately correct answer.

Sutton stayed with us for a week in June 1973, when the World's Greatest Jazzband played at Mr. Kelly's in Chicago. He occupied the room of our son, Joe, who was 13 at the time and away at camp for the summer. Ralph couldn't wait to unpack and put his clothes neatly in the dresser and closet. Throughout his visit, he made a point of not wanting to put anyone out in any way. He subtly let it be known that he preferred doing things for himself and being by himself to a certain extent—but he obviously enjoyed knowing that people were around who cared about him.

"I knew Ralph would be an easy guest because of what Sunnie had told us about him," Ruth said. "I didn't know how easy. He helped out when he could and expected nothing, but he was pleased to accept extra services—Jim's going up to the delicatessen and getting him a corned beef sandwich when he arrived earlier than we expected him; our taking him to a luggage repair shop to have the handle of his suitcase fixed; my doing his laundry; Jim's getting his check cashed for him at the bank; our having his roommate, Bob Wilber, up for dinner; our driving him to Mr. Kelly's the last night, even though we didn't hear the band that night. He couldn't seem to believe that there were people who wanted to do all these things for him."

Millions of Americans spent hours watching the televised Watergate hearings that summer, and Sutton was no exception. He forgot about taking his usual daily walks and listened to much of the testimony. Almost every night after coming home, Ralph drank one or two glasses of buttermilk, liberally seasoned with salt, pepper, and paprika. He has done this on the road for years, wherever buttermilk has been available. He carries innumerable varieties of pills with him and swallows the designated number of each daily. One of the pills eases the discomfort of the gout that he picked up after moving to the mountains, and the rest are vitamins. "Sunnie and I got on a health kick," Ralph explained. "With the life we lead in saloons every night, we gotta have something to make up for what we lose in the food department."

Sutton startled Ruth and me one night after the three of us had come home from Mr. Kelly's. He had a slug of Scotch instead of buttermilk, and we began chatting in the living room. Suddenly, Ralph became infuriated while telling us about the band's rule providing a $100 fine for getting drunk on the job. He said he had been threatened with a fine about a week earlier and declared that he would quit the band if his next paycheck were any smaller as a result. (It wasn't.) Ralph raved on for several minutes, using virtually every profanity in the English language. Ruth and I sat silently, nodding occasionally in agreement. Having seen mild-mannered men turn into vicious characters after drinking too much, I became apprehensive about the possibility of Ralph's causing physical damage to our home or to us. But Ruth couldn't imagine his doing anything harmful. She was right. The raving stopped as suddenly as it had started. Ralph stood up and announced quietly that, having gotten everything off his chest, he was going to bed. He went into the kitchen, downed a glass of buttermilk, and called good night. His door closed a moment later.

"I have a high boiling point most of the time," Sutton said. "The only time I lose my temper is when I feel that some injustice is being done to me or to a good friend of mine. I believe in live and let live. When something disturbs that situation, I blow up."

Ralph likes to joke about what he considers most important in life: "The three most basic things are loose shoes, a tight pussy, and a warm place to take a shit." But he is completely serious when he says that the title of his favorite tune sums up his philosophy toward life—"'Tain't

Nobody's Bizness."* This attitude explains his great annoyance at people who ask him to play certain tunes.

"I think it's none of their damn business what I play," he insists. "If they come to hear me play, I'll play what I want to play. If they don't like it, they can get out. Some people ask me to sing, but I'm not that crazy about singing. I won't do anything that doesn't come naturally to me.

"I just can't go out and promote myself or have myself promoted either. I hate anybody who's overbearing, and you need an overbearing booker or manager to put you across with the public. You need somebody who's really obnoxious. I've never cared to go that route. I've always preferred to do it my own way."

Ruth thinks Ralph reacts with the philosophy of a concert pianist toward people who request various numbers: "A concert pianist certainly doesn't expect to accept requests. He plays his program, which *he* has chosen. If the audience requests an encore, *he* decides what he'll play. No one asks him to play any particular number. If an artist is known for a certain favorite, perhaps he'll play it—but that would be *his* decision.

"When Ralph sits down at the piano in one's home, he plays everything—'Echo of Spring,' 'Love Lies,' and even the swinging jazz numbers—as concert pieces. He plays them so dramatically and so spectacularly that no one dares utter a word. In a club, people are drinking and have no inhibitions about talking or yelling out requests. But when this guy plays in a home situation, you're forced to listen and not say a word—if you care at all about Ralph. His complete seriousness about his playing compels you to be completely quiet, even if you don't want to be. It's like watching a concert pianist at work."

Sutton also has great resentment of authority, which he believes started after he was drafted: "I really resented that goddamn Army. The blacks were segregated from the whites, and I used to think how we were fighting

---

*During a 1941 interview, Fats Waller named "'Tain't Nobody's Bizness" as the first tune he had recorded. Excerpts from the interview appear in *"Fats" in Fact*, Laurie Wright's book on Waller published in 1992. Wright, the editor of *Storyville* magazine, points out that Waller erred. The biodiscography section of the book shows that Waller recorded "'Tain't Nobody's Bizness" and "You Got Ev'rythng a Sweet Mama Needs but Me," accompanying vocalist Sara Martin on both tunes, about December 1, 1922. He had recorded two piano solos, "Muscle Shoals Blues" and "Birmingham Blues," around October 21, 1922. Maurice Waller, in his biography of his father, also lists "'Tain't Nobody's Bizness" on Fats Waller's second recording date.

for democracy and at the same time we had a bunch of asshole Southern crackers in the cadre at Camp Roberts who ordered me around. I made up my mind that no son of a bitch was going to give me any trouble after I got out.

"I've often wished I had been born black. I started out listening to Fats, of course, and I've had so many dear friends who were black. They always seemed to know how to have a good time. It's a lot more fun playing for blacks who are really hip and swinging than it is to play for the majority of whites. I have such a warm feeling with blacks. There's a lot of love between us, and you can't beat that."

Ralph vetoed only one thing about his biography. I had originally chosen John Theobold's first words to Sutton—"You sure don't play like a white boy"—as the title of the book. Ralph had no objection to using the Theobold quote as a chapter heading, but he felt strongly about seeing it on the cover. "The title is good in many ways, but I would prefer a different one," he wrote me. "Sunnie thinks it sounds like putting the white race down; but the race thing never occurs in my thinking, though I despise a lot of vanilla people. Jim, when John Theobold said that to me, it was a hell of a compliment and I loved him immediately. But it's such a personal, down deep thing with me. I don't want to spread it around too much."

The generation gap closed a bit during the 1973 gig at Mr. Kelly's, where the World's Greatest Jazzband shared the bill with a country-rock group called the Mission Mountain Wood Band. One night, a table of about a dozen teenagers made as much noise cheering for jazz as for the music they admittedly had come to hear. They sat just a few feet from the piano, and I asked two of them what they thought of Ralph's playing. I also asked them, though they had never heard of Sutton, what kind of a person they thought he was, based solely on his playing.

Steve Giese in particular was bowled over by Sutton's artistry: "He amazed me, the way his fingers moved so fast up and down the keyboard. He stood out because the piano seems like such a rigid instrument that creativeness coming from it is more enthralling than when it comes from other instruments.

"He seems to be a man who would pick up the special things in life—like noticing a flower growing out of a junk pile, or a certain pattern in a cloud in the sky. Just the special little beautiful things that some people don't notice. He struck me that way because of his sensitivity with music. I think music is one of the special beautiful things in life, and he's so much a part of music that there'd be no way he couldn't pick up those other things."

The dissimilar music of the two bands affected Debbie Kasinecz in slightly contrasting ways: "When I hear Mission Mountain, I've got to clap my hands. I couldn't sit still if I wanted to. But jazz is the greatest stuff in the world. It isn't the type of music to clap your hands to; it's the type to sway your body to. I watched the pianist's fingers, and he excited me and everybody else in the place with the fastness and lightness of his playing. He looks real serious when he plays the piano, but I have a feeling that he's a blast. He looks like he can really live life."

Ralph got a big kick from the teenagers' comments, especially one of Giese's remarks. "He's right," Sutton murmured. "I *would* see a flower growing out of a junk pile."

Marge Kathan, a professional artist, spent a couple of evenings at Mr. Kelly's with Ruth and me. Sutton impressed her deeply as both man and musician: "He struck me as one of the few people you meet along the way whom you feel is worthwhile, with a depth that would take some time to get to know. He is a dignified person and appears sophisticated—but it is a sophistication born of an agreeable shyness rather than worldliness. He is charming in an almost old-fashioned, courtly way—and very attractive!

"His intimate knowledge of the piano is so expressive that it seems the keyboard is part of the man. His style seems perhaps more lack of a style. He is not flamboyant; one is impressed by his sensitivity and strong control. His power at the piano is so controlled and part of the whole that it is difficult to isolate him from the rest of the band when an ear not so attuned attempts to do so.

"I kept wishing I had the musical background to fully appreciate technically and intellectually the imagination behind what he was doing, in addition to enjoying the emotional impact of the music. When he had a solo, I was mesmerized by the facility of his fingers and the almost casual ease with which he faultlessly ripped off fast, difficult passages. He seems very dignified and almost reticent. Taking a bow appears to be an obligation he would like to eliminate."

My mother, a clinical psychologist in Chicago, had looked forward to meeting Ralph ever since she learned that I was writing a book about him.

Helen S. Shacter, upon being introduced to Sutton, noted what she described as his gentle, diffident smile and his firm, nondiffident handshake. She thought "his quiet, pleasant manner held a kind of wariness," and she wondered if he had once been kicked hard and had never been too sure when another painful experience might occur.

"Ralph plays with complete assurance," she said, "and he must find considerable satisfaction and pleasure in what he does. Music is undeniably a large and enjoyable part of his life, but it is not his whole life. He is a very human, sensitive person and enjoys telling others of the great pleasure he finds in long walks alone through the woods and in the beauty of his surroundings at home—the mountains, the trees, and the wildflowers. Perhaps he finds a special satisfaction there, with no possible criticism, disagreement, or rejection. His dogs provide silent companionship and the devoted affection and complete acceptance needed for true contentment.

"With people, he possibly is merely cautious, preferring to try out a relationship before venturing into any involvement, however casual. Yet, with all the caution, he seems to find scarcely concealed enjoyment in personal contact that is responsive. He finds such contact pleasant and desirable—and he relishes it."

Ralph thoroughly relished reading some of the letters and transcribed tape manuscripts that had accumulated for the Sutton Project. He read Sunnie's comments first, and later he asked to hear the tapes made by the other musicians in the band. Bennie Morton's thoughts almost made him cry. Ralph said the experience of having other people describe their feelings about him had made him a stronger person. He added that he realized he was not all he wanted to be as a human being.

Sutton said again that he had been extremely dubious about the whole project at first. My terrific and continued enthusiasm, he declared, had made him keep going with it. He said he had no idea that his life could be so interesting, but he believed it now and was more than anxious to read the book. Ruth felt that if Ralph could get excited about anything beside Sunnie and the Saint Bernards, he certainly was excited about the prospect of the book.

Ralph also had no idea that *Who's Who in America* had carried a brief entry about him since its 1960-1961 edition. "That's strange," he said. An asterisk indicated that the information on Ralph Earl Sutton was compiled by someone in the publisher's office, not furnished by the subject himself.

A few weeks after leaving Chicago, Ralph played at a jazz party in

Huntington, Long Island, at the home of Thomas J. Morley and his wife, Jane. Whenever Ralph performed in New York, the Morleys were likely to throw a party, with Sutton and several other top jazzmen as playing guests. Billy Butterfield, Bob Wilber, Milt Hinton, and Mousie Alexander also played at the 1973 affair.

Morley, a physician, first met Ralph at Condon's as a Princeton freshman: "I play piano and understood enough about music to appreciate that something very special was happening on the stand. After we got to know each other, Ralph used to let me sit up there in the late hours, after the club had thinned out. I'd watch his left hand in awe. One night, just before closing, I played a more or less verbatim version of his recording of 'Keepin' Out of Mischief Now.' It amused him, and he commented that it was 'very flattering.'

"I had a great interest in his style and technique and must have badgered the poor man endlessly with questions. If they ever bothered him, he never let me know it; he always maintained the big grin and tried to cooperate. But I never was able to learn anything detailed about the music from Ralph. It seemed to be something he simply couldn't describe."

The guests at the party included Marty Bruehl, an old friend of Ralph's, who made Sutton grimace by jokingly asking him while he was swinging away, "What's stride piano? Is that it?" People had bugged Ralph with such questions through the years, but he still found it difficult to understand why the answers were not obvious. "My first reaction is that I wish they wouldn't bother me with questions like that," he said. "But then I try to explain what stride is. I tell them it's got a swingin' left hand that you walk with—but then I have to explain what walkin' with it means. It seems so obvious to me what stride piano is that I can't see why everybody doesn't know. It's just swing piano."

Ralph stayed with Ruth and me again one night in October 1973 during a long tour of the band. Our son, who had been at camp during the gig at Mr. Kelly's, was understandably eager to hear Sutton play a little at home. After I had finished a session of interviewing, Joe asked Ralph if he would mind playing a number or two sometime before the end of his visit. Sutton jumped up and asked, "What's the matter with right now?" He strode, rather than walked, to the piano and began to play "Willow, Weep for Me" before I could even get the tape-recording equipment set up. Then he tore into a version of "Handful of Keys" even lustier than the one that had set the audience on fire the night before in Lincoln, Illinois.

Joe asked Ralph about his habit of sometimes moving his lips while he plays. On many of Sutton's records, he can be heard grunting or muttering along with the music. Bill MacPherson, in the liner notes for one of the Blue Angel albums, described the sound as a "subterranean mumble." Ralph does this especially when he is going all out on a number or ripping off a solo. "I think I began doing it in St. Louis when I was just starting out," he said. "I guess it helps me concentrate; but I'm not always conscious of it, and sometimes I catch myself doing it. I'm just making up licks and swinging along with myself."

Ralph has a charming description of himself at the keyboard: "When I play, I'm making love to the piano. There's a certain rapport between the instrument and me."

Ruth, Joe, and I drove Ralph up to Waukegan the next night and helped him get settled in his room in one of the crummiest hotels any of us had ever seen. As he always does on the road, Sutton checked the bathroom first, to make sure it had an adequate supply of toilet paper and a toilet that worked. Then he gazed sadly at the whistling steam radiator and the faded paint on the walls of the narrow room. He sat down on the bed and sighed, "And you wanted to be a musician, Ralph."

Joe was enthralled by the whole experience of spending so much time with Sutton and hearing him play with the band two nights in a row, in Lincoln and Waukegan. He wrote down his thoughts: "When Ralph plays, he doesn't play with gusto. His hands do, but he doesn't. He's like a train plugging along. He never looks at the audience; he looks away, unlike the others. I don't think he likes to bow more than necessary. In Lincoln, Yank had to tell him to bow again after one of his solos. He tries to be a showman, but I think he is just too timid. At Waukegan, for instance, he walked over to Gus during 'Carolina in the Morning' with a mind to do something, but he didn't. He walked back to the safety and security of the piano.

"When he was at our house, he didn't talk much most of the time. He let others do the talking, and he answered in monosyllables if someone asked him a question. He always seems to be thinking of someone else. For example, as soon as we got home after driving up from Lincoln, he apologized for taking over my room. Also, after working one-nighters for two months, he played the piano for me immediately after I asked him to. When he played, he just sat there.

"Ralph seems to be able to relax with people he likes. We had dinner at a restaurant in Waukegan, and he talked like Maudie Frickert and told all sorts of jokes. I think he gets lonely, especially when he waved to us from backstage before the concert. I think he gets emotional rarely, but he did when we said good-bye backstage. He shook hands with me, but then he got a little choky and hugged me, too. He was something else!"

During the backstage farewell, Ralph first hugged Ruth and kissed her. "Joe, you old son of a gun," he said as he bent to hug the boy. Then Ralph turned to me. "Goddammit," he said, "I'm going to kiss you, too." And he did.

In November 1973, a remarkable woman named Leslie Johnson did the world of traditional jazz a tremendous favor. She published the first issue of *The Mississippi Rag*, inaugurating an abundant and matchless monthly source of news items and feature stories about musicians and events and everything related to them.

Johnson grew up in Bloomington, Minnesota, a Minneapolis suburb, and enjoyed going to the Emporium of Jazz to hear the Hall Brothers band and the visiting musicians, including Ralph, who played there. She wanted to learn something about the musicians but found herself stymied.

"I knew nothing about them, and there wasn't a good resource," she said. "The library had *Jazzmen* and other old books that were very good, but they had nothing on any of the younger musicians or current information about people like Turk Murphy. The Minneapolis and St. Paul papers do a poor job covering jazz, and there were no periodicals. There wasn't anything."

The 31-year-old Johnson had met Butch Thompson shortly before getting the idea of starting a publication devoted to traditional jazz. Thompson played both piano and clarinet but at the time was on clarinet with the Hall Brothers. He later became known as an outstanding pianist and a featured performer on Garrison Keillor's radio program "A Prairie Home Companion." Thompson was an editor for a suburban newspaper, and Johnson asked him what he thought of her idea and if he would write for her.

Thompson went for the idea, noting that no periodical existed of the type she envisioned. He introduced Johnson to Paige Van Vorst, an auditor by trade, whom she called a "walking encyclopedia of jazz." Thompson and Van Vorst worked with her on the first issue and continued to provide invaluable assistance through the years. So did Jody Hughes and Debbie Peterson, her sisters. Her husband, Dennis, from whom she was later divorced, also worked with her from the beginning. The Johnsons, both journalists, had two children, Tony and Renee, who were 6 and 3 years old when their mother started the *Rag*. They lived with her after the divorce.

Leslie Johnson named her publication for the first published rag, which came out in 1897 and was written by William H. Krell, a Chicago bandleader. One day while Johnson was trying to decide on a name, she and her husband were listening to Turk Murphy's record of "The Mississippi Rag."

"Dennis asked me the name of the tune," she said, "and when I told him he yelled, 'That's it!' I wanted the name of the paper to have something to do with the Mississippi River, which flows down to New Orleans and has its headwaters in Minnesota. I was going to be publishing a tabloid newspaper, and newspapers are sometimes called rags. It all seemed to fit."

Starting with the third issue, the *Rag* carried a subtitle, *The Voice of Traditional Jazz and Ragtime*. The name of the editor and publisher appeared as Leslie Carole Johnson until the April 1979 issue, in which she dropped her middle name.

"I had never used 'Carole,' but I added it because people wouldn't have known I was a woman," Johnson said. "It was strange to be called Leslie Carole by so many people. As soon as the *Rag* got well enough known and I was well enough known, I dropped it because I don't care for that name.

"I wanted to be known as a woman at first because 'Leslie' is ambiguous and I can't stand getting letters addressed to 'Mr. Johnson.' I also wanted to make an impression on people that a woman could make a dent in traditional jazz, which is a male-dominated world.

"I had to get over a lot of traditional thinking on my part because I grew up in the era when it was a man's world. Butch was the first man I ever called. Women didn't call men in the old days, and I had always waited for men to call me. It was a big thing to go to the bank and negotiate a loan for the *Rag* and then, when they said it had to be cosigned, have a fight with the bankers.

"Dragging a lot of those people into the 20th century was a real challenge, and so was dealing with the printers. The printer that I dealt with since the third issue worked only with me. But when I started out, all the men wanted to deal with Dennis or Butch. A lot of subscribers would not address a letter to me. They addressed it to Butch, even though he wasn't the editor. They just couldn't handle dealing with a woman."

Johnson's greatest pleasure from the *Rag* came through many friendships she developed with subscribers and musicians, especially Eubie and Marion Blake. The legendary pianist and composer delighted her because he not only read the paper but genuinely liked it. His wife, one of her favorite people, remembered the details of a number of articles from the *Rag*.

Through the years, Johnson's regard for Thompson and Van Vorst deepened as they worked together. Thompson told her how much he liked Ralph's playing, which was unusual because he didn't like many musicians at the time she began publishing the *Rag*.

"Ralph was one of the few who passed the test," Johnson said. "Butch told me he really swings. He always goes to hear him play when Ralph is at the Emporium or anywhere in the neighborhood. Ralph is one of the few musicians whom he'll go out of his way to hear.

"Butch taught me how to listen to the music. He didn't analyze it, but our tastes are very similar. I liked the music that he liked, but I didn't know why. We spent hours together listening to records. Ralph was one of the people he liked, and I could tell from Butch's reactions what to listen for."

In 1974, for the first time in his career, Ralph became a piano teacher. His student was Bob Hirsch, an academic adviser at the University of Wisconsin in La Crosse, who also led a jazz combo and played at jazz festivals in various parts of the country. Hirsch had admired Sutton's work for almost 25 years. He first heard Ralph play in 1961, in Cincinnati, and did not see him again until 1973. That year, Hirsch got the idea of applying to the National Endowment for the Arts for a grant to study with Ralph. To his great surprise and delight, Sutton enthusiastically agreed to work with him for a week in Pine.

The grant came through, but Hirsch and Sutton almost found themselves without a piano for their week together. The Steinway grand in

Ralph's living room belonged to Jack Lesberg's stepson. It had been there for more than two years, with the understanding that the owner could claim it at any time. On the morning that Hirsch's plane was due in Denver, Lesberg's stepson called and said he would be over that afternoon with a truck to pick up the piano. Ralph managed to persuade him to let the piano stay a while longer.

"Through the years," Hirsch said, "I had tried to emulate Ralph's style of playing. But he does an awful lot of things that I just couldn't pick up off his records. I wanted to learn how to play those things correctly and with the proper fingering. Ralph taught me some of the great classic Fats Waller figures that he does with his right hand. I brought a tape recorder along, and so now I can practice those licks at home. I had never learned to be a really good piano player because I played by ear and never studied correctly. I just played what I heard on records. But Ralph told me the most important thing to do was to practice scales. He got out the Czerny book of scales that he has used for years, and I practiced them every morning for about an hour before we had our session together. I've been practicing them faithfully ever since.

"Ralph's a beautiful guy. I've never been so proud in my life—not only to have been able to study with him, but to be a personal friend of his. I love him."

Sutton thoroughly enjoyed his week with Hirsch: "The teaching really interested me. I showed him some stuff I do in the right hand and how to get into the stride bit. We did some fingering work, and I told him to get a book of Hanon exercises to practice along with the Czerny scales. He was having trouble with the third and fourth because he played a lot of octaves instead of using all the fingers. We spent about three hours together at the piano every day and had a ball."

Late in 1973, the Saint Bernard population at the Suttons' place rose to four again for a few months. A customer at the Navarre told Sunnie he was moving from a house into an apartment. His frolicsome Saint Bernard pup, who had the unlikely name of Bogart, was too big to go along; and so Sunnie took the dog home to Pine. She quit her job in January 1974, shortly before the Navarre was padlocked for nonpayment of taxes. A few weeks later, she started tending bar at the Pump and Derrick, a new club in downtown Denver. At about that time, the Suttons discovered that Mahalia had cancer; a veterinarian put her to sleep. "It makes us very sad, and I get big lumps in my throat," Ralph wrote Ruth and me. "We had to have the same thing done for her mother, Amy, and it took me a long time to get over that."

Ralph was in Honolulu with the World's Greatest Jazzband when Sunnie left the Navarre. Several of her old customers bought her a plane ticket so she could join him there. A friend, Dick Weyrich, called Bob Wilber and told him she was coming. "Everyone in the band knew about it except Ralph," Sunnie remembered. "The guys were going to bring him to the airport to meet my plane, but they were sure he'd suspect something if they gave him some phony reason for driving out there. So I took a cab to the hotel and went up and knocked on Ralph's door. He opened it and just stood there looking at me. He kept saying, 'Honey... Honey... Honey...' I finally asked him if he wasn't going to invite me in."

Ralph said the sight of Sunnie at his door was "the biggest and happiest surprise I've ever experienced."

A few weeks later, in March, the band added Bobby Hackett and Bucky Pizzarelli to its ranks for a record date with Teresa Brewer. Pizzarelli called this record one of the most memorable of his career. His guitar complements the rhythm section beautifully, and he and Sutton are especially pulsating together behind Brewer's vocal on "Keep Your Sunny Side Up." He had first played with Ralph at the Odessa Jazz Party years before.

"I was overwhelmed," Pizzarelli said. "I don't judge musicians on notes. I judge them on the energy they put out when they play. I guess I haven't been wrong, because my favorites have been energy players like Zoot Sims, Benny Goodman, and Yank Lawson. They're all playing the drums at the same time they're playing, and that's what comes to mind about Ralph because he gets that thing going with both hands. He can do it with or without a band, and that's what he was doing all the time. It's all energy, that whole record with Teresa Brewer singing.

"I can sit there and play with Ralph all night long. He listens to you, and you listen to what he's doing, and things start to happen. The fire starts to come out. Ralph starts to roll. He bounces. He gets going. He gets it off the ground. That's the whole ball game—that energy. There's only one guy like that. When he gets it rolling, he never misses."

In a way, Pizzarelli returned to his roots at the Odessa party where he met Sutton. He had eagerly looked forward to seeing that Texas area because of his father's experiences as a teenage cowboy on a ranch there. The cowboy connotation came out when his father gave the nickname Bucky to John Pizzarelli II. Bucky's son, John III, known professionally as John, Jr., became a jazz guitarist, too—and often his partner on gigs. *He* has a son, John IV. It would be nice to relate that John IV, Bucky's grandson, also played guitar. But he was just a year old when *Loose Shoes* was published.

Chapter **24**

My Marriage Comes First and Music Second

A new chapter of Ralph's career began in September 1974, when he left the World's Greatest Jazzband. The grind of spending most of the previous six years on the road had become too much for him to take any longer. That fall, Peanuts Hucko moved back to Denver from Los Angeles. He asked Ralph to join him in a quartet that would have its home base in Denver. Sutton happily accepted the offer from his old friend.

Ralph had been trying for some time to establish such a home base. He wanted to play regularly near his home and go on the road for occasional guest appearances with the WGJ, as Billy Butterfield, Bobby Hackett, Vic Dickenson, and Maxine Sullivan did. Ralph and Gus Johnson had taken a leave of absence from the band in April so they could play what was scheduled to be a steady gig through June at the Oxford Hotel in Denver.

Things looked good the first week at the Oxford. "Gus and I are doing very well," Ralph wrote Ruth and me. "The audience is most receptive. Sunnie and I leave notes to each other on the kitchen table. This Oxford deal is developing into a home base, and it's an opening I've been looking for." But the crowds fell off during the next three weeks, and the hotel canceled Sutton and Johnson.

A couple of years before, Ralph had expressed doubt about leaving the band, despite his dislike of the road. He valued not only his close personal friendship with all the men, but also the incomparable rapport that exists among top performers in any field. Another factor also influenced his thinking. "It's a real drag to be on the road so much of the time," Ralph had said. "But I've committed myself to the band, and I enjoy playing with all the guys. Sunnie and I have talked it over, and we both know that if I stayed around Denver, I'd become just another local piano player. You can't stay in one spot in the music business—unless it's like New York used to be—and I don't make enough for Sunnie to be able to travel with me. I'd be happy to get out of music and get a job that would let me be home all the time, but I don't know what I could do. We might be able to see our way clear one of these days; but in the meantime, it's a damn drag."

The goal of getting off the road was uppermost in Ralph's mind when we spent a week with him in Pine in June 1974. But the ambivalence in his feelings were obvious. One evening, after spending the day going through Ralph's photo albums and scrapbooks looking for possible illustrations for the book, the three of us took a walk with the Saint Bernards. Ralph wanted to show us his "thinking rock," on which he liked to sit and contemplate things in general during walks in the woods. This huge rock had a natural seat that fitted Sutton's rear end perfectly. Ralph suddenly stopped on the dusty dirt road to the woods and told his companions, "Just breathe that air." Then he pointed silently to some beautiful cloud formations. Later, we sat outside listening to Fats Waller's music pour from the living room. Sutton sighed deeply. "This is all I need," he said. "Good music and people I love, like you and Ruth."

On the other hand, Ralph was eager to rejoin the band in New York early in July. "There's nothing I'd rather be doing than playing with those guys," he said. "When the band's really swinging, there's nothing like it. I'm looking forward to seeing all the guys again and playing with them." He took us for a drive one afternoon and commented on a member of a highway construction gang who was waving a red flag at approaching cars. "That wouldn't be a bad way to make a living," Ralph said dryly. "The next time you two come out here, you might see me waving one of those flags."

Bogart, the most playful of the Saint Bernards, apparently developed a crush on Ruth during our visit. He tried to mount her one afternoon in the Suttons' backyard while Ralph and I stood laughing nearby. She finally managed to push the amorous dog away, a task made rather difficult by his size. Ruth laughs about the incident today but did not find it too humorous at the time, especially when neither her husband nor host did anything to help her because they were enjoying the spectacle so much.

Ralph had offers that week to appear in July as guest star with two bands. Buzzy Drootin called from Boston and asked him to appear with the Drootin brothers' combo. Then Peanuts Hucko, who at the time was fronting the Glenn Miller band, wanted Sutton to play with that group at Elitch Gardens. Ralph chuckled when Hucko told him that the pianist with the Miller band "wants to play a concerto every time he has a solo." Sutton had to turn down both offers because he was going to play a jazz festival in Nice, France, with the WGJ.

Ralph renewed friendships with a number of musicians at the festival. They included Bill Coleman, who played trumpet with Fats Waller intermittently in the 1930s and 1940s and had lived in Europe for years; Lucille Armstrong; and Panama Francis. Sutton also wrote that he "had a nice talk with Eubie Blake on the way to the concert one evening. What a great gent."

In Nice, Ralph's affection grew for a couple whom he and Sunnie had known a relatively short time and who became two of their closest friends: "Kenny Davern and his charming wife, Elsa, were there. I kept an eye out for them because it was so relaxing and comfortable to be with them. They are two wonderful people."

Some bad news awaited Ralph upon his return from Nice to Pine. "We are going to have to put in a new septic tank," he wrote. "Seems when I come home the shit hits the fan." He reported shortly: "Our septic system should be finished today. That's a relief. Now we'll have a warm place again."

In September, at the London House in Chicago, Ralph played his final gig with the WGJ before joining Hucko. He had changed his mind about being "just another local piano player" in Denver. After thinking over the whole situation, he said, he didn't think it would work out that way. He also was sure he would be better off financially without having to be concerned about expenses on the road. Most important, of course, he would be living at home.

Ralph felt bad about leaving the band. With his departure, four of the original members—Lawson, Wilber, Freeman, and Haggart—remained. Wilber dropped out a few months later. "We're all buddies in the band and very good friends," Sutton said. "It took a little thought for me to come to this decision because we've been together a long time. It's hard to believe that I made the decision, but I'm glad I did. I had to do it. The guys are sorry I'm leaving, but they know my reasons and they understand. The deal with Peanuts just happened to come along at the right time."

My Marriage Comes First and Music Second

During lunch at a Mexican restaurant near Pine that summer, Sunnie had commented that Ralph's drinking caused "the only trouble we have between us." In Chicago, I asked Sutton to comment on this problem. Ralph grinned sheepishly and asked me to turn off the tape recorder. He said he preferred not to discuss his drinking, but he changed his mind immediately after Ruth and I noted that it was part of his story. "I can understand Sunnie's viewpoint, and she's right," he said. "That goddamn booze. I started drinking when I was about 10 years old. They made home brew in Missouri, and I used to drink it. Dad always had a whiskey bottle up on a shelf. When he came home from work, he'd pick me up and let me lick the cork after he had taken a drink. I've never lost the taste for the stuff. But I guess that as you get older you can't consume it like you used to, and I've cut down on it now."

Sutton hoped that living at home most of the time would enable him to see more of his sons than had been possible during his years with the band. When Ralph left the WGJ, all three sons were living in the San Francisco area. Jeff was 26 and playing drums in a rock band. He also played guitar, bass, and piano. Pete, 22, the only nonmusician of the three and the only son who had married, was a ceramics craftsman. Nick, 19, had three jobs. He played piano in a jazz combo, he was a ceramics craftsman, and he worked as a shingler as well.

Nick had been only 9 when his parents separated. He never had an opportunity to become close to his father until 1973, when Ralph visited Barbara and Hal Curtis in Ukiah. Nick, then 18, saw him there: "Dad asked me to take a walk with him. He told me, 'Forget I'm your father. Let's just talk man to man.' I said I had wanted to do that ever since I could remember. We walked and talked, and for the first time in my life I really felt I knew my father. The feeling was so good. I'd like to see much more of him. One of these days, when Dad has the time, my brothers and I are going to take off into the mountains somewhere and spend about two months with him, making up for all those years we missed. One of these days!

"My father is like an idol to me—somebody I really look up to. Whenever I hear him play, I just lie back and close my eyes and feel each beautiful riff. My dream is to sit down at the piano with him and really wail. Man, wouldn't that be something! I'm so damned proud that I'm one of Ralph Sutton's sons, and I've thought of that many times, especially when I listen to one of his records or one of Fats's. I want him to teach me a few little licks and riffs. I hope to be an accomplished jazz pianist like my father. To be that—wow! Then I could sit down with him and play and play and play."

Nick had an unforgettable experience in 1974 when he went to hear Eubie Blake. He wrote his father about it: "After all the autograph freaks were finished, I walked over and said, 'Mr. Blake, I hope I'm not interrupting, but my name is Nick Sutton, the youngest son of Ralph Sutton.' He said, 'Ralph Sutton! Man, your daddy sure can play that piano! The next time you write, you tell him what I said.' I thanked him very much and thought that would be it. But after he had played a few songs, he told the audience that there had been some great pianists—like James P., the Lion, and Fats—and Ralph Sutton is up there with them. He said he hoped I realized that, and I sure do hope I realize it!"

The new quartet, fronted by Peanuts Hucko, opened at the Continental Denver Hotel on October 1, 1974, with Sutton, Cliff Leeman, and Colin Gieg, a Denver bass player. Hucko's wife, Louise Tobin, sang with the group. She had been a top vocalist of the Big Band Era, when she sang with a number of top bands, including those of Benny Goodman, Will Bradley, and Harry James.

Barry Morrison, in his *Denver Post* review of the group's opening night, lauded the performance. He praised Sutton as "the unbeatable pianist [who] ripped up everybody with his 'Honky Tonk Train,' which has become a classic for him."

Ralph thoroughly enjoyed working in Denver and being home every night. "I feel so goddamn free!" he wrote Ruth and me. "It's wonderful to be home and enjoying life again. My marriage comes first and music second. Even though Sunnie and I see each other so little during the week, we make up for it on weekends. The dogs are enjoying it no end, having me home during the day and Sunnie home at night. They seem to wonder where this bonus came from.

"Everything is going great at the Continental Denver. It's a real pleasure to play with Peanuts, Cliff, and Colin. We're doing a terrific business, and I'm doing better financially than when I was with the band because I've got fewer expenses.

"We are booked through January. I shudder to think that if I were still with the band I would be in New York over the Christmas holidays. I can't call that living. So all in all, I'm very happy with the whole new situation. The quartet is swinging, the customers like it, and everything is fine."

Hucko wanted to open his own jazz club, featuring the quartet, at the Sheraton Denver Airport Hotel. This setup would have been ideal for Ralph. In addition to having steady and lengthy employment, he could have continued playing nightly with old friends at a classy establishment that was only about an hour's drive from his home. Hucko met with Sheraton officials late in 1974 to discuss the plan, and Ralph wrote in December that "it looks like Peanuts will get the saloon going in February." However, the target date was pushed back several times, eventually to the end of April.

In January 1975, Sutton reported that the quartet had been held over indefinitely at the Continental Denver. But the size of the audience dropped off on week nights during Lent, prompting his whimsical thought that "people should give up water." On March 21, he wrote tersely that "we are closing on the 29th." More bad news followed early in April: "Peanuts gave up on his club idea, so I don't know what's going to happen next."

What happened was that Ralph, at the age of 52, embarked on a fulltime career as a free-lance musician. Almost all his peers in traditional jazz had been performing as free-lancers for years. Like them, Sutton expected to free-lance indefinitely. It meant returning to a life spent to a large degree on the road—and with far more time away from Sunnie and Morning Air Ranch than he would have chosen. He had little choice.

Piano Man was published in May 1975, and I gave Ralph an advance copy of the biography at the Odessa Jazz Party that month. His great pleasure while skimming through the finished product must have been dampened by the recent death of Boozer, who had suffered a stroke and had to be put to sleep. After reading the book at home, Sutton sent me his thoughts about it.

He wrote touchingly of his favorite pet: "So glad the picture of Boozer and me on the thinking rock is in the book. I had forgotten about that shot. He was my close buddy."

Chapter **25**

You Have to Prove Yourself to Ralph

alph made several recordings and played a number of engagements as a free-lancer with the World's Greatest Jazzband after Peanuts Hucko's hopes for a jazz club fell through. The first of these gigs came in early May 1975, when the band recorded an album of Cole Porter tunes. Tommy Newsom played tenor sax for the session, taking time from his chair in the band on "The Tonight Show."

On trombone was George Masso, who had joined the WGJ in January. He had done little previous recording, though he started his career in 1948 with Jimmy Dorsey. Masso entered Boston University in 1950, earned bachelor's and master's degrees in music education, and then taught music in high school and at the University of Connecticut. Bobby Hackett, a friend of his father's, became the catalyst that led Masso to leave academia and return to the life of a jazz musician. He accepted Hackett's offer to play a one-week gig with him in 1973 and worked with Benny Goodman and then Hackett again before joining the WGJ.

Masso had admired Sutton's playing for years but met him for the first time at the Cole Porter record date. He felt both excited and jittery about making his first professional recording after almost 25 years as a college student and then a teacher.

"I was very impressed with Ralph," Masso said. "As a person, he seemed easy to get to know—that nice, easygoing manner of his. It was quite awesome for me to be in that company of musicians, and Ralph did a lot to alleviate the situation. He went out of his way to talk with me and tell me that I wasn't the only one who gets a bit uptight at such times. He certainly helped me get through the session.

"When I heard Ralph play, I was delightfully surprised to learn how versatile he is. I had always pictured him as a two-fisted, hard-swinging Fats Waller-type piano player. I wasn't aware of the lighter side of his playing—how sensitive he could be and how perceptive to what Bob Haggart wanted in his arrangements. Most of the tunes in the album are show tunes, not the ones I had associated with Ralph. Tunes like 'All of You,' 'It's All Right with Me,' 'Let's Do It,' 'I Concentrate on You,' 'Just One of Those Things,' and 'Love for Sale.'

"I have a great deal of admiration for the way Ralph can state things so simply and effectively at the piano. He has a lot of technique, but you don't hear it. He uses it very sparingly. He won't show a display of great technique at the expense of good musical taste.

"One of the first characteristics I admired about Ralph was his honesty and integrity. There's just no bullshit there. He's straightforward and a very warm human being. He doesn't say anything that isn't true or anything that he doesn't mean. He's a very good person to have as a friend. He's not a fair-weather friend; he's a true friend. The better I got to know Ralph, the more I realized that my first impression was right—that he's a very sensitive human being, very sensitive to people's feelings.

"One time when the band was playing in Harbor Point, Michigan, my luggage didn't show up. Being new on the road and new to flying and traveling, I was very upset. I had no idea if I'd ever see it again. Ralph and I happened to be roommates, and as soon as we got to the room he said, 'Sit down, man, and relax.' He assured me that this happens quite often and the baggage would show up in a few hours and everything would be OK. It was nice of him again to take the time and show some compassion. My luggage finally showed up around 3 o'clock the next morning.

"Another thing I admire is Ralph's dislike of unfairness. He's quite verbal if he sees unfairness, not only to himself but to others. He'll speak up for them as well as himself, and he won't be passive about it.

"I'm so happy anytime I see that man. Ralph can always make me smile with his dry, quiet sense of humor. Sometimes when we leave the stand, I'll tell him how much I enjoy playing with him. He'll grin and say, 'It's pari-mutual, man.' "

Ed Polcer, while earning an engineering degree and playing cornet professionally at Princeton in the mid-1950s, frequently heard Ralph at Condon's. He didn't meet Sutton until the Odessa Jazz Party of 1975.

When Polcer stepped up on the stand for his first set at the party, he automatically assumed leadership of the group on stage with him. As leader, the cornet or trumpet player traditionally chooses the tunes and the key in which each is played, and also sets the tempo of every number.

"Ralph was the piano player," Polcer recalled. "I was this young kid. He didn't know who the hell I was. I had spent an hour or two that afternoon picking out what I thought were the three or four best tunes for the set, including the tempos. I had the set well paced when I got on the stand.

"Everybody was ready to go, and I said, 'OK—"Rosetta."' Then I gave the tempo—'one-and-one-two-three-four.' And nothing happened. Ralph looked up at me and said, 'I'll set the tempo.' My first meeting with him, and he had let me know that I had to prove myself to him first. Right in front of everyone. I was the new guy in town. It really took me aback.

"Then I realized that he had never heard me play and he was not going to entrust me with setting tempos. You have to prove yourself to Ralph before he'll open up and accept you into his inner circle. He's demanding. His standards are so high that a lot of other players would be lucky if they could play as well as he does on an off night. When he knew I could play and that I was coming at the music the same way he was, we were fine. We're the best of friends.

"My original recollections of Ralph were primarily as a solo piano player. He's still a marvelous soloist, but I've seen him grow as a band pianist. I didn't realize he's as good as he is in making the rest of the band sound good. He knows what to do behind the horn players. When he gets into his solos he can change the mood, but he doesn't mess around with the horns. He does what he's supposed to do, which is make *you* sound good."

Peanuts Hucko and Sheraton officials met again during the summer of 1975 and renewed their talks about setting up a jazz club. He told Sutton in June that the deal was "98 percent set" for the club to open at the end of October. Both musicians had agreed to go to England with the World's Greatest Jazzband in late September and then make a three-week European tour with the band. Ralph had also contracted to stay on for a solo tour through the first week of December. He expected to join Hucko and Gus Johnson at the Sheraton Denver Airport Hotel at that time.

Hucko returned to Denver a week before the opening of his Jazz Joy'nt at the Sheraton on October 29. Unfortunately, the club closed after a little less than three months. Sutton and the hotel failed to reach agreement on his salary, and so he did not play at the club during its brief existence.

Toward the end of the WGJ's European tour, the band played three nights at the Atlantic Club in Stockholm. Exceptionally fine examples of the collective and individual artistry of these superlative musicians appear on two records of live performances from the final night. The group includes Al Klink, who shared the tenor sax solo with Tex Beneke on Glenn Miller's celebrated record of "In the Mood," and Maxine Sullivan. Sutton rarely uses the pedal, but he does so briefly while bouncing through his third chorus of "St. Louis Blues." Then he takes an additional 12 bars after Yank Lawson calls out, "One more, Ralph."

The band completed its tour in Oslo the next night, October 22, with everyone exhausted from the many bus trips between cities on the schedule. "All long, ass-tiring trips," Ralph reported, "but I did enjoy looking at the countryside." The rest of the band returned to the United States the following day while he flew to Amsterdam and started his solo tour. Sutton "breathed a sigh of relief" after the WGJ played its final date, but for him the work had just begun. Between October 23 and November 15, he played concerts, recording sessions, or both, in Amsterdam, Milan, Geneva, Genoa, Milan again, Bologna, Milan and Genoa again, Zurich, Lucerne, Zurich again, and Bern.

"My solo tour has been quite successful," Ralph wrote from Bern. "Looks like I'll return over here next year. Lots of jazz fans and great reception. I love Switzerland."

Ralph flew to London on November 16 and played that night at the Fox and Hounds, a jazz pub in Haywards Heath. Appearing with him was the Benny Simkins Sextet, established by Simkins on tenor sax, his son Pete on piano, and Roy Bower on trumpet. The group also included Pete's younger brother, Geoff, on alto sax. Pete Simkins, who started collecting Ralph's records in the mid-1950s, met Sutton when the WGJ played in Brighton in 1971. He remembered that Ralph "performed magically on 'Carolina Shout' and 'Viper's Drag.'"

Bud Freeman had appeared in Brighton earlier in 1975, and his agent arranged Sutton's gig in Haywards Heath. For the English musicians, the opportunity to share the bandstand with such idols was a dream come true.

Pete Simkins told a fine story on himself when describing his experience with Ralph:

"The room, at the back of the pub, was small. If you got 100 people in there, you needed a shoehorn to get to the bar. On that night it was absolutely packed, with people standing on chairs in the back just to *see* Ralph. I started off the evening on piano and made way for him after two or three numbers. Ralph then played a couple of tunes with the band before doing his first solo set.

"Our bass player and drummer, Alan Kennington and Bernie Godfrey, though a little in awe of Ralph, soon settled down into a good groove. At the end of their first tune with him, which was 'California, Here I Come,' Bernie turned to me and said, 'With all due respect, Pete, why don't you make the band swing like that?' Any comment from me would have been superfluous.

"Ralph seems to generate a tremendous impulse when he gets up a head of steam. It always reminds me of a huge steam locomotive at full power. But most of all, I respect Ralph as what we Brits would call a bloody good bloke. At one of his appearances with us I announced him as the Gentle Giant of the Piano. That's the best way I can think of to describe him. Quiet, strong, and capable of making the hair stand up on the back of your neck with a happy right-hand phrase or a stomping piece of left-hand power."

A record of Sutton solos from the concert includes a rousing medley. Ralph strides through "Honeysuckle Rose" and "Handful of Keys" and then, with Pete Simkins leading a shout from the audience, winds up with "Somebody Stole My Gal."

From November 17 through December 6, Ralph's concert and recording engagements took him to Bracknell, London, Bristol, Nottingham, Glasgow, Aberdeen, Hatfield, the Isle of Wright, Southampton, and Blandford Forum. In London, he played at a poorly ventilated club where the World's Greatest Jazzband had appeared in October. "Still no ventilation," he remarked after his return visit. "Phew!"

In Blandford Forum, on the final night of his tour, Ralph performed at the inaugural concert presented by the Blandford Jazz Circle. This jazz fan organization was the dream child of Russell Barnes, a former policeman and later a probation officer. Its story began in London in 1949, during one of Barnes's visits to Charing Cross Road, the home of many secondhand bookstores. The neighborhood's record shops had not yet recovered completely from the bombs dropped by Hitler's Luftwaffe. However, a few jazz lovers among the bookstore owners were importing records from New York. As a result, some of the most unlikely bookstores had alcoves with a handful of jazz records.

The proprietor of one such shop looked like a character from Dickens, with his black suit and stiff winged collar. Barnes was astonished to see a neatly handwritten card—"Jazz Records for Sale"—in the window. He asked if the stock included any records by Art Tatum or James P. Johnson, but those names meant nothing to the Dickensian character. The proprietor explained that his son, who was out at the moment, dealt with the records. But he remembered the son's saying something about an American jazz pianist.

"Searching through a heap of records on a table, he withdrew one and handed it to me," Barnes said. "It was Circle J1052, 'Carolina in the Morning' and 'Whitewash Man,' piano solos by Ralph Sutton. I had never seen the label and I certainly hadn't heard of the artist, but I took a chance and bought it.

"Who was Ralph Sutton? No one knew. But during the weeks that followed, I played that 78 record so much that I swear you could almost hear each tune coming through from the other side. As a frustrated jazz piano player, I couldn't believe what I was hearing. What a hell of a player that man was! But as for finding out anything about him, he might as well have been from Mars. As the years passed, meager information came my way, plus a handful of his records that I learned about from catalogs."

By 1974, Barnes had become involved part-time with a jazz record program on the Southampton radio station of the British Broadcasting Corporation. The producer heard that Sutton had been booked by a nearby club and asked if Barnes would be interested in hearing him.

"Was I interested!" Barnes laughed. "Hell hath no fury like someone trying to get a ticket to hear and perhaps even meet Ralph Sutton. He turned out to be a most polite and charming man. We chatted at great length about many things, and I mentioned a long-cherished hope of presenting jazz concerts in the old Georgian market town of Blandford Forum, where my family roots run deep for generations. Ralph asked if he could be the first musician to play for us. He had a deal!

"The next day, the whole idea seemed preposterous. Blandford was the domain of conservative, reactionary, stuffy landowner-farmers. Who would buy tickets to hear Ralph Sutton? But I pushed ahead. Three friends joined me in putting up enough money to get started. The date for Ralph's concert was set, the advertising was printed, and a group of us started going door to door promoting the idea of live jazz.

"How do you convince people to pay to listen to a jazz piano player they'd never heard of and who lived on the other side of the world? I wanted to take jazz out of noisy, smoke-filled pubs and present it in a relaxed but formal setting—present it as the art form it is—to an appreciative, quiet, attentive audience.

"We had the support of the staff of our local school. We used their hall and, above all, their grand piano, which was once owned by the great classical pianist Arthur Rubinstein.

"Every ticket was sold. On the night of the concert, a line of people waited for the doors to open. Panic quickly replaced my exhilaration and self-congratulation, and I raced around imagining every possible catastrophe. Then a firm hand grasped my shoulder. It was Ralph. With a knowing and reassuring grin, he told me: 'I'm the guy who should be worrying. I've got to go out there and play the piano.'

"He played like the master he is, and they gave him a standing ovation.

"We never looked back. The Blandford Jazz Circle took hold and grew into one of the largest live jazz organisations in southern England.

"That first night, we arrived at my home tired but happy. I left the house on an errand at 10 the next morning. Ralph was sound asleep in his bed, and Puggles, our part Welsh collie, was the same in his basket. When I returned, both were in Ralph's bed with their heads on the pillow and his arms around the dog's neck.

"That day, Ralph gave Puggles a new name: Muggles."*

Sutton returned to Blandford Forum for another concert in June 1976. A record called *Jazz at the Forum* features highlights of the two performances. Ralph gives the piano an especially vigorous workout on "The Sheik of Araby."

---

*Muggles is a jazz musician's term from the 1920s meaning marijuana cigarettes.

Barnes summed up the spirit of the organization in his invitation letter for a 1981 concert by the Pied Pipers, fronted by Peanuts Hucko, with Sutton, Jack Lesberg, Jake Hanna, and Peter Appleyard. "We have fun in the Blandford Jazz Circle," Barnes wrote. "Why don't you come and join us?"

Ralph and Sunnie took a vacation in Mexico after he wearily flew home from England in December 1975. He wrote about his long solo tour in glowing terms, again comparing the audiences in Europe with those in the United States:

"Everywhere I played the reception was great. The people over there know what it's all about, from the working people on up through the ranks to the rich ones. There is much respect for a jazz musician. I met so many nice people and made a lot of new friends. It certainly is more fun to play over there than it is in this country.

"Each night I played with different musicians. Some bands were good and some were fair, but everything came off great.

"I played two 45-minute sets a night, starting off with about 20 minutes solo. Then I'd bring up the bass and drums for 10 minutes, and then the rest of the band would join me. We broke it up everywhere."

From early March to late April 1976, the Suttons both worked at the BBC, a Denver restaurant and lounge. Ralph played a light schedule, finishing at 8 o'clock, and Sunnie had the same hours behind the bar. The job became especially pleasant after the BBC bought a 60-year-old rebuilt Mason & Hamlin grand piano that he had turned up.

Ralph flew to Zurich in early May and played in Switzerland, England, and France through June. While he was playing at a club in Geneva, a Swiss artist came up and introduced himself. Pierre Terbois had heard Sutton on records before attending art school in New York in 1953 and 1954. He spent much time going to jazz clubs there with prominent musicians, including Willie the Lion Smith. The Lion urged him to "stop at Eddie Condon's and you'll hear one of the most talented young pianists." Terbois went to Condon's several times but was disappointed because of the noise, with people "talking almost louder than the piano."

Although Terbois did not meet Ralph while in New York, he was one of the few who defied the torrential rain on April 17, 1954, and heard

Sutton's concert For Listeners Only at Town Hall. The music that afternoon was one of the highlights of what Terbois called his "golden days" in the city. He and Sutton became friends after meeting in Geneva. While visiting the artist's home, Ralph was amazed to see a copy of the concert handbill that Terbois had saved. Terbois' handbill became the back endsheets of this book.

A few years later, Terbois and his wife, Catherine, drove to Acqui, Italy, to hear Ralph. Thick fog covered the city, and Terbois suggested "In a Mist" for the opening number. Sutton thought that was a fine idea but changed his mind when a nearby campanile went into action just before he started playing. He opened with "Ring Dem Bells" instead.

In 1976, Ralph arranged for Lou Stein to play at the BBC during his absence in Europe, followed by Dick Wellstood and then George Van Eps. The final substitute headliner, Ralph's sister Barbara, got a big thrill from sitting in for him. As she prepared for the engagement, she said her piano "has been crying 'Uncle' for the past couple of weeks." Barb received considerable praise from the public and the media.

"Needless to say, I am proud that I handled the job as well as I did and that I came across with most people as a pianist in my own right," she said. "It was a tremendous experience for me, especially with that gorgeous piano. I was high for weeks afterward."

Sunnie had flown to London and met Ralph there, and she went with him on the remaining European dates. Ralph described the grand reception that greeted them when they flew home on July 4: "As we crossed the United States from New York, the cities sent up rockets and fireworks welcoming us back. That's what comes from being a jazz musician. The people in this country are becoming very knowledgeable and showing respect after all these years."

One evening at the BBC, two women who appeared to be in their 40s were sitting at a table directly in front of the piano. As Ralph finished a tune, a man at a nearby table heard one of them ask him to play "Canadian Sunset." Sutton replied that he didn't play the number, adding that it was featured by Erroll Garner. The woman seemed surprised, as though she expected him to play anything requested. Then the man heard her invite Ralph to join her and her friend during his next break. He declined with thanks, saying he had already made plans. After the set, Sutton astounded the man, his wife, and their four or five companions by walking over to their table and sitting down with them.

The dumbfounded customer was Bob Livesay, a cousin of Barbara Alderson's. She had been the California teenager who years before became a Sutton fan and corresponded briefly with Ralph when he played at Condon's. Shortly after Alderson introduced Livesay to Ralph's music via a record, the Korean War broke out and the Army sent Livesay to Japan. He spotted Sutton's *Piano Moods* record at the PX one day and bought it immediately. Like his cousin, he got hooked for life. He and Ralph had never seen each other until the evening at the BBC. Livesay and his wife, Hazel, and their friends were on a trip from California, and he had learned from a pamphlet in their hotel room that Sutton was playing in Denver.

"I'm sure he came over to our table because he had seen from our faces—especially mine—how much we appreciated his music," Livesay said. "He just sat down and asked, 'How're you guys doing?' One of our friends was George Oram, a retired judge from Boise, Idaho, who was quite bald. Ralph teased him and said he looked just like Joe Venuti.

"We had a pleasant conversation for about 10 minutes, and then he got up and went back to the piano. After he had played a few numbers, he looked over and asked me, 'What would you like to hear?' I requested 'Honeysuckle Rose,' and Ralph grinned and said, 'I guess you want me to work, huh?'

"I can't imagine 'Honeysuckle Rose' being played any better than Ralph played it that night. I couldn't believe the stuff he added with each new chorus. He tore that thing up. And as he did it, he knew the impression it was making on me because he'd look over with a big grin. It was a moment to remember. Every chance he got, he'd stop at our table and say a few words."

About a year later, in 1977, the Livesays and Oram passed through Denver on another trip while Ralph was playing at a downtown hotel. They went to hear him, and he recognized them and told Oram, "God, you look like Joe Venuti." Then he directed them to some empty seats next to the piano. A patron began keeping time with the music by beating with a fork on the arm of his chair, and Livesay asked Sutton if the racket didn't bother him. "Hell, no," he replied. "Silly son of a bitch doesn't know what he's doing. I just ignore him." Later, Ralph wanted to know if Livesay had a request. When asked for "Sweet Lorraine," Sutton told him he hadn't played it for years.

"He started playing it very nicely," Livesay said, "but he couldn't remember the bridge. He went through some pretty chords and then back into the main melody. He glanced at me when he did this, and I grinned and shook my head, No. Ralph grinned back and said just loud enough so the crowd couldn't hear him, "Hell, they don't know the difference."

A cabdrivers' strike took Denver's cabs off the streets after midnight, and a friend of Ralph's heard the Livesays and Oram talking about how they would get back to their motel. The friend not only took them in his car, but also played Sutton tapes of Fats Waller tunes en route.

The Livesays traveled to England in 1979. A friend gave them the name of a record shop in downtown London that he said might have records by Ralph unavailable in the United States. The store owner surprised them with the news that Sutton would be playing that night at a club just outside the city. The Livesays caught a train, but another passenger told them it did not go to the town where Ralph was performing. On top of that, rain started pouring down. The other passenger, an attractive young clothes designer, came to their rescue. Her husband, who met her at the station, drove the Livesays the additional 10 miles to the club.

Bad news awaited them. The place had been sold out. Luckily, two customers canceled and the Americans got a table. Before the performance, Livesay asked the owner to take him to Sutton's dressing room.

"I'll be darned if he didn't recognize me," Livesay said. "Ralph has a fantastic memory for faces: 'My God, look who's here. I can't believe it. You're here in England?' Later he grabbed Hazel and gave her a bear hug and a kiss, and introduced us to several of his English friends.

"The last train back to London left at midnight, which meant we would miss about an hour and a half of Ralph's playing because we'd have to leave at 11 o'clock to get a cab to the station. This was during the gas shortage, and one of the Englishmen said he would drive us to London if we bought the gas. So we got to stay for the entire performance. We were overwhelmed by the hospitality of all these people."

In August 1979, Sutton played at a hotel in downtown San Francisco. Bob and Hazel Livesay took his 83-year-old father, who loved Ralph's music and had played piano and fronted small dance bands, to hear him. They arrived early, and Livesay took a walk to kill some time.

"I walked into the foyer just as Ralph came in the front door," he said. "He spotted me right away and threw up his hands: 'Jesus Christ, what are you doing here?' I asked him if he would stop at our table and meet my father, and he came right over. He gave Hazel a hug and a kiss again and was talking with my dad when someone came up, put a hand on his shoulder, and told him, 'Ralph, you know we've got somebody up here who you're supposed to meet.'

"Ralph turned around, looked the guy right in the eye, and said in a very even tone, 'I'm busy with some friends here. I'll be free a little later, and we'll take care of it.' Then he continued to chat with my dad and Hazel and me. I'll never forget it. It meant so much to me because Dad passed away six months later."

Sutton returned to the BBC in July 1976 and played there through October. The employees signed a petition to keep him, and a number of patrons also urged that his contract be renewed, but nothing came of these appeals.

Edna Sutton died in August, about three months after her 80th birthday. Barb had written Ralph in March that their mother was going downhill, and he predicted that he would be a basket case when she passed away. Her death, plus the end of his stint at the BBC, could have contributed to his mood in October when he wrote: "Every once in a while lately I have been glancing through the book, especially when I am feeling a little low. You know what? It picks me up."

Ralph obviously felt much better when he reported in November that he and Sunnie were "in the middle of a real estate deal you would not believe. Going for big casino! I get the shakes just thinking about it." On December 1, the Suttons bought a new home on 37½ acres—compared with 9 acres in Pine—with huge spruce and pine trees all around it. They moved down the highway to Bailey later that month. But the one-hole outhouse had to be left behind.

Bailey, an unincorporated community somewhat larger than Pine, has a population of about 300. Around 85 percent of the people work in Denver and commute the 45 miles by car or bus. The rest are retired or run their own businesses. Large numbers of visitors come to the area for its camping, hiking, hunting, fishing, skiing, and horseback riding.

A lively mountain river, formally called the North Fork of the South

Platte River, flows through the Suttons' property with simple and audible elegance. It crowns the beauty of their place and quickly seduces anyone who likes lovely scenery or abundant fishing. Ralph and Sunnie added to the charm of their home by naming it Morning Air Ranch, after the famous piano solo by Willie the Lion Smith.

Chapter **26**

Words Cannot Express What Ralph Has Meant to Me

ntil Joe Sample heard Ralph at Condon's, he considered intermission pianists "nuisances to be tolerated until the band returned to the stand." Sample quickly realized that Sutton was of another breed. He bought his records and enjoyed his music as much as that of the band.

Sample moved from Chicago to Billings, Montana, in 1954, and his trips to New York became relatively infrequent. He lost track of Ralph until the early 1970s, when he went to Denver for the regional conference of the National Association of Broadcasters. As he and some friends were walking past the Navarre after a meeting one night, he saw a billboard next to the door that said, "Ralph Sutton at the Piano." Sample couldn't believe his good luck.

"I dragged my reluctant companions in, and no one left until the lights went out for the night," he recalled. "I introduced myself to Ralph and asked him to play 'Keepin' Out of Mischief Now,' not realizing that he had the same affection for requests that he reserved for horned toads and pit vipers.

"He played it. I asked him about his current activities and what he had been doing since leaving Condon's. His answers seemed somewhat terse and discouraged further conversation. I felt almost as if I had intruded on his privacy. It was not a promising beginning."

In the fall of 1976, Sample was back in Denver and learned that Sutton was playing at the BBC. He ducked out of the broadcasters' meeting in midafternoon and went over. Ralph was much more relaxed this time and readily accepted an invitation to play a party in Billings given by Sample and his wife, Miriam.

"As a result," Sample said, "Ralph came to Billings on January 28,

1977, with Gus Johnson, Jack Lesberg, and Kenny Davern to play for about 150 of our friends and a couple of special guests. One was Russ Davis, a member of the Billings Symphony and a former big band musician who lent Jack his bass. The other was the manager of the Northern Hotel, where we held the party. He was a former musician, and I had suggested that if he liked Ralph's work, he should book him into the hotel lounge. The party was a great success, the manager was ecstatic, and Ralph and Gus had a month-long engagement there every year for the next seven years."

The musicians played in a room called the Golden Belle, which served as a meeting place for Billings people and ranchers from the area. A 5-foot-long oil painting of the Golden Belle herself hung over Johnson's drums. Her natural endowments more than compensated for what she lacked in clothing.

"We liked to kid Gus about her," Sample said. "Sometime later when we had another party in the hotel ballroom, we moved the painting upstairs over his drums to keep him company.

"I had no idea how the first month-long engagement would go. Ralph and Gus came up in April. They certainly weren't overpaid, but they were a bit of a strain on the hotel's modest entertainment budget. The room wasn't large, and we couldn't convince the manager to raise the price of drinks while the musicians were there. We were presenting world-class entertainment, and he insisted that we had to be competitive with a dive across the street that had a jukebox. Fortunately, the crowds held up and the bar grossed $45,000 for the month, so the entertainment costs weren't any higher as a percentage of sales than for any of the other acts that the hotel booked.

"Furthermore, never underestimate the loyalty of the Sutton fan club. Ralph attracted a lot of people who didn't ordinarily come to Billings. Many came from Denver, the Dakotas, Los Angeles, and who knows where else. They stayed at the hotel, of course, and that fact was not lost on the manager.

"Misfortune befell one avid fan, a very good European modern jazz pianist who was playing at the nearby Sheraton Hotel. He became so entranced with Ralph's playing that he forgot about his own time schedule. The Sheraton fired him."

Sample's toughest job was to persuade the Northern's board of directors to buy a new piano so Ralph did not have to play one of its two well-worn spinets. Being a part owner of the hotel, he made sure the piano was purchased despite a shortage of funds.

Sample bought a new grand piano from a local dealer and former bass player named Curt Jarratt, who had earned a music degree by playing his way through college. He later was a high school band director and then owned a music store before entering the piano business. Jarratt virtually gave up playing for 38 years because his first wife did not share his enthusiasm for music. After selling the piano to Sample, he delivered it to the hotel and was tuning the new grand when Ralph entered the room.

"I mentioned that I had played bass in the past, and he insisted that I sit in with him and Gus," Jarratt said. "That was when I decided to get back into playing music, regardless of the consequences with my wife. Playing had always been a lifetime dream for me. Ralph encouraged me and gave me the determination to practice and try to regain what 38 years had cost me."

Jarratt brought his bass to the hotel every night, and Ralph let him sit in for a couple of numbers. As his technique improved, he played more and more until he became a regular six nights a week. Jarratt joined Sutton and Johnson on every gig they played in Billings. Upon arriving in town, Sutton would call and ask, "How's your chops?" The hotel could not afford to pay Jarratt, and he never asked for compensation. The musicians' union looked the other way.

"One night, Ralph paid me the greatest compliment when he said I sounded like Walter Page," Jarratt said. "Soon afterward, I got divorced. Ralph helped me through a difficult time. He told me, 'A person has to marry a second time to know how to marry.'

"My second wife shares my love for music and encourages me to follow my dreams. In Billings, Mildred was so enthralled with Ralph's playing that she always arrived early so she could sit at the piano bar and not only hear him best but also watch his hands.

"Words cannot express what Ralph has meant to me. I owe so much to him and also to Gus. They were my stepping-stones to much happiness and the realization of my dreams. I'll always treasure the inspiration that Ralph gave me to get started in music again."

Sample took a picture of Jarratt playing with Sutton and Johnson. He titled it the Curt Jarratt Trio and had it enlarged and autographed. Sutton,

Johnson, and Sample then presented the picture to Jarratt, who was delighted. He later joined the band of Frank Bettencourt, Jan Garber's pianist and arranger for 20 years. Bettencourt's group played private clubs in Fort Worth and Houston.

In December 1979, Ralph persuaded the hotel manager to let Kenny Davern join him and Johnson for two weeks. Sunnie came up from Denver, and they all went to the Samples' home for dinner one night. Johnson and Miriam Sample cooked ham hocks and black-eyed peas, and Ralph whipped up a batch of his hot sauce.

Every afternoon, Sutton took a long walk and Davern often joined him. One day, Davern decided to buy a pair of boots. The two men went into a large bootery and Davern tried on what he guessed was every pair in the store. Ralph sat watching him silently. None of the boots satisfied Davern, who spent more than an hour slipping them on and off. The same thing happened in another boot store, Sutton quietly watching his friend try on pair after pair. As they were about to enter a third store, Ralph told him, "I think I'll just mosey on." That experience started a running gag, Davern continually asking if Sutton wanted to go with him and look at boots.

Even though Davern struck out in his quest for Montana boots, he found an expert clarinet repairman. Russ Davis not only played bass in the Billings Symphony, but also clarinet and sax on club dates. Davern's clarinet required some repair work, and a couple of local musicians recommended Davis. From then on, Davern sent his horns to Davis for repairs and recommended the Montanan to other musicians as well.

The Samples gave another party in December 1980. Davern had been playing with Sutton and Johnson, and he stayed over an extra night even though he was scheduled to start an engagement in New York 24 hours later. Yank Lawson, George Masso, and Eddie Miller joined them. So did Milt Hinton, who flew out for the one-nighter while playing a regular gig in New York.

"When you give a jazz party," said Sample, "there are two magic words: Ralph Sutton. When you say them, the other musicians will break their backs to get there."

A person living in Bismarck, North Dakota, could get pretty lonesome for good jazz, even if he emceed a radio program called "Dixieland North." Jasper Kleinjan had played drums through college and then in local dance bands. After the Army discharged him in 1957, he sold his drums and forgot about playing. In fact, he pretty much forgot about jazz until Gene Mayl and his Dixieland Rhythm Kings came to Bismarck in 1974.

"Hearing them awakened a smoldering fire," Kleinjan said. "I started buying records and tried to find out what was happening in the music world. Then, late in 1979, I read that Gus Johnson, Kenny Davern, and Ralph Sutton would be playing in Billings. I had heard Gus on records, but I didn't know the other names."

Kleinjan and his wife, Colleen, drove the 440 miles to Billings. They checked in at the Northern Hotel and walked into the room where the trio was playing.

"I was overwhelmed," Kleinjan said. "I could hardly say a word to Colleen. We just sat there spellbound. I had never heard anything like it. The mood changed with the type of tune, and when they played 'Black and Blue' I cried like a baby. The harmonies of Kenny's clarinet and Ralph's incredible chords were an emotional fulfillment, happiness at its highest.

"It's difficult to express why Ralph's piano makes me feel so wonderful, but the sensation gets better through the years. His chords and the things he does with that great left hand bring a fullness and feeling that is missing with most piano players, and his rhythm is powerful and driving.

"Ralph plays the music he loves, rather than knuckling under to the pressures of the media money god. I admire him for doing what he believes in, even though he no doubt could have had greater fame and earned more money if he had capitulated to the changing whims of the music manipulators. He is fiercely independent in what he does and how he lives, but he cares deeply for people. His playing reflects his inner beauty and strength."

The Kleinjans met the musicians that night and drove out to the Northern annually until Ralph's gigs ended with the sale of the hotel in 1983. The new owners had no interest in jazz.

Around 1980, Kleinjan started to practice drums to Ralph's records. As Sutton, Jarratt, and Johnson took a break on a Saturday night in 1982, Johnson told him, "You're a drummer. Get up here and play the next set." Kleinjan felt trapped, but he followed orders.

"I sat down at the drums," he said, "and looked to my right at Ralph, who was sitting at the piano grinning. All I could think was that I wasn't good enough to play with him. He asked what I'd like to play, and I replied, 'Black and Blue,' which was how I felt. Playing drums to his piano is beyond description."

Ralph liked to tell about the Sunday afternoon that he and a friend, Doc McBride, took a drive and stopped at the Atlas Bar in Columbus, Montana. Several old ranch hands were playing poker in a corner. After a drink or two, McBride suggested that Sutton play a tune on the upright piano that stood nearby. Ralph did so and soon was swinging away. The music got better and better until one of the poker players walked over to Ralph, tapped him on the shoulder, and said, "Say, bud, would you mind not making so much noise?"

On another Sunday, Sutton and Johnson drove out to Bill Mackay's ranch in Roscoe. Mackay had heard Ralph at Condon's and got to know him at the Northern Hotel. The rancher noticed immediately how much Ralph liked the rugged country. He enjoyed not only the outdoors, but also the solitude and quiet of ranch life.

Mackay's son, Bill, Jr., came over and the men got to talking about horses. Ralph preferred walking, but Johnson said he'd like to ride a horse and asked if the Mackays had one that he could try.

"Sure, we've got just the horse for you, Gus," Mackay's son told him.

"What's his name?" Johnson wanted to know.

"His name is Killer," Mackay's son replied.

"I'm not getting on any Killer!" Johnson stated emphatically.

But the Mackays got him on a suitable horse, and the drummer did very well as he rode off through the tall grass. Mackay suspected that Johnson must have had a lot of experience with horses in Texas, where he grew up.

During one of Ralph's engagements at the Northern, George Winston also performed in Billings. Winston, a New Age pianist, returned to his native Montana and played an annual series of benefit concerts that repeatedly sold out and raised considerable funds for local charities. He displayed still more class when he began his Billings concert with a couple of numbers and then turned to the audience.

"I don't know why you're here listening to me while the finest jazz pianist in the world is playing down the street at the Northern," Winston told the crowd.

Ralph was playing in New York in 1988 when Joe Sample discovered a place in Glen Cove, Long Island, that restored old player pianos. Sample asked Sutton to check out the pianos there and give him a professional opinion, for which he would receive a consultancy fee and expenses. Ralph drove out to the store with Sunnie and Jack Lesberg, examined every piano, and called Sample with his report.

"He refused to accept a dime for all that effort," Sample said. "There is a great sense of love about Ralph, and it flows from that big, rugged man without a hint of embarrassment. He is proud, genuine, and generous."

Sutton played in Denver, at Herby's Bar in the Executive Tower Inn, from February through March 1977. Business at the bar picked up greatly during that period, and Herby's booked him to return for the rest of the year after a European tour in May and June. Before Ralph and Gus Johnson went to Billings for their month-long gig in April, I speculated in a letter that perhaps he had mellowed a bit. Sure enough, he encountered virtually no static from the patrons at the Golden Belle.

"I had trouble with only one asshole," Ralph wrote from the Northern Hotel. "By the time I got through with him, he didn't know whether to shit or go blind. Otherwise, I guess I might have mellowed somewhat. When a person comes up and makes a request, I usually have my list of tunes on cards sitting on the piano. I tell the customer I'll get around to his request as soon as I play all the others. That seems to satisfy people."

In May, Ralph and Wild Bill Davison recorded an album in Copenhagen with a group of Danish musicians. Digby Fairweather observed in his liner notes that "Davison's music is as original as Armstrong's [and] Sutton is a giant who guards the irreplaceable flame of jazz piano tradition in perfect trust."

The album, called *Together Again!*, was not issued until 1982. I bought it before Ralph obtained a copy, and he heard it for the first time with Ruth and me in Chicago. Sutton listened intently to the entire record, nodding occasionally but saying not a word. He was thinking of Wild Bill, a close friend and still blowing his cornet at the age of 76, who had extolled him to Eddie Condon after hearing him play in St. Louis years before. Ralph nodded once again at the end of the record and, with eyes glistening, expressed his reaction: "That's a good one." It is indeed.

Ralph returned to Herby's in July 1977. Late that month, he played at a cocktail party in Vail at the home of Gerald and Betty Ford. Sutton was recruited for the affair by Larry Burdick, who owned a Vail club called the Red Lion where he had played many gigs. A Ford aide asked Burdick to recommend a piano player for the party, given for Republican bigwigs during a golf tournament sponsored by the former President and his wife.

"I played an out-of-tune spinet for about three hours with the place in a roar with talkers," Ralph said. "After the party I told Larry that for such a big shindig I wanted $500. He paid me and collected the money from Ford's right-hand man the next day.

"Larry said the guy almost shit when he found out my fee. I told Larry that if they wanted someone who tours other countries and is well known all over, they shouldn't have any qualms about the fee. He told the right-hand man that, and I'll bet the guy will never forget me. It did my heart good to get some of that Republican money.

"A lot of golf pros were there, plus guys such as Bob Hope, Clint Eastwood, and Jack Lemmon hanging around the piano, along with Betty Ford. I got Jack to play the piano and had a good talk with him. He's a hell of a guy."

I learned another interesting expression from Ralph's childhood a few months later. Sutton wrote about a newspaper story that had suggested he was still growing musically. "Mercy!" he began, using one of his—and Fats Waller's—favorite humorous expletives, "I didn't know I was still growing. It's time they bought me some long pants so I'll stop dragging it through the gravy." I requested a translation, which Ralph supplied with obvious relish.

"Concerning the long pants and the gravy," he wrote, "it goes like this. Out in the farming area in Missouri when boys are growing up, they have a hell of an appetite and don't always wait for someone to pass the food. They sometimes stand up and reach across the table for something. If the young studs are wearing short pants when they use a boardinghouse reach like that, the dick may slip out. If the gravy is in the way, look out!"

Ralph was more than a little surprised one stormy night that winter when he looked up from the piano at Herby's and saw two friends from St. Louis. Roger and Mary Ann Altvater had left their home by car at 2 o'clock that morning. They planned to drive straight through to Denver and hear Sutton play before continuing on to Aspen to do some skiing. At the Kansas-Colorado border they hit a snowstorm that became a blizzard, with trucks forced off the highway and motorists taking early shelter in motels. Ralph couldn't believe the Altvaters had made it all the way. They didn't realize how bad the storm was until they set out for Aspen the next morning. Every highway was closed except those going west.

Ray Bolger, who was playing in Denver, came into Herby's during the last set on that snowy night. Ralph immediately swung into "Once in Love with Amy," Bolger's great song-and-dance number from the musical comedy *Charley's Aunt* and the movie version, *Where's Charley?* Then, as a climax to Roger Altvater's busy day, he, Bolger, and Sutton sang the tune together.

The Altvaters had first heard Sutton at Condon's in 1953 on their honeymoon. They started skiing in 1960 in Aspen and had been to the Rendezvous before it became Sunnie's. They met Ralph there in 1964 during his first winter at the club and returned for numerous annual reunions with the ski slopes and Sutton. The World's Greatest Jazzband played for Roger Altvater's 45th birthday party in 1972.

"Ralph called three or four days before the party and told us the band had no dates until then," Altvater said. "He asked if we could put him up if he came to St. Louis early. That was the first time he was our houseguest, and it brought us even closer together. I think one of the reasons Ralph and I hit it off so well is that we both can go for long periods without saying much. I'd be with Ralph, and I didn't have to talk and he didn't have to talk."

The Altvaters went to their first Gibson party in 1967. They met other hometown fans of Ralph's there and soon found themselves part of the inner circle of his St. Louis friends.

"If you've got him for a friend, you've got a good friend," Mary Ann Altvater said. "I had five children, two dogs, and a housekeeper in the house, and Ralph could just sit in the kitchen. People would come and go, and he didn't have to say anything. The kids would bring their friends over: 'Look, there he is!'

"The children loved him. He talked to them, and they'd sit on the floor with their friends and listen to him play. One of our daughter's friends sat on the piano bench and played with Ralph one night. It was the biggest thrill in that child's life. He still talked about it when he was a man in his 30s."

Roger Altvater once saw Ralph use a novel method to squelch a pesky member of his audience. While he was playing at a private party in St. Louis, a woman sat down on the piano bench and began talking to him. She made some requests and kept bugging him. Finally, as Sutton finished a number, he played up to the treble end of the keyboard as far as he could. He then moved up on the bench and pushed the woman off.

"She went plop," Altvater recalled. "She was speechless and not amused."

Chapter **27**

It Was Inspiring to Play with Him

hen Ralph goes on the road, he never knows what the population of Morning Air Ranch will be when he returns. Sunnie sometimes adds to the household without his knowledge—but always with his subsequent delighted approval. In January 1977, for example, Ralph got home and reported:

"Another Newfoundland pup arrived while I was away. We now have three Newfoundlands and one Saint Bernard—Clancy, Mollie, Ella, and Bogie—and two cats, P.C. and Nina. Jesus Christ!!!"

That was small potatoes—or small animals—compared to Rufus' arrival in 1978. A veterinarian in Bailey had become involved in a project to remove a number of burros from the Grand Canyon. Park rangers had been relocating burros for years because the animals ate much of the canyon's vegetation, taking food from the bighorn sheep, deer, and other wildlife there. Burros had no natural enemies in the Grand Canyon, and so their population kept growing. The vet brought many of them to Bailey and put an ad in the local newspaper announcing an Adopt a Burro program.

"I put my order in for a burro and chose Rufus," Sunnie said. "He had a number 7 tattooed in his ear, which meant he was the seventh burro in his group that they brought from the canyon. Ralph was away when Rufus arrived. He misses out on a lot of things I do, and it's always a surprise for him when he comes home. He never knows what's going to be here. This time it was a burro."

Sunnie gave Rufus temporary quarters in the dog pen next to the house, and Ralph saw him for the first time when he got home. He couldn't have been happier.

"I loved him immediately," Sutton said. "But you have to get acquainted with these animals very slowly because they're wild. Rufie and I got acquainted and worked everything out."

Rachel arrived in 1979. Ralph was on the road when Sunnie learned that the government planned to shoot some burros that lived near an Air Force base in China Lake, California. She figured Rufus must be lonesome, so she acquired one of them to keep him company in the pasture and barn on the other side of the river. Rufus and Rachel produced a daughter in 1981. The Suttons called her Chayo, a Mexican name meaning "sweet thing." Perhaps not coincidentally, the next year Ralph and Vic Dickenson recorded a seldom-heard tune called "Sweet Thing." Fats Waller had recorded it, and the 1982 version features one of Sutton's rare vocals.

Ralph and Sunnie also acquired a new friend and neighbor the year that Rufus joined them. Kristy Rohloff, an artist, moved in nearby. Her friendship with the Suttons began when she rented the cabin that stood on part of their property a short distance from the house and just off the highway. Rohloff opened an antique and art shop there. She later succeeded Florence Cole as interim keeper of the Sutton menagerie after Cole moved from Denver. Rohloff began tending the animals when both Ralph and Sunnie were away from home and continued to do so after giving up her shop in 1985.

From the beginning of their friendship, Rohloff regarded the Suttons in a somewhat different light than did many of their friends. The relationship was based on day-to-day living, rather than centering around jazz.

"When I first met Ralph and Sunnie, I knew less than nothing about jazz," Rohloff said. "I grew up without any knowledge of the music. They promptly took me under their wing and began educating me to this new world. I found it quite wonderful.

"Prior to meeting Ralph, I had been told that he was a world-famous jazz pianist. I don't know what I expected, but I was very surprised when I met him. Here was this huge, gentle, soft-spoken man wearing a flannel work shirt, jeans, and tennis shoes. He looked a lot like a man who had spent the entire day, and much of his life, working outdoors on physical jobs. Since then, I have seen him perform many times. I have watched him captivate every audience and have been awed by what he draws from the piano. But I still think of him as I did when we first met.

"People are always praising Ralph for his strength at the keyboard and his genius for stride piano playing, and the list goes on and on. But to me, Ralph's power lies in his complete personality. His genius is the ability to pour his entire being into the keyboard. This is Ralph's *real* magic! It is why his music is so pure and his fans so addicted. It is why we are awed."

Rohloff arranged for Ralph to play at the community elementary school for the more than 500 children in kindergarten through fifth grade. He entranced his unlikely audience, even though the youngsters might have come up with more than 500 meanings of the word *jazz*.

"As Ralph walked out of the school, Sunnie and I watched as children of all ages—mostly girls but also a few boys—corralled him," Rohloff recalled. "They gazed at him with adoring eyes and asked for his autograph. Quite an accomplishment for a 45-minute appearance, when one considers the circumstances.

"When Ralph is home, he spends much of his time working outside. He thrives on it. He's always busy doing large and small jobs around the house and on their property, like gathering wood, mowing the grass, or working on the driveway. In the winter he shovels snow. He loves tending the animals, especially the burros. I once watched him from my shop and asked if he ever got tired trying to catch up with everything when he wasn't on the road. He told me: 'No, never! I could do all this day after day and never get tired of it. I just love it.' "

Ralph's sense of humor impressed Rohloff as warm, unique, and occasionally subtle. Sunnie dropped into her shop several times one day, appearing somewhat frustrated and flustered, and feeling as though she was going around in circles. Ralph stopped by later that afternoon and burst out laughing when Rohloff asked if Sunnie was having a better day.

"'One of Sunnie's pet peeves,' he explained, 'is toilet paper that's put on the dispenser forward instead of backward. I changed all the rolls this morning and watched her change them back as she noticed them. I've done that four times today when she's not looking. Keeps her going!'"

Sunnie told me years later that she knew Ralph was the culprit but decided to go along with the gag. She finally got tired of the game of changing the rolls back and forth, and thereafter left the paper whatever way Ralph put it.

Rohloff spent more time with Sunnie than with Ralph because of his being away on the road so much. Sunnie's ability to misplace her glasses or keys provided many chuckles. After prolonged searching, the two women found them in such unexpected places as under a pile of weeds, in a planter, and on the roof of Rohloff's shop. A pair of glasses disappeared one September and turned up the next June when Sunnie unpacked her summer clothes.

Sunnie could be bluntly outspoken at times. Rohloff thought this trait resulted from her caring so deeply about people and things:

"She says exactly what's on her mind but never refuses to listen to the other person's point of view. She can also be very emotional. When I opened my shop, I had spoken to Sunnie only a few times. She came in with a plant for the shop, looked around, and burst into tears because she was so happy for me.

"It was a common sight to see Sunnie driving her small Toyota pick-up around town with five Newfoundlands in back. Sadly, they all died. She and Ralph have had a parade of animals, not only dogs, cats, and burros, but also chickens, ducks, and geese. And rabbits, rabbits, and rabbits."

Sunnie gives a lot of her time to the Intermountain Humane Society as a volunteer worker. Whenever the organization needs her, she spends a week with its answering service. People call the service to report losing or finding a pet. They provide a description and other information about the animal, and she writes a report and tries to match the owner with his or her missing pet.

Plants rank a close second to animals with Sunnie. Many flowers add to the beauty of the land around the house, and her garden provides carrots, spinach, lettuce, tomatoes, and herbs for the table. Sunnie gets busy planting with the arrival of spring, but no one in the area knows when spring will arrive. Almost a foot of snow fell on the first day of summer in 1989 while I was with the Suttons. A heavy snowfall in late June, they assured me, was not uncommon in the Rockies. When I woke up that morning, Ralph was shoveling snow from the deck that extended from the living room of the house. He kept wood crackling in the fireplace all day as the temperature stayed around 30 degrees.

Ralph played at Herby's in the Executive Tower Inn in Denver until mid-April 1978 and then went to Switzerland for a week. Before flying overseas, he had three dates in New York, including one with the band at Condon's.

Ain't Misbehavin', the musical hit featuring tunes by Fats Waller, opened on Broadway in May. It won many awards, including the Tony for best musical of 1978. The show introduced a new generation to the music that Waller composed and played. Ralph was deeply touched when he and Sunnie saw it: "The tears were rollin' down my face."

Sutton and Gus Johnson spent July with the Golden Belle in Billings. A letter sent from the Northern Hotel, where business boomed during the gig, reflected Ralph's eagerness for the months in Bailey that he knew lay ahead while he played at Herby's for the rest of the year:

"The garden at home is doing real well, and I'm anxious to spend some time pulling weeds and watering the plants. I'm also going to do some fishing. No place like home." After a few days at the ranch he wrote happily that "it feels good to be here with the suitcase put away."

Ralph started 1979 on a novel note by making his first player piano rolls. He had a lot of fun with the player piano used by the manufacturer, Play-Rite Piano Rolls of Turlock, California. Sutton made six rolls at the January session. Three are medleys of, respectively, two tunes by Willard Robison, two by Willie the Lion Smith, and three by Fats Waller. The other three rolls consist of one number each—"Brother, Can You Spare a Dime?," "Honeysuckle Rose," and "Sophisticated Lady."

In April, Sutton went to Australia, another first for him. He booked a flight to Sydney, where he planned to relax for a day before going on to Brisbane for a jazz festival. Unfortunately, no one had told him he needed a visa, and that requirement did not occur to him either. As a result, Ralph left San Francisco a day later than scheduled after frantic telephone calls to the U.S. consulate and Brisbane. He received a warm welcome at the festival and also enjoyed petting some kangaroos and koalas while down under.

The festival audience included Mark Hewitt, who flew more than 600 miles from his home in Sydney. Hewitt had met Bud Freeman there during the Christmas season in 1976. The two men became friends and spent much time together during Freeman's three-week stay. Hewitt was familiar with the work of such pianists as James P. Johnson, Luckey Roberts, Jess Stacy, Joe Sullivan, Fats Waller, and Bob Zurke, and he asked Freeman many questions about them.

"Bud taught me the importance of the rhythm section in jazz," Hewitt said. "He told me that the rhythm section was the motor in the music. If the motor wasn't well tuned, the thing would never run right. He told me why the bands he had worked with early in his career sounded like they did and why the soloists played as they did. Because they had piano players like the ones I knew about; bass players like Bob Haggart and Jack Lesberg; and drummers like Jo Jones, Gene Krupa, Buddy Rich, Zutty Singleton, and George Wettling. That was why those bands had the drive that they did. It came from the engine room.

"He said one of the major reasons why the World's Greatest Jazzband had worked as well as it did was that they had Ralph Sutton on piano. He told me a little about Ralph, and what he told me made me want to know about this man. In the band, whether Bud was playing as a soloist or in an ensemble passage, he could venture as far and wide as he wished on any amount of tricky ground; but when he put his feet back on the doorstep, Ralph had the welcome mat there for him. That was what impressed Bud most.

"When I learned that Ralph was coming to Brisbane, I decided to hear him. He played there with a band and his playing knocked me out, especially the way he supported the other artists. He had such empathy for them."

Hewitt did not have a chance to meet Ralph at the 1979 festival. But he more than made up for lost time a few years later.

Mat Geiger had been a Swiss exchange student in 1966 when he heard Ralph, then working nearby with the Bob Cats, play a couple of numbers in an impromptu performance at Condon's. During the following years, Geiger established friendships with many top American musicians—chief among them Sutton—whom he heard at jazz festivals and clubs in Switzerland and elsewhere in Europe. He earned a master's and a doctor's degree in economics and played trombone on frequent gigs.

He also went to numerous jazz concerts, including one in Zurich in the spring of 1978 featuring Sweets Edison and Lockjaw Davis. There, Geiger ran across Margrit Burtscher, who became his wife. He had invited the band and a number of others to his house after the concert, and "somebody brought Margrit along. I was cooking for my guests when she came into the kitchen and offered to help. We started talking, and that was that." Burtscher—assisted by Ralph and Gus Johnson—made 1979 a memorable year for him.

Geiger had met Sutton in November 1975 at a Zurich club where

Ralph was playing. He went there with two old friends, jazz writer Johnny Simmen and his wife, Liza, who had known Sutton for years. That night, Ralph played with a rhythm section of Peter Schmidli, Isla Eckinger, and Rolf Rebmann, all members of a Swiss band called the Tremble Kids.

A couple of days later, Geiger got a call from Werner Keller, the clarinetist and leader of the Kids. Someone who spoke English was needed to bring Sutton to a Zurich radio station for a recording session. At Keller's request, Geiger picked up Ralph at his hotel and drove him to the studio, where a 9-foot Bösendorfer concert grand, one of his favorite pianos, awaited him.

"Ralph hadn't spoken much on the way to the studio," Geiger recalled. "He played a few bars to try out the piano and then sat quietly until he began recording. The session lasted only about two hours, and he did all the tunes in one take except 'Viper's Drag' and the Willard Robison medley, which he recorded twice. He remained at the piano between tunes and said hardly anything. He didn't even take his jacket off, though the studio was very warm.

"As we left, Ralph seemed pleased with the session but he didn't say a word about it. We went to a jewelry store so he could buy a watch for Sunnie. Somehow we had become friends."

Ralph returned to Switzerland in late April 1979 for the annual jazz festival in Bern. Geiger and Burtscher had decided to get married and to have Sutton and Johnson be best men. The couple planned to fly to the United States for their wedding without telling anyone at home that it would be the highlight of a vacation trip.

During the Bern festival, Geiger asked Ralph to be one of his best men and Burtscher invited "Uncle Gusti" to be the other, with their wives attending as witnesses. Both musicians accepted with obvious pleasure.

At a Bern club the following weekend, George Masso and the English trombonist Roy Williams met for the first time and had one of the richest experiences of their lives. Various small combos were delighting the audience in the packed room late that Saturday night. Masso and Williams joined one of them, a trio consisting of Ralph, Johnson, and bassist Dave Green of England.

"The trio swung like hell and provided an ideal backing for those two superb trombonists," Geiger said. "What George and Roy did on 'Tea for

Two,' 'I Can't Believe That You're in Love with Me,' and 'Polka Dots and Moonbeams' was some of the best trombone playing I've ever heard—swinging, relaxed, inventive, smooth. Just perfect."

The combo, now a quintet, created one of those incomparable but unheralded moments in jazz. Masso remembered the session vividly:

"It was very late, maybe 1:30 in the morning, when we're very relaxed. We were listening to the trio and they sounded wonderful. Ralph was in great form. I don't remember what they were playing, but it was very inspiring to Roy and me. Roy caught my eye and said, 'You feel like playing?' I said, '*Yeah.*' I think both of us were dying to play. We weren't getting much to play in the groups with which we were performing.

"So we got our horns out and went up on the bandstand, and the rest is history. It was just one of those nights when we locked into each other's playing and worked off each other—not only Roy and me, but also Ralph, Gus, and Dave. It was a great evening of dialogue. That's how I like to remember it—like chamber music. You're working off one another.

"A lot of things contributed to it. First of all, the hour—being so relaxed, the informality of the situation. When we started to play, you could hear a pin drop. That was very flattering to us. When Roy and I get together, we always relive that night in Bern. I think that will be true for as long as we live.

"Ralph was one of the reasons we wanted to pick up our horns and just enjoy. It was inspiring to play with him."

Mat Geiger and Margrit Burtscher were married in Denver in August 1979. They sent their families and friends a wedding announcement consisting of a postcard with a photo of the wedding party—themselves, Ralph and Sunnie Sutton, and Gus and Mildred Johnson. In the picture, the "Lacey" on the piece of cardboard held by the Suttons refers to Lacey Green, a mythical trumpet player invented by Ralph and some English friends of his and Geiger's.

It seems that after Sutton had played a gig near London, he and the friends drove through a village and past an alley named Lacey Green. "Lacey Green," Ralph said. "How's he doing?" They began telling stories about the legendary Lacey, and Geiger later joined them in swapping yarns verbally and in letters to one another. Lacey had been seen here or there. He had surfaced somewhere else. He was still blowing his horn. He was trying to get his chops in shape. But then the booze hit Lacey again. He landed in trouble and lost a gig.

Ralph stayed at the Geigers' home near Zurich during many of his tours in Switzerland. One day, while taking his usual long walk with their Belgian sheepdog, he became friendly with a young bull in a pasture. Somehow he persuaded the bull to leave its herd and come to him for some pats on the head. Sutton demonstrated this achievement with great pride.

"Animals just love him," Mat Geiger said. "That is one of Ralph's greatest gifts—making animals and people feel good."

Ralph calls himself a whorehouse piano player, but he has never played piano in a whorehouse. Neither has Jay McShann. No matter. An idea of Dick Gibson's blossomed into some fine albums and numerous gigs by the two master pianists performing under a colorful sobriquet, the Last of the Whorehouse Piano Players.

During Gibson's annual jazz party in Colorado Springs in September 1979, he got the idea of scheduling a two-piano set featuring McShann and Sutton. They brought down the house and had a ball playing together. Hearing them at the party inspired Ralph's old friend Charlie Baron to produce the two albums. "It was a gasser," Sutton said in describing the experience of recording with McShann. Milt Hinton and Gus Johnson provided stellar support for Sutton and McShann on the albums and on almost all the gigs that the Whorehousers played following their inaugural performance at the Gibson party.

Baron, who thought up the name of the Last of the Whorehouse Piano Players, didn't stop with the two albums by McShann and Sutton. From 1979 to 1982, he issued 14 LP albums and a cassette on his newly created Chaz Jazz label. Ralph is featured on 11 of the LPs and the cassette, and Dick Wellstood on the others. One of the Wellstood albums consists of two LPs.

Two of Sutton's recordings for Chaz Jazz consist entirely of solo piano. One of them is called *The Other Side of Ralph Sutton,* for which I wrote the liner notes:

> . . . The title of this album, *The Other Side of Ralph Sutton,* came from Ralph's desire to make an album composed almost entirely of tunes that he had rarely played for audiences and had never recorded. . . .

When I asked Ralph why he had chosen the tunes, his answer was simple—he likes them. Here are his other answers, equally unpretentious and to the point, characteristics of the man himself:

"Stan Wrightsman was a close friend of mine, and he wrote a couple of tunes—'Cattin' on the Keys' and 'Stanley's Waltz'—that I thought should be recorded.

"I've always loved Eddie Miller's rendition of his 'Lazy Mood,' and so I thought I'd take a stab at it in the hope I wouldn't mess it up too much.

"A few people are acquainted with Fats Waller's 'Jitterbug Waltz,' but even fewer know that he also wrote another waltz, 'Say Yes,' and I would rather get a 'yes' than a 'no' anytime.

"As for 'Brother, Can You Spare a Dime?,' the breadline seems to be getting closer than we realize—and besides, it's a beautiful tune.

"I like the way 'When Gabriel Blows His Horn' swings along—and Fats wrote it.

"I recorded 'Keep Your Temper' many years ago, but that record is out of print now. As the result of some urging from the one I love, I did it again here. Now I can rest easy.

"I heard a recording of Fats's playing 'Willow Tree' on the organ and liked it, and so I decided to include it in the album.

"One of the tunes that George Barnes and I used to play at Sunnie's Rendezvous in Aspen was 'I'm Always in the Mood for You.' It brings back some fond memories, and I am always in the mood for Sunnie.

"The next tune, 'Bond Street,' is from Fats's *London Suite*. 'Nuf said.

"I thought I'd include 'If It Ain't Love' because if it ain't love, forget it.

"And, of course, 'Honeysuckle Rose' has always been a favorite of mine...."

Ralph's other Chaz Jazz recordings highlight him with one or more musicians whom Baron called "major jazz artists who have not received recording exposure commensurate with their stature." In addition to McShann, Hinton, and Johnson, the Chaz Jazz roster has Ruby Braff, Kenny Davern, Peanuts Hucko, Bud Freeman, Eddie Miller, Vic

Dickenson, George Masso, Jack Lesberg, Cliff Leeman, and Bobby Rosengarden. Wellstood plays solo piano on one of his Chaz Jazz albums, and the other is by the Blue Three—Davern, Wellstood, and Rosengarden.

The Last of the Whorehouse Piano Players recorded for Chiaroscuro in 1989, again accompanied by Hinton and Johnson. That year, Chiaroscuro bought Chaz Jazz. Chiaroscuro began to reissue the Chaz Jazz recordings in 1992, starting with a CD of the two-piano tunes by Sutton and McShann. One of the numbers, "Truckin'," features a lusty Wallerlike vocal by Sutton. Two previously unissued numbers were added to the CD, with the regrettable exclusion of a solo by each pianist. One of the tunes omitted from the CD is "I'll Catch the Sun," a beautiful ballad sung by McShann. The other solo is Sutton's "Ain't Misbehavin'."

Ruth and I received a letter from Ralph shortly after New Year's Day in 1980: "I know where the time goes, but I wish it wouldn't. Sunnie and I wish you a swingin' New Year and everything that goes with it. Think of you often and decided to sit ratt down and write yourselves a letter. Christmas was nice and quiet with Sunnie's folks here. Dad and I played checkers with hot buttered rum on the side. Sunnie makes a hell of a good batter for that stuff. Very filling though...." The letter ended with Sutton's frequently expressed directive to "Keep breathin' and keep swingin'."

Ralph related a few weeks later that "the Sutton menagerie now has four Newfs—Mollie, Ella, Tatum, and female pup Boots—and Bogie the Saint Bernard." Basie subsequently joined the Newfoundland contingent. "It's so nice to be home again where it's peaceful and away from the assholes," Ralph wrote in his next letter.

Sutton flew to England in late April for a concert in Manchester with Al Casey and Claude (Fiddler) Williams. Then he went to Switzerland for the Bern festival, which was "a huge success and a sellout." He played there in a band with Pee Wee Erwin, George Masso, Johnny Mince, Jack Lesberg, and Gus Johnson. After the festival, Ralph toured England, Scotland, and Switzerland with Peanuts Hucko's Pied Pipers, a combo that also included Lesberg, Johnson, and Peter Appleyard. He sent an enthusiastic though wistful account:

"The quintet is really swinging. Jazz fans all over Europe. Most rewarding. Switzerland is such a beautiful country. Wish I had the money to retire here. But I can still dream."

The quintet dates ended shortly after mid-May, and Ralph played in Barcelona, Stuttgart, and Munich before winding up the tour in England and Scotland in late June. He had hoped for some dates in Italy but didn't sound too disappointed when they failed to come through: "It's a long enough tour to be away from Sunnie."

Ralph arrived home in early July, but, as Sunnie wrote, "it didn't last long. Had him for only a week and he was gone again," this time to New York for a gig at Hanratty's, a jazz club. George Shearing dropped in one night and sat in with Ralph for a duet that broke up the crowd.

On Labor Day weekend in 1980, radio station KWNE in Ukiah, California, had a surprise for jazz fans in the community. The first program of "The Jazz Show" went on the air, with Hal Curtis, the husband of Barbara Sutton Curtis, as host. Ralph's brother-in-law, who taught high school English in the city, welcomed the chance to resume the radio work he had enjoyed at St. Lawrence University. Hal worked at the campus station as a student and then as a teaching assistant in the university's Radio Department. He later managed a classical music station in San Francisco.

A couple of years before Hal went on the air in Ukiah, the station—then licensed as KLIL—had taken a shot at jazz programming. The show lasted about a month before bowing to the rock and country-and-western music that pervaded the area. One Ukiah station played nothing but country-and-western. The sale of KLIL resulted in a new call sign, KWNE, and brought Hal into the picture. He and the new owner of the station knew each other slightly.

"I asked him if he would let me do some jazz programming," Curtis said. "He surprised me by saying he liked jazz and had been hoping I'd host a show for him."

Hal's show aired on Sunday night from 9 to 11 o'clock for about four years, when the station switched it to Sunday morning. He questioned the wisdom of the change but was told that the demographics for a morning show were better because he would attract the audience he wanted, people from 30 to 55. Sure enough, he got a lot more comments than before and received mail about the program for the first time.

"I don't feel it's important to play the newest and latest kinds of jazz, and I don't play them," Hal said. "The recordings of guys like Louis Armstrong, Earl Hines, Duke Ellington, Bix Beiderbecke, and Jelly Roll

Morton are our musical heritage. If we don't preserve them and play them so people know who these great players were, we're going to lose both the musicians and their music.

"I usually start with a big band track, follow it with something a bit more modern, and then maybe play a record from the '20s or '30s. One thing I like to do that listeners enjoy is to play something fairly contemporary and follow it with a recording that may be 50 years old. They mix together much better than people might realize. I also try to include a vocal or two. Of course I can play Ralph's records, which I do regularly.

"The show reaches the audience we want it to reach, and it also gets people in their 30s who grew up on rock and are looking for something else. My teenage students take great pride in telling me they hate jazz and don't listen to it—but that their parents do listen to the show."

Hal gets a special kick from putting on a show for Easter. He uses his imagination to compensate for the dearth of Easter jazz with timely tune titles and musicians' names, and fine puns. One year the show included "Cottontail" by Duke Ellington; "Bunny" by Shorty Rogers; "Easter the Sun and West of the Moon" by Tommy Dorsey, with a solo by Bunny Berigan; "Eggsactly Like You" by Ralph and Wild Bill Davison with a Danish combo; "I'm Putting All My Eggs in One Basket" by Louis Armstrong and Ella Fitzgerald; "Candy" by Don Byas; "Lollipop" by Woody Herman; and "Stompin' at the Savoy" by Chick Webb.

Chapter **28**

A Better Trick Is Not to Be Had

ne of the biggest disappointments of Ralph's career occurred, ironically, during a highly successful engagement. In January 1981, he and Jay McShann were performing as the Last of the Whorehouse Piano Players, along with Milt Hinton and Gus Johnson, at Rick's in Chicago. They attracted large, enthusiastic crowds to the club, in a lakefront hotel, and received excellent reviews.

Late one day, someone from Rick's told the musicians that CBS planned to tape a segment for "60 Minutes" at the club that night. The men were given the impression that the segment would feature Sutton and McShann. Ralph called me and urged that Ruth and I come down even earlier than usual so we wouldn't miss any of the action. We joined him in his hotel room, and he called Sunnie and told her the good news about the taping and the expected appearance of the Whorehousers on a perennially top-rated television show. I had never seen Ralph more pleased about anything.

Harry Reasoner, the veteran "60 Minutes" reporter, showed up with a camera crew and took considerable footage of McShann, Sutton, Hinton, and Johnson. However, he did not interview any of them. The manager of Rick's, savoring the prospect of the jammed club's appearing on "60 Minutes," announced the cancellation of the cover charge for the last show and the reduction of drink prices to normal levels.

A few days later, a *Chicago Tribune* columnist reported that Reasoner and the camera crew had been at Rick's to film the room itself for a segment about the movie classic *Casablanca*. The club's full name was Rick's Cafe Americain, and it was a replica of the club of that name in the film. At the entrance to the jazz club, a life-sized cardboard figure of Humphrey Bogart, who plays Rick, the club owner, welcomed guests to the room.

On a Sunday evening the following fall, while Ralph was touring in Europe, Reasoner appeared at the beginning of "60 Minutes" and previewed the segment. I called Sunnie, and we watched a very interesting piece on *Casablanca*. It included the briefest of shots—unidentified—of McShann, Hinton, and Johnson, but none of Sutton. All the musicians felt more than a little let down.

"There really ought to be a law against having as much fun onstage as Jay McShann, Ralph Sutton, Milt Hinton, and Gus Johnson are having...," the reviewer for the *Chicago Sun-Times* wrote when the group returned to Rick's in February 1983. "If they're 'whorehouse' piano players, a better trick is not to be had."

The four musicians agreed with that appraisal. Said McShann:

"It's a gas working with Ralph. He says something on the keyboard to me, and I say OK. Then I say something to him, and he says OK. Back and forth. That's the way we talk to each other, and that's how we stay out of each other's way. And what more can you ask for than Milt and Gus in the rhythm section?

"I never knew that Ralph sang, and I was so surprised the first time I heard him. He sounded exactly like Fats, and he's got Fats's expressions. I told him I thought I was hearing Fats. I was glad I was there so I could see for myself that it was Ralph singing. He should do more of it. It adds so much variety.

"I'm not a singer," McShann maintained, though long famous not only for his piano artistry but also for his singing, especially the blues. "Years ago, people demanded that someone sing this tune or that tune. No one else wanted to do it, so I had to."

Hinton remarked that the four men "really love one another, and I think it sort of projects. Anybody who sees us and hears us knows that. Every time we play together it's a joy.

"The variety is great with Ralph and Jay playing," Hinton said. "They play a few choruses together, and then each does something with the rhythm section. Then Gus and I do one of the routines we've cooked up to be entertaining. Sometimes we look back and forth at Jay and Ralph when they're playing fours. Or we pretend to get ourselves screwed up. The public likes that sort of thing, and we're just trying to please the people and play good music."

Johnson first played with McShann when he joined the latter's band in Kansas City in 1938. He enjoyed hearing Sutton and McShann "give each other a lift when they're playing. Milt and I feel great playing with them because they go together just like ham and eggs."

Sutton seldom shows emotion. But his face lights up when he talks about the Whorehousers.

"Jay and I make a beautiful team," he said. "It's the best team I've ever worked with. I've played with a lot of piano players—Dick Wellstood, Roland Hanna, Dick Hyman, Dave McKenna—and they were all great to work with. But this thing with Jay, we really have something going there. The two albums we did for Charlie Baron turned out real well. I don't see how we could have done them any better.

"We listen to each other and we keep an eye on each other. I know that when Jay plays a solo chorus, I'll stay below him and back him up and play rhythm. If I feel he's going into a second chorus, I'll continue playing rhythm behind him. Then he hands it over to me and does the same thing behind me.

"Maybe we'll play four bars or eight bars each, back and forth, and Milt and Gus will take the bridge. On the rompin' choruses going out, if Jay's in the middle of the keyboard I'll go up high in the treble. If he's up in the treble, I'll stay down in the bass so there's some variety.

"Jay may hear my voice differently than I do. Singing sounds different to the listener than to the singer. Fats has always been a favorite of mine, but my voice doesn't have the range that his had. I'm very conscious of the way I sound, and when I hear it played back it really sounds funny to me. But at least I sing in tune.

"We had a ball when we did the first two albums. All of us had friends in the engineer's booth who came to the studio to catch the sessions. They had never heard anything like it. They enjoyed it so much it was unbelievable. The four of us are all dear friends, and we had such rapport with one another. It was so easy. We did a lot of the tunes in just one take.

"After we finished the session, I told Jay as we were leaving the building that if this doesn't make it, I'm ready to quit the music business."

During the next few years, the group played many engagements in the United States and Europe. Ralph served as m.c. at the performances.

"It just happened to work out that way," he said. "When we sat down on our first opening night, I had a list of the tunes we had recorded. Later I added some others. After the first tune I looked at Jay and thought I'd better say something because I figured he wouldn't."

In April 1981, Ralph played some solo dates in Switzerland. He joined Peanuts Hucko, Jack Lesberg, Jake Hanna, and Peter Appleyard at the Bern festival in May, after which the quintet went to Stockholm for four engagements. One of those Stockholm gigs could have been the time that Ralph found himself stuck with what Hanna remembered as "a pretty bad piano."

"It was a real fancy place," Hanna said. "The piano was painted white, but they forgot to tune the thing. Ralph found a couple of bad notes, and he played them all night. Peanuts would say, 'Can't you go around those notes?' Ralph told him, 'Nope, those are the ones I'm playing.' He found a way to play them as many times as possible on every chorus. Most guys would try to avoid them, but Ralph went out of his way to use them. He sounded like Thelonious Monk."

The men went to Germany and played in Frankfurt and Stuttgart after leaving Stockholm. Then they flew to England for a tour of cities from south to north.

One evening in Hereford, the musicians had dinner with Eddie Cook and his wife. Cook had succeeded Sinclair Traill as publisher and editor in chief of *Jazz Journal International*. Cook had talked to Ralph only a few times but found him "friendly and warmhearted, with a great—almost British—sense of humor.

"His personality didn't come over very strongly at the concerts I've attended," Cook said, "perhaps because he was always part of someone else's band. But he has always been very popular with the audience."

Sutton, Hucko, Lesberg, and Hanna flew to Texas from London on May 18 for the Odessa party. The plane landed in Odessa late at night at about the same time that Sunnie arrived from Bailey. After the party and a week at Morning Air Ranch, Sutton returned with Gus Johnson to the Northern Hotel in Billings. He wrote that "Gus and I are back to kickin' tires and spittin'. Made some hot sauce yesterday at a friend's house. It beats ketchup."

Ralph flew to Australia with Ruby Braff in October. He reported that they "broke it up" in Brisbane. Sutton returned to Switzerland late that month and again teamed up with Hucko, Lesberg, and Hanna. He performed there and in Germany through the first week of December, playing 17 concerts within a 21-day period.

Starting in 1982, the skies became ultrafriendly for jazz fans on Swissair's long-haul flights from Switzerland to the United States and other countries. Jazz writer Johnny Simmen, a troubleshooter in the airline's passenger sales promotion department, began creating programs for travelers listening to the Inflight Entertainment jazz channel. Simmen prepared the programs with his own records, and a recording studio put them together into cassettes.

Swissair gave Simmen complete freedom in choosing the musicians and tunes he used on the tapes. The programs were changed every two months. At first, each program lasted an hour and had no commentary. The running time was eventually extended to an hour and a half, and then to two hours. After more than a year of persuasion, Simmen bowed to requests that he add some commentary to the music being presented.

Simmen featured such artists as Louis Armstrong, Bob Barnard, Count Basie, Sidney Bechet, Ray Bryant, Kenny Burrell, Benny Carter, Henri Chaix, Doc Cheatham, Buck Clayton, Bill Coleman, Wild Bill Davis, Vic Dickenson, Tommy Flanagan, Erroll Garner, Lionel Hampton, Coleman Hawkins, Earl Hines, Milt Hinton, Johnny Hodges, Billie Holiday, Illinois Jacquet, James P. Johnson, Guy Lafitte, Ole (Fessor) Lindgreen, Dave McKenna, Kid Ory, Jimmy Rowles, Willie the Lion Smith, Art Tatum, Joe Turner, Fats Waller, Chick Webb, Dick Wellstood, and Teddy Wilson. Several programs of various jazz anthologies were also presented for the passengers.

While flying home from Switzerland in December 1987, Ralph and Sunnie listened to the program featuring Sutton. They heard Simmen praise Ralph not only as "justly famous for his authentic, impeccable re-creations of the works of some of the greatest stylists in jazz piano history, such as James P. Johnson, Willie the Lion Smith, Fats Waller, Bob Zurke, and Meade Lux Lewis," but also as "a great inventive pianist in his own right."

During more than 60 years of "jazz appreciation," Simmen has written over 3,000 jazz articles for about a dozen publications. "I write only about musicians, bands, and records that I understand and love," he said. "I'm not a critic, but a jazz lover who shares his pleasure with his readers."

Simmen expressed a deceptively simple philosophy when he wrote that "It's up to each individual listener to get a maximum of fun and joy out of the music. . ." His statement brought to mind the people who have come up to me at jazz parties and declared that X, Y, or Z is "better than Sutton." Almost without exception, they seemed surprised when I replied that everyone should decide whom he or she likes on the basis of what his or her ears tell them. Ralph agreed strongly.

A perceptive article on Sutton appeared in *The Denver Post* in January 1982. Written by Zeke Scher, it began:

> If you want to hear "a pianist of legendary stature who holds the real jazz tradition in his enormous hands," you can visit Italy, Austria, and England during the next four weeks.
>
> On the other hand, if you just want to see this "jazz immortal," you can ride up U.S. 285 to Bailey, on the banks of the North Fork of the South Platte River some 50 miles west of downtown Denver, where Ralph Sutton lives between worldwide gigs.
>
> Those appraisals as "legendary" and "immortal" come from Danish and Dutch music critics who, like many other jazz fans around the world, treat pianist Sutton with royal reverence. In his home state of Colorado, however, Sutton gets only an occasional offer (last weekend it was a wedding reception in Denver). On Saturday, he was off to Europe again for a series of concerts and jam sessions. . .

In April, the Suttons and Gus Johnson flew to Minneapolis. They were joined by Al Grey, Kenny Davern, Flip Phillips, and Milt Hinton for dates there, followed by gigs in Eau Claire and River Falls, Wisconsin. Ralph called it "a real swingin' band."

Sunnie's father, Arthur Anderson, had been hospitalized with cancer before she and Ralph left Bailey for Minneapolis. He died in late April. "I'll sure miss him," Ralph wrote. "We were good friends and had a lot of fun together."

The Suttons branched out that summer and added poultry to their menagerie. They found themselves with 20 chickens and 2 ducks in addition to 3 burros, a rabbit, and the usual assortment of dogs and cats.

"We have four roosters, all singing away," Sunnie told us. "Such a symphony!"

In December, Sunnie underwent a mastectomy. Her morale remained high throughout the ordeal, and she sounded as perky as ever when Ruth and I called shortly after the surgery. She came to Chicago with Ralph in February 1983 and enjoyed the Last of the Whorehouse Piano Players as he and Jay McShann, Milt Hinton, and Gus Johnson delighted big crowds night after night at Rick's.

Later in February, Sutton and Johnson again returned to the Northern Hotel in Billings. It turned out to be their final gig with the Golden Belle.

"Things are a little slow there," Sunnie wrote. "The hotel has been sold, and I doubt if they'll book Ralph and Gus again.

"I'm really missing Ralph. Gee, we had December, January, and most of February together! Oh, well, he'll appreciate me when I pick him up in Billings."

Ralph was the first featured artist at the Cafe des Copains in Toronto when the club started its piano jazz policy in June 1983. The policy began as a 13-week experiment. It became so popular, however, that pianists were highlighted until the club closed in March 1991 following a failure to negotiate a rent renewal agreement. Sutton performed there a number of times, as did Barbara Sutton Curtis beginning in 1987.

A superb recording presents tunes that Ralph played at the Toronto club through 1987. John Norris, publisher of the Canadian jazz magazine *Coda*, supervised the Cafe des Copains recording and wrote the liner notes. When listing the production credits, he paid tribute to the pianist in an unusual way: "Production coordination by John Norris, who wishes to thank Ralph Sutton for the privilege of being able to release his music." The photo of the pianist on the cover of the liner notes was taken by Paul J. Hoeffler, who contributed the portrait on the jacket of this book.

Mark Hewitt went into action as soon as he learned that his friend Bob Barnard, also of Sydney, Australia, planned to fly to New York in August 1983. Hewitt had heard Ralph at the Brisbane jazz festival in 1979, where Barnard and Sutton met and played together. Barnard and his band greeted Ralph at the Brisbane airport that year, when Sutton made his first trip to Australia.

Ralph played in Brisbane again at the 1981 festival, and he and Hewitt met there. The program also featured Barnard and his band. Ruby Braff had come over with Ralph, and Barnard and Sutton did not work together until the final day of the event.

"Ralph played with Bob's band and they were fantastic," Hewitt said. "They sounded like two lovers who hadn't seen each other for a long time and had gotten back together."

As Hewitt listened to Barnard and Sutton, he decided to make a record featuring the two artists. He started to plan the session in 1982 but could not arrange to bring Ralph back to Australia, as he wished. Then Hewitt learned that Barnard would be going to the jazz festival in Edinburgh, Scotland, in August 1983, with a stopover in New York.

"I wrote to Ralph and told him that Bob was coming through the States on his way to Edinburgh, and would he like to make a recording with him," Hewitt related. "Ralph said he'd love to, and for his normal recording fee.

"I told him I needed a bass player and asked if he could recommend someone. Ralph said, 'I'll give you a telephone number. When the phone is answered, introduce yourself, tell the person what's involved, and say I told you to call.'

"So I called and told the man who answered what Ralph said to tell him and that Ralph had given me his number. The man told me his name was Milt Hinton, and I almost fell over. He said he'd be delighted to play the recording session, that it had to be fine if Ralph had told me to call him. I asked about his fee, which I thought would be high, and Milt told me he'd do it for scale. I wanted to pay him half in advance, but he wouldn't take my money."

Hewitt had a friend in New York named Horst Liepolt, a nightclub owner who had lived in Australia for about 30 years. Liepolt served as coordinator for the recording session, renting a studio and making sure the musicians arrived on time. He asked for no payment, which was fortunate. Hewitt did not have enough funds at that time to fly to New York after paying for the studio and the four musicians, who included Barnard's brother, Len, on drums.

"Every tune on that record is a first take," Hewitt said. "They recorded 'Slow Boat to China' first as a run-through, and it sounded so good that they kept it. The last tune they played was 'Swing That Music,' which I used as the opening number. The reason there's such a long bass solo at the beginning and also a bass solo later is that Milt told me he used to do it that way as a feature with Cab Calloway."

The recording is called *Partners in Crime.* During Sutton's first visit to Australia, in 1979, he had given Bob Barnard a photo of himself and inscribed it, "To Bob, my partner in crime. Ralph."

The Sutton menagerie lost a rooster in October with the banishment of Louie. The bird always greeted Sunnie and Ralph with loud crowing, and so they named him after the immortal Armstrong and his incomparable trumpet. Unfortunately, Louie began to stalk Sunnie whenever she approached. He probably thought she intended to harm the hens in the flock when she came near to feed the rabbits.

Louie attacked one day when Sunnie bent down with the rabbits' dinner. He gave her a black eye with his bill, and Sunnie retaliated by giving him to a neighbor. But Louie turned against the neighbor and her two daughters as well, and she gave him to Gus and Mildred Johnson. The Johnsons decided not to mess with Louie. They passed him along to one of their daughters, who eventually cooked him.

Anyone who savored excellent skiing and fine jazz could start every New Year with the best of both, beginning in 1983. Tom Brownell and his wife, Elisabeth, provided the doubleheader at Thunderbird Lodge, their resort in Taos Ski Valley, New Mexico.

When Brownell walked into Hanratty's to hear Ralph during a business trip to New York in 1982, he had no idea that he and Sunnie Sutton had gone to high school together. He had never met Ralph nor heard him in a live performance. But Brownell loved stride piano, and a friend had sent him some of the Chaz Jazz records. So when he saw that Ralph was playing at Hanratty's, he dropped in to hear the pianist whose recordings had given him such a kick.

"I introduced myself to Ralph and talked to him at intermission," Brownell said. "The liner notes of his records said he lived in Bailey, which isn't too far from Taos. I asked if he might be interested in coming down to play a gig, and he said sure.

"Ralph and Sunnie came to the lodge for a week in January 1983. We had horrible snowstorms that week, though, so very few people who weren't guests at the lodge could get up to hear him, which was a shame. But Elisabeth and I became friends of the Suttons', and Ralph came for two weeks in 1984 with Kenny Davern, Milt Hinton, and Gus Johnson. Herb Ellis joined them during the gig.

"Sunnie and I discovered that we had been in high school together. Where are you from? Chicago. North Side. What high school? Senn. What year? She graduated in June of '43 and I got out in January of '44. I have the yearbooks with her picture in them. Senn had about 4,500 students, and we never met until Sunnie and Ralph first came to the lodge."

Brownell bought a 7-foot grand piano prior to the 1984 engagement, and the Thunderbird's jazz roster expanded in 1985 with Buddy Tate and Bucky Pizzarelli. Through the years, the lodge presented such other notables as Conte Candoli, Warren Vaché, Jr., Carl Fontana, Jim Galloway, Scott Hamilton, James Moody, Flip Phillips, Eric Schneider, Buddy Tate, Monty Alexander, Eddie Higgins, Ross Tompkins, Gerald Wiggins, Howard Alden, Barney Kessel, Ray Brown, Phil Flanigan, Bob Haggart, Brian Torff, Jake Hanna, and Butch Miles.

Brownell billed the musicians as the Jazz Legends. He produced limited editions of cassettes of the Thunderbird performances, one in 1984 and two in 1985. Guests of the lodge paid nothing to hear marvelous jazz nightly. Others were charged a small admission fee. A number of ski enthusiasts who had never heard of Sutton acknowledged after hearing him play that they were drawn equally each succeeding January by the skiing and the wonderful jazz.

Sutton and some of his cohorts, notably Vaché, Davern, Hinton, and Johnson—until the drummer retired because of illness—returned to Taos Ski Valley year after year. Every January 7, Davern celebrated his birthday at the lodge.

Few of the musicians experimented with skiing, though Torff, Johnson, Miles, and Elsa Davern ventured onto the slopes. I asked Vaché during our interview for this book whether he had ever skied there. He looked at me as though I were out of my mind and replied, "If somebody told you to strap a couple of boards to your feet and slide down that mountain, would you do it?" Definitely not, I said. "Me neither," said Vaché. "I break too easily."

Ralph's hot sauce became almost as popular as his piano playing among the Thunderbird staff and some of the guests. He brought a jar of it along early in his tenure at the lodge, and the sauce soon disappeared. Whereupon Sutton began going next door to the Brownells' home every January to concoct a few jars of the stuff in their kitchen. The staff loved the sauce, but it was served to guests only upon request. "It scares too many of them," Brownell said.

Elisabeth Brownell's mother, Emmy Schlegl, came from her home in Munich, Germany, one year and assisted Ralph with the hot sauce besides taking in every set of the music. They brewed about 15 quarts of it. Sutton warned Schlegl to wash her hands thoroughly and not rub her eyes, because the ingredients burned some people's skin. She was immune to the sauce, but Vaché wasn't.

"When we go to Taos, they put Ralph to work in the kitchen making his hot sauce," Vaché said. "The sauce is great, but I'll never understand how anyone can cut up jalapeño peppers with bare hands. He's got skin like an alligator. He must be an alligator to have his hands in jalapeños and feel nothing. That oil gets me, but Ralph has no pores in those hands. They're made of concrete."

Postscript: One of Ralph's favorite tunes is "Alligator Crawl," the great piano solo by Fats Waller.

Chapter **29**

The Two Pianos Did Everything but Fly

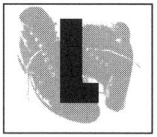ike most performing artists, Sutton frequently plays in surroundings he would avoid if he did not need the income. When such engagements come along, he tries to follow the policy of playing, taking his pay, and then leaving the scene as soon as practicable. Ralph expresses this philosophy by jokingly but determinedly quoting a Yiddish phrase, "Nem de gelt," which means, "Take the money (and get out)."

In April 1984, Sutton played two weekends of solo piano at a club in a Denver suburb. A writer named Alex Katz dropped in to hear him, and his discerning impressions appeared in a *Denver Post* article under the headline, "Sutton out of place, but never out of style":

> Saturday night at the Cafe Kandahar in Littleton, one of the world's great stride piano players had finished playing his first number, "Between the Devil and the Deep Blue Sea," when a patron approached him.
> "Do you take requests?" the customer asked.
> "I take 'em, but I don't play 'em," Ralph Sutton replied.
> So the man offered a dollar bill to the pianist who has recorded with Sidney Bechet, Jack Teagarden [Katz was mistaken; Sutton never recorded with Teagarden], and dozens of the world's greatest musicians, and whose record *The Last of the Whorehouse Piano Players*, which he recorded with Jay "Hootie" McShann, has been hailed as one of the best piano albums of recent years.
> "Man, I can't buy anything with a dollar," said Sutton.
> Such is the fate of this 61-year-old artist who owns a home in Bailey and who is respected by audiences and musicians worldwide,

but who never has received proper recognition in Denver.

A tall man with a large, open face, thick spectacles, and a broad grin, Sutton's brilliance was wasted at the Kandahar. It's an attractive restaurant that doubles as a ski museum, and it's a fine place to listen to background music. But the Kandahar isn't set up for a musician of Sutton's stature. The area around the piano seats only about 20, and most of those seated last night had a poor view. With another 20 people standing nearby, the place seemed crowded and stuffy, and the din from the bar across the room detracted from the music.

But it was still worth it. Sutton plays stride piano in the tradition of James P. Johnson and Fats Waller. . . . With his extraordinary coordination, he can play two complicated runs at once, with elements of stride, swing, and boogie woogie. In his first set, he played "Supposin'," "Jubilee," and, perhaps in deference to the Kandahar crowd, "As Time Goes By." When he felt inspired, the music heated up. When he felt like resting, he played high-class cocktail music.

Before the evening began, Sutton was asked how he felt about being a relative unknown in Denver. He grinned. "I just say 'F— it! Get the money! They don't know any better!' The waitresses bring me martinis. I don't feel any pain."

Sunnie's widowed mother, Irene Anderson, moved from Denver to Morning Air Ranch early in April. She lived with the Suttons until her death seven years later. Sunnie greatly appreciated Ralph's willingness to let his mother-in-law stay in their home. The older woman cut into their privacy when he was not on the road, and she and Sunnie did not always see eye to eye. Sutton never complained about her, and Sunnie found pleasure in her mother's fondness for Ralph: "She adores him."

Ralph flew to Japan in late April for his first engagement in the Far East. He played a series of solo gigs and also teamed up with Japanese musicians for dates in Tokyo and several other cities. "I really loved it," he wrote after returning home. "The hospitality and food, etc., were great. I hope to go back next year." Sutton went back to Japan not only in 1985 but annually for years thereafter.

During the summer of 1984, Flip Phillips spent three days with Ralph and Sunnie in Bailey. Phillips, a man of almost as few words as his host, often electrified audiences the way Sutton did. Both repeatedly brought crowds to their feet applauding and shouting for encores of brilliant, swinging improvisation. At the ranch he enjoyed himself thoroughly, especially when the two old friends went fishing in the river together.

"Ralph is a man after my own heart," Phillips said. "He's quiet, minds his own business, and plays his ass off. I felt his left arm once and it was like feeling a baseball bat. That, of course, is from playing stride piano, which he does better than anyone.

"We play many concerts together, and when we get to play in the same set I enjoy yelling at him to 'Get it!' and go all over that piano. He responds very well. I can tell by the smile on his face, and does he 'get it.' He shakes things up.

"Ralph doesn't laugh loudly. When he hears a funny story, his face puffs up and gets red and his eyes start squinting. He's hilarious."

Some time after his stay in Bailey, Phillips gave the Suttons a wooden clock that he had carved himself. Ralph and Sunnie hung it in a prominent spot on a wall of their music room, and whoever entered saw it immediately. Phillips carved "Skip and Harry" on the face of the clock, but neither man knew why they called each other by those nicknames.

"He calls me Skip and I call him Harry," Phillips said. "For three days at his place he called me Skip. After the third day I told him, 'You want to be like that, I'm calling you Harry from now on.' It's been that way ever since and will be forever.

"I hope it will be forever. There is only one Ralph Sutton. Harry, that is!"

The Denver Post published a lengthy profile of Sutton in its *Empire Magazine* section on a Sunday in October 1984. The writer, Stephen Singular, had heard Ralph and Jay McShann perform together earlier in the year. He described that experience and followed with a number of observations about Sutton. The article was called "Piano Man" and had an appropriate subtitle, "Ralph Sutton has always called his own tune."

> . . . Sitting at the piano opposite McShann, Sutton was ramrod straight, his face locked into a frown. He didn't appear to be having

any fun at all. The only way to discover what kind of time he was having was to listen. The two pianos did everything but fly. The music was happy—there is no better word for it—and that is precisely how it makes people feel. The audience listened, wriggled in their seats, moved their feet without thinking about it. . . .

The first thing that stands out in Sutton's playing is the range of his dynamics. He can play with a deft, soft, lyrical touch, but when he unleashes his left hand, Sutton has a power and confidence that few pianists can approach. . . . The second thing is his taste, his attraction to simplicity and beauty. In decades past, taste might have been something that one would have assumed a good jazz musician, or any other artist, would have. Now, many great jazz artists have been troubled or confused by the problem of incorporating the more dissonant—or ugly—sounds of the contemporary world into their playing. Sutton seemingly has never been bothered by this. Ask him his opinion of "fusion," one of the more recent movements in jazz, and he says, "Fusion? That's con-fusion." For the past half century, he has played music that is more devoted to swinging than to making any other kind of statement. In the world of modern music, that is more of an achievement than might at first seem obvious. . . .

(Sutton's playing) embodies a contradiction: How can a person who shows so little happiness on the outside produce such joyful sounds? . . .

In March 1985, Ralph starred in both of the top-billed attractions at the Mid-America Jazz Festival in St. Louis. The festival was headlined by the "Return of the Bob Cats"; and Sutton and McShann were on the program as the Last of the Whorehouse Piano Players, along with Milt Hinton and Gus Johnson.

The Bob Cats featured five members of the combo from the old Bob Crosby band—Yank Lawson, Eddie Miller, Nappy Lamare, Bob Haggart, and Ray Bauduc. Another Bob Cat alumnus, Billy Butterfield, had been scheduled to be with the group, but illness prevented him from appearing. George Masso, Johnny Mince, and Ralph filled out the Bob Cat lineup.

Haggart and Bauduc teamed up on "Big Noise from Winnetka" and received a standing ovation. They especially delighted those in the audience who had heard the two creators of the famous bass-drums novelty number play it during the Big Band Era.

Jess Stacy had been billed as "Honored Guest" at the festival, but poor health sidelined him as well. Sutton recalled a visit to Stacy's home, where the older pianist told him, "I love music but I hate to play it." Ralph professed to be starting to feel the same way. The Bob Cats, including Sutton, went from St. Louis to Indianapolis, where they played to another packed house.

Ralph was badly upstaged one hot Saturday in August. He had offered his services for the community's annual Bailey Day celebration, consisting of fun, food, games, shopping at roadside booths, and a variey of live entertainment.

Sutton found himself playing an out-of-tune spinet on Main Street at the foot of Crow Hill, across from a Standard station. At the other end of the street, near the old post office, the volunteer Bailey Fire Department staged its own brand of live entertainment. Firemen shot a spout of water high into the air and balanced a large ball on the top of it. The spectacle attracted a sizable crowd all day. The pianist did just the opposite. It was the first and last time he donated his musical talent to Bailey Day.

Ralph flew to Bern in October 1985 for several weeks of gigs with Jim Galloway, Hinton, and Johnson. They played at Jaylin's Club in the Hotel Schweizerhof in Bern, the Widder Bar in Zurich, and in several other cities, including Lucerne, Lausanne, and Biel. "It feels so good to be back in Switzerland," Sutton wrote. "Everything is first class. We were met at the airport in Bern by a Mercedes limo from the Schweizerhof." Everything became even better when Sunnie joined him during the tour.

Manfred Selchow, a German teacher, took time off from working on *Profoundly Blue,* his bio-discography of Edmond Hall, to go to Bern to hear the quartet. He and his wife, Renate, drove about 600 miles from their home in Westoverledingen. Selchow had been in contact with Ralph since 1978, when he asked for assistance with the Hall project. Sutton responded with a long letter containing not only information about Hall, but also personal thoughts and memories of the clarinetist, who had been a close friend. The two men began corresponding, and Selchow developed a desire to meet Ralph.

The Selchows went to the United States during the summer of 1983 to research his book. The highlight of the trip came when Ralph played a solo concert in Carnegie Hall in late July. Selchow had written that he and his wife would be in the audience, and they joined the many people who went backstage after the concert to chat with Ralph or to get his autograph.

"Ralph looked at my face while he was talking to some other people," Selchow remembered. "Although he had never seen a photo of me, he pointed his finger at me. A broad smile spread over his face, and he said, 'Mannie.' I still don't understand how he could have known me.

"Ralph played at the Waterloo Village Jazz Festival in New Jersey the next two days, and we had a chance to talk. I loved this man from the moment I first saw him, and my feeling for him did not come from my admiration of him as a musician. I was drawn to characteristics of his that are dying out or that people often hide because they do not seem to fit our time—honesty, openness, compassion, and great interest in others."

In November 1983, the Selchows drove to Bern, where Sutton was playing with Peanuts Hucko's Pied Pipers. The combo also included Jack Lesberg, Gus Johnson, and Lars Erstrand. Selchow had remarked to Ralph that "Should I" was one of his favorite tunes. That night, Sutton played the number, accompanied by Lesberg and Johnson. The experience was unforgettable for Selchow, who called it "a dream come true."

Ralph gave Selchow an encore of "Should I" in Bern in 1985. The two men got together for a chat one night before Galloway, Sutton, Hinton, and Johnson started their first set. Selchow mentioned the tune again, and the quartet played it. Perhaps it was more than coincidental that Hinton had given Selchow his portable recorder to make a tape of the evening's performance for himself.

From Switzerland the Suttons went to Italy, where Ralph played in Rome, Milan, Genoa, Trieste, Ferrara, and Cosenza. Sunnie was convinced that she and Ralph had eaten enough in Switzerland for the next six months. She much preferred the Swiss pasta, salads, and desserts to the Italian variety: "Even the bread was disappointing. I suppose we ate in the wrong restaurants."

In March 1986, the incomparable Jim Cullum Jazz Band made its first appearance at the Mid-America Jazz Festival in St. Louis. The Last of the Whorehouse Piano Players were also on hand.

The Cullum band was established in 1962 as a father-son partnership by Jim Cullum, Sr., who played clarinet, and Jim Cullum, Jr., on cornet.

The Two Pianos Did Everything but Fly

Originally called the Happy Jazz Band, it took its new name after the death of Jim, Sr., in 1973. John Sheridan, the group's splendid pianist and arranger, wrote many of its charts, including tunes by Louis Armstrong, Jelly Roll Morton, King Oliver, and other legendary jazz figures that through the years helped give the band its matchless reputation.

Sheridan and Sutton teamed up for some two-piano duets on the final day of the 1986 festival. The crowd gave them a rousing reception. Ruth and I went with Ralph to his room after the festival ended, and his phone rang while we chatted. The caller was Sheridan, who told Sutton what a thrill and privilege it had been to play with him again. The two had performed together for the first time the previous September at Summit Jazz in Breckenridge, Colorado.

Ralph, unsurprisingly, remained virtually silent while Sheridan poured out praise and veneration for him. As Sutton hung up, he grinned at me and said, "Whew!" I remarked that Sheridan obviously didn't think much of him, and Ralph laughed. "I've been trying to figure out what's wrong with John," he deadpanned.

Sheridan, about 23 years younger than Sutton, grew up in Columbus, Ohio. He became interested in playing piano, particularly jazz, at the age of 11 or 12 when his father brought home the *Bing with a Beat* record by Bob Scobey.

"Most of the record is Bing, of course," Sheridan said. "But on almost every tune I wondered, 'Who's that piano player back there behind him?' Ralph played especially beautiful things on the verse of 'I'm Gonna Sit Right Down and Write Myself a Letter.'

"I didn't think much more about it and didn't get much exposure to him until I was 14 or 15. I started listening avidly to Bill Culter's radio show, and one day he played Ralph's record with Arthur Trappier of 'When You're Smiling.' I felt like I had been reborn. It was like God had looked upon the earth and smiled, because I had never heard piano played quite like that. I thought, 'Wow, that's the way the instrument ought to sound.' Ralph has been one of my big heroes ever since."

Sheridan graduated from Capital University and played in the Navy band in Washington for four years. Then he earned a master's degree in music theory at North Texas State University, in Denton, and also worked as a teaching assistant. Every Sunday night he drove about 30 miles to Dallas and played with Tommy Loy's Upper Dallas Jazz Band, which had a gig at a steak house called the Railhead. After receiving his graduate degree, Sheridan free-lanced in Dallas six nights a week in addition to playing at the Railhead on Sundays.

The Cullum band, based in San Antonio, was a fixture at the Landing, a club on the city's Riverwalk. The group sometimes played one-nighters in Dallas, and Cullum would sit in at the Railhead. Sheridan met Cullum about 1976 and joined his band in 1979.

"At that point I decided to study piano again," Sheridan said. "I wanted to study with somebody in the business who could coach me in what I wanted to do, instead of studying the classical composers. The first person who came to mind was Ralph. I cooked up a scheme that would have involved flying to Denver about once a month on Sunday, taking a lesson from him, and then coming back to San Antonio. Jim was kind enough to book Ralph at the Landing for a weekend.

"I had never met Ralph, but I called him up and told him about my plan. He thought it was a great idea and thanked me for thinking of him. Just as nice as he could be. I picked him up at the airport when he came down for the weekend, and he played marvelously on Friday and Saturday nights. Then, on Sunday, I drove him out to my apartment at about 2 o'clock and we spent the rest of the day there.

"Ralph played for me, I played for him. Back and forth for six hours. He said, 'I'm no teacher, but you don't need any lessons. There's only one thing I'm going to tell you. Get your foot off that pedal. It covers up your left hand. Other than that, you got it goin'. I can't tell you anything.' He could have, but I sat there listening to him play and watching everything he did. I couldn't have gotten any more if I had asked Joseph Levine or Vladimir Horowitz to do the same thing.

"Later we played records and went out and got some pizza. We had a great time and have been close friends ever since. Ralph and I don't solve the problems of the world when we get together, but we sure as hell get them defined.

"He's one of the great giants of the piano. When you hear Ralph's records, you know he's good. But when you play duets with him, you sit right in the middle of it. His time is absolutely impeccable, his choice of notes is impeccable, and he gets a *sound* out of a piano that I really can't describe with words. It's kind of like having a steamroller come at you at 95 miles an hour. When he comes to play, there is no messing around. He is perfect. I feel the same way when I play with Dick Hyman."

The Two Pianos Did Everything but Fly

Sheridan said he probably loved arranging even more than playing the piano. He or any other musician might play a fine chorus on a particular occasion, he pointed out, but it was gone forever if nobody recorded it. On the other hand, something written down could be preserved. Sheridan realized this vividly when he wrote the charts for a Jack Teagarden radio show presented by the Jim Cullum Jazz Band. Three guest stars played with the band—Teagarden's sister, pianist Norma Teagarden, and trombonists Dan Barrett and Bob Havens. Sheridan received a supreme compliment from Norma Teagarden.

"I think the biggest thrill you can have as an arranger," he said, "is to cook something up in your head, take it into rehearsal, and have it work just the way you wanted it to. It's like giving birth. It's your child. It stands on its own two little feet and nobody can knock it down. On the Teagarden show, we did 'I Got a Right to Sing the Blues' with three trombones. Mike Pittsley of our band joined Dan and Bob.

"Norma listened to those charts and the way I had worked the trombones, and she said, 'You listened to Jack when you were a little boy, didn't you? You really learned Jack's music, didn't you?' I said, 'You bet.' She told me, 'It sure shows.'"

Ralph's record of "Drop Me Off in Harlem" gave Sheridan the idea of doing a chart of that tune for the Cullum band. He also credited Sutton with giving him the incentive to get to know a woman whom he met at the St. Louis Ragtime Festival on June 13, 1986. Benny Goodman, Sheridan's first musical hero, had died that day, and the musicians and members of the audience were toasting him at the hotel bar.

Sheridan noticed two attractive women sitting on a couch in an adjoining lounge. He caught their eye and they smiled. He smiled back, said hello, and asked if he could join them. They agreed, and the three introduced themselves. The women were Karen Kambestad and Shireen Nygren, who had been fans of the Cullum band for years and knew that Sheridan was the group's pianist.

"I thought they were friends or roommates, maybe working at the same office," Sheridan said. "I was surprised to learn that Karen was Shireen's mother. Karen was sitting next to me on the couch and told me she was partial to piano players. I asked her if she liked Ralph Sutton and, much to my surprise and delight, she immediately said he was one of her favorites. She loved jazz parties, always caught Ralph's sets, reeled off the names of his albums that she owned, and told me how much she had enjoyed my set with Ralph at the Mid-America Festival a few months before.

"I was delighted to meet a lovely lady by chance, bring up the name of one of my musical heroes, and not have to answer the perennial question, 'Ralph who?' That's what convinced me. I figured she must be pretty hip. If she knew who Ralph was, maybe I'd better take a second look at her. Karen was a widow at the time, and several months later we began the beautiful relationship we still have to this day.

"Benny Goodman and Ralph Sutton both grabbed my attention early in life. They helped shape my musical taste and direction and influenced me to become a professional musician. But never in a million years would I have thought of them as matchmakers."

Ralph traveled about 22,000 miles on 13 airlines in June 1986 for an Australian tour with engagements in Sydney, Brisbane, Coffs Harbour, Adelaide, and Melbourne, and in Hobart, Tasmania. Dick Hughes wrote a glowing review for the Australian magazine *Jazz* after hearing a performance in Sydney, where Ralph appeared with Bob Barnard, Wally Wickham, and Len Barnard. The quartet played a Duke Ellington medley of "In a Sentimental Mood," "Sophisticated Lady," and "Ring Dem Bells," and the review ended with some advice for Sutton.

"'Ring Dem Bells' just took off and romped and stomped for chorus after chorus," Hughes wrote. "Ecstatic music. Take it easy, Ralph. It's only a job, man, and you're only playing for people, not gods. For this was music for the gods."

Sutton spent several days at home following the Australian tour and then flew to England. Sunnie summed up their feelings about all the time he spent away from the ranch: "What one has to go through to pay the mortgage!" During Ralph's brief stay in Bailey, he and Sunnie drove to the airport to meet his son Pete, who, with his second wife, Clare, and 9-year-old son, Nathan, was coming for a visit. Unfortunately, the younger Suttons were not due until the next day. Sunnie's sense of humor came in handy again: "We miss the airport when we don't see it for a few days."

While in England, Ralph played solo at a piano party in Cambridge for an audience limited to about 50 people. He made the hot June evening extra memorable for Jim Levermore, a fan who had collected Sutton's records for several years but had never met a musician of his stature.

"Ralph was the first jazz giant whom I managed to meet and talk to in an informal setting," Levermore said. "My first impression was of someone very easy to approach; pleasant and easygoing; and happy to greet new faces, answer questions, and sign autographs. He showed interest in the records I brought to be autographed and took the trouble to provide interesting answers to my questions even though they related to recordings made many years ago, which are of great interest to collectors but less so to the musicians involved.

"Ralph returned to Cambridge in 1987, this time with Jack Lesberg and Jake Hanna. He seemed to recognize me and happily autographed another batch of records and my copy of *Piano Man*. We stood talking by the bar and I intended to buy us a drink, but Ralph insisted on buying them. It was another great evening—fine music and interesting conversation with a master jazz pianist who was quite happy buying a drink for a fan. That was only a small incident, but I think it provides insight into Ralph's character and personality."

As part of a European tour in the fall of 1986, Ralph played on a Mediterranean jazz cruise. The cruise wasn't too jazzy, but it did land him in a most unlikely place—on a camel. He and Sunnie, along with Milt Hinton and Gus Johnson, boarded an Italian ship in Venice in October. However, the musicians did little playing—six times during the 10-day cruise. Only a handful of the passengers knew or cared to know anything about jazz. Ralph had a thorough rest aboard ship and a grand time ashore at the various ports of call in Greece, Egypt, Israel, and Cyprus before heading back to Italy.

In Egypt, the Suttons and Johnson visited the pyramids. Ralph and Sunnie, figuring they probably would not have another chance to do so, climbed on a couple of camels for a ride. One of the camel drivers took a photo of Ralph clad in desert garb and perched atop his steed with Sunnie standing alongside. The expression on Sutton's face suggests that a camel hump was goosing him when the picture was taken.

People who knew Ralph and knew about the photo got a laugh from the thought of his riding a camel, especially if they had a chance to view the scene. Jake Hanna had an especially fitting reaction: "First it was Lawrence of Arabia. Now it's Ralph of Egypt."

Chapter **30**

Ralph Is a Living Legend, of Course

alph flew to Toronto in late January 1987 for a gig at the Cafe des Copains. A review by Mark Miller in *The Globe and Mail* noted that his playing "can be incredibly powerful. He can also be remarkably gentle." During that engagement, Sutton played a concert in Kitchener, Ontario, on a Sunday night. Another reviewer, John Kiely of the *Kitchener-Waterloo Record,* commented not only on Ralph's playing but also on his choice of tunes:

> (Sutton) is simply one of the most expressive jazz pianists ever to grace this planet. His playing moves through a song the way the seasons move through a year, and the subtleties he brings to his craft often go unnoticed except to those who make a point of hearing them.
>
> His repertoire includes songs by the classic stride pianists, but he also has sought out and nurtured some of the most underplayed and beautiful songs from the days of the great American art song. His repertoire hasn't changed in content for nearly two decades, but neither has it grown stale. No one else plays these songs, so there is no way to tire of them, and even if others may flirt with the same tunes, they don't play the songs the way Sutton does.
>
> There is no one else who plays the songs of Willard Robison ("Old Folks," "Cottage for Sale," "'Tain't So, Honey, 'Tain't So"), nor does anyone else play the achingly gorgeous "Love Lies" or Willie Smith's "Morning Air" and "Echo of Spring." There hasn't been a piano player of any stripe who has approached Bix Beiderbecke's piano music, such as "In the Dark" or "In a Mist," with such devotion and sensitivity....

There is a difficulty in discussing the art Ralph Sutton brings to his playing because there is a seemingly artless ease to the manner in which he goes about it. Yet, it is not stretching a point to say that Sutton creates a world apart on the piano. It's a world in which these often gentle and romantic songs are still vibrant.

In mid-February, Ralph played for the jazz society of Eugene, Oregon. He also visited the building in which he had bunked during his Army days at the University of Oregon. "Those were my goofing-off days trying to stay clear of the second lieutenants and sergeants," he wrote. "Must say I did a pretty good job at it."

Sutton had dates in Switzerland and France in May. The day after he returned, he and Sunnie went to Odessa. Sunnie reported from Bailey early in June that "everything is OK here, except Ralph is in Japan. He hardly rested from Switzerland and then the Odessa party." A postcard from Tokyo told us that the tour "has been most enjoyable. Good pianos. Weather is nice."

Sutton returned to Toronto late that month and played in a combo with Yank Lawson, Jim Galloway, George Masso, Milt Hinton, and Gus Johnson at the Harbourfront Festival. There, Paul Hoeffler took a charming photo of "three great stride players," as the caption in *The Jazz Report* called them. The picture shows Ralph watching with approval as Dick Wellstood and Dick Hyman play four-handed piano. Tragically, that photo was one of the last taken of Wellstood.

As musical director of the Peninsula Jazz Party in Palo Alto, California, since it began in 1983, Ralph had the responsibility of designating the musicians who played each set. He and Dick Wellstood, whom he affectionately dubbed "Wellstride," were the pianists for the 1987 party. Although Ralph had played in all four previous Peninsula parties, it was the first for Wellstood. Sutton assigned himself to play the opening set on Friday night, July 27.

That afternoon, Wellstood had just arrived from New York and was registering at the hotel when Ruth and I said hello to Ralph in the lobby on our way to take a walk. Sutton heard Wellstood's voice and went over to greet him. They talked for a while, and Ralph gave his old friend the sheets with the musicians' sets written on them. The two pianists then walked to the elevator, and Wellstood went up to his room. Ralph was the last musician, and possibly the last person, to see him alive.

Wellstood had not shown up in the hotel ballroom toward the end of the first set, and no one had seen him since he took the elevator to his room. Victor Horwitz, a member of the party committee, had picked up Wellstood at the airport and now went to his room to see if he was all right. The door was locked, and Horwitz' knocks and calls brought no response. He summoned a member of the hotel's security force, and they entered the room and found Wellstood's body in a chair. His coat hung on the back of the chair, and the set sheets that Ralph had given him lay on the floor.

Kenny Davern had just left the stand after playing the first set. He had been close to Wellstood for years, and Horwitz notified him immediately. Kenny and Elsa Davern, together with Mona Hinton and Denisa Hanna, Jake Hanna's wife, went to the room and identified Wellstood's body. He had died of a heart attack at the age of 60.

Ruth knew something terrible had happened when she saw Kenny Davern's face as he headed upstairs. I had left the ballroom and ran into Sunnie Sutton, who also looked stricken. She said she had just heard a rumor that Wellstood had been found dead in his room.

The news of Wellstood's untimely death spread through the ballroom, but the musicians overcame their grief and played up a storm for the two nights of the party. Barbara Sutton Curtis came down from her home in Ukiah and filled in for Wellstood on Saturday night. The audience and the musicians contributed a fund of about $1,000, which Elsa Davern sent to Wellstood's widow, Dianne. Some people also mailed checks to her.

Ralph's sister, who had played at the first four Peninsula parties, had spent Friday house painting. Barb and her husband, Hal, were busy redecorating their home, and she kept wondering whether they might have made a wrong decision or two. The upheaval in the house annoyed her, and she was tired of the whole mess.

Barb went to bed early that night and was asleep when Sig Kriegsman, chairman of the jazz party committee, called to ask her to substitute for Wellstood. Hal woke her up after talking to Kriegsman.

"I don't think Hal realized what a shock it was to be wakened from a sound sleep to learn that Dick Wellstood had died," Barb recalled. "It felt like a bad dream. I knew right away that I would fill in at the party, but I also called myself a jerk for spending all my time painting instead of practicing my piano technique every day.

"I felt kind of numb when Hal and I drove down to Palo Alto, and I was worried that I might not do a good job. But Flip Phillips let me know Saturday night that he had told Sig to call me, and I learned that Ralph wasn't the only other musician to tell him that. Flip still scared me with his breakneck tempos. Those are the times that I know I'm really playing with the *big* boys.

"I have a wonderful memory of the '84 party, when I played in the dining room during dinner. All the musicians ate in a side room, and I felt so far removed from them. Trummy Young looked through the door a couple of times to let me know he was listening, and I appreciated that so much. Later he did a vocal and I played behind him. Trummy came over and gave me a big kiss after the tune. He told Hal later, 'That wife of yours, she saved my ass!' [Young died a few weeks after the 1984 Peninsula party.]

"I don't know how the musicians could have even played on the Friday night after Dick's death. That is one mark of professionalism, I guess. Ed Polcer was visibly shaken up in the musicians' room on Saturday, and I wondered if Kenny broke down later. Sunnie and Elsa were terribly concerned because they knew it could happen to any of the men, especially being on the road so much. All the musicians were very nice to me. There seemed to be more spontaneous touching and hugging than usual, especially with Milt Hinton and Jack Lesberg."

Barb subbed for Wellstood not only at Palo Alto, but also on a lengthy European tour that started in early October and extended into November. She and Ralph played a number of two-piano sets on that tour, which they made after his first trip to New Zealand and a return visit to Australia.

The musicians' roster for The Jazz Party in Minneapolis the year before, in September 1986, included three marvelous pianists—Dick Hyman, Ralph Sutton, and Dick Wellstood. I found myself sitting between Wellstood and Clark Terry in the hotel shuttle bus that picked up the musicians at the airport. Wellstood was annoyed because he had neglected to bring his tux shoes and would have to buy a pair for the black-tie performance Saturday night. After berating himself several times, he graciously told me that he owned two or three copies of the Sutton biography and had enjoyed the book very much.

In February 1988, seven months after Wellstood's death, Ruth and I went to Pine Bluff, Arkansas, for the 60th birthday party of Al White, an old friend of many musicians, including Sutton. Our son, Joe, lived in Little Rock at the time, and the three of us drove down at the invitation of Al and his wife, Ann. Ralph, Kenny Davern, Bob Haggart, and Gus Johnson provided the music at the party.

Al White told me that Wellstood had envied Ralph because a book had been written about him. According to White, Wellstood wished somebody had such strong feelings for him and his piano playing. He considered the book a tremendous tribute to Sutton. Wellstood's remarks, as quoted by White, touched me deeply. Davern confirmed that his close friend had been envious of Ralph because of *Piano Man*. He then related what he called a "Wellstood on Sutton" story:

"Dick and I were talking on the phone, and he said he didn't understand why so few people came to hear him play at Hanratty's. People waited in line there every night to hear Judy Carmichael, Dick said, and Ralph packed the joint and called everybody who made noise a motherfucker—and they applauded.

"I asked Dick how many postcards he sent when he went on the road. He said, 'None.' I told him that Ralph not only sent postcards to people, but when he passed through their hometowns he picked up the phone and called them. I told Dick, 'Ralph fills that room with his friends, or at least people who consider themselves his friends. Each one of them feels he or she had been personally invited by Ralph to attend that particular performance of his.

"'So when he yells out, "Bunch of motherfuckers!," everyone turns around to see the jerks he's talking about because they know he's not talking about *them*.' This enormous revelation came to Dick and he said, 'They do?' I told him, 'That's why Ralph can go into Hanratty's or anywhere else and call somebody a motherfucker and nobody takes umbrage.'

"Ralph cultivated those people—not because he didn't like them. He *did* like them. He has his own groupies, his own groups of groupies, and they'll travel for miles to hear him play. Each group does different things. Some just drink with him. Others have enough money to fly him wherever they want him when they want him, and he'll be there. One senses this loyalty. The word *loyalty* keeps coming back. Ralph is loyal to his friends, and his friends are loyal to him."

Late in 1976, Ralph and Sunnie Sutton moved down the highway in the Rockies after buying this house in Bailey, Colorado. They named their home Morning Air Ranch. The dirt road leading to the house, like the one at their former home in nearby Pine, has signs to ward off unwanted callers.

Loose Shoes

The Curt Jarratt Trio played an annual month-long gig at the Northern Hotel in Billings, Montana, from 1977 to 1983. Joe Sample, a friend of Ralph's, named the trio for the bass player who joined Sutton and Gus Johnson regularly though informally. They played in a room called the Golden Belle, where a painting of the belle hung over Johnson's drums. (*Joe Sample*)

Swiss sweethearts Mat Geiger and Margrit Burtscher were married in Denver in 1979, accompanied by Ralph and Sunnie Sutton and Mildred and Gus Johnson. The couple had gotten together following a jazz concert in Zurich. A few months later, they invited Ralph and "Uncle Gusti" to be best men, with the two wives as witnesses. (*Collection of Mat and Margrit Geiger*)

Loose Shoes

The Last of the Whorehouse Piano Players brought down the house everywhere they played. The combo of, *left to right*, Ralph, Milt Hinton, Jay McShann, and Gus Johnson also made some fine records. McShann and Sutton performed together on two pianos for the first time at Dick Gibson's jazz party in 1979. (*Al White*)

Ralph told Al White that of the countless photos White had taken of him, this one of Sutton and Milt Hinton was his favorite. (*Al White*)

Loose Shoes

Teddy Wilson joined Ralph for some two-piano numbers at the jazz party in Odessa, Texas, in 1983. (*Al White*)

Ralph played many gigs with, *center and right,* Yank Lawson and Bob Haggart after leaving the World's Greatest Jazzband. In 1984, they formed part of a band that performed in Pine Bluff, Arkansas, where this photo was taken. (*Al White*)

Loose Shoes

Flip Phillips spent some time with Ralph and Sunnie at Morning Air Ranch during the summer of 1984. The river that flows through the Suttons' property is well stocked with trout, and Ralph watched his guest reel in a few of them. (*Lyn Alweis*)

After visiting the Suttons, Phillips carved a wooden clock for them. On the face of the timepiece, above a photo of the two great musicians, he put the men's nicknames for each other. Sutton called Phillips "Skip," and Phillips called Sutton "Harry," but neither knew why. The clock hangs in the Suttons' music room.

Sunnie Sutton loves it when Ralph sits down at the piano in their music room. On the rare occasions that he practices at home, he usually plays finger exercises and then Bach fugues and preludes before swinging into some stride. (*Lyn Alweis*)

Loose Shoes

The poster to Ralph's left expresses one of his strongest sentiments. Under it, a photo of Lou McGarity smiles at him. A portrait of the band at Condon's is to the right. Throughout his career, Ralph has wished that people would heed the advice of the sign standing on the piano. It is shown on the next page. (*Lyn Alweis*)

Loose Shoes

When Ralph has a chance to spend some time at home, he thrives on tending the Suttons' three burros, which occupy a pasture and barn on the other side of the river from the house. This photo shows him brushing Rufus while Rachel and Chayo, *left and center,* graze nearby. Rachel and Rufus produced Chayo on the ranch. Their daughter has a Mexican name meaning "sweet thing."

Ralph's expression here reflects the complete contentment he finds on Morning Air Ranch with Sunnie and their beloved animals. It's a good bet that Sutton has high regard for anyone whom he looks at like this. (*Lyn Alweis*)

Loose Shoes

Ralph wore desert clothing for a camel ride in Egypt in 1986. He and his steed both looked uncomfortable when a camel driver took this photo while Sunnie held the reins. "First it was Lawrence of Arabia," said Jake Hanna. "Now it's Ralph of Egypt." (*Collection of Ralph Sutton*)

Howard Alden, one of the brightest younger stars of jazz, and Milt Hinton delighted the audience with a duet at a jazz party in Wilmington, North Carolina, early in 1987. Hinton always got a big laugh when he declared, "I've got shoes that are older than Howard." (*Al White*)

Loose Shoes

Manfred Selchow, a German teacher moonlighting as jazz promoter, was open-mouthed with joy and surprise when the two-piano performance by Ralph and his sister Barbara received a boisterous ovation in Westoverledingen, his hometown, in 1987. Until then, Selchow had thought the people in the audience were "rather reserved." (*Courtesy Manfred Selchow*)

Sutton liked what he heard when Dick Wellstood and Dick Hyman, *center and right*, sat down at the same keyboard during the Toronto Jazz Festival in July 1987. This photo showing the three great stride pianists together was one of the last taken of Wellstood, who died later that month at the Peninsula Jazz Party in Palo Alto, California. (© *Paul J. Hoeffler, Toronto*)

Loose Shoes

Two couples who are among the firmest friends in jazz got together during a gig in Pine Bluff in 1988. Elsa Davern and Sunnie Sutton regard each other almost as sisters, and Kenny Davern and Ralph are also close pals. (*Al White*)

Ralph and Kenny Davern toured New Zealand and Australia together in 1988. While they were in Sydney, this drawing accompanied a newspaper article about Sutton by Joya Jenson, host of "The Joy-A-Jazz," a radio program broadcast from there. (*Illustration by John Shakespeare*, The Sydney Morning Herald)

Loose Shoes

Jim Galloway showed his pleasure when Ralph belted out "'Tain't Nobody's Bizness" during a performance in Toronto in 1988. Galloway, a leading figure on the jazz scene in Canada, always asks Sutton to do the tune. (© *Paul J. Hoeffler, Toronto*)

Kenny Davern and Warren Vaché were swinging away when this photo was taken in 1989 at Thunderbird Lodge in Taos Ski Valley, New Mexico. Milt Hinton is in the rear, and Gus Johnson can barely be seen behind Vaché's cornet. Ralph is out of sight behind the piano at the left. (*Roger Altvader*)

Loose Shoes

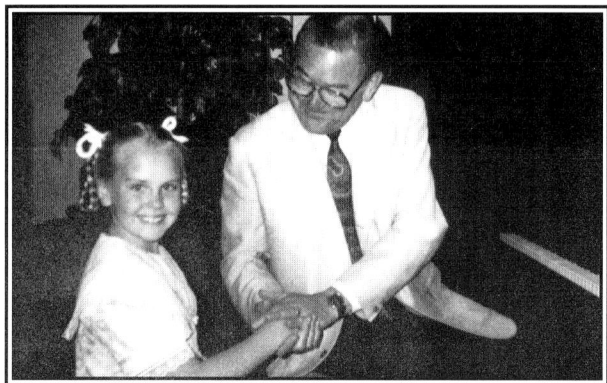

Eight-year-old Madeleine Nichols had been a fan of Ralph's even before meeting him in 1989 at her first jazz party, *above,* in Santa Fe, New Mexico. Her grandmother often played a tape of which one side, as Maddy described it, "was mostly all Ralph Sutton." (*Jane Eddy*)

Ralph always looks forward to a visit with Johnny and Liza Simmen whenever he plays in or near Zurich, as he did in December 1989 when Sunnie Sutton took this photo. Simmen, one of the world's most respected jazz writers, and his wife met Sutton in 1952. (*Sunnie Sutton*)

Ralph unknowingly became a matchmaker when John Sheridan, the sterling pianist and arranger of the Jim Cullum Jazz Band, met Karen Kambestad, *second from left*. She impressed him immediately because Sutton, one of his musical heroes, was a favorite of hers, too. Kambestad and her daughter, Shireen, posed with Sheridan and Sutton in 1990. (*Al White*)

Loose Shoes

Ralph and Jay McShann have a ball together whenever their paths cross. They shared the same piano bench for this photo, taken at the 1990 DuMaurier Jazz Festival at Harbourfront in Toronto. (© *Paul J. Hoeffler, Toronto*)

One of the finest rhythm sections in jazz—Milt Hinton, Gus Johnson, and Ralph Sutton—played together for the last time in 1990, when Alzheimer's disease forced Johnson to retire. (© *Milt Hinton*)

Loose Shoes

At the recording session that followed the 1991 Triangle Jazz Party in Raleigh, North Carolina, Dan Barrett demonstrated some piano dissonance in one of the tunes for Ralph. The other musicians broke up when Barrett commented, "Jesus Christ, here I am showing Ralph Sutton how to play piano!" (© *John Callahan*)

Randy Sandke and Ralph took a breather during the Triangle recording session. Arbors Records produced the recording for Friends In Need (FIN), the nonprofit charitable organization that sponsored the party. All the musicians at the session donated their talent. FIN gave part of the recording proceeds to Gus Johnson, whom Alzheimer's disease had forced to retire. (© *John Callahan*)

John Sheridan called up a request for "If Dreams Come True" during one of Ralph's sets at the Lake of the Ozarks Festival in 1992. Sutton promptly invited him to the piano, and they swung through a duet on the tune. (*Photo © 1993 by Leslie Johnson,* The Mississippi Rag)

Ralph and John Sheridan played a two-piano set at the 1993 Summit Jazz, accompanied by Don Mopsick and Frank Capp. At Sutton's suggestion, they performed an unscheduled set the next day. Ralph had never before asked another pianist to play an encore set with him. (*Karen Kambestad*)

Loose Shoes

Ralph gets together with his three sons and their families when he has a gig in the San Francisco area. This photo was taken at Nick's home in 1992. Nick, Jeff, and Pete, *left to right,* love their father deeply and are extremely proud of his fame as a jazz pianist. But they have always wished he had spent much more time with them. (*Sunnie Sutton*)

Sunnie and Ralph (*Collection of Ralph Sutton*)

Loose Shoes

One of Ralph's solo records is called *The Other Side of Ralph Sutton.* However, this unique artist has many sides. The contrasting photos on these two pages show a couple of them. (© *Paul J. Hoeffler, Toronto*)

Loose Shoes

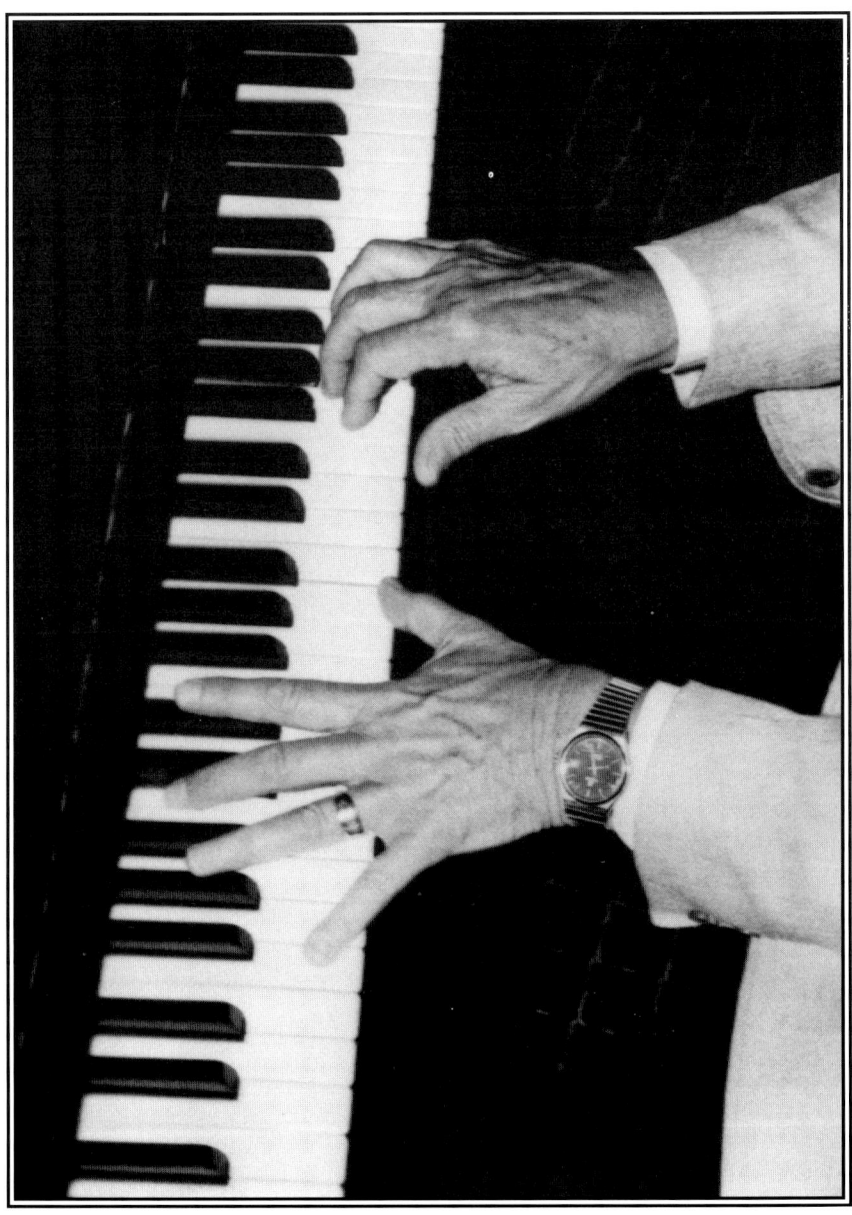

The hands of Ralph Sutton (*Al White*)

Dick Wellstood's early death deprived traditional jazz of a top stride pianist. It may have lengthened the life of another. John Sheridan, a mainstay of the Jim Cullum Jazz Band, weighed more than 300 pounds when Wellstood died in 1987. He and Wellstood had become friends in January of that year when the Cullum band played at the tribute to Turk Murphy at Carnegie Hall in New York. Wellstood appeared there as a member of Vince Giordano's Nighthawks.

"I was good friends with Dick Hyman and Ralph," Sheridan said. "It was big bear hugs with us whenever we got together. We played duets and admired each other's talent. That happened immediately. Dick Wellstood was another kind of bird. You had to prove yourself to him pretty hard over a period of time. That night at Carnegie Hall, he decided to be friendly. 'John,' he told me, 'you're playing your ass off.' We got real friendly."

Sheridan and Wellstood got together again later in 1987. The Cullum and Giordano groups performed on the Jazz in July program, directed by Hyman, at the 92nd Street Y. Wellstood died six days later in Palo Alto.

"Dick's death got to me," Sheridan said. "Then I learned about the autopsy report and that he had been doing things like eating two quarts of ice cream a day on the road. That got my attention right then and there, and I decided to do something about it.

"Karen begged me not to gain any more weight. I thought I might as well clean up my act so maybe I'd be around a while longer. Jim Cullum came to my rescue. I went on a strict diet that he told me about, and the pounds just dropped off me. By Christmas that year I was under where I ought to be."

The change in Sheridan's appearance was dramatic. He weighed about 180 pounds when Ruth and I heard him with the Cullum band at the Mid-America Jazz Festival in St. Louis in March 1992. After the band's final set, Ruth told him that she had again detected a bit of Sutton in his playing. The grinning Sheridan did not dispute her.

Ralph's first visit to New Zealand came early in August 1987, a week after the Wellstood tragedy. He spent a short but busy time there, playing two engagements on successive nights in Auckland and Wellington before leaving for Australia. The Sunday night audience at Auckland's Cotton Club included John Williams, who, with his wife, Julie, took his father's advice and traveled about 100 miles from their home in Hamilton to hear the solo concert by Sutton. His parents, Norman and Beatrice Williams, met Ralph's plane at the Wellington airport the next afternoon.

Norm and Bee Williams had long been fans of Sutton's but had never heard him in a live performance. A month before Ralph flew to New Zealand, Norm wrote Ralph a letter introducing Bee and himself. He closed by telling him: "You will never go anywhere where you'll find yourself quite as welcome. We look forward to a dream coming true."

The Williamses awaited Ralph's arrival even more eagerly after their son John called and raved about hearing him play the previous night in Auckland. The club manager was a friend of theirs and had taken John Williams backstage during the intermission to meet Ralph. John recounted this "exhilarating experience":

"Having been utterly entranced by the first half of the concert, though feeling a bit cheated because I had not been able to watch his hands, it was with some trepidation that I asked if I might meet Mr. Sutton. I had read *Piano Man* with more than a little interest and was a bit perturbed at the possibility of perhaps finding him in the 'Do not pester me' frame of mind I had read about. Nothing could have been more incorrect. There was the man, sitting by himself, sipping orange juice through a straw. When he stood up smiling, surprising me with his height, all my trepidation disappeared immediately.

"The warmth of his smile and the grip of his handshake were enough to make anybody feel welcome. Ralph's first words were, 'Hello, John. I just received a lovely long letter from your dad. He told me all about you.' Before I knew it, we had chatted away the entire 30-minute intermission. This most pleasant and warmhearted man left me with the wish that I might share with him and my environmentalist brother, Peter, the calm company of a country man when tramping through the bush or casting for rainbow trout."

Norm and Bee Williams and Bill Hamer, president of the Wellington Jazz Club, met Ralph's plane in the capital. That same afternoon, Hamer took Sutton to meet the United States ambassador to New Zealand, Paul M. Cleveland. As a high school boy more than 40 years earlier, Cleveland had gone to Condon's many times "to hear the man who played like Fats Waller." Now he wanted to welcome that man to New Zealand.

The Williamses later suggested that Sutton might like to run through some tunes with the two Wellington musicians scheduled to accompany him that night at Victoria University, Paul Dyne on bass and Roger Sellers on drums. "No need," Ralph said. "We'll just go up there and play." The concert confirmed his confidence in Dyne and Sellers. He complimented both as great players whom he would like to have in all his performances, and they praised him lavishly.

"Ralph is a living legend, of course, which is obvious in his playing and in his personality," Dyne said. "He's without doubt a master craftsman. That becomes obvious as soon as his hands hit the piano. Roger and I enjoyed him because he's that rare class of master musician who makes his rhythm section feel totally at ease. We felt comfortable when we met him and when we played with him. We were impressed by his great sense of dynamics, his wonderful sense of time, and his superb technique.

"We were also impressed by his warm personality. And we were very pleased that he complimented our support. We felt that we had met him in that international space where we could all contribute something to the music. Ralph is at the level of musicianship where he can do his thing and leave us a little space to have a bit of a say as well.

"He came to us with a reputation that he can sometimes get a little angry, that he's often a hard taskmaster, and that he would have extremely high expectations. We had some uneasiness, but he was a total gentleman. We found him an inspiration to play with and joy to share music with."

Following the concert, Ralph went to dinner with Norm and Bee Williams, Dyne and Sellers, and several other admirers. He had to catch an early morning flight to Australia, and the Williamses reluctantly took him to his hotel around midnight.

"After reading so much about Ralph and what people think of him, everything fell into place once I had met and listened to the man," Norm Williams said. "The realization was greater than the anticipation, which does not happen very often. Bee and I cannot see and hear too much of this boy from Missouri—with or without the piano, but preferably with the instrument that is almost part of him."

The Williamses saw and heard Ralph again a year later. He returned to New Zealand in August 1988, this time with Kenny Davern, and again played with Dyne and Sellers. While in Wellington, he and the Williamses went to the mansion of the U.S. ambassador, where Ralph brought back Paul Cleveland's memories of Condon's by playing for him and his wife,

Carter. Cleveland wrote to Norm Williams expressing his great appreciation for arranging "Ralph Sutton's memorable visit."

Barbara Sutton Curtis had been booked before Dick Wellstood's death to play her first gig at the Cafe des Copains in the fall of 1987. She later was asked to replace Wellstood on a German tour that overlapped it. Barb arranged a short postponement of her Toronto engagement, and early in October she flew to the Dallas-Fort Worth airport and joined Ralph, Jim Galloway, Jack Lesberg, and Jake Hanna, who had just finished playing the Midland Jazz Classic. They were headed for Germany, where they hooked up with the other musicians in one of the two bands on the tour—Yank Lawson, Jackie Coon, George Masso, Christian Plattner, and Carrie Smith. Barb had never toured with her brother before.

Mannie Selchow, the moonlighting German teacher, directed the first part of the tour. This part was called A Tribute to Fats Waller and opened in Selchow's hometown, Westoverledingen. The band, fronted by Lawson, played the first set and then was joined by Smith, who sang several tunes.

The second set featured two-piano duets by Ralph and Barb, backed by Lesberg and Hanna. The audience, composed of people whom Selchow described as "rather reserved," gave the brother-sister team a boisterous reception. Supplemented by yelling and stamping, the applause did not stop until the surprised Selchow called for an encore, which received a similar ovation. The band then returned for the final set, which included more vocals by Smith.

In Lüneburg, the mayor gave the musicians a welcome that included a tour of the town hall. One room in the building dated from about 1550, and in it stood a Steinway grand. The piano had been donated by a wealthy citizen and was used for occasional classical concerts. Ralph sat down at the keyboard and played "Ain't Misbehavin'," and Barb described the reaction of his companions: "As always happens when he plays, everyone listened with admiration."

The Flat Foot Stompers, a German group led by clarinetist Peter Bühr, joined the tour on the fourth day. Mannie and Renate Selchow returned to Westoverledingen, as they had planned, and Bühr directed the rest of the trip. Barb and Ralph teamed up in the second set after the intermission on this part of the tour. They played to enthusiastic audiences night after night, but she still had misgivings about her playing.

"The Germans loved Ralph and me!" Barb said. "The brother-sister two-piano team really went over, but I felt I was playing in Ralph's shadow. His talent can be intimidating, and he definitely was the star. He has made many friends over there and is so well liked. He was very thoughtful about not taking pieces at breakneck tempos, except once when he started 'Dinah' in A-flat at a fast clip that really got me. I usually play it in F. I later asked him not to do *that* again.

"Ralph was very protective and understanding of how the tour was affecting me—the newness and strangeness of it, and the audience tending to make me nervous. I cherish the good times we had, like going back to the hotel on the bus after a concert and talking about old times in Howell. Or having him look at me across the pianos, smiling and encouraging me, and mouthing the word, 'Relax.'

"It was good that Hal didn't come with me, as much as I would have liked it. I learned a lot. It was a new experience for me, and I came to like looking after myself with no worries about Hal or the house or the pets."

Barbara flew home in early November, after being away about a month, and went to Toronto 11 days later. She was a little jittery during her first few performances at the Cafe des Copains, as if on trial, but then began feeling good about her playing and her reactions to the audience. Barb felt especially pleased when she learned that some of the people didn't know she was Ralph's sister.

"The first weekend brought the talkers, which I found very difficult to put up with," she said. "I tried to play to the people who were listening. The talkers stopped talking after one tune, even though they hadn't heard a thing. The second week got better. My playing improved, and I handled the audience warmly."

Barb's second week at the club satisfied her greatly because she surmounted the traumatic incident that preceded it. On Sunday, she had tripped and fallen on the sidewalk while walking to her apartment after taking a bus tour of Toronto. A large swelling sprouted over her right eye, and the wound bled heavily. She called two friends of Ralph's, Olive and Jim Loney, who had invited her to dinner that night, and they took her to the emergency room of Toronto General Hospital. A physician put in two sutures, and X rays showed no further injury.

"I was able to play on Monday but had to get a pair of dark glasses to hide the mess above my eye," Barb said. "I also had to write my tune lists in large letters, and make them even larger the second night, because I could hardly read them without my prescription glasses, which broke when I fell.

"The last three nights were great. I received many compliments and felt in command. The audiences were wonderful, and the people who came during the weekend actually listened."

Ralph couldn't have been more tickled when a letter arrived from Jack Hutton, an official of the Ontario Secondary School Teachers' Federation:

> For many years I have told people that Ralph Sutton is the most popular pianist to appear at Des Copains. Unfortunately, that is no longer true and I'm sorry to pass on that news.
>
> Your sister, Barbara, is now the reigning favorite.
>
> I only noticed in the paper yesterday that she was playing in town (her last day) and made it a point to get down to Des Copains last night. After listening to her for two sets... I wished that she lived closer so I could take lessons from her. I've never heard anyone play "Davenport Blues" better.
>
> More importantly, however, she won everybody over immediately with her open friendliness. People are so used to "important" piano players passing through there, playing material you have to strain to understand (let alone like) that it was sheer joy to have Barbara tell them about the music and the composers. She turned the whole place into a family living room....
>
> Looking forward to hearing you here again one of these days, Ralph, but in the meantime Barbara is welcome anytime she wants to come up!

Like her brother, Barb became a repeat headliner at the Cafe des Copains. After it closed, she, too, returned to Toronto for gigs at the cafe's successor, the Montreal Restaurant Bistro.

Chapter **31**

I'll Just Have to Get Out of the Way of Ralph's Left Hand

he 1988 concerts of the Traditional Jazz Series at the University of New Hampshire jumped off to a swinging start with a February performance by the Last of the Whorehouse Piano Players. Ralph and Jay McShann played without accompaniment by bass and drums. Their appearance, the program notes declared, was "one of those rarities that usually occurs only in wishful thinking, imaginative fantasy, or prayer.

"On the more practical level," the notes went on, "we have long wanted to have Ralph Sutton on this series, and have also hoped to appropriately observe Black History Month with an artist of Jay McShann's stature. For various logistical reasons neither result has been previously attained, so their convergence, as well as the instrumental format, confers a double blessing....

"Jay and Ralph typify and dramatize the highest qualities of human interaction through which America's indigenous contribution to the musical art of the world has developed and flourished."

Sutton and McShann got together again later in February for a concert in Kansas City, Missouri, where McShann had been a favorite son for years. They played at the Folly Theater, on two 9-foot Steinway grand pianos, and the sell-out audience gave them a standing ovation.

Ralph performed in Switzerland and France in March and April. His schedule called for a Japanese tour next, but he wrote from Bern that he had canceled it so he could "have the gearbox worked on." Sutton underwent surgery for prostatic cancer late in April. He hit the road again less than three weeks later and played a concert in Medford, Oregon, for the Southern Oregon Traditional Jazz Society. The Odessa party came two days after that.

The whole Whorehouse group opened the following week in New York at Carlos I, the city's self-proclaimed best Caribbean restaurant. Praising Sutton and McShann, one reviewer speculated that if they "played in the parlor of a bordello, none of the customers would want to go upstairs."

Jazz critic John S. Wilson of *The New York Times* wrote a glowing review. His final paragraphs summarized the music of this unusual quartet:

> . . . Along with their duets, there are solo ballad spots for each of the pianists when Mr. Sutton turns to a gentle lyricism, although Mr. McShann, on Wednesday evening, retained his blues instinct sufficiently to cap a feathery, long-lined exposition of "Willow Weep for Me" with some gently nudging boogie-woogie. Mr. Hinton's bass steps into solo spots from time to time and Mr. Johnson has some rocketing drum breaks.
>
> But this is a quartet that is at its best—an unparalleled best—when it is functioning as a full foursome with the two pianists picking up on each other, trading leads and rollicking through bubbly, buoyant lines over the pulsating rhythmic foundation poured out by Mr. Hinton and Mr. Johnson.

In June, Ralph performed in the Stride Piano Summit at Davies Symphony Hall in San Francisco. An ad called the program "a celebration of Harlem stride and classic jazz piano. . .featuring and inspired by the music of Fats Waller and James P. Johnson." Sutton, McShann, Dick Hyman, and Mike Lipskin played solo and in various combinations. Hyman also played organ on some piano-organ duets with Lipskin, recalling similar performances by Waller and Johnson. Ruby Braff shared the billing, along with Red Callender, Eddie Marshall, and Sam Shaffer.

In a preconcert interview with Jesse Hamlin of the *San Francisco Chronicle*, Hyman said he was looking forward to the gig. Then he kidded himself: "I'll just have to get out of the way of Ralph's left hand." Hamlin's review declared that the concert "paid the greatest possible tribute to classic jazz. It showed how vital the music is and always will be when played with the right mix of talent, respect, sentiment, and imagination."

The final number of the Stride Summit was an eight-hand version of "Honeysuckle Rose" with all the musicians taking part. McShann and

Sutton shared one of the two pianos, and Hyman played the organ. "It was unruly," Hamlin wrote, "but a happy closer to a concert dedicated to this joyous music."

A week later, many of the same stride fans went to Watsonville, south of San Jose, for the second annual Fats Waller Memorial Jazz Festival. Ralph and his sister Barbara played both solo and two-piano sets. The festival also featured a number of other pianists, including Sutton's former student Bob Hirsch and about a dozen jazz bands.

Ralph and Kenny Davern spent most of August 1988 touring together in New Zealand and Australia. The spectacular talents of these two jazz masters are highlighted in a recording they made in Adelaide. Accompanied by drummer Bill Polain, Davern and Sutton complement and play off each other beautifully. Ralph also shines on a solo Ellington medley of "In a Sentimental Mood," "Sophisticated Lady," and "Ring Dem Bells." He starts the latter tune as a third ballad, then goes into a light swing tempo, and climaxes with some stomping stride.

While the two friends were away, Elsa Davern didn't need more than one invitation from Sunnie to exchange the sweltering heat of New Jersey for Morning Air Ranch and some time doing nothing. Sunnie sent her an airline ticket, but the two women wound up splitting the cost of the flight. They regard each other almost as sisters and had a delightful time together. Sunnie summed up their sentiments when she wrote that the only things missing were Ralph and Kenny.

"It was incredible," Elsa said. "Sunnie and I didn't get in each other's way at all. We could just sit there without saying a word, the way she and Ralph do, but we talked a lot, too. We walked and we cooked some good meals or went out. It was very loose and relaxed. I felt like I lived there.

"One of the nicest things about jazz is meeting people like Ralph and Sunnie. I'm glad it brought us together and that I have people like them to love. When I first met Sunnie, I knew I'd love to be friends with her. The very bottom of our relationship is absolute trust. It takes her a long time to love someone and to accept a person totally. After that, she'll trust you with anything, no matter what you do. I feel very secure with her, and it's a nice feeling.

"I'm a twin, and anything that I might say to my sister would be forgiven. That's been a given in my life. To find Sunnie and be able to have that sort of relationship with her is kind of a miracle. It's a rare thing to know someone you can say anything to and have it accepted with love and silence. I would do anything for her.

"We're very supportive of each other because we understand each other's life style and have the same feelings. It's difficult when our husbands are away on the road and we're left at home to take care of things. Then they come home, and there are adjustments both ways. Sunnie and I have had many healthy talks about that, which has helped a lot. We laugh about it, too."

Their husbands have the same loving, supportive relationship. Most people believe Kenny and Ralph have opposite personalities, but Elsa thinks they are much alike. Ralph, of course, rarely says anything on the stand. But Kenny frequently breaks up the audience with his quick wit about almost anything and his caustic comments about poor sound systems, glaring lights, or other frequent inadequacies in the physical setup.

"The most interesting thing about Ralph is his credo that silence is the best policy," Elsa said. "He is silent about things, and Kenny is verbal—in public. Ralph loves it when Kenny goes on one of his tirades about microphones, the music business, politics, world affairs, or anything else. I think he encourages Kenny to be as bad as possible. Ralph claps his hands and gets that little grin on his face, wanting Kenny to be verbal.

"If I get pissed off at something Kenny says, Ralph sometimes calls my name or puts his finger to his lips and says, 'Shhh.' Then the two of us laugh, because we know it's silly to get upset about such things. He's telling me to take it easy and relax."

At home, Kenny is not the gregarious wisecracker who obviously enjoys making others laugh. Many people have told Elsa how lucky she is to live with him and have her days filled with laughter. She generally takes the easy way out and agrees with them. But Kenny is very quiet when the two of them are alone. He loves to read and listen to music, and he spends considerable time tinkering with his clarinet and its accoutrements.

"Kenny is gentle, sweet, and sentimental," Elsa said. "His sense of humor comes out a lot because he's expressing his view of the world. He has a cynical, humorous response to most things. He does make me laugh, but certainly not all day. That aspect of his personality blossoms when he's in public. He loves to perform, but he doesn't perform with me."

Elsa became known in her own right as a creator of beautiful necklaces, and Kenny took great pride in her skill and in her graduating summa cum laude with a degree in fine arts history. She had been visiting her twin, Laina Corbalis, whose real name is Elaine, in Albuquerque in 1987 and saw an Indian necklace made of little red glass beads. Elsa wanted to buy it but couldn't afford the $1,000 price.

"I found the beads and things to string them with, and I made up a necklace just like it," she said. "Kenny and I were in England a few months later, and I bought some old ivory and made up an ivory necklace for myself. A lot of people liked those two necklaces and asked me to make one for them.

"I had some old beads, and one weekend I was just sitting around and I thought, 'Why not?' So I made up a few necklaces and started looking in antique stores. I had gotten together 14 necklaces by the time of Dick Gibson's party about four months later. I sold 12 of them at the party, and that's how it started.

"I buy beads and other stuff at flea markets and antique stores wherever we happen to be. I also buy a lot of things that are broken. I took jewelry courses in college, and I solder and rivet and saw and repair. The work gives me a lot of pleasure and keeps me out of trouble."

During the 1987 Jazz Party in Minneapolis, Kenny and Elsa, Ralph and Sunnie, and Joe and Miriam Sample went to a restaurant for dinner one night. Ralph began talking to Elsa about Fats Waller, and she recalled it as one of their loveliest conversations.

"Ralph told me that when he was young, he wanted the world to be like he felt when he listened to Fats play," Elsa said. "Ralph would have liked to perceive the world as Fats made him feel inside. He wanted it to be like that, with everybody happy and thoughtful and having a feeling of wellness."

As Ralph talked about Fats in the restaurant that night, a quartet—violin, viola, cello, and piano—was playing Strauss waltzes. The musicians left the stand after finishing the set, and Sutton gave his companions what Elsa described as a wonderful moment. Without a word, he walked over to the piano, played one Fats Waller tune, and returned to the table.

"It was so unlike him to do that," Elsa said. "Sunnie's mouth dropped open."

A headline in *The Mississippi Rag* said it all: "Hot Jazz, Good Cause."

The head appeared on a review of the Triangle Jazz Party, held in Raleigh, North Carolina. This was an unusual party, largely because its founder, Steve Blades, was an unusual man.

The first Triangle party took place in the fall of 1988, only seven months after Blades and his wife, Dottie, drove from their home in Greenville to the southeast corner of the state for a jazz party in Wilmington. She had bought the tickets as a surprise birthday present. He was not thrilled, though he had loved jazz for years.

"I figured this would be something weird," Blades remembered. "I wouldn't know what they were playing, I didn't know if I would like it, and what a way to spend money we couldn't afford. But I didn't say anything because it was a really sweet idea."

Blades had started a love affair with the trombone in seventh grade, when he joined the school band. The director gave him a choice of baritone, tuba, or trombone. He had never heard of the baritone and didn't want to haul a tuba around. Trombone sounded neat, and he began taking lessons. He later began to search out trombone music, primarily jazz.

"The Wilmington party was great, and Dan Barrett's playing captured me," Blades said. "I bumped into him in the elevator and introduced myself. That night I went up to him during a break and we talked for about an hour and a half. We were friends by the time he had to play again. Meeting Dan was the key to starting the Triangle party.

"Driving home, I told Dottie, 'I think we could do a jazz party as a fund raiser for the Multiple Sclerosis Society.' She said she had been thinking the same thing. I wrote a letter to Dan and said I hadn't mentioned that I have MS. At the time I wasn't limping much or using my cane. I told Dan that having MS was beside the point, that I wanted to put on a jazz party and hook it up to the MS Society. The party would raise funds to accomplish two things—expose people to jazz and contribute to the MS society without being a benefit function for the society. It would be put on *by* the society *by* people with MS. To me, that has a more positive effect.

"Dan called me as soon as he got the letter. He said, 'First off, let me say I'm sorry you've got MS.' I told him, 'There's no reason to be. It's just the luck of the draw. I look at it as a challenge. If I can do all the things I'm doing *and* have MS, I can feel pretty good about myself. I'm always doing 50 projects at once, usually with 100 ideas and 3 good ones. Enough said. Let's talk about the party idea.'

I'll Just Have to Get Out of the Way of Ralph's Left Hand

"Dan said, 'I'd love to do it. Let me help you put it together.' We talked about some hard realities, such as jazz musicians' not making enough money to be able to play a party as a charity. About a week later, I got a 12-page, single-spaced letter. Dan laid everything out and really got excited. He came to Raleigh in May to play a gig, and Dottie and I drove over to hear him. The three of us got together the next day and had a brainstorming session.

"We made Dan the music director of our party and came up with a list of the musicians we wanted. He began contacting them, and I put together the details of the party. About a week later he called and said all our first choices were available and would love to come. I attribute a lot of the party's success to Dan, though he won't take credit for it."

On the last weekend in September 1988, an impressive lineup of artists played at the first Triangle Jazz Party: Ed Polcer, Dan Barrett, George Masso, Kenny Davern, Ken Peplowski, Dick Hyman, Ralph Sutton, Howard Alden, Marty Grosz, Major Holley, Jack Lesberg, Gus Johnson, Jackie Williams, and Polly Podewell. The same group performed at the 1989 party, except that Warren Vaché replaced Polcer.

Blades was a departmental administrator at the East Carolina University medical school when he started the Triangle party. He had been hit by MS nine years earlier at the age of 29. As he—and his wife and their two young sons, Josh and Mike—learned to live with the incurable neurological disease, he began to resent what he perceived as the tendency of such organizations as the National Multiple Sclerosis Society to take care of victims of a disease rather than working to involve them in the process of solving the problem.

Soon after the 1989 party, Blades formed a nonprofit volunteer organization called Friends In Need (FIN). The group set its goal as helping victims of a chronic disease or disabling condition who could not afford the health care equipment or services that they required. FIN took over the Triangle sponsorship in 1990. Ralph missed the party that year but returned to Raleigh in 1991 for the fourth one, which was dedicated to Major Holley. The popular bassist, whose comic humming-singing in unison with his bowed solos always brought wild applause, had died shortly after the 1990 gig.

Seven of the musicians at the 1991 party—Randy Sandke, Barrett, Chuck Hedges, Rick Fay, Sutton, Lesberg, and Jake Hanna—made an excellent recording the next day for Arbors Records. Billed as the Triangle Jazz Party Boys, all donated their talent to Friends In Need. In turn, FIN gave part of the recording proceeds to Gus Johnson, who had been forced by Alzheimer's disease to retire. The second of two $500 checks was sent to Mildred Johnson at Christmas 1992.

Trombonist George Broussard, a music faculty member at East Carolina University, plays on one of the tunes recorded. He and other local musicians, including Steve Blades, had joined some of the featured performers in the 16-piece band that played for the patrons' brunch at the party. Ralph has a prominent role throughout the recording. His piano behind Broussard and Barrett on "Just Friends" is a particularly fine example of his extraordinary comping.

While the musicians were warming up on another of the recorded tunes, "Triangle Jazz Blues," Barrett walked over to Sutton and commented on the dissonance in the piano segment of the intro. He made a stab at the desired effect with his right hand, and Ralph quickly picked it up. Barrett began laughing and broke up the others as he returned to his place: "Jesus Christ, here I am showing Ralph Sutton how to play piano!"

Blades reluctantly canceled the 1992 Triangle party after accepting the position of administrative director of a cardiology practice in Kingsport, Tennessee. He started the new job that spring and for more than a year drove home to Greenville every other weekend, a seven-hour trip each way. His wife and sons joined him in Kingsport in 1993. Blades reestablished FIN there that year and resurrected the Triangle party in 1994. The original party had been named for the triangle formed by Raleigh, Durham, and Chapel Hill. Blades looked forward to working with Barrett in staging an annual gig in the Tennessee triangle of Kingsport, Bristol, and Johnson City.

The Suttons and some close friends planted the seeds of their own jazz party shortly after Ralph played at the first party in Raleigh. Peter and Barbara Guy owned one of Aspen's top restaurants, the Steak Pit, and had known Sunnie since she bought the Rendezvous and, later, ran it with Ralph. In October 1988, the two couples were sitting on the deck of the Guys' home with Eve Homeyer and a few other friends. They began reminiscing about the jazz parties that Dick Gibson had put on at the Hotel Jerome, beginning 25 years earlier.

Peter Guy remembered the fun that everyone had at those early parties. He still found it hard to believe that Gibson could attract the superlative musicians who played at those affairs. Aspen wasn't used to having that kind or quality of music.

"Peter," Sunnie said to Guy, "wouldn't it be great if we could have a party at the Jerome?"

"Yeah," he replied, "it would be great."

"Well, why don't we try?" Sunnie said, having the same thought at the same time that her friend did.

The Guys, the Suttons, and Homeyer went to work immediately. They wanted to have a party that was smaller than Gibson's and more informal and relaxed. They also wanted to have fewer musicians and to give the players plenty of time to enjoy the town and the weather.

Ralph, as co-musical director with Jack Lesberg, lined up the musicians. Sunnie started calling or writing to people about the planned event, and her enthusiasm came across in the postcards she sent with the news about the inauguration of Jerome Jazz. Many people were intrigued by the thought of going to a party at the hotel where the jazz party idea had started, especially with the newly renovated Hotel Jerome's celebrating its 100th anniversary in 1989. Other attractions included the skiing and scenery of Aspen, plus having one of the most brilliant and popular jazz musicians and his wife as prime movers in staging the event.

"Whenever Ralph and I go to Aspen, we get very excited," Sunnie said a couple of years later. "We love the town and we miss being there in a way, and we've always loved the party that Gibson started at the Jerome. We thought Aspen was the greatest place to have a jazz party."

"The more we talked about it that day on our deck," Guy recalled, "the more enthusiastic we got about the idea of going back to the Jerome where jazz parties began and seeing if the hotel people were interested in helping us put on a party. When we first contacted them, they thought we were crazy. They had never heard of this kind of format and weren't sure how we were going to get the guests to come. I'm sure they thought we'd probably go away and not show up again.

"We drew up a list of musicians that same day, and also a list of people to contact. I wanted Ralph to invite the musicians because he knows them and he knows the music. I had total confidence in his ability to put together a group that not only would be compatible but would have a lot of fun playing together."

It was indeed quite a group that he put together to perform in September 1989 at the first Jerome Jazz: Yank Lawson, Randy Sandke, Snooky Young, Dan Barrett, Al Grey, George Masso, Kenny Davern, Scott Hamilton, Flip Phillips, Marshall Royal, Dick Hyman, Ralph Sutton, Howard Alden, Milt Hinton, Jack Lesberg, Jake Hanna, and Gus Johnson.

"Sunnie's personal contacts were instrumental in the success of our party," Guy said. "She kept being her own inimitable self and pushing hard, and the enthusiasm grew. Every time she went to a jazz party or somewhere else, she'd talk the thing up and give out information. We started getting calls even though we didn't even have the invitations ready. People wanted to send their checks and kept asking how soon they'd get some notice of the event and was the date firm for September 1989.

"We may have burned up a few phone lines between Aspen and Bailey with all the calls we made back and forth. The invitations finally went out in late May. By then, the party was half filled. The checks started coming in and we continued working with the Jerome to try and get suitable arrangements. The hotel people began to come around when they found out we really were planning to bring a crowd of 300 into their ballroom. They had never held 300 in there and were worried about that. We told them it wouldn't be dinner service, that we just wanted to serve drinks and to be able to listen to the music. One thing led to another, and it all eventually fell together.

"The Jerome was going through a change in management, and so the hotel personnel were coming and going. We'd go back to firm up some details that we had talked through previously and not always be able to talk to the same person. So we'd have to start from square one again and convince them that we were real and were going to do it.

"Eve's role was to work with the hotel. She's a detail person and is sensitive to timing and people's problems. Barbara was essentially the secretary of our group. She's dynamite at this kind of thing, thorough and so eager. Without those three ladies, the party wouldn't have happened. Sunnie because she contacted all the people. Eve because she was so good at working with the Jerome and making the arrangements. Barbara because she kept everything straight and in order.

"I'm not being modest when I say I can't remember what part I played. I just tried to keep everybody happy and didn't do anything specifically. If Eve had a problem, I'd sit down with her and help her work it out. Or I'd go with her when things got a little sticky at the hotel at times. I just kind of pursued things when the others needed some help.

"Those three women did all the work. It was a dynamite group and a lot of fun, but an awful lot of work. We had no idea that the whole thing would evolve into so much work. But the parties were great, so that made it worthwhile."

Sunnie filled in some details of the Guys' role in Jerome Jazz: "We were very successful in 1989, the first year, when we sold out. The second year we didn't sell out and we lost money. We had made money the first year, and that saved us in 1990. I never thought Peter would go for a third party, and heaven knows Ralph and I can't afford to throw a party and lose money. Peter and Barbara have a very successful restaurant, but I can't see their wanting to take the money that they make working hard and throw it out on a jazz party. I was resigned to not having a third party until I talked to Peter in January. He felt badly about the thought of not doing it again in 1991 and said, 'Let's go!'"

Chapter **32**

His Music Jumps Up and Grabs You

alph faced twin frustrations at the Pensacola Jazz Party in January 1990. First, a flight delay made him late for the gig. The party promoter, Gus Statiras, asked John Sheridan to sit in for him with the World's Greatest Jazzband. Sutton arrived while the Jim Cullum Jazz Band was playing. Later, Sheridan got a kick during the prelude to a two-piano set featuring Ralph and himself.

"It's always a lot of fun for Ralph and me to play two pianos," Sheridan said. "This time, the pianos were at opposite ends of the stand. Ralph told me, 'That's not gonna work. Go talk to Gus and have him push the pianos together.' I said I had planned to do so. I talked to Gus, who told me, 'It's impossible to do that. Too many wires there, and the drums are in the way. You'll have to play the pianos where they are.'

"I went back to Ralph, and that jaw of his came out. 'Bullshit!' He grabbed me by the elbow. 'Come with me! Let's go talk to this guy.' Ralph told him, 'Gus, you've got to push the pianos together.' Gus said they couldn't be pushed together. Ralph insisted, 'You've *got* to push them together. How do you expect us to play?' The two of them went back and forth, and finally Gus walked away. Ralph stood there with the balloon with a question mark over his head. 'Didn't the guy hear what I said?' Then he looked at me and said, 'Fuck him!'

"'Let's go play anyway,' Ralph told me. He grabbed my cheek and said, 'We're pros. You know what you're doin', and I know what I'm doin'. We've done this before. Come on.' We went ahead and played, and everything was fine."

Statiras laughed when recalling the incident: "It didn't bother me at all. Ralph and I have been friends too long for me to get upset by something like that. I would have pushed the pianos together if it had been possible, but it was a physical impossibility. John and Ralph sounded great together, as always."

When I interviewed Jay Leonhart for this book, he had written and stashed away at least 2,000 humorous poems. At the rate of one a day—and in the extremely unlikely event that he did not bolster his stockpile—it would have taken him well over five years to turn all of them into his uniquely witty songs. He regaled audiences with these tunes, singing to the accompaniment of a combo or just himself on bass.

As a teenager in the 1950s, Leonhart developed great respect for stride pianists and became acquainted with the records of Fats Waller, James P. Johnson, Art Tatum, Dick Wellstood, *and* Ralph Sutton." He heard his first live Sutton performance in March 1989 at the Paradise Valley Jazz Party in Phoenix.

"I had known about Ralph for so long that I found it interesting to be playing with him," Leonhart said. "I was thrilled that he knew who I was. He was very sweet, very nice. Ralph's a phenomenal pianist. And to think I'm actually playing with the guy. His syncopation, his time are extraordinary. He swings *so* much. I don't know if anyone else plays like that now."

At Bill Muchnic's San Diego Jazz Party in February 1990, Leonhart voiced his pleasure at being on the program with such giants as Bob Haggart and Milt Hinton. He also expressed the hope that he would not lose his reputation as a bassist as the result of his success as a composer-singer. That reputation started when Leonhart moved to New York in 1961. One day, he dropped into Jim and Andy's, a musicians' hangout. Hinton, whose nickname, The Judge, reflected the respect and affection bestowed on him by other musicians, happened to be there. Leonhart told what happened:

"Milt saw me there by myself and was very kind to me. He said, 'Why don't you come out to the house?' Mona cooked a lovely meal. It couldn't have been nicer. I went downstairs and played a couple of notes on Milt's bass. He said, 'Yep, OK, you can play.' He started recommending me for gigs, and I was never out of work because of that. Milt made me feel accepted right away. He'd get a gig he couldn't do and would recommend me. You work for the right people right away, and all of a sudden your name is well known. It's magic."

Leonhart paid tribute to Hinton by composing a song that he sang at The Judge's 80th birthday celebration at Town Hall on June 23, 1990. This was Hinton's actual birthday, which made the event especially touching. The song was one of Leonhart's finest:

The Judge*

It's been over 30 years
Since I overcame my fears
Packed my bags and moved to New York City.

Got myself a little place
Just room for me and my bass
No time to wallow in self-pity.

Head to Jim and Andy's bar
That's where the musicians are
Give lady luck a little nudge.

Open the door and I walk in
Right away luck does begin
'Cause on that day I run into The Judge.

No sooner am I in the place
When I am standing face to face
With one of the great bassists in the land.

I start getting very nervous
What did I do to deserve this
A feeling that I think you'd understand.

No hidden motivations lurk
The Judge knows that I need to work
He knows the hungry look of a beginner.

So we talk for a little while
Until I see The Judge's smile
And he invites me out to the house to dinner.

* © Chancellor Music Company. Reproduced by permission of Jay Leonhart.

His Music Jumps Up and Grabs You

So I call on the telephone a
Woman by the name of Mona
Answers and says Sunday would be fine.

So merrily to Queens I trudge
For dinner with Mona and The Judge
I'm laden down with flowers, gifts, and wine.

(Well, flowers and gifts . . .
(OK, just flowers . . .
(So I brought nothing. I was very young.)

But nonetheless I was on time
And Mona's dinner was sublime
Real home cooking the genuine stuff.

And after dinner I play the bass
A stern look on The Judge's face
After three notes he says, "That's enough."

Oh, no, I've failed my first audition
In my quest for a position
Someplace in New York where I could play.

I didn't need anything real big
I just needed a simple gig
Didn't care what it might pay.

So I say goodnight to Milt and Mona
Once again I'm all alone, a
Young man with those great big city blues.

But next week it was the strangest thing
My telephone began to ring
With gigs for me such wonderful news.

Loose Shoes

He helped me so when I got started
Such wise counsel he imparted
And he taught my telephone to start to ring.

And there's simply no debating
That he helped my credit rating
In itself a monumental thing.

Perhaps I need a new perspective
Or lenses just a bit corrective
But to me The Judge stands 10 feet tall.

Up from the primordial slime and sludge
Occasionally evolves a Judge
To help us find some meaning in it all.

He's shown me how to lead my life
How to deal with stress and strife
Living with a minimum of fuss.

He shows us how to share our lives
He shows us how to care for our wives
While they in fact are taking care of us.

Imagine that a jazz musician
Could achieve such a position
Where he is beheld a national treasure.

But before the birth of Branford and Wynton
I was friends with Milton Hinton
A fact I note with great pride and great pleasure.

Another birthday comes and goes
But on The Judge it never shows
He must have friends in higher places.

Or maybe it's just because he's wise
And gets a lot of exercise
Chasing planes and trains and lugging basses.

So here I stand before you folks
With a minimum of jokes
Just a chance to play the bass and sing.

And from this stage I will not budge
Until I get to tell The Judge
Happy Birthday, Judge, and thanks for everything.

You make every rhythm section swing
Imagine what the next 10 years will bring
We love you, Judge, and thanks for everything.

On March 28, 1989, the Last of the Whorehouse Piano Players finished their first recording for Chiaroscuro. That same day, Sutton, Hinton, and Gus Johnson recorded the first tune for a Chiaroscuro album featuring The Judge with a large assortment of his peers. For this album, called *Old Man Time*, Hinton sang the song of that title, which he had performed throughout the world.

Hinton selected an ageless ballad to record with Sutton and Johnson for the album. When Ruth heard their lovely version, with its interplay by Sutton and Hinton, she suggested that it could have been called "Love Affair Between Piano and Bass" if it didn't already have a title, "Time on My Hands."

In May, Ruth learned firsthand about the affection showered on Sutton by his European fans. She was traveling through southern Italy with a family friend who was a professional Italian tour guide, and had arranged to stop in Cosenza and meet jazz pianist Raffaele Borretti. Ralph had played a recorded concert with Borretti and his combo, the Cosenza Jazz Workshop, in 1982.

The combo's guitarist, Franco Beltrano, told Ruth that all the musicians considered Ralph a giant. They and their wives had taken Sutton to the airport, and everyone cried when they said good-bye to him. Borretti's wife called Ralph a wonderfully warm person and said being with him had been one of the greatest experiences of their lives. Borretti felt insignificant at the piano in comparison.

Thirty-eight years had gone by since Barbara Alderson, as a teenager in Santa Ana, California, initiated a brief correspondence with Ralph, then playing his fourth year at Condon's. Excerpts appear in Chapter 9 of this book.

Alderson remained a fan of Sutton's through the years but never had a chance to hear him in a live performance. Then, in the spring of 1989, some friends who shared her love for his piano told her that Ralph would be playing nearby in June at the Glenn Ranch Jazz Party. She and five of them went to hear him on a Sunday afternoon in the San Bernardino Mountains of southern California.

"I didn't know whom he was playing with or even if he was playing with anyone," Alderson said. "It could have been an elementary school accordion band for all I cared. I just wanted to hear Ralph play. I had kept his letter and postcard all those years, and I read them every once in a while. So when I had an opportunity to hear him, I took them along. I thought he'd get a kick reading them.

"What a group he had with him—Gus Johnson, Milt Hinton, and two young fellows who were new to me, Kenny Davern and Warren Vaché. Two of us kept trading seats so we could watch Ralph's fingerwork. Oh, those chords! Not only his solos, but the background things he played just destroyed me. He did 'Viper's Drag,' one of my favorites and one of the first tunes I ever heard him play on a record. A woman sitting behind us tapped me on the shoulder and said, 'I'm sorry you're not enjoying yourself.'

"It was very difficult for me to approach Ralph. He had so many people talking to him and was very gracious with all of them, but I kind of froze when I realized it was really Sutton. One of my friends had to almost shove me up to him. I eventually introduced myself and we chatted a while. I handed him the letter and the postcard, and he kept shaking his head as he read them. 'I can't believe I bared my soul like that,' he said. It was the most enjoyable day of the year for me."

Jazz writer Floyd Levin, in a glowing review for *West Coast Rag*, noted that Vaché, Davern, Sutton, Hinton, and Johnson were the only performers at the four-day party. He added that "the word *only* could never apply to such world-class musicians." Levin lauded each individually, with these impressions of Ralph:

> Sitting almost sphinxlike, the implacable Ralph Sutton extracts a fervent swing from his keyboard. When the tempo rises, his grin broadens as he bolsters the rhythm with an exhilarating stride that provides a throbbing cushion beneath the soloists. He has played 'Honeysuckle Rose' a zillion times, yet finds a freshness that makes Fats Waller's masterpiece seem new.
>
> "Sutton transforms the familiar bridge into a launching pad that explodes into a romping chorus ('So sweet when you stir it up') and a concerto ending. His love and admiration for Waller flows from every chorus, every note. As a contrast, Ralph later offered a pensive, introspective treatment of the Bix Beiderbecke piano solo, 'In the Dark,' and applied his personal stamp to the lovely arcane ballad, 'Love Lies.'"

In July 1989, Ralph played at the Montauban Jazz Festival in France. "What a show!" proclaimed one review. "To see Ralph Sutton jam on his keyboard at unheard-of speeds and give birth to such melodies by his numerous finger gymnastics. It's hard to believe he only has 10 fingers!"

On the last night of the festival, an incident occurred that prompted an indignant editorial commentary by Laurie Wright, the editor of *Storyville* magazine:

> During a recent visit to France, we visited the Montauban Jazz Festival, where we were made most welcome by the festival organizers and the Hot Club of France, who use the occasion to hold their annual meeting and banquet. We were most impressed with the amount of good music on offer.
>
> To my ears, the star of the festival proper was Ralph Sutton, both with and without drummer Jackie Williams, who confirmed that he is one of the few really thoughtful and tasteful drummers around these days. Ralph excelled whether playing as featured artist or as backing for other artists, but I felt that the way he was treated on the final evening was disgraceful.
>
> Having finished his set, he played a well-deserved encore and was then asked to play a couple of more numbers (to the delight of the

audience) as the Lionel Hampton Big Band was not quite ready. That was fine, except that the band then began to drift on stage to set up their instruments and Sutton, having finished the requested two numbers, waved good-bye and left. Hardly the way to treat one of your star artists, and I hope that apologies were rendered to him and that it won't happen again.

Johnny and Liza Simmen, who were at the festival, agreed with Wright that Ralph had been treated shabbily. Sutton shrugged the whole thing off, however. No apology had been offered, he said, expressing mild surprise at Wright's reaction.

Sutton performed in Vienna in November and then went to Germany. Mannie Selchow had arranged two concerts, in Bremen and in Westoverledingen, his hometown. Ralph played a solo set each night and was joined by clarinetist Peter Müller and drummer Helle Peters for two sets. Sutton and Müller, an admirer of Edmond Hall's, played several numbers that Hall and Ralph had done together years before, including "Dardanella" and some Fats Waller tunes.

Peters did nicely on drums when playing behind Müller and Sutton. But Selchow kidded him for botching some of his solos. Peters got so carried away by his excitement in working with Ralph that he forgot to count the bars while soloing and finished on the wrong beat. After Selchow's two concerts, Sutton played in Zurich and then wound up the tour at Jaylin's Club in Bern.

Madeleine Nichols went to her first jazz party in 1989 at the age of 8. She lived in Santa Fe, New Mexico, where the party was held during the Memorial Day weekend. Maddy had been listening to the music for several years, courtesy of her mother, Catherine, and her grandmother Jane Eddy. Her earliest jazz memories included hearing Fats Waller's famous record of "Your Feet's Too Big." Her grandmother also liked to play what the little girl called "a tape with 'Big Noise from Winnetka' on one side, and on the other side it was mostly all Ralph Sutton."

Maddy took piano lessons, which enhanced her pleasure at hearing jazz, especially Sutton. She was thrilled when her grandmother took her to the Santa Fe party. Seven months later, in January 1990, Maddy and her mother and grandparents ignored a heavy snowstorm and went up to Taos

Ski Valley to hear Ralph, Warren Vaché, Kenny Davern, Milt Hinton, and Gus Johnson at Thunderbird Lodge.

"I really enjoy listening to someone who can play the piano so beautifully," Maddy said. "I like to sit up front so I can see how Ralph plays. After I hear him play, it makes me want to play, too, and I usually end up playing a little better. His music jumps up and grabs you and makes you want to go crazy."

Most of Maddy's friends did not know about her musical tastes. She kept her preferences to herself because she thought the other kids would laugh at her for liking what they considered old-time music.

"They think, 'Who wants that junk?'" she said. "They say, 'Modern music's better.' Well, it's not. Modern music is loud and it's got bad words and all that junk. Take any rock hit or heavy metal. It's complete dodo brain. I'm surprised people actually like it. I hope it'll go out someday and jazz will come back in because it's so wonderful."

"Just finished my round-the-world trip," Ralph wrote in late May 1990. "Bailey, San Francisco, Osaka, Hong Kong, Frankfurt, Zurich, Atlanta, Dallas, Odessa, Bailey. How does that grab ya? For the time being, I'm taking it easy. Mercy!"

Sutton returned to Japan in July and played two parties and a concert in Tokyo. He played with a band led by trumpeter Yoshio Toyama and enjoyed himself thoroughly both on and off the stand: "The hospitality is the end, and the music is really appreciated. They know what is going on. If only the Americans would catch on. But I guess it's the difference between class and ass."

That difference manifested itself again when Ralph came to Chicago in October to play a private party given by an old Army buddy. He brought Yank Lawson, George Masso, Phil Bodner, Howard Alden, Bob Haggart, and Gus Johnson with him. Unfortunately, virtually none of the businessmen who made up the audience realized—or cared less—that they were hearing a rather formidable array of jazz talent. The crowd was the noisiest, drunkenest, and rudest I had ever heard, despite repeated appeals for quiet from Ralph and the other musicians. The band, accustomed to such boorishness, played beautifully. Sutton's mood became increasingly less beautiful as the evening progressed.

The jazz world was saddened that same month by the death of Major Holley. Ruth and I had enjoyed his marvelous talents in September at the

Triangle Jazz Party in Raleigh. After one of his sets, Holley showed Josh Blades, the 9-year-old son of the party's founder, Steve Blades, how he bowed his bass in unison with his humming and singing. The boy watching the large man with the giant bass made an unforgettable picture. The previous weekend, at the Hotel Jerome in Aspen, the major had created another memorable scene when he sprawled on the floor and played with Dan Barrett's little son, Andy.

Holley greatly admired Ralph's stride artistry and said it was "beautiful" to play with him. But he and his fellow bassist, Brian Torff, like many of their peers, felt that Sutton had such a powerful left hand that he didn't need a bass.

Joya Jenson, an Australian jazz broadcaster and writer, celebrated Ralph's 68th birthday by presenting a special program on her Sydney radio show, "The Joy-A-Jazz," in November 1990. The program, called *Piano Man,* featured tunes from the *Partners in Crime* album by Sutton, Australians Bob and Len Barnard, and Milt Hinton. It also included segments of a Sutton interview by Jenson. She invited me to send her a tape of my favorite Sutton recording and to say a few words about it. I sent two tunes, wishing to give her listeners a sample of Ralph's talents as both accompanist and soloist.

The tunes came from the 1969 live recording at Elitch Gardens in Denver by the Ten Greats of Jazz, the precursor of the World's Greatest Jazzband. One is a tenor sax solo of "Lady Be Good" by Bud Freeman that displays Ralph's superlative comping. The other is a Sutton solo warhorse, "Viper's Drag" by Fats Waller.

Jenson added a clever twist to her Sutton birthday observance by playing two tunes based on Ralph's devotion to Waller and Jack Teagarden. During her interview with Sutton, she had asked him to mention some highlights of his career. Ralph named two—meeting Teagarden and playing with him for the first time, and "when he sent for me to come to New York."

So Jenson played Waller's 1929 recording of "Handful of Keys," his famous piano solo and a Sutton staple. Then she closed with "I'll Be Glad When You're Dead, You Rascal, You," recorded in 1931 by a band fronted by Teagarden and including Waller. Teagarden sings his distrust of Waller, the rascal whom he suspects of dallying with his wife. Waller repeatedly proclaims his innocence and also plays a swinging solo.

On the morning after the 1990 Aspen party, Gus Johnson could not find his flight ticket. He and I shared a cab to the airport, and I mentioned the Sutton biography and again expressed my thanks for the interview he had given me. The great drummer did not seem to know what I was talking about. He appeared confused and sat staring straight ahead, saying hardly a word. He apparently had no concern about how he would get to Denver without a ticket. Sunnie made a quick trip from the airport back to the Hotel Jerome in the vain hope that someone had found Johnson's ticket. It turned up in one of his pockets at the last minute.

A week and a half later, at the private party in Chicago, Johnson had great difficulty setting up his drums and misplaced some parts. Ralph, who was becoming increasingly concerned, had to help him.

The two friends flew to Bern together in November as they had done so many times. But Johnson had much trouble playing, and Sutton reluctantly put him on a plane for home a week later. Alzheimer's disease had ended the career of one of the finest drummers–and nicest people—in the history of jazz. He had just passed his 77th birthday.

The Denver Jazz Club, which booked Ralph for one or two concerts every year, had scheduled him for February 1991. At Sunnie's suggestion, the club turned the gig into a benefit for Johnson. Peanuts Hucko, Colin Gieg, and Jake Hanna played the concert with Ralph. Sunnie had an 8- by 10-inch photo of Johnson blown up to 4 by 5 feet, and the enlargement stood on the bandstand. Gus and Mildred Johnson were in the audience. The benefit raised more than $8,300 for them to help meet medical expenses.

Ralph shared some reflections with the audience:

> "... Gus is a compassionate man, played perfect time, and is an impeccable dresser. He has a great sense of humor, loves children, and at the age of 70 he adopted his grandson to raise.
>
> "When we were traveling, we always looked out for each other's well-being. We were like brothers.
>
> "Gus was not a flashy drummer. His drums were the heart of all groups he played with, large or small, and he listened to the individual soloists and backed them perfectly. What more could you ask for? I love him."

Chapter **33**

What a Bargain! Three Hours of Ralph Sutton for $10

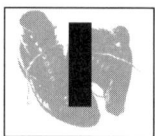n January 1991, John Sheridan made his first recording under his own name. This fine mixture of piano solos and combo tunes on the Triangle Jazz label features Randy Reinhart, Freddy Salas, Howard Elkins, and Don Mopsick, the latter two, like Sheridan, from the rhythm section of the Jim Cullum Jazz Band. The album has the intriguing name *Butterscotch*, which came from the title tune, written by Sheridan. As Marty Grosz explains in his liner notes, Sheridan named it for his favorite ice cream topping.

"Unlike many contemporary keyboard players," Grosz wrote, "(John) places as much emphasis on the role of the left hand as he does on that of the right, an approach that enlists him in the ranks of the two-fisted jazz pianists, a vanishing breed of players who sound as good alone as they do with rhythm backing. There's about a shot-glass full of top-notch jazz pianists who can claim that distinction. Ralph Sutton, Dick Hyman, and Dave McKenna come to mind; a distinguished company, more like a snifter-full actually."

Sheridan also got together with Dan Barrett for a recording whose title hardly reflects the zany story behind it. In May 1992, Barrett spent two weeks as the guest of Sheridan and Karen Kambestad while playing with the Jim Cullum Jazz Band at the Landing in San Antonio. The two musicians discovered that they both wore the same kind of red plaid tartan pajamas and robes. Barrett proposed that they make a duet album, pose in their pajamas for the cover photo, and call the project *Two Sleepy People*. They recorded the album for Arbors Records in September.

Bill Wolfe of Lakeport, California, wanted to hear his piano teacher play piano, and so in March 1991 he flew to St. Louis. His teacher hap-

What a Bargain! Three Hours of Ralph Sutton for $10

pened to be Barbara Sutton Curtis, and she and her brother Ralph were headlining the 10th Mid-America Jazz Festival.

Barb had played a concert in Lakeport a few months earlier. A newspaper article told Wolfe about the concert and mentioned that Barb gave lessons and was Ralph's sister. Wolfe had been a Sutton fan for some time. He went to Barb's concert and was so impressed that he introduced himself and asked if they could talk about her giving him lessons. She agreed, and he drove to her home in nearby Ukiah a couple of weeks later.

Wolfe had taken a few piano lessons when he was in fourth grade, but he didn't learn to read music. He had a natural ear that enabled him to play whatever he heard his teacher play. She mistakenly thought she was teaching him to play.

"I fooled around by ear until I went into the Air Force in 1950," Wolfe said. "I played a little until they asked me to transpose something from C into another key. I didn't even know what the key of C was, let alone what I was going to transpose into. My career as a part-time piano player was very short-lived. For more than 20 years I didn't play at all. Then, when Barbara came to town, I thought, well, I've got a lot of music in my soul, and before I die I want to get it out.

"Barbara told me she had never taught anybody who couldn't read music. I told her I would learn to read if she taught me to play better by ear. I played for her, and she told me to come back on Thursday for my first lesson."

Teacher and student agreed that she would not play any tune for him. Wolfe could pick up by ear what she played, which would work against his learning to read.

"She doesn't play for me at all," he said. "If I have to fly to St. Louis to hear her, it's well worth the trip."

After about a month of lessons, Barb asked Wolfe to give her the names of all the pianists whose records he owned. His list included Ralph, and Wolfe baited his teacher a bit by telling her that Sutton was one of his favorites. Barb soon learned that Wolfe knew she was Ralph's sister. He had not mentioned it because he didn't know how the two of them got along. Perhaps disharmony existed between this brother and sister, as it did with many siblings.

"I stayed away from the subject because I didn't want to anger her as the result of my feelings about Ralph's playing," Wolfe said. "You tread lightly on thin ice, especially when he's one of the greats of jazz. Barbara expressed a great deal of warmth and love and support and awe for her brother, and she has done so continually ever since. It's a tribute to both of them that they're as close as they are.

"I couldn't believe what I heard when the two of them played together. Their fingers melded. It sounded like one piano with 20 fingers on it, not like dual pianos."

Wolfe could not say enough about his teacher: "Barbara Curtis is a big piano player, but she's a bigger woman and a bigger human being. She's a warm, wonderful person."

Barb and the audience both relished her first appearance at the St. Louis festival. She was greeted by a number of people whom she hadn't seen since their childhood days in Howell. Many in the crowd had never heard Barb and Ralph play together. People kept complimenting her and saying they realized that something special was going on.

"I hope they caught the joy that was coming from Ralph and me," she said. "That's really what it's all about—the sheer happiness of being together, of listening to each other and responding to the other's ideas, and making the music work as best we can. That is joy to me."

Jay McShann was also on the program, but he and Ralph were not scheduled to play together. McShann plugged that hole during his final set by calling Sutton up to the second piano. The audience burst into applause, and Ralph walked to the stand. A man followed and started talking to him as he sat down at the keyboard. Ralph ignored him. The crowd quieted, and McShann and Sutton got ready to kick off their first tune. The man kept talking. Ralph finally turned around and glared at him. The man shut up instantly. He stared at Sutton with an expression reflecting fear and awe—and retreated. Ralph hadn't said a word.

Sunnie drove Ralph to the airport as usual on April 7, when he flew to France. She arrived home to find her mother lying dead in bed. Irene Anderson had been in deteriorating health for some time. The Suttons were saddened by her death, but it lifted from them great emotional stress and financial responsibility.

Ralph wrote that he returned from France "with a hell of a cold, and then Sunnie caught it. She just wouldn't stay away from me. Mercy!" He played a benefit for Gus Johnson in Colorado Springs in late April before flying to Japan with Marty Grosz for gigs in Kobe, Onomichi, Tokyo, and Chiba. Sutton went to Australia on May 9, 1991. He played the next 10 days in Adelaide, Melbourne, Hobart, Sydney, and Cairns, and then Wellington, New Zealand. On May 19, he flew to the Odessa party via Auckland, Honolulu, Chicago, and Dallas.

Upon arriving in Wellington, Sutton was met at the airport by Bill Hamer, president of the Wellington Jazz Club, and Ralph Sutton. It was the first time that the pianist had met someone with the same name. Hamer introduced him to Ralph Lionel Sutton. A story, including a photo of the two Ralph Suttons smiling together, appeared a couple of days later in the *Evening Post* of Wellington.

The New Zealander Sutton was born three months after the American. He lived in Wellington, and short-wave radio had long been one of his hobbies. Shortly before his namesake arrived, he had heard two other hams conversing. One was Hamer, who told about the jazz club's activities and mentioned that the pianist would soon be in town to give a concert.

"I thought it would be interesting to meet him," the New Zealander said. "I called Bill and suggested that it might be good publicity for his club and the concert. He agreed and arranged for the two Ralphs to meet.

"I had heard of Ralph, of course, although I'm not really a jazz enthusiast. I enjoy jazz, but no more than any other type of music—though far more than the rubbish that has been dished up in recent years. Whenever Ralph is on the air, a friend of mine calls and tells me to tune in.

"Until I met Ralph, I had heard of only two others of the same name. One is a Methodist clergyman in New Zealand. And the day after I arrived here from England in 1947, a story in the Auckland newspaper reported that Ralph Sutton had been convicted of 'converting a motor vehicle to his own use.' Strangely, just one week to the day after Ralph's latest concert in Wellington, the paper had an advertisement about someone seeking the right to take ground water for farming use by Ralph Gordon Sutton. He was news to me!"

Arild Wideröe, a Swiss promoter, presented his first Ralph Sutton concert in 1980 in Villingen, Germany, a village near the border with Switzerland. That engagement was held in a small church, and Jack Lesberg and Jake Hanna played with Ralph. Milt Hinton and Gus Johnson accompanied Sutton in Wideröe's second concert, and Jim Galloway appeared with him in the third one. Wideröe then moved to Baden and took his concerts along with him. In November 1990, he presented the Last of the Whorehouse Piano Players, plus Bob Barnard. Highly respected among jazz musicians, Wideröe cares deeply for them and their music.

John Norris, the publisher of *Coda* magazine and a close friend of Wideröe's, heard Ralph and Barbara Sutton Curtis play together at the Mid-America Jazz Festival in March 1991. He was so impressed with the brother and sister at dual pianos that he urged Wideröe to have Barb join Ralph in Baden in November. Barb and her husband, Hal, had planned a European vacation trip for October, but she hesitated only a moment before accepting Wideröe's offer.

"I didn't relish the thought of another transatlantic flight so soon, but I would not let this opportunity slip by," Barb said. "I don't know how Ralph does it. I have to admire his stamina."

Ralph and Barb, accompanied by the Swiss bassist Reggie Johnson and Jake Hanna, split the bill with a quartet consisting of Kenny Davern, Sutton, Johnson, and Hanna. The four men arrived in Baden from Bern, where they had been playing. Wideröe brought in a Bösendorfer grand to join the theater's Steinway grand.

"Ralph gave me the Bösendorfer for our hour," Barb said. "I sure appreciated that from big brother. Someone told Arild I must be crazy to come over for just one hour of playing. I agreed that I was, but I wouldn't have missed that concert for the world.

"The audience was something else. Very warm and generous with their applause. Ralph played all the intros, and on 'Fine and Dandy' he got off track and started 'Crazy Rhythm,' which had been our first tune. It's easy to do that; the two tunes are in the same key. I told him later that I thought we were going to die out there. The first chorus was a battle of wills. I tried to get him back where he belonged because I couldn't see playing 'Crazy Rhythm' again. By the second chorus we were OK, and the rest of the piece was really good.

"I call the final version 'Crazy Fine and Dandy Rhythm.' Ralph told me that I had saved his ass. Trummy Young said the same thing after I played behind a vocal of his at the Palo Alto party in 1984."

The *Bulletin of the Hot Club of France* printed a review by Konrad R. Korsunsky under the headline, "The Sutton Family in Baden":

Right from the start, it was crystal clear that this evening was going to be devoted to piano jazz. In this happy instance it meant the physically strong, ever vital and swinging stride piano that the stoic-looking Ralph Sutton has always managed to bring into full bloom. As a novelty for Swiss audiences, Ralph also introduced his striding sister Barbara, an amazingly good piano player, admittedly not quite filling her brother's enormous shoes. They played together at two concert grands, achieving both amusing and exciting moments....

In 1993, Norris produced the first commercial recording featuring the brother-and-sister team. He issued it on the Sackville label under Barbara's name. The recording consists of Barbara and Ralph's duets from the Baden concert and solos played by her at the Cafe des Copains in Toronto. Norris paid tribute to Barbara as he had to Ralph in Sutton's album recorded at the club, thanking her for the privilege of releasing her music.

While Ralph was growing up in what his son Pete called the "small, backwoods hamlet" of Howell, another Missourian, Willard Robison, was composing some of the tunes that became Sutton staples years later. Robison came from Shelbina, a slightly larger community in the northeast part of the state. Ralph developed great affection for both Robison's music and the man himself. Their deep appeal to Sutton is explained in Brian G. Boyd's *Willard Robison and His Piano: A Discography*. In this monograph, published in 1990, Boyd wrote:

> Robison was a prolific composer, lyricist, arranger, vocalist, pianist, and dance band leader, active primarily in the 1920s and 1930s... (His) compositions reflect a variety of musical influences which are deeply rooted in the American experience, including jazz, blues, folk, and spiritual music.... At a time when America was undergoing a process of rapid urbanization, his lyrics often demonstrate a distinctly nonurban sensibility and a nostalgia for the simpler values of rural life....

During a 1971 tour of the World's Greatest Jazzband, Derek Coller had met Ralph in England. He got together with Sutton several times through the years and, in November 1991, came across a cassette of early recordings by Robison. It featured the composer singing and accompanying himself on the piano, and also included his Deep River Orchestra. Sutton frequently played a number of the tunes on the recording.

Coller thought Ralph would like to hear Robison perform such numbers of his own as "A Cottage for Sale" and "'Tain't So, Honey, 'Tain't So." He sent the cassette to me, and I passed the thoroughly enjoyable recording on to Sutton.

Referring to side A of the cassette, Ralph commented that "I was 4 years of age when these [recordings] were made. Willard was his own man and I loved him. Quite a range to his voice." Regarding side B, Sutton noted that "My age now goes through 5, 6, and 7. Mercy!

"I liked the way Willard plays and also how he accompanies his vocals, this gentleman from Shelbina, Missouri. It's the first time I heard his Deep River Orchestra and I like it. He was a dear man and I have some fond memories of the times we were together."

Early in 1992, Ralph was elected to the American Jazz Hall of Fame. He and nine others—Mildred Bailey, Betty Carter, Bill Evans, Budd Johnson, Horace Silver, Zutty Singleton, Slam Stewart, Billy Strayhorn, and Dave Tough—were inducted on May 1. Sutton felt honored by his election, but he could not attend the ceremony because he was on tour in Japan. The number of jazz artists elected to the Hall of Fame reached 109 that year.

Warren Vaché, Sr., a charter board member of the New Jersey Jazz Society and editor of *Jersey Jazz*, its monthly publication, proposed in 1980 that jazz should have a Hall of Fame. The hall, created jointly by the society and the Institute of Jazz Studies of Rutgers University, held annual induction ceremonies on the Rutgers campus in New Brunswick. The first members were inducted in 1983: Louis Armstrong, Count Basie, Bix Beiderbecke, Benny Carter, Duke Ellington, Dizzy Gillespie, Benny Goodman, Earl Hines, Jelly Roll Morton, Charlie Parker, and Art Tatum.

Pat Hawes, an English jazz pianist and vocalist, excelled not only at the keyboard but also at kidding himself. He wrote to me in April 1992 about his "great pleasure" in working a recent gig with Ralph at the Pizza Express in London.

"My part of the proceedings," Hawes explained, "was to warm up the piano for him. It's a brave man who sits down after Ralph! He has long been one of my heroes. Happily, I've had the opportunity of hearing him live over the years in a number of varied musical situations. He has always been never less than wonderful, to slightly paraphrase the title of a Fats Waller tune ['Slightly Less Than Wonderful']."

Hawes wrote the liner notes for one of Sutton's best albums, recorded for the J&M label during an April 1990 concert in Woking, England. Ralph came up with especially beautiful renditions of two compositions by Waller, "Clothesline Ballet" and "Honey Hush," which the recording presents back-to-back. Hawes commented that hearing him in a live performance "is a quiet joy for the eyes as well as the ears, with much to learn for the rest of us about how to play the piano . . .

". . . He uses his long arms and massive hands and his extraordinary technique to conjure up from the piano an instantly identifiable sound," Hawes said. "Ralph's playing, for my money, epitomizes all that is good in our music; it's exciting but controlled, always tasteful, melodically and harmonically top class, and it *swings*. . . . No one plays stride piano better than Ralph . . ."

Thirteen years had gone by since Bob and Hazel Livesay last heard a live Sutton performance, and so they drove to Watsonville for the Fats Waller Festival in June 1992. This time, Ralph proved he was only human. He didn't immediately recognize the couple whom he had greeted upon spotting them in England years before. He later recalled their past meetings and told the audience about running into the Livesays overseas.

Barbara Sutton Curtis was on the Watsonville program as well as Ralph. Their two-piano duets delighted the crowd, especially the interplay between brother and sister.

"Barbara kept looking up at Ralph as though she was asking him what they were going to do next," Livesay said. "He'd just grin at her and nod and give her thumbs up. Ralph was very proud of his little sister. He turned to the audience while they were playing and said he couldn't believe how good she sounded. He told the crowd he might retire and become her manager. They got standing ovations after all their sets."

Toward the end of one of Ralph's sets, the band that followed him on the program drifted in and sat down. The cornet player took an empty seat next to Livesay in the front row. During one of Sutton's numbers, he turned to Livesay and said, "Tell me that man doesn't have three hands." The band's pianist kept his eyes pinned on Ralph's hands. When Sutton tore into "Honeysuckle Rose," the other man shook his head and declared that what Ralph was playing was impossible to play.

"Ralph had a list of tunes in front of him and referred to it during his sets," Livesay said. "I had never seen him do that before. He'd turn to the audience and announce the next number. On occasion he asked for requests, which surprised me. He'd also stop and ruminate with the audience. He talked about working on his father's construction crew as a boy and earning a nickel and going down to play the jukebox. And how he heard Fats Waller and decided that was all he wanted to do—just play like that from then on."

Sutton recorded with the Oscar Klein International Chicago Jazz Orchestra in Zurich in July. This excellent recording is replete with Ralph's comping, and he plays a lovely solo version of "I'm Always in the Mood for You." Oscar Klein puts down his trumpet and blows two harmonica choruses of "St. Louis Blues," and Bill Allred sings "Struttin' with Some Barbecue" in addition to contributing some gutsy trombone.

Heinz Bigler, the group's fine clarinetist, wrote the liner notes. Thirty years earlier, he had been a scholarship student at the Berklee College of Music in Boston. During his two years in the United States, Bigler played with such top performers as Roy Eldridge, Coleman Hawkins, Illinois Jacquet, Howard McGhee, Jimmy Rushing, Clark Terry, and Sir Charles Thompson.

Bigler told how he "nearly played with Ralph" on his last night before returning to Switzerland late in the summer of 1962. He found himself listening to Sutton play solo at a New York club: "I sit there as if frozen and keep repeating to myself, 'Now you have to join him. This is your last chance.' The clarinet lies at my feet, but I cannot bring up the courage, am not relaxed, and I am broke. I manage to convince myself that it is better and safer to go home."

In October, the audience at the 1992 edition of Jerome Jazz applauded long and loudly when Sunnie took the stand to introduce the musicians playing the first set. She got a big laugh when she presented the piano player: "My favorite pianist except for Dick Hyman."

In the middle of the final session, the crowd gave Sunnie another lusty reception when Jack Sheldon persuaded her to sing a tune. She did a grand job with "I Guess I'll Have to Change My Plan" and never had a better supporting cast—Sheldon, Dan Barrett, Scott Hamilton, Ralph, Bob Haggart, and Jake Hanna.

Ralph was playing "Viper's Drag" when the first presidential debate between George Bush and Bill Clinton began at 5 o'clock. During the next and final set, Hyman mentioned the debate and told the audience, "We're very grateful to all of you for having no interest in politics." There might have been a subliminal message in his selection of the tune that followed, "Jive at 5."

All the musicians took the stand for the final tune of the party, as was customary. Rumors had been floating around that, for financial reasons and despite the capacity crowd, this might be the final year for Jerome Jazz. Sunnie set off sustained applause when she announced that the Hotel Jerome had already been booked for the 1993 party.

As always, the audience marveled at the astonishing array of talent, old and young, that was helping to keep traditional jazz as vibrant as ever. Those who might have been partial to pianists got their usual special kick watching two such masters as Dick Hyman and Ralph Sutton cut up together while sharing the piano bench.

A week later, about 75,000 football fans converged on Mile High Stadium in Denver to watch the Denver Broncos play the Houston Oilers. A couple of blocks away, on that same Sunday afternoon, a much smaller crowd gathered in a motel to hear Ralph play the piano. The Broncos won the game, 27-21, in the final two minutes, setting off a roar from the stadium crowd. The roar of the motel crowd listening to Ralph and his rhythm section of Colin Gieg and Chris Lee easily matched it in enthusiasm, if not in volume.

The Denver Jazz Club, which presented the concert, had to fold back the walls of the motel ballroom to provide seats for all who wanted to hear Sutton. The crowd included Jan Redfield, who hadn't heard him since the previous weekend in Aspen. Neither she nor, in all likelihood, anyone else at the motel would have changed places with anybody at the stadium. When Ralph dedicated the trio's performance of "Sweet Lorraine" to Gus Johnson, the audience was obviously touched.

Redfield succinctly expressed her sentiments about the concert: "What a bargain! Three hours of Ralph Sutton for $10."

In November 1992, shortly after his 70th birthday, Ralph flew to Italy, where he gave six concerts, all one-nighters, in Bari, Genoa, Bergamo, Trieste, Ferrara, and Forli. Then he went to Switzerland for a two-week gig with Milt Hinton and Butch Miles at the Hotel Innere Enge near Bern. During that engagement, the trio played what Johnny Simmen called a "marvel" of a concert in Baden. Simmen said the musicians enjoyed working together so much and played such swinging music that the audience, a full house, "vibrated with them right away, and there was a formidable ambience all through the concert."

Ralph spent the 1993 New Year weekend playing a jazz party in Palm Springs, California. Then he and Sunnie went to New Mexico for the customary January gig at Thunderbird Lodge in Taos Ski Valley. Bob Haggart played this engagement for the first time, joining Warren Vaché, Kenny Davern, Ralph, and Jake Hanna.

The Suttons flew to Switzerland on January 26 with Jake and Denisa Hanna, Milt and Mona Hinton, and Jack and Linda Lesberg to play a birthday party in Bad Ragaz. The couples returned home on February 1. Ralph spent the following weekend in North Carolina, playing a party in Wilmington and a Sunday jazz buffet and evening concert in New Bern. Then, on February 8, he flew back to Switzerland for three weeks of gigs, winding up in Baden for a concert with Jay McShann.

"I spend my time commuting," Ralph wrote.

Chapter **34**

He's Never Anything but Right

s a free-lance pianist since leaving the World's Greatest Jazzband in 1974, Ralph has performed mostly as a soloist, either unaccompanied or with a rhythm section. Following are the impressions of some of the musicians who have played with him at jazz parties, concerts, and private engagements, and on other gigs.

Dick Hyman: I always look forward to playing two pianos with Ralph because we share an awful lot of common vocabulary about the music. I love to go in the direction that our mutual knowledge propels us, which is often toward the memory of Fats Waller. That's a great deal of fun, and Ralph, of course, to me is the exemplar of that kind of playing. He can do it better than anybody, and I try to learn from him. Ralph has many ways of playing, and not only Fats. Even in the Fats stuff, he's made it his own. He plays it like Ralph Sutton plays it.

He has a sweetness in his playing. You can sense it generally in his character even if he's not playing the piano. You hear it in the way he plays ballads and the Beiderbecke things and the Willie the Lion things. That kind of playing is very sweet and pure and unadulterated. I love to hear him do that on his own, solo.

I got to know him and Sunnie thanks to Dick Gibson's parties, though I probably heard him back when he was at Condon's. Ralph's a nice, sweet guy. He's very comfortable to be with, and absolutely unpretentious and honest. He will not bullshit you.

Ralph has a wonderfully delicate touch. And he has a nice sound on the piano, even when he's playing hard, which is very difficult to do. He gets a sound out of the piano; not everybody does. Some people play very inventively, but their tone is kind of harsh. Ralph's is always gentle and rounded. There aren't too many people who know how to do this, or even know what the concept is.

[At a Midland party, I was sitting with Sunnie in the back of the room while Hyman and Sutton played a two-piano set. They finished with "Honky Tonk Train." On his way out of the room, Hyman passed us and shook his head. "It's like trying to hold down a freight train," he said.]

I think it was probably ill advised for us to choose that number because that's one of Ralph's great vehicles and there wasn't any great need for a second piano. When Ralph wants to, he can unleash tremendous power at the keyboard. You'd best get out of the way or try to complement him in some way, not compete with him.

[Even with all the playing he does, Hyman goes to the piano before a performance and plays finger exercises.]

It helps me to do that. I really admire people who don't need to do it. Ralph, for example, and Dave McKenna. I do it systematically because I feel I need it. If I don't, I regret it. Unless I *know* I'm in good shape—that I've played several nights before or have practiced for several days before—I feel that it's necessary. To play the way I like to play and not have to worry about technique and just get into ideas as they come to mind, I have to do some exercising.

["Dick Hyman is a genius," Ralph told me early in our association. I heard Sutton praise few musicians, and Hyman was the only one he called a genius. "I'm highly complimented, if that's true," Hyman responded when I shared Ralph's comment with him. I assured him that it was. "I believe you, and thank you for telling me," he said.]

Dave McKenna: It's always a pleasure to run into Ralph. I had met him before I started going to Gibson's parties, but then our paths began to cross two or three times a year. What are you going to say about the guy? He plays stride so accurately and so swingingly and so hard. It's just powerful stride piano. There's more to him than that, though. He swings away on swing tunes and can tear up a piano. I don't know how he got all that power and accuracy he gets into his stride. That's a tough thing to do.

I play a little bit of stride once in a while. It seems to me I can do it if I play it light. I can be a little more accurate that way. But if I chomp down, I can get some spirit into it but I can't hit the notes accurately. Ralph must have taken to it naturally, because he sounds like it's all natural.

When you play two-piano things with Ralph, you've got to work hard because he's so strong. But it's easy musically because you know he's going to swing like a son of a gun and it's going to come out right. All you've got to do is tag along. He generates a lot of swing.

Ralph can be a very funny guy at times. We've always gotten along great, and he's one of my favorites.

Howard Alden: Ralph is about my favorite pianist to play with in a rhythm section because of his flawless sense of time. He plays many styles, whether he's doing a full stride accompaniment or just comping lightly à la Count Basie. I love sitting in front of the piano and hearing that sound come over my back. Sometimes I can't believe I'm sitting in front of him and hearing the things he plays.

Whenever he's in a rhythm section, everything seems to come together rhythmically. The sound he gets out of a piano is very strong and unlike anyone else's. He always gets that full, clear, ringing sound. Just hearing it inspires me and makes me play better. He's about the closest thing to Fats, but he's got his own way of playing. I can't think of a better stride piano player living today.

I think the first time I played with Ralph and a lot of the other guys was at the Midland party. I savored every moment of it because if I never played another gig with them, I would have relished that all my life. It's like a dream come true just to play regularly with guys like Ralph, Milt, Flip, Jack, and Kenny.

Ralph has always been very congenial and supportive of a lot of the younger musicians. Very open and friendly, just like his piano playing.

Marty Grosz: My first impression of Ralph was hearing him at Condon's after he replaced Joe Sullivan. A gang of us went down. We had never heard him play, and we were very pleasantly amazed that there was somebody as young as he was who hadn't succumbed to playing block chord bebop solos. We were tickled to death that this guy was playing James P. and Fats tunes and some rags and things like that. He knocked out all of us.

What's nice about Ralph is he sits down and he's got the happy attitude that goes with the music. You don't come to unload your troubles on the bandstand. You come to dispel them. That kind of thing is very helpful to the music. I've often thought that, to use a Wellstoodian term, the grease and funk have gone out of jazz. A kind of wonderful insane, manic energy came out of it in the old days. Ralph's got sort of a barrelhouse feeling about him when he plays, and I think that's what a lot of people like.

Once when Ralph was playing at the London House in Chicago during the '50s, my wife and I took him to our house. We played records until about 5 in the morning. I had a record of Fats Waller's that we played over and over, "Hallelujah! Things Look Rosy Now" and "'Tain't Good (Like a Nickel Made of Wood)." It was a South American issue without the vocal; so instead of a piano chorus and a vocal, you got two piano choruses. Ralph had a phonograph in his hotel room, and he called me up and said he was playing it over and over there, too.

[Grosz wrote about Sutton at the London House in the liner notes for the two Chaz Jazz records that Ralph made with Kenny Davern and Gus Johnson: "They used to put cards on the tables asking you to write in who you would like them to bring back. Several of us would gather up as many cards as we could and write Ralph's name in, but for some reason they didn't get him back; so we wished a curse on the place. Today it's a Burger King."]

Milt Hinton: Ralph is one of a kind. Like I said before, I thank God that I was spared to have met a man like this and to be associated with him and work with him. He's a most passive person. He loves people, he loves to play. I love people and I love to play, so that makes us compatible. We have the same crazy sense of humor about things. We like a good joke. And a good drink together. So we have reasons to have an association. I love him, and it's a mutual admiration society between us.

Thank you for writing about Ralph. It's wonderful that people can read this story and really know something about this remarkable man. He's such an inspiration to so many of us, and he has such a great niche in the world of music.

Jack Lesberg: [Lesberg and Sutton met in 1947 while with Jack Teagarden's band. Their close friendship began shortly after Ralph recommended Lesberg to organize Dick Gibson's first jazz party, in 1963.]

Ralph trusts me, and I'm always honest with him. I love him very much, and if I can help him or steer him in a certain way, I always feel good when I can do that. If he steps over the line once in a while here and there, I'll tell him and he appreciates it. If I say, "You did this or you did that," he'll listen to me. I feel very good that he feels that way about me. He asks my advice about which way to go sometimes, but he certainly doesn't need much help. He appreciates friends, and he knows who his friends are when he needs them.

Gus Johnson: Ralph's as nice a person as you'd want to meet. We've never argued about anything. He's been the same for as long as I've known him. He hasn't changed. He's the same all the time. If he doesn't like something, he'll say what he doesn't like. He likes what he likes, and I like what I like. We both like the same things and we get along fine.

We'll be walking down the street together, and he might walk a little faster and tell me to catch up with him—that he's getting away from me. I know exactly why he walks fast away from me. Because he's my friend. He's a wonderful guy and a wonderful piano player. I love him.

["Don't forget the $2,000 you owe me," Johnson said after our interview. I told him, "Milt charged me only $1,500." Said Johnson, "That's Milt. My interview costs more. Drummers get more than bass players. I have all those drums. Milt has just one little fiddle."]

Butch Miles: One night in Odessa, there was a party going on after the music. I walked in and Ralph was standing in a corner by himself. He had a drink in one hand and was smiling for no particular reason. Then he wandered into the bar area where everybody was fixing drinks. He started helping people make drinks and serving them. Never said a word. He went back to the corner about 40 minutes later. People were talking to him, but he didn't say anything. Just smiled, leaning against the wall. I went over to get a drink, and Ralph put his drink down. He grabbed my hand, squeezed it in that bear grip he's got, then grabbed my arm and squeezed it. Looked me dead in the eye and smiled, turned around and walked out the door. Nobody saw him the rest of the night.

It was a little odd. He was completely happy just standing there watching everything going on around him. Never said anything. When he was ready to leave, he just left. Didn't say good night to anybody.

I met Ralph and played with him at my first jazz party, in Odessa in 1980. But I had known about him for years. Ralph was very famous in a lot of jazz circles, but I hate to say that the general public wasn't even aware of him—and they still aren't aware. The people I knew and had worked with were *very* aware of Ralph Sutton, so it was an absolute pleasure to finally meet him.

It's so enjoyable working with him because he puts everything out there and makes it so easy for another musician. I look forward to playing with Ralph whenever I can. I know it's going to be a wonderful set.

I could listen to Ralph play under any condition—out-of-tune piano, no lights in the room, total darkness, anything like that because he's such a great pianist, such a great musician. I just love to hear him play. He always surprises me. I might hear him play a tune 25 or 30 times, but each time he plays it a little differently. He accompanies beautifully, which is a talent in itself. He's at the top of his game when he plays in his own inimitable style that he loves so much. He's an absolute master.

Randy Sandke: He's such a great piano player. He's part of the stride tradition that so few people are carrying on, but he has his own way of playing it. I think I could always identify Ralph's playing. He's got a great feel, a great sense of time.

You cover the keyboard constantly in stride, but it's important that it sounds relaxed. That's what is wonderful about Ralph. He's done it for so long, and he's so great at it, that all the hard technical stuff is second nature to him. He's completely in control and relaxed. He reminds me of Fats Waller, who played this incredibly technical stuff but tossed it off so casually like it was nothing.

Ralph's a power to have playing behind you. You don't need anyone else. He's a one-man band. You feel a lot of support and sympathy, like everything is laid down there. It's kind of done for you. It's like you're riding in a Mercedes. You don't worry about the car breaking down, and it's going to be the smoothest ride you ever had. No problems.

I met Ralph at the first jazz party I played, in Odessa in 1985. I knew who he was, of course. I had heard him on records and was aware of his career. I was the new kid on the block. I knew about all the other guys, but they didn't know who I was. And I was supposed to tell them what to play and count off the tempos, because it's always assumed that the trumpet player does that. It was very intimidating for me, and I was kind of quaking in my boots. But we did it.

Ralph has always been nice and supportive. He's said some nice things to me and has been very encouraging, which of course means a lot coming from someone like him. I always look forward to playing with him.

One thing I love about playing this music is that I get to play with people like Ralph who are an immediate link to the past. I appreciate who these people are and what they've done. To play with them and feel all those years of experience—it can't help but rub off in some way. I think the music will always be around. Music, when it's valid and good, is timeless. As more time passes, I think the value and uniqueness of the music will become clear, especially compared to the dreck that's going on now.

Warren Vaché, Jr.: When I was a kid, my dad had a large record collection and I almost wore out a couple of them, Ralph's *Salute to Fats* and *Piano Moods*. I guess the same reason you're writing the book made me wear those records out. He's got an infectious sense of time and his touch is unique, the harmonies he uses and everything else. He's a natural. It's all innately right.

It's wonderful to have him play behind you. You get that time and that sense of harmony. A lot of pianists mess with the harmony every 15 bars or even every bar. Ralph doesn't like all those substitutes. It's the same way all the time with him, and it's usually right. When Bobby Hackett was in one of his scholarly moods, he would say, "Simplicity is the essence of good taste." Ralph's a master at keeping things simple. He doesn't waste any movement, he doesn't waste any words, and he doesn't waste any notes. When it comes out of Ralph's fingers, it's usually right.

On a professional basis, he's never anything but right. He's always got a smile for you, and he's always on your side. Ralph is always paying attention. There've been times when we've both been tired and one or the other of us hasn't paid attention to what's going on, and the result is a train wreck. But that's kind of natural. He's a very good soloist, and he's got the ability to play that particular sound as a soloist and be an accompanist at the same time. Ralph's thinking about it and putting a lot of care into what he's playing behind you. He's always very supportive.

He's kind of a quiet character. You don't get too much out of him on or off the bandstand in terms of verbiage. He doesn't offer a whole lot of commentary about the world. He shows up to go to work. He shows up to swing. I'd like him to talk a little more. I'd like to find out what's going on in Ralph's mind. But he's got that country boy quiet, and I don't think it's going to change.

Dan Barrett: I first met Ralph in 1977 at the international festival in Breda, Holland. He was featured as a soloist, but he also appeared with various groups. I was playing with a group called the Sunset Music Company, and Ralph was a guest with us.

A few years later, Ralph and Gus Johnson and Red Callender appeared in Torrance, a suburb of Los Angeles. They played in a shopping mall called the Old Town Mall. In the middle was a gazebo, a little circular bandstand surrounded by fast-food booths. You'd order food, take it to the middle area, sit down and eat, and presumably watch the band playing in the middle.

I worked there in a Dixieland band on Saturday afternoons. One day we heard that Ralph Sutton was going to play there. We couldn't believe it. Ralph Sutton at the Old Town Mall playing for a bunch of people eating lunch? It turned out that a gentleman of Ralph's acquaintance had put together a real jazz festival featuring Ralph, Gus, and Red. Groups from various jazz societies in southern California were featured, but I was there for only one reason—to hear Ralph Sutton. They brought in a grand piano and put it on the gazebo. There was barely room for the drums and bass.

Although we had met in Breda, I reintroduced myself to Ralph. We started chatting, and much to my surprise he asked if I'd like to play a tune with his group. I was frightened to death. I thought I had no business on stage with Gus Johnson, Red Callender, and Ralph Sutton. I graciously declined, but finally he twisted my arm.

I had never played with musicians of that caliber before. I tried to be polite, so I played a couple of choruses and got out of the way. Ralph said, "Come on, man, play. We got you up here to play." That scared me even more. I played a couple more tunes and thought that was enough, but Ralph said, "Come on, blow." So I kept playing. That was one of my more exciting musical experiences, having Ralph and Gus and Red behind me.

It's great to play with Ralph. When you're beginning a solo with him in back of you, it's sort of like getting on one of those motorized treadways at an airport. You just step on and you're sucked into the pull of things. A lot of piano players know how to accompany certain musicians in certain idioms. But Ralph can adapt his own style to accompany soloists and complement them to their fullest and make them sound their best. He's always listening and always responsive. I'll play an idea, and Ralph will play the perfect response to that idea, which will lead me into the next phrase. It's sort of like a little cat-and-mouse game, but Ralph never leads you wrong. If the soloist gets into trouble, he'll set the person straight by various harmonic guideposts or things he does that show the soloist the direction.

Ralph has always been very encouraging and friendly not only to me, but to many of the other relatively younger musicians—Ken Peplowski, Randy Sandke, Howard Alden. People who wonder where this music's going shouldn't despair, because there are more younger musicians out there than you might think trying to play it. We represent the tip of the iceberg. So I wouldn't worry about the future of the music.

Al Grey: The first time Ralph and I played together, I heard little splinks and other things of Count Basie's. I said, "Hey, Chief!" and Ralph smiled. I knew it was a great get-together because Basie let soloists have their freedom and so did Ralph. They didn't cover me up trying to help me like many piano players do. They had the same type of playing. Ralph loved Basie. He didn't study Basie; he just felt him and played him.

After Jimmy Forrest told me about Ralph's getting him in to play that club in St. Louis, he talked about Ralph so much that I felt I knew him before I met him. Years later, Jimmy and I were playing at a nightclub in Denver. I saw Ralph and Sunnie in the house. He came up to play one number with us and played the whole set. That really tears you in your heart. After that, there was no wrong that Ralph could ever do.

Ralph gave me a lot of help one year at the Odessa party. I had to make long-distance phone calls to France about a job. The hotel gave me the runaround, and I knew it was because I wasn't the right color. They didn't know whether I could pay for the calls. They acted like they didn't know how to get France, so I went down to the front desk. A lady from Denver heard me going through this problem, and then Ralph came up. As soon as they said something, the call went through just like nothing had ever happened. If people who know you care about you, they say something. If they don't care about you, they just pass by and overlook it. Ralph was never like that.

Kenny Davern: Ralph plays stride piano on a level with James P.

Johnson, Fats Waller, Luckey Roberts, and Willie the Lion Smith. "Echo of Spring" and "Honeysuckle Rose" are his concertos. He does not play them like Willie the Lion or Fats. They are pure Ralph Sutton, and they vary from night to night. But when he wants to win over the audience, he'll play "Honky Tonk Train."

Ralph plays completely differently when he has a bass with him than when he doesn't have one. When there's no bass, Ralph plays full piano because he's supplying the bass. That's what he does best. It may be harder work than comping with a bass and drums behind a soloist, but Ralph *excels* when he plays without a bass, as witness the recording he made with Cliff Leeman in 1953. That was a startling performance.

Ralph pisses and moans about a few things, but for the most part he's about as easygoing as anyone I've ever met. He certainly looks like a strong, imposing person whom you wouldn't want to cross. He dismisses humanity and says he loves animals because he can't stand two-legged creatures. I once told him he was full of it on that one. He looked at me very sheepishly and said, "You can't live without them, can you?"

Elsa and I met Ralph and Sunnie at the Odessa party in 1973 or 1974. We were drawn together through some kind of unspoken magnetism, and a very special relationship ensued.

Jim Galloway: My first knowledge of Ralph came through records while I was growing up in Scotland. I met him in 1983 when John Norris and I started booking the Cafe des Copains in Toronto. We turned it into a club that became known as a great jazz piano room. Ralph got it going.

It was no surprise to discover that we got along because we have the same sort of love for a number of things. We both revere the traditions of the music and we both love *good* songs. Outside of music, we share a love of the simple life.

[Galloway's wife, Rosemary, plays bass. She, too, is a full-time professional musician and has played gigs with Sutton.]

Rosemary and I own a farm that's about a two-hour drive northwest of Toronto. I get there whenever I can. I know how happy Ralph is to be at the ranch with the burros, and he knows how happy I am to get to the farm and just listen to the grass grow. That's a real bond between us.

It's odd that we spend our lives chasing around the world, being with people and being in noisy, smoky places. Given our druthers, both of us would probably be sitting in a field somewhere if we were removed from making our music.

The way a band plays can be largely dictated by how the pianist plays. You can have a good band, but if the piano player doesn't cut it, you're going to have a long 45 minutes up there. Ralph provides a cushion that a horn player can lean on. How can you not play well? It's just *there*. If you're getting into the out choruses of a tune and it's really swinging along but you need that little oomph on the out, there's *nobody* who can kick ass on piano like Ralph. He's uncanny at that.

I sometimes get a little depressed about the future of our kind of music. A handful of younger musicians have chosen to play it; but for every one of them, how many thousands are there who don't even know who Louie was? I think the music will always be around, but more and more of it will become a sort of historical, nostalgic thing.

I dearly love the music and am saddened when I see how few places there are that can present it and make it viable. You have all the pressures of the music industry against you. The music business has nothing to do with music. It's got to do with making money. And jazz suffers because the first rule of North America is: It has to be new. We ain't.

Scott Hamilton: When I came to New York in 1976, I played with other pianists who played the two-handed style; but Ralph's the real thing. He's probably the greatest living practitioner of stride piano. I've been listening to him all my life. My father has all the Eddie Condon records.

Ralph has the relaxation that a lot of the other guys don't have. He is one of the few stride pianists who doesn't have a stiff feel, so that I'm able to phrase the way I would normally phrase, rather than having to make my phrasing more rigid. Ralph's a very good band pianist. He knows what to do and is easy to work with. And even more wonderful to listen to.

Most of the guys who play stride or any derivative of it tend to be younger pianists who learned it from records. They tend to be either incredibly sloppy or incredibly rigid. They produce a stiff, square kind of rhythm because they're so busy hitting the notes. They don't swing. That's a difficult thing to do. It doesn't just happen. Ralph grew up immersed in that style, and it's second nature to him. It's also the marvelous sound he gets. Those gigantic hands. Unfortunately, there are a lot of guys playing piano who are not real pianists. Ralph is a real pianist. You've got to get a sound out of the instrument. He gets that chime sound.

The relaxation is something that can't be bought. There's a way of playing stride that floats, that swings. There's another way of playing it that's all square edges and nothing's happening. Ralph is on the good side of that spectrum. He's probably the best. It's like driving a truck with a square wheel. You're not going to be able to perform with a rigid feeling behind you. If you have a pianist who's not with you rhythmically, you're out of luck.

Ralph's a funny guy. Sometimes I laugh just looking at his face, and I mean that in the most complimentary sense. He's always been very kind to me. When I arrived on the scene, I was about 21 and didn't know what I was doing. Ralph was very tolerant, very nice.

A lot of the older guys who were on the scene when I came to New York are dead now. The music still goes on. There's a fairly large group of young musicians playing basically in this style. It's not a bunch of purists who are interested *only* in playing the way it was played in 1920 or even 1940. But musicians who are heavily influenced by tradition like to keep that tradition alive in their playing. The music will never be the same again, but some good things are happening. I play a lot of gigs where I see a large young following. They may listen to other kinds of jazz or to pop or classical music, but they're still interested in hearing something like this if it's properly done.

There's no more reason to worry about the future of this music than there was to worry about the future of classical music in the 18th century. Great music has to be preserved and it has to be continually played. It can't just be preserved on paper or on records. It has to be played. I think there will always be an audience for it because it's wonderful music and it offers a lot to people.

Ken Peplowski: I was born in Cleveland and used to go to a Chinese restaurant called Chung's where Ralph played many gigs. I'd never heard piano played like that before. He was a real two-handed piano player with so much internal swing and drive. I told myself, jeez, if I could play like that, with that sense of time on the clarinet or saxophone, I would really have something.

He's Never Anything but Right

As much as I've been influenced by clarinet players and saxophone players, I've been equally influenced by piano players like Teddy Wilson and Art Tatum, and Ralph is one of that kind of people. He's got great time and taste. He plays some of the most beautiful music on the piano, and I guess that's probably where you get most of what Ralph is really like—through his music.

It's inspiring to play with him. He has an absolutely perfect sense of swing and rhythm. When you play with him, you get a sense of forward motion. It never lags. It just keeps rolling along. He's got impeccable time. The combination of him and Gus Johnson was unbeatable. Those two guys were the best drums-piano duo I've heard in a long time. You could plug in just about any bass player; it didn't matter because Gus had the same sense of time as Ralph.

You can hear Ralph play the same songs over and over, but he always comes up with fresh things to do with them. When I play with him, I like to hear him first so he inspires me to do something. He's got a great sense of humor as a musician. It's the lively way he plays, and he does unexpected things in unexpected places. He'll toss off a great solo full of sparkling wit, and he gives you that boyish smile and winks at you. He's got a lot of a little kid inside him, and he gets a kick out of playing.

We have to find some way of getting a younger audience. We make a lot of our living at jazz parties, where I don't see many young faces. When we go to the schools, we find that the kids don't even recognize the names of Duke Ellington and Louie Armstrong. Once they hear us, they like the music. But they have to hear it first. That's the problem, getting the music to them. They don't have that option with radio, so we have to get out there and start taking initiatives. The musicians can't do it alone. We need the help of the promoters and people with money. We can't just sit back and say, gee, I hope this music survives.

Chapter **35**

I'm Happy Being a Hermit with *Very* Loose Shoes

alph's three sons, recounting their relationships with him, expressed many of the same feelings they had disclosed almost 20 years earlier in *Piano Man*. Jeff, Pete, and Nick Sutton and their families all live in Petaluma, California, about 40 miles north of San Francisco. They almost always get together with Ralph when he has a gig in the San Francisco area, and all have visited Sunnie and him in Bailey.

The Sutton brothers love their father deeply and have tremendous pride in his achievements as a master jazz pianist whose artistry is admired throughout the world. As has been true through the years, however, those feelings are tarnished by their unhappiness at his not spending nearly as much time with them as they would have liked as both boys and men.

Jeff Sutton, the oldest of Ralph's sons, played drums in and was co-producer of a rock band from 1972 until 1980. He got a good taste of the music entertainment business and found it hard to believe that his father had been in it so long. Jeff started an automotive-marine repair business in 1980 and got married that same year. His wife, Doreen, is a computer programmer. They have two daughters—Amanda, born in 1983, and Tara in 1986.

"Both girls are very musical and artistic," Jeff said, "and I wanted to be as close as possible to them and be there when they needed me. I've always wondered if Dad wanted that for me.

"He and I were very close before my parents' divorce, and I believe he wanted that closeness to continue. Circumstances kept us apart—my growing up in the rebellious '60s, the distance between California and Colorado, and Sunnie. She and I disagreed on just about everything at first, but over the years we learned to give and take. I think we have mutual respect for each other.

"Sunnie has given Dad exactly what he's needed—weaned him from heavy drinking, been a good business partner, and cared for his life and health. They are a real team, and I respect her for what she has done for him.

"I know a lot of musicians' families suffer because a gifted artist has a tough row to hoe. A family has to understand this, and I've come to understand what Dad is all about. He is a strong and simple man with a sensitive heart, and he has believed that the way to other people's hearts is through his music.

"If you've ever spent time with Ralph Sutton and met the close friends and musicians whom he invites to his home; if you've seen his kindness, generosity, and love of animals and nature, you wouldn't think he was an international celebrity pianist. You would think of him as a person who likes the peace and quiet of open country and wants to keep to himself.

"Dad and I are worlds apart, and sometimes we don't talk the same language. But the morals and respect he taught me have survived, and my understanding of him and his world has grown through the years. He taught me an appreciation of the few precious musicians of his era who are still active. They are like fine wine. I met Ben Webster, Jimmy Rushing, Duke Ellington, and many other incredible musicians who were friends of Dad's.

"I remember his taking me to hear Andrés Segovia when I was about 12. I happened to look at Dad during a passage that brought him to tears. His sensitivity has been passed on to me, because I often turn to mush when the music is right. He also taught me that there are only two kinds of music—good and bad. When I hear Jack Teagarden sing one of Willard Robison's tunes, it breaks me down and I know Dad feels the same thing. There's no language barrier there.

"It seems like yesterday that the two of us drove around Belvedere together and he tried to explain the birds and bees to me. Sometimes I wish I was footloose so I could spend more time with him, but I make the best of it when we're together."

Nathan Sutton, Ralph's oldest grandchild, made a surprising discovery during the summer of 1991. He and his father, Pete, were spending a week at

Morning Air Ranch. Nathan, then 14, woke up one morning "and heard this wonderful piano playing coming from downstairs. I thought it was the radio or the TV. But when I went down, I was amazed that it was Grandpa Ralph warming up. Ever since then I've appreciated his marvelous talent."

Nathan is the son of Pete and his first wife, Laura. Pete and Clare, his second wife, have two children. Alexander was born in 1988, and Madeline in 1992. Pete owns a contracting business and sees himself as following in the footsteps of his grandfather, for whom Ralph packed shingles as a boy. He likes to fly-fish in his spare time and does a lot of it when visiting Ralph and Sunnie at Morning Air Ranch. Pete puts up with his father's preference for bait fishing.

"Dad frequently walks his beat along the river, clippers in hand, ready to cut off any offending branch that might snag his guests," Pete said. "I call him the 'riverkeeper' after the practice of the upper-class English who employ caretakers, or riverkeepers, to guard and maintain their private trout-filled rivers. He lives in beautiful country. The clouds and the mountains seem to compete for top visual honors.

"As a son looks to his father for clues on how to live his life, the father serves, in one respect, as a great role model. Dad taught me to do what you love, and success—and hopefully money—will follow. People get bogged down in unsatisfying work simply to put bread on the table.

"I think it is a great accomplishment to come from a small, backwoods hamlet and become a world-class, globe-trotting jazz pianist, especially in America where jazz is not revered as it is overseas nor as lucrative as rock and roll. I'm sure Dad has paid a price for this success, as I know I've had to by not having him near as I was growing up. He was either very stubborn or simply had no choice, really, but to play his music. I think we're all the richer for it."

Clare Sutton, who has a background in floral design, landscaped her home beautifully. She enjoys Ralph's visits and likes to tell how he is quiet around the family but beams when with his grandchildren.

"We treasure the time we spend with Ralph and Sunnie," Clare said. "I always feel his warmth and love. He seems to take great pride in each of his sons, as different as they are."

Nick Sutton, the youngest son, works for Pete's contracting firm. He and his wife, Jean, have two children—Nicole, born in 1986, and Spencer in

1988. Jean is a certified massage therapist. Nick plays jazz piano with a combo on an impromptu basis. He and the others in the group have played together since high school and hold jam sessions a couple of times a month. Nick expects to play for the rest of his life because he is sure he would not feel right if he didn't.

"What can I say about my father other than he is my hero, but in an absent sort of way," Nick said. "Whenever I hear him play, all the thoughts of the nonexistent father don't seem to matter. I wish he had showed some interest early on in my being attracted to music. I've decided that it's OK and that I don't blame him, but somehow I know deep down that I needed a father to relate with and to be there. There have been occasions when I've tried to relate to him, but either it was the time factor or he just didn't know how to relate on that level.

"I know Dad's a quiet fellow, but when he sits down at the piano, man, can he relate! I love my father dearly despite all the misgivings. I sure would like to be with him more, not only to make up for lost time, but also because I miss him. One of my fondest memories was the time I flew to New York while he was playing at Hanratty's. I got there for his last set, and I'll never forget the look on his face when he saw me.

"Maybe I've expected too much of Dad—wanting him to be a certain way when he could only be himself. But one thing I'm sure of is that whenever I hear him play, the world is all right, I'm very proud he's my father, and I love him very much."

Nick and Jean knew each other as little children through their parents. They lost touch for about 15 years until she dropped into a bar with some friends to celebrate her 21st birthday. Nick was playing piano there. They recognized each other, renewed their friendship, and were married the following year.

"I remember when I met Ralph and Sunnie," Jean said. "All the Sutton brothers felt the excitement of his coming to town. Ralph greeted me very warmly. Nick had told me so much about him, and it was clear that Ralph had a very important part in Nick's life even though they never had a lot of time together.

"I always notice Ralph's great warmth, the twinkle in his eyes, and how comfortable he seems to be in any surrounding. Our children often talk about Grandpa Ralph and Grandma Sunnie. We listen to his albums, and Colie and Spencer know it's their grandpa playing the piano."

Ralph and Sunnie celebrated their 25th anniversary in 1990. She kidded that the marriage had succeeded because he was on the road so much. Sunnie estimated that Ralph had been away from home for a total of at least 15 of their 25 years together.

"Whenever he comes home, it's kind of like another honeymoon," she said. "It's been a great life. We've had a lot of fun, and the last few years I've been able to travel with Ralph a little more. I'm grateful for that. It gets lonely when he's not home, and I'm sure this kind of life will continue for as long as we're alive.

"When I had a major illness, it put me in tune with my mortality. If you have something like cancer, you feel it's just a matter of time before it could reoccur and you might cash everything in. I felt the need of having to go with Ralph and be with him more. People have been very nice and have included me a lot of times, paying for my transportation so I could travel with Ralph. I appreciate that.

"Ralph's been growing all the time I've known him. He's much more tolerant than he was when we were married. He's learned to handle his anger much better when he's confronted by stupid people who pull on his coattail when he's trying to concentrate or by pianos that don't work. I think he's a happier person.

"Sometimes when we're out riding along, I wish I had a pen and paper to jot down some of the little things that he comes out with. He'll see something, and it tickles him and he'll say something cute. I've never written anything down, but I wish I had. I'm much more serious and uptight now than he is. I'm always stewing about something. It used to be just the opposite. He was the one who was much more serious and let things get under his skin.

"Ralph is a wonderful husband. He's sweet, accommodating, and thoughtful. He picks up after himself. He'll eat anything I fix, and he'll go out if I want. I couldn't ask for a nicer man. He's perfect."

Ralph's feelings for Sunnie are pari-mutual, though typically expressed in fewer words: "Our years together sure have gone by fast. They've been wonderful, and I've been very fortunate to have her. Sunnie's been a great inspiration to me, and I wouldn't be in the position I'm in without her help. She steers me. We clash every once in a while, but what the hell; all couples do. She's a strong gal and I'm a strong guy. Things work out because we love each other so much."

I'm Happy Being a Hermit with Very Loose Shoes

Ralph and Sunnie foresee no significant change in their way of life. He joked that his time on the road would continue unless a big lottery payout fell in his lap. Johnny Simmen expressed the thoughts of the legion of Sutton's fans: "Ralph is as precious a human being as he is an authentic artist. It's sad that after these decades of demanding activity he cannot afford to sit back, relax, and work only when *he* wants to."

Ralph had to take things easy following a minor stroke in March 1993. He canceled engagements in Canada, Germany, Austria, and England but thoroughly enjoyed a couple of months of relaxation while recuperating at Morning Air Ranch. He swung back into action in May at the annual Odessa party. In June, Ralph recorded for the Maybeck Recital Hall series sponsored by Concord Jazz. He and Dick Hyman joined forces at Maybeck in November on a two-piano recording, also for Concord.

Sutton philosophically accepts the prospect of continuing to spend much time away from Sunnie and the ranch. He also has some positive thoughts about that likelihood.

"Even with all the traveling, things are all right after I get to wherever I'm going," Ralph said. "The airports and the crowds and stuff like that can be a little tiring at times, but the music business is never boring. I travel all over the world and I've got friends all over the world. That's very important. I mean real friends. If I'm stuck somewhere in Australia or Japan or wherever, I know whom to call."

The enthusiasm of audiences for Sutton's playing has never wavered, and people continually tell him he has never sounded better. In June 1993, shortly before this book went to press, Ralph received a letter from a woman who heard of him for the first time a few months earlier while browsing at a thrift shop near her home in Florida. Eleanor Anderson bought a used copy of his *Big Noise from Wayzata* record because Sutton's picture on the front and the Wayzata story on the back of the album caught her eye.

"That's the only record I've ever heard of your work, and it made me decide that you play the socks off a piano," Anderson told Ralph. "If I were to tell you how many second-hand record stores, music stores, libraries, and other places I have been to in order to find some more of your recordings, I don't think you'd believe me.

"I admire your work on that record more than any other jazz pianist I've ever heard, and I've heard more than a few. I was born in August 1922, three months before you, so both of us have been around a bit."

Anderson recalled her high school days in the late '30s and 1940 in Montclair, New Jersey, during the Big Band Era. She spent countless hours at the famous Meadowbrook ballroom in nearby Cedar Grove:

"Almost every afternoon after school, I sat at a table there with some of my sorority sisters. I'd buy a nickel Coke and watch the big bands rehearse. The band leaders and their orchestra gentlemen would also buy nickel Cokes and, at break time, sit at our table and chat.

"Glen Gray was my favorite. I liked Glenn Miller, too, but he was quite shy. I met the Dorsey brothers and Frank Sinatra, and then there were Larry Clinton, Guy Lombardo, Benny Goodman (of course), Sammy Kay, Vaughn Monroe, Artie Shaw, Hal Kemp, Charlie Barnett, Woody Herman, and Harry James. I'm sure I've forgotten many others.

"For years I have played at playing the piano, which makes me realize what a great jazz artist you are," Anderson wrote in her letter to Sutton. "I would love to know where I could buy some of your other recordings. What a pleasure it is to hear you play!"

Ralph had a somewhat oblique explanation for his steadfast appeal: "I think my belief gets stronger. What I believe in, whatever it is, gets stronger. I hear different things happening with all the instruments, and I figure that I'm going to stay with my roots.

"Everybody's going off in different directions. I'm sticking with what I believe in. I'm going to go straight ahead, and 'tain't nobody's bizness if I do. I just keep it easy and keep swingin'. I remember what Fats said: 'You get that right tickin' rhythm, man, and it's on.' That's the best way I can say it. Just keep that right tickin' rhythm. Don't get too cerebral. Keep it simple, have fun, and enjoy life."

More than most people, Ralph is a different person at home than on the job. "At home, everything's loose," he said. "I like it loose." He feels far more relaxed at the ranch than during jazz parties and other gigs, where someone almost always seems to be coming up and talking to him. Unless the person is a good friend, such conversation occasionally drives him up the wall. Ironically, despite the universal appreciation of audiences for his playing, Ralph would rather be by himself when at the keyboard.

"It's the freedom," he said. "You're perfectly free when you're alone. You're not tied down by anything around you to distract you from your thinking. I enjoy playing for friends and other people. But my favorite times are when I'm sitting there all by myself. When nobody's around. I'm happy being a hermit with *very* loose shoes."

The microphones provided on some gigs, especially the amplification at various jazz parties, annoy Sutton and many other musicians. Kenny Davern has been known to get furious with the mikes. At the piano, Ralph has trouble hearing his own playing about half the time because "everything from the horns" comes at him through the speakers.

"It's not a natural sound, and it's very uncomfortable for me," he said. "The band at Condon's had no microphone. We just played. I think we've got too much electricity today, and I can do without it. It's not necessary at all."

Ralph acknowledges that many people, including old friends, have pushed him for years to add new tunes to his repertoire instead of playing some of the same ones so frequently. Joe Sample, for example, noted that at jazz parties Sutton is limited to a certain number of solos and, naturally, wants to make the best possible impression and feels more secure with his warhorses. "He plays the hell out of them," Sample said, "but they do get a little repetitive."

Johnny Simmen advised Sutton to consider playing different tunes more often, "especially because he is so gifted and can play *everything*." In 1988, prior to Ralph and Sunnie's arrival in Switzerland, Simmen drew up a list of what he called "not-overexposed numbers," some of which Sutton had recorded early in his career. They included such Fats Waller tunes as "Ain't Cha Glad?," "Concentratin' on You," and "Take It from Me I'm Takin' to You." Sutton reacted favorably to most of Simmen's suggestions, but the project died after Sunnie accidentally left the list in a phone booth.

Ralph did the unexpected at The Jazz Party in Minneapolis in 1990 when he ripped off a torrid solo on "Nagasaki," which many in the audience had never heard him play live. He said he "just happened to think of it." Then he noted with more than a little logic that he frequently gets requests for the old familiar tunes that he plays. "Who else plays those warhorses?" he asked.

At the 1993 Summit Jazz in Denver, Sutton again showed his penchant for doing the unexpected. The groups on the program included the Jim Cullum Jazz Band and the Ralph Sutton All Stars, a band comprised of Bob Barnard, Dan Barrett, Kenny Davern, Sutton, Bucky Pizzarelli, Milt Hinton, and Frank Capp.

The program called for Sutton and John Sheridan to play a two-piano set on the second day of the party. They were accompanied by Don Mopsick, Cullum's bass player, and Capp. Mopsick had not played with Ralph previously and was thrilled by Sutton's invitation.

Immediately after the set, which received a standing ovation, Ralph thanked Sheridan and suggested that they play a second—and unscheduled—set the next afternoon during the final session of the party. The astonished and delighted Sheridan agreed on the spot, as did Mopsick and Capp. Juanita Greenwood, who had founded Summit Jazz 15 years earlier, approved Ralph's proposal that the pianists play one of the two Sutton All Star sets.

The second piano, a white instrument, was pushed into place a few inches from the standard black one that had been used throughout the party. A man in the audience got a big laugh when he called out, "Did you get Jesse Helms's OK for that?"

The crowd raised the roof even higher than after the two pianists' first set. Sheridan expressed his thanks and appreciation to the grinning Sutton, who replied, "It's pari-mutual."

I asked Ralph if he had ever before requested another pianist to play an unscheduled encore set with him.

"First time," said Sutton. "I like playing with John. He makes me feel good."

In 1922, the year Ralph Sutton was born, King Oliver sent a telegram to 22-year-old Louis Armstrong in New Orleans, inviting him to join the Creole Jazz Band at the Lincoln Gardens in Chicago. That same year, a group of Chicago boys organized a jazz band after hearing a record of the New Orleans Rhythm Kings in an ice cream parlor near Austin High School. The group included Bud Freeman, who was struggling to learn the C-melody sax and who half a century later would be playing in the World's Greatest Jazzband with the infant who had just been born in Hamburg, Missouri.

During Sutton's boyhood, the men he later idolized were playing, recording, and writing much of the music that he would include in his own repertoire. Before Ralph was 7 years old, Meade Lux Lewis wrote and recorded "Honky Tonk Train," Fats Waller and Andy Razaf collaborated on "Honeysuckle Rose," Bix Beiderbecke composed "In a Mist," and Waller wrote "Handful of Keys." Willie the Lion Smith wrote "Echo of Spring" the year that Ralph celebrated his 13th birthday.

Many of Ralph's peers in jazz died during the 19 years between the publication of the two editions of his biography. He had played with three of them—Billy Butterfield, Vic Dickenson, and Bud Freeman—in the World's Greatest Jazzband. Others who passed away, and with whom he had performed, included Red Callender, Al Cohn, Eddie (Lockjaw) Davis, Wild Bill Davison, Louise Duncan, George Duvivier, Bobby Hackett, Major Holley, Nappy Lamare, Cliff Leeman, Lou McGarity, Jimmy McPartland, Eddie Miller, Joe Schirmer, Zoot Sims, Maxine Sullivan, Joe Venuti, Dick Wellstood, and Trummy Young. Some of them had been dear friends of Ralph's.

"It's very sad," Sutton said. "But at the same time that all these good friends go on, I kind of feel like they're still here. When you play a job and they're not on the stand, that's when you really miss them. And then Gus got Alzheimer's. I still can't believe it. But we're all gonna go when the wagon comes."

As Ralph passed his 71st birthday, the development of a number of younger musicians made him more optimistic than he had been about the future of traditional jazz. He once believed that many of the next generation were technically skillful on their instruments and could play up a storm—but could not swing. "There's a difference between the way they play and playing from the balls," Sutton had said, "and I don't know if there are many coming along with balls or not."

Ralph's doubts, shared by many older players, were largely dispelled by the extraordinary talent of such younger musicians as Howard Alden, Dan Barrett, Jim Cullum, Phil Flanigan, Chris Flory, Scott Hamilton, Joel Helleny, Jay Leonhart, Butch Miles, Ken Peplowski, Ed Polcer, Randy Sandke, John Sheridan, Allan Vaché, and Warren Vaché, Jr.

Fats Waller used to say, "One never knows, do one?" But the artistry of the above—and other—swinging jazz musicians seemed to assure the longevity of Ralph Sutton's kind of music.

Discography

This discography consists of commercial and private recordings on which Ralph Sutton has played. The data on the commercial recordings are based—with great appreciation—on the discographies prepared by Jorgen Jepsen, Walter Bruyninckx, Erik Raben, and Tom Lord.

Abbreviations used for names of record companies and instruments are listed below.

Record Companies			
Aff	Affinity	Mos	Mosaic
AoH	Ace of Hearts	MPS	MPS
Atl	Atlantic	NOR	New Orleans Rarities
Aud	Audiophile	Ome	Omega
BA	Blue Angel	PA	PhonAcord
Bar	Barclay	Pan	Panachord
Bare	Bare	Parl	Parlophone
Bru	Brunswick	PC	Pony Canyon
Cen	Century	Phi	Philips
Chiar	Chiaroscuro	Phoe	Phoenix
Cir	Circle	Proj	Project 3
CJ	Chaz Jazz	Que	Queen
Col	Columbia	RA	Rarities
Com	Commodore	RCA	RCA-Victor
Con	Concord	Riff	Riff
DC	Dawn Club	Riv	Riverside
Dec	Decca	Rou	Roulette
DH	Down Home	SA	Solo Art
Dia	Dialogue	SP	SP
Dur	Durium	77	77
88UR	88 Up Right	SK	Sackville
Emb	Ember	Sav	Savoy
ES	Elite Special	Sham	Shamrock
Esq	Esquire	Sig	Signature
FDC	For Discriminate Collectors	Solo	Solo
FIN	Friends In Need	Stv	Storyville
Fly	Flyright	Supra	Supraphon
Fon	Fontana	Ti	Timeless
Geo	Georgian	Troc	Jazz in the Troc
GTJ	Good Time Jazz	Ver	Verve
Har	Harmony	Vic	Victor
Herw	Herwin	Voc	Vocalion
HMV	His Master's Voice	Vog	Vogue
IAJRC	International Association of Jazz Record Collectors	WGJB	World's Greatest Jazzband
Jans	Jansco	WJ	World Jazz
JazAr	Jazz Archives	WhLa	White Label
JazHi	Jazz in the Hills	WRC	World Record Club
Jazl	Jazzology		
Jazt	Jazztone	(Au)	Australian
Jazum	Jazum	(C)	European Continent
KJ	Kings of Jazz	(Can)	Canadian
Lon	London	(Cz)	Czechoslovak
Lyr	Lyragon	(Dan)	Danish
MCA	Music Corporation of America	(Du)	Dutch
		(Eng)	English
Main	Mainstream	(F)	French
Mem	Memories	(G)	German
Mile	Milestone	(I)	Italian
MM	Musicmasters	(Sw)	Swiss
MoEv	Monmouth-Evergreen		

Instruments			
ah	alto horn		
as	alto sax		
b	bass		
bas	bass sax		
bcl	bass clarinet		
bj	banjo		
bs	baritone sax		
bsn	bassoon		
cel	celeste		
cl	clarinet		
cnt	cornet		
cond	conductor		
d	drums		
fid	fiddle		
flgh	flugelhorn		
g	guitar		
har	harmonica		
man	mandolin		
o	organ		
p	piano		
sop	soprano sax		
sous	sousaphone		
t	trumpet		
tb	trombone		
ts	tenor sax		
tu	tuba		
vcl	vocal		

Discography

JOE SCHIRMER TRIO   Spring 1946   Chicago

Ralph Sutton (p), Joe Schirmer (g), Jack Stern (b).

Mary Lou	Standard Radio Transcriptions Q212 D5-MM 2221-2222
Begin the Beguine	-
Flying Home	-
Honky Tonk Train	-
Missouri Waltz	-
Boogie Joys	-
Shades of Anitra	-
Backroom Boogie	-
Minute Waltz	-
Doo-Wah	-
Coquette	Standard Radio Transcriptions Q213 SRR 2431-2432
On the Sunny Side of the Street	-
Christopher Columbus	-
Sweet Lorraine	-
Just You, Just Me	-
Out of Nowhere	-
She's Funny That Way	-
Royal Garden Blues	-
Memories	-
I Can't Get Started	-
Three Blind Mice	Standard Radio Transcriptions Q228 D6-MM 1436-1437
How High the Moon	-
Who Dunnit	-
Ooh That Kiss	-
Hollywood at Vine	-
Slipped Disc	-
You Go to My Head	-
Please Don't Talk About Me When I'm Gone	-
St. Louis Boogie	-
Tea for Two	-
In an 18th Century Drawing Room	-
My Bonnie	Standard Radio Transcriptions Q229 SRR 2060-2061
'Deed I Do	-
Wild Man	-
Symphony	-
Soft Winds	-
Sleepy Time Gal	-
Hong Kong Blues	-
Boogie Down Broadway	-
Where Has My Little Dog Gone?	-
Avalon Town	-
Always	-
London Bridge	-

THIS IS JAZZ   June 28, 1947   New York

Wild Bill Davison (cnt), Jimmy Archey (tb), Albert Nicholas (cl), Ralph Sutton (p), Danny Barker (g), Pops Foster (b), Baby Dodds (d).

Shine	Stv SLP4067	
Black and Blue	Stv SLP4068	
The Five O'Clocks (Montana Taylor solo)*		
I Can't Sleep (Montana Taylor solo)*		
Struttin' with Some Barbecue		
Tishomingo Blues	-	Jazl JCD42 [CD]
I Found a New Baby	-	

*These titles are on the "This Is Jazz" air checks only.

Loose Shoes

THIS IS JAZZ   July 5, 1947   New York

Wild Bill Davison (cnt), Jimmy Archey (tb), Albert Nicholas (cl), Ralph Sutton (p), Danny Barker (g), Pops Foster (b), Johnny Blowers (d), Chippie Hill (vcl).

Rosetta	Stv SLP4067		
Save It, Pretty Mama*			
How Long Blues	-		
Skeleton Jangle	-		Jazl JCD42 [CD]
Careless Love	-		
Dill Pickles	-		
Shim-Me-Sha-Wabble	Cir J1040 L402	Riv RLP12-211	-

THIS IS JAZZ   July 19, 1947   New York

Wild Bill Davison (cnt), Jimmy Archey (tb), Albert Nicholas (cl), Ralph Sutton (p), Danny Barker (g), Pops Foster (b), Baby Dodds (d), Chippie Hill (vcl).

12th Street Rag*		
Darktown Strutters' Ball*		
I'm Sorry I Made You Cry*		
Oh, Lady Be Good*		
Whitewash Man*		
Lonesome Road	Cir 12004	Esq(E)10-201
Muskrat Ramble*		

THIS IS JAZZ   July 26, 1947   New York

Wild Bill Davison (cnt), Jimmy Archey (tb), Albert Nicholas (cl), Ralph Sutton (p), Danny Barker (g), Pops Foster (b), Baby Dodds (d), Chippie Hill (vcl).

NY43	Eccentric	Cir J1023	L402	Riv RLP2514	RLP12-116	Esq(E)10-110 Jazl JCD42 [CD]
NY44	Tishomingo Blues	-	-	-		Esq(E)10-030
NY45	Hotter Than That	Cir J1025	-		RLP12-211	Esq(E)10-039 Jazl JCD42 [CD]
	Don't Leave Me, Daddy*					
NY46	Big Butter and Egg Man	Cir J1024	L402			Esq(E)10-039
NY47	Baby, Won't You Please					
	Come Home	-	-			Esq(E)10-110
NY48	Sensation	Cir J1025				Esq(E)10-030

THIS IS JAZZ   August 2, 1947   New York

Wild Bill Davison (cnt), Jimmy Archey (tb), Albert Nicholas (cl), Sidney Bechet (sop), Ralph Sutton (p), Danny Barker (g), Pops Foster (b), Baby Dodds (d).

NY70	I Never Knew	Cir J1042	Riv RLP12-216	RLP-139		
	Dardanella	Cir L405	-	-	Jazl JCD42 [CD]	KJ(I) KLJ2003
	China Boy*					
	Love for Sale		Riv RLP12-149		KJ(I) KLJ20033	
	Dear Old Girl		Stv SLP4068			
	Wolverine Blues		-			
	California, Here I Come		Stv SLP4067			

Discography

THIS IS JAZZ August 23, 1947 New York

Wild Bill Davison (cnt), Jimmy Archey (tb), Albert Nicholas (cl), Ralph Sutton (p), Danny Barker (g), Pops Foster (b), Baby Dodds (d).

NY67	Ballin' the Jack*				
	Four or Five Times	Stv SLP4068			
	As Long as I Live	Cir 12003 S19	Riv RLP12-211	Esq(E)10-201	Jazl JCD42 [CD]
	Trombone Preachin' Blues		Riv RLP2514		-
	Mandy*				
	Peg o' My Heart*				
	Nobody's Sweetheart*				

THIS IS JAZZ August 30, 1947 New York

Wild Bill Davison (cnt), Jimmy Archey (tb), Albert Nicholas (cl), Ralph Sutton (p), Danny Barker (g), Pops Foster (b), Baby Dodds (d), Chippie Hill (vcl).

At the Jazz Band Ball	Stv SLP4067	Sham 1809
Sometimes I'm Happy		-
Some of These Days		-
Just a Gigolo		-
Put Your Arms Around Me, Honey		-
Blues		-
The World Is Waiting for the Sunrise		-

MILT HERTH TRIO** September 4, 1947 New York

Milt Herth (o), Ralph Sutton (p), Hy White (g), Gary Chester (d), Bob Johnstone (vcl).

74079	The Little Old Mill	Dec 24199

September 5, 1947

74077	Herthquake Boogie	Dec 24450
74078	Peggy O'Neill	Dec 24199
74080	12th Street Rag	Dec 24450

**All titles labeled as Trio despite number of musicians.

THIS IS JAZZ September 6, 1947 New York

Wild Bill Davison (cnt), Jimmy Archey (tb), Edmond Hall (cl), Ralph Sutton (p), Danny Barker (g), Pops Foster (b), Baby Dodds (d).

NY59	Clarinet Marmalade	Cir 12003 S-19 Riv RLP2514 Esq(E) 10-191 Jazl JCD42 [CD]
	Tishomingo Blues*	
	'S Wonderful*	
	Ol' Man River*	
	Maple Leaf Rag*	
	Georgia on My Mind	Stv SLP4069
	Bugle Call Rag*	

343

Loose Shoes

BUNK JOHNSON September 6, 1947 New York

Bunk Johnson (t), Jimmy Archey (tb), Edmond Hall, Omer Simeon (cl), Ralph Sutton (p), Danny Barker (bj), Cy St. Clair (tu), Fred Moore (d), Huddie Ledbetter (vcl).

Introduction	NOR Vol. 3	WhLa(E) 102
Tiger Rag	-	-
Panama	-	-
Ain't Misbehavin'	-	-
Ja Da	-	-
Muskrat Ramble	-	-
Someday, Sweetheart	-	-
Sister Kate	-	-
Baby, Won't You Please Come Home	-	-
Basin Street Blues	-	-
Royal Garden Blues	-	-
Yellow Girl	-	-
Bottle Up and Go	-	-
Jazz Me Blues	-	-
After You've Gone	-	-
Finale (Blues)	-	-

THIS IS JAZZ September 13, 1947 New York

Wild Bill Davison (cnt), Jimmy Archey (tb), Edmond Hall (cl), Ralph Sutton (p), Danny Barker (g), Pops Foster (b), Baby Dodds (d).

It's Right Here for You**	Cir J12004	Riv RLP2514	Jazl JCD42 [CD]	
Jelly Roll		-	-	
I'm Coming, Virginia	Stv SLP4069			
Can't We Be Friends?	Cir J1042			
Skeleton Jangle		-		
Blues	Cir 12003		Stv SLP4069	Que 020
Muskrat Ramble			-	

**Announced by Rudi Blesh as Crazy Blues.

THIS IS JAZZ September 20, 1947 New York

Wild Bill Davison (cnt), Jimmy Archey (tb), Edmond Hall (cl), Ralph Sutton (p), Danny Barker (g), Pops Foster (b), Baby Dodds (d).

Indiana	Stv SLP4069
Sunday*	
Liza*	
I Can't Believe That You're in Love with Me*	
St. Louis Blues*	
All of Me*	
Dippermouth Blues	-
Tiger Rag**	-

**Steiner-Davis Christmas 1949 private recording under Davison's name.

THIS IS JAZZ September 27, 1947 New York

Wild Bill Davison (cnt), Jimmy Archey (tb), Edmond Hall (cl), Ralph Sutton (p), Danny Barker (g), Pops Foster (b), Baby Dodds (d).

Jazz Me Blues	Stv SLP4069		
Royal Garden Blues*			
Take Me Out to the Ball Game*			
Avalon	Cir J1041	Riv RLP12-211	Jazl JCD42 [CD]
Wrap Your Troubles in Dreams*			
Swinging Down the Lane	-	-	-
High Society*			

Discography

THIS IS JAZZ   October 4, 1947   New York

Wild Bill Davison (cnt), Jimmy Archey (tb), Edmond Hall (cl), Sidney Bechet (sop), Ralph Sutton (p), Danny Barker (g), Pops Foster (b), Baby Dodds (d).

Sensation	Stv SLP4069		
Ja Da*			
St. Louis Blues	Riv RLP149	KJ(I) KLJ20033	
Laura		-	
Big Butter and Egg Man	Stv SLP4069		
Sweet Lorraine	Riv RLP 149	Jazl J35	
Farewell Blues	Stv SLP4069	KJ(I) KLJ20033	

TONY PARENTI   November 22, 1947   New York

Wild Bill Davison (cnt), Jimmy Archey (tb), Tony Parenti (cl), Ralph Sutton (p), Danny Barker (bj), Cy St. Clair (tu), Baby Dodds (d).

NY49	Grace and Beauty	Cir 1030	
NY50	Hiawatha	Cir 1031	Vog(E) V2114
NY51	Praline	Cir 1030	
NY52	Swipesy Cake Walk	Cir 1031	-
NY53	Hysterics Rag	Cir 1029	Vog(E) V2115
NY54	Sunflower Slow Drag	-	-

All titles also on Riv RLP12-205, Lon(E) LTZ-U15072, and Jazl J15.

PUNCH MILLER   December 16, 1947   New York

Punch Miller (t, vcl), Jimmy Archey (tb), Edmond Hall (cl), Ralph Sutton (p), Ernest Hill (b), Arthur Trappier (d).

PM121B	Just Can't Help Myself	Sav MG12038	Esq 32-121	
PM122B	She's Funny That Way	-	-	
PM123E	Shine		-	Cen 4005
PM124B	Some of These Days	Sav MG12050	-	Cen 4006
PM125B	Cool Kinda Papa	-	-	Cen 4019
PM126B	Cock Robin	-	-	

WILD BILL DAVISON   December 27, 1947   New York
Wild Bill Davison Showcase

Wild Bill Davison (cnt, vcl), Jimmy Archey (tb), Garvin Bushell (cl, bsn), Ralph Sutton (p, cel), Sid Weiss (b), Morey Feld (d).

NY61	Just a Gigolo	Cir J1032
NY62	She's Funny That Way	Cir J1034
NY63	A Ghost of a Chance	Cir J1033
NY64	Yesterdays	-
NY65	Why Was I Born?	Cir J1032
NY66	When Your Lover Has Gone	Cir J1034

All titles also on Cir L405, Riv RLP12-211, Lon(E) LTZ-U15068, and Jazl JCD83 [CD].

PUNCH MILLER   December 30, 1947   New York

Punch Miller (t), Edmond Hall (cl), Ralph Sutton (p), Ernest Hill (b), Jimmy Crawford (d).

PM131A	Squeeze Me	Sav MG12050	Esq 32-121		
PM132B	Small Hotel	-	Esq 32-121	EP240	Cen 4005
PM133	Weary Blues*	Sav MG12038	-		Cen 4019
PM134D	Panama	-	-		Cen 4014
PM135C	Down by the Riverside	-	-		-
PM136A	Exactly Like You	Sav MG12050	Esq 32-121		Cen 4006
PM137A	Informal Blues (Snag It)	-	-		

*Labeled as Shake It and Break It on Sav MG12038.

Loose Shoes

TONY PARENTI January 22, 1948 New York

Tony Parenti (cl), Ralph Sutton (p), George Wettling (d).

NY73	Crawfish Crawl	Cir 1056		Lon(E) EZU19022
NY74	Entertainer's Rag	Cir 1054	Esq 10-048	
NY75	Lily Rag	Cir 1056		
NY76	Cataract Rag	Cir 1054	-	
NY77	Nonsense Rag	Cir 1055		-
NY78	Redhead Rag			

All titles also on Riv RLP12-205, Lon(E) LTZ-U15072, and Jazl J15.

THIS IS JAZZ February 17, 1948 New York

Wild Bill Davison (cnt), Georg Brunis (tb), Edmond Hall (cl), Ralph Sutton (p), Sid Weiss (b), Morey Feld (d).

Hotter Than That   Stv SLP4067

RALPH SUTTON January 22, 1949 New York
St. Louis Piano

Ralph Sutton (p).

NY79	Dill Pickles	Cir J1053	Riv RLP12-212	Vog(E) V2112	
NY80	Whitewash Man	Cir J1052	-	-	
NY81	Carolina in the Morning	-	-	Vog(E) V2113	Herw403
NY82	St. Louis Blues	Cir J1053	-		

EDDIE CONDON March 19, 1949 New York

Sidney Bechet (sop), Ralph Sutton (p), Eddie Condon (g), Jack Lesberg (b), Buddy Rich (d).

I Know That You Know   Que 029

EDDIE CONDON April 16, 1949 New York

Bobby Hackett (cnt), Cutty Cutshall (tb), Peanuts Hucko (cl), Sidney Bechet (sop), Ernie Caceres (bs), Dick Cary (ah), Ralph Sutton (p), Eddie Condon (g), Jack Lesberg (b), J.C. Heard (d).

Fascinating Rhythm	Que 030
I've Got a Crush on You	-
'S Wonderful	-
They Can't Take That Away from Me	-
The Man I Love	-
Embraceable You	-
I Got Rhythm	-
But Not for Me	Que 031

EDDIE CONDON June 4, 1949 New York

Hot Lips Page (t), Sidney Bechet (sop), Cutty Cutshall (tb), Peanuts Hucko (cl), Ernie Caceres (bs), Dick Cary (ah), Ralph Sutton (p), Jack Lesberg (b), Sid Catlett (d).

High Society   Que 029

GORDON JENKINS August 12, 1949 New York

Orchestra and chorus. Musicians include Ralph Sutton (p) and Carl Kress (bj).

California   Dec DL78011

Discography

RALPH SUTTON November 1949 San Francisco
Backroom Piano

Ralph Sutton (p).

DH13	The Villain	DH 7	1003	MGD4		
DH14	Cataract Rag	-	-	-		Col(E) LB10065
DH15	Climax Rag	DH 8	-	-		Herw H403
DH16	Chromatic Rag	-	-	-		Col(E) LB10056
DH17	Frog Legs Rag	DH 9	-	-		Vog(E) V2108 JS812
DH18	Black and White Rag	-		-		Herw H403
DH19	The Cascades	DH 10	-	-		Vog(E) V2108 JS812
DH20	Grace and Beauty	-		-		Col(E) LB10089
	Cannon Ball Blues			-		
	Down Home Rag			-		Col(E) LB10056
	Harlem Drag			-		Col(E) LB10065
	Black Bottom Stomp			-		Col(E) LB10076
	Shoe Shine Boy			-		-
	Jelly Roll Blues			-		
	Christopher Columbus			-		
	Hindustan			-		

All titles from MGD4 also on Ver MGV1004, Col(E) 33CX10061, and Bar GLP3594.

HOT LIPS PAGE January 14, 1950 Philadelphia

Hot Lips Page (t, vcl), Cutty Cutshall (tb), Peanuts Hucko (cl), Ralph Sutton (p), Charlie Traeger (b), Eddie Phyfe (d).

The Blues in "B"	JazAr JA17	
Muskrat Ramble	-	
Squeeze Me	-	

SIDNEY BECHET March 11, 1950 Philadelphia

Wild Bill Davison (cnt), Cutty Cutshall (tb), Sidney Bechet (sop), Ralph Sutton (p); others unknown.

I Found a New Baby	JazAr JA37	
After You've Gone	-	

RALPH SUTTON March 13, 1950 New York
Bix Beiderbecke Suite

Ralph Sutton (p).

A4944	In the Dark	Com 639	FL30001	Com(E) 625525	Com XFL16670	Mos MR20-134
A4945	Flashes	-	-	-	-	-
A4946	Candlelights	Com 1525	-	-	-	-
A4947	In a Mist	-	-	-	-	-

March 17, 1950

Ralph Sutton (p), Arthur Trappier (d).
Piano Portraits

A4938	Boogie Joys	Com 636	-		-
A4939	Them There Eyes	-	-		-
A4940	Sweet Lorraine	Com 640	-		-
A4941	Three Little Words	-	-		-
A4942	When You're Smiling	Com 641	-		-
A4943	Squeeze Me	-	-		-

EDDIE CONDON March 20, 1950 New York

Wild Bill Davison (cnt), Cutty Cutshall (tb), Peanuts Hucko (cl), Ralph Sutton (p), Eddie Condon (g), Jack Lesberg (b), Buzzy Drootin (d).

75988	Maple Leaf Rag	Dec 27035	DL5195	DL8282	Bru(E)	LA8549	AoH(E) AH100
		MCA BA212	(F)510206	Herw 104			
75989	Dill Pickles	Dec 24987	DL5195	DL8282	Bru(E)	04506	-
		MCA BA212	(F)510206				

347

Loose Shoes

TOMMY REYNOLDS　　April 26, 1950　　　　New York

Chris Griffin (t), Cutty Cutshall (tb), Tommy Reynolds (cl), Ralph Sutton (p), Jack Lesberg (b), George Wettling (d).

A411	Crazy Words, Crazy Tune	Atl 910
A412	Did You Come Back to Say Good-bye	-
A413	Oceana Roll	Atl 921
A414	Valentina	-

SIDNEY BECHET　　April 27, 1950　　　　New York

Wild Bill Davison (cnt), Wilbur de Paris (tb, vcl), Sidney Bechet (sop), Ralph Sutton (p), Jack Lesberg (b), George Wettling (d).

4948	Jelly Roll Blues	Com 637	Jazt J100	
4949	At a Georgia Camp Meeting	Com 638	Ome 78613	
4950	National Emblem March	Com 637		
4951	Hindustan	Com 638	-	Fon(E) TL5294 Vog(F) INT 40028 Mile 56009
4986	I'll Take That New Orleans Music*	Lon(E) HMC5015		

All titles also on Lon(E) HMC5015, Com XFL15774, Mos MR20-134, and Com FL20020 except (*).

EDDIE CONDON　　June 9, 1950　　　　New York

Wild Bill Davison (cnt), Cutty Cutshall (tb), Peanuts Hucko (cl), Ralph Sutton (p), Eddie Condon (g), Jack Lesberg (b), Buzzy Drootin (d).

76475	Yellow Dog Blues	Dec 27106	DL5196	MCA BA212	(F)510206

RALPH SUTTON　　July 5, 1950　　　　New York
Piano Moods

Ralph Sutton (p), Jack Lesberg (b), George Wettling (d).

CO44052	Oriental Tones	Col 39458	CL6140	Har HL7019	Fon(E) TFR6002
CO44053	Jitterbug Waltz	Col 39459	-	-	-
CO44054	Tia Juana	Col 39460	-		
CO44055	Keep Your Temper	Col 39457	-	Herw H404	
CO44056	Ain't Misbehavin'	-	-	Har HL7019	-
CO44057	I Used to Love You	Col 39460	-		

　　　　　　　　　　July 6, 1950

CO44058	Muskrat Ramble	Col 39459	-
CO44059	Deep Henderson	Col 39458	-

All titles also on Col(E) 33S1018.

EDDIE CONDON　　September 26, 1950　　　　New York

Yank Lawson (t), Cutty Cutshall (tb, vcl), Edmond Hall (cl), Ralph Sutton (p), Eddie Condon (g), Bill Goodall (b), Buzzy Drootin (d).

76895	Ragging the Scale	Dec 27408	DL5196	MCA2-4071
76896	Grace and Beauty	-	-	AoH(E) AH100 MCA BA212
		(F)510206		MCA2-4071
76897	Everybody Loves My Baby	Dec 27409	DL5196	MCA2-4071
76898	A Hundred Years from Today*-	-	-	-

*Johnny Windhurst (t) replaces Lawson.

Discography

EDDIE CONDON 1950-1951 New York

Wild Bill Davison (cnt), Cutty Cutshall (tb), Peanuts Hucko (cl), Ralph Sutton (p), Bob Casey (b), Buzzy Drootin (d).

The Saints	Jazum 77	
She's Funny That Way	-	
After You've Gone	-	
When Your Lover Has Gone	-	
When You're Smiling	-	

Bobby Hackett (cnt) replaces Davison, Jack Lesberg (b) replaces Casey, Buddy Rich (d) replaces Drootin. Sidney Bechet (sop) added.

Thou Swell	-
September Song	-
I Know That You Know	-
This Is Romance	-
Cottontail	-

JAMMING AT RUDI'S January 23, 1951 New York

Dick Smith (cnt), Conrad Janis (tb), Tom Sharpsteen (cl), Bob Wilber (sop), Ralph Sutton (p), Danny Barker (g), Pops Foster (b), Fred Moore (d, vcl).

NY116	Panama			
NY117	Weary Blues			
NY118	Maryland, My Maryland			
NY119	See See Rider	Cir L404	Riv RLP12-215	Lon(E) LTZ-U15095
NY120	High Society	-	-	-
NY121	That's a Plenty	-	-	-
NY173	The Saints I	-	-	-
NY174	The Saints II	-	-	-

RALPH SUTTON February 7, 1951 New York
Salute to Fats (Ralph Sutton Plays Music of Fats Waller)

Ralph Sutton (p), Bob Casey (b), Buzzy Drootin (d).

CO45128	Alligator Crawl	Col 39374	CL6180	Har HL7019	Fon 662004TR
CO45129	Viper's Drag	Col 39375	-	-	-
CO45130	Clothesline Ballet	Col 39372	-	-	-
CO45131	Ain't Cha Glad?	Col 39373	-	-	-
CO45132	Take It from Me	-	-	-	-
CO45133	Blue, Turning Grey	Col 39375	-	-	-
CO45134	Sheltered by the Stars	Col 39374	-	-	-
CO45135	Keepin' Out of Mischief Now	Col 39372	-	-	-

All titles also on Col(E) 33S1025 and Fon(E) TFR6002.

DIXIELAND CLAMBAKE NO. 2 March 13, 1951 New York

Lee Castle, Wild Bill Davison, Pee Wee Erwin, Andy Feretti, Bernie Glow, Max Kaminsky, Rex Stewart (t), Will Bradley, Cutty Cutshall, Vince Grande, Lou McGarity (tb), Hank d'Amico, Peanuts Hucko, Jimmy Lytell (cl), Phil Olivella (as), Bud Freeman (ts), Ernie Caceres (bs), Frank Signorelli, Ralph Sutton (p), Carl Kress (g), Benny Mortell (bj), Bob Haggart (b), Joe Tarto (tu), Ray McKinley, Chauncey Morhouse (d), Mildred Bailey (vcl), Harry Sosnick (cond).

Dixieland Parade
Rockin' Chair
I Can't Give You Anything but Love

A U.S. Treasury Department radio program, recorded for release April 29, 1951.

GEORGE WETTLING May 4, 1951 New York

Wild Bill Davison (cnt), Cutty Cutshall (tb), Edmond Hall (cl), Ralph Sutton (p), Eddie Condon (g), Bob Casey (b), George Wettling (d).

CO45686	As Long as I Live	Col CL6189		
CO45687	A Good Man Is Hard to Find	-	CL2559	Fon(E) TFE17083
CO45688	Indiana	-	-	-
CO45689	Memphis Blues	-	-	-

All titles also on Col(E) 33S1019 and Har HL7080.

349

Loose Shoes

RALPH SUTTON June 11, 1952 New York
Ralph Sutton at the Piano

Ralph Sutton (p), George Wettling (d).

Fascination	Cir L-413	Riv RLP12-212	Vog(E) LDE014	Bar BLP6827
African Ripples	-	-	-	-
"A Flat" Dream	-	-	-	-
I'm Coming, Virginia	-	-	-	-
Drop Me Off in Harlem	-	-	-	-
Sugar Rose	-	-	-	-
Love Me or Leave Me	-	-	-	-
Bee's Knees	-	-	-	-

RALPH SUTTON June 1952 London

Ralph Sutton (p).

Three Little Words	Lyr AF2
No Local Stops	-
Oh, Baby	-
Concentrating	-
Drop Me Off in Harlem	-
Morning Air	-
Blues for Chuck	-
African Ripples	-

RALPH SUTTON July 5, 1952 Basel, Switzerland

Ralph Sutton (p).

E4934	Morning Air	ES 9113
E4935	Maple Leaf Rag	ES 9114
E4936	Effervescent	ES 9113
E4937	Christopher Columbus	ES 9114

RALPH SUTTON June 3, 1953 New York

Ralph Sutton (p), Cliff Leeman (d).

W84644	Jeepers Creepers	Dec ED2112	DL5498	Br(E) OE9286	LA8719
W84645	Eye Opener	Dec ED2111	-	Br(E) OE9285	-
W84646	Snowy Morning Blues	Dec ED2112	-	Br(E) OE9286	-
W84647	'Tain't Nobody's Bizness	-	-	-	-
W84648	Sneakaway	Dec ED2111	-	Br(E) OE9285	-
W84649	Fussin'	Dec ED2112	-	Br(E) OE9286	-
W84650	I'll Dance at Your Wedding	Dec ED2111	-	Br(E) OE9285	-
W84651	I Got Rhythm	-	-	-	-

All titles also on AoH(E) AH39, Aff(E) AFS1020, and Mos MR20-134.

Discography

LEE COLLINS/RALPH SUTTON'S JAZZOLA SIX   August 1, 1953   San Francisco

Lee Collins (t), Burt Johnson (tb), Pud Brown (cl, sop, ts), Ralph Sutton (p), Dale Jones (b), Smoky Stover (d).

These four sessions are air checks from the Hangover Club.

Panama	RA31
After You've Gone	-
Little Rock Getaway (Joe Sullivan solo)	-
West End Blues	-
Indiana	-
	August 8, 1953
Down in Jungle Town	RA31
St. James Infirmary	-
Honeysuckle Rose (Joe Sullivan solo)	-
Johnson Rag	-
On the Sunny Side of the Street	-
Hindustan	-
	August 15, 1953
I Found a New Baby	RA32
Buddy Bolden's Blues	-
Muskrat Ramble	-
Monday Date	-
Clarinet Marmalade	-
	August 22, 1953

Bob McCracken (cl) and Don Ewell (p) replace Brown and Sutton.

Fidgety Feet	RA32
Chinatown, My Chinatown	-
Viper's Drag (Ralph Sutton solo)	-
Basin Street Blues	-
Big Butter and Egg Man	-

RALPH SUTTON   February 10, 1954   New York

Edmond Hall (cl), Ralph Sutton (p), Walter Page (b), Cliff Leeman (d).

85849	Oh, Baby	Mos MR20-134		
85850	Dardanella	-		
85851	Up Jumped You with Love	-	Dec 29081	Bru(E) 05564
85852	Sweet and Lovely	-	-	-

June 8, 1954

86401-5	Ain't Cha Got Music	Mos MR20-134
86401-4	Ain't Cha Got Music #2	-
86401-3	Ain't Cha Got Music #3	-
86401-1	Ain't Cha Got Music #4	-
86404-2	Cross My Heart	-
86404-1	Cross My Heart #2	-
86404-3	Cross My Heart #3	-

RALPH SUTTON   July 24, 1954   San Francisco

Edmond Hall (cl), Ralph Sutton (p), Walter Page (b), Charlie Lodice (d).

These two sessions are air checks from the Hangover Club.

Oh, Baby	Stv SLP4009	Stv(E) SLP253
Keepin' Out of Mischief Now	-	-
Basin Street Blues	-	-
Coquette (Meade Lux Lewis solo)*		
I Found a New Baby	-	-
Dardanella	-	-

*These titles are on the air checks only.

July 31, 1954

St. Louis Blues	Stv SLP4009	Stv(E) SLP253
Sweet and Lovely	-	-
Blues My Naughty Sweetie Gave to Me		
Home (Meade Lux Lewis solo)*		
Up Jumped You with Love	-	-

Loose Shoes

RALPH SUTTON August 7, 1954 San Francisco

Clyde Hurley (t), Edmond Hall (cl), Ralph Sutton (p), Walter Page (b), Charlie Lodice (d).

These two sessions are air checks from the Hangover Club.

Black and Blue	JazAr JA45
I Found a New Baby	-
Between the Devil and the Deep Blue Sea	-
Jelly Roll (Meade Lux Lewis solo)*	
Honeysuckle Rose	-
Sheik of Araby	-

August 14, 1954

St. Louis Blues	-
Tin Roof Blues	-
Love Is Just Around the Corner	-
Four or Five Times (Meade Lux Lewis solo)*	
I Got Rhythm	-

RALPH SUTTON January 3, 1956 New York

Vic Dickenson (tb), Ralph Sutton (p), John Giuffrida (b), Buzzy Drootin (d).

89101-1	Christopher Columbus	Mos MR20-134
89101-2	Christopher Columbus #2	-
89101-4	Christopher Columbus #3	-
89102-1	St. Louis Blues	-
89102-2	St. Louis Blues #2	-

EDDIE CONDON February 23, 1956 New York

Billy Butterfield (t), Cutty Cutshall (tb), Peanuts Hucko (cl), Ralph Sutton (p), Eddie Condon (g), Walter Page (b), George Wettling (d).

CO55587	Duff Campbell's Revenge	Col CL881	Phi(E) BBL7207	Phi(C) BF322214	
				BO7226L	
CO55588	I've Got a Crush on You	-		Phi(C) BE429233	
CO55589	I Found a New Baby	-	Phi(E) BBE12365	Phi(C) BF32214	
				BE429233	
	Original Dixieland One-Step	Col CL1020	Phi(E) BBL7184	Phi(C) BO7260L	

All titles from CL881 also on Phi(E) BBL7131 and Phi(C) BO7193L.

BOB SCOBEY Summer 1956 San Francisco
The Great Bob Scobey (Vols. I & II)

Bob Scobey (t), Jack Buck (tb), Bill Napier (cl), Ralph Sutton (p), Clancy Hayes (g, bj, vcl), Hal McCormick (b), Bob Short (tu), Fred Higuera (d).

My Honey's Lovin' Arms	Jans JLP6250
Then I'll Be Happy	-
I Can't Give You Anything but Love	-
I'll See You in Cuba	-
Blue, Turning Grey Over You*	Jans JLP6252
Five Foot Two	-
Maple Leaf Rag	-
I'm Sorry I Made You Cry	-

*Labeled as Scobey's Trumpet Has Boots.

The liner notes for these two records identify the pianist as Sutton on some of the tunes and Jesse (Tiny) Crump on the others, without naming the specific numbers on which each man plays. The identification of Sutton on the above eight tunes was made by the author.

Discography

BOB SCOBEY   August 13, 1956   Los Angeles
Beauty and the Beat

Bob Scobey, Manny Klein (t), Jack Buck, Abe Lincoln, Warren Smith (tb), Bill Napier, Matty Matlock (cl), Ralph Sutton (p), Clancy Hayes (bj, vcl), Bob Short (tu), Phil Stephens (b), Fred Higuera (d).

G2JB4812	Rose of Washington Square	Vic LPM1344	HMV DLP1146	
G2JB4813	The Girl Friend	-	-	
G2JB4814	Linda	-	-	
G2JB4815	Mickey	-	-	
G2JB4816	Alice Blue Gown	-	-	RCA(F)430549
G2JB4817	You Must Have Been a Beautiful Baby	-	-	
G2JB4818	Calico Sal	-	-	
G2JB4819	Miss Annabelle Lee	-	-	RCA(F)430549

August 14, 1956

Moe Schneider (tb) and Wayne Songer (cl) replace Smith and Matlock.

G2JB4820	Lulu's Back in Town	-	-
G2JB4821	Mandy Is Two	-	-
G2JB4822	Sweet Substitute	-	-
G2JB4823	Sweet Lorraine	-	-

BOB SCOBEY   January 21, 1957   Los Angeles
Swingin' on the Golden Gate

Bob Scobey, Dick Cathcart (t), Jack Buck, Abe Lincoln, Warren Smith (tb), Matty Matlock (cl), Ralph Sutton (p), Clancy Hayes (bj, g, vcl), Bob Short (tu), Red Callender (b), Sammy Goldstein (d).

H2JB0209	New Orleans	Vic LPM1448	RCA(E) RD27031
H2JB0210	Carolina in the Morning	-	-
H2JB0211	Snag It	-	-
H2JB0212	Waiting for the Robert E. Lee	-	-

January 22, 1957

Manny Klein (t) and Phil Stephens (b) replace Cathcart and Callender.

H2JB0213	Ain't Cha Glad?	-	-
H2JB0214	Wabash Cannonball	-	-
H2JB0215	Come Back, Sweet Papa	-	-
H2JB0216	I Can't Get Started	-	-
H2JB0217	Sunny Disposish	-	-
H2JB0218	Feet Draggin' Blues	-	-
H2JB0219	Let's Dance the Ragtime	-	-
H2JB0220	It Happened in Sun Valley	-	-

BOB SCOBEY   February 1957   Los Angeles
Bourbon Street

Bob Scobey (t), Jack Buck (tb), Bill Napier (cl), Ralph Sutton (p), Clancy Hayes (bj, g), Bob Short (tu, b), Fred Higuera (d), Lizzie Miles (vcl).

On Revival Day	Ver MGV1009	Co(E) SEB10088	Ver(G) EPV7003	EPV5060
Make Me a Pallet	-	-		-
Baby, Won't You Please Come Home	-	-		
Ain't Misbehavin'	-	-		EPV7004
Frog-I-More Rag	-	Col(E) LB10078	-	
Deep Henderson	-	-		
Jimtown Blues	-	Col(E) SEB10082		
Down and Out Blues	-	-		
Squeeze Me			*	
Wild Man Blues	-			-
When You're Smilin'	-			EPV5060
Tiger Rag	-			

All titles also on Bar GLP3589. Col(E) SEB10088 issued as by Lizzie Miles.

353

Loose Shoes

BING CROSBY & BOB SCOBEY February 19-20, 1957 Los Angeles
Bing with a Beat

Bob Scobey, Frank Beach (t), Abe Lincoln (tb), Matty Matlock (cl), Dave Harris (ts), Ralph Sutton (p), Clancy Hayes (g), Red Callender (b), Nick Fatool (d), Bing Crosby (vcl).

H2JB0321	Dream a Little Dream of Me	Vic LPM1473
H2JB0322	Some Sunny Day	-
H2JB0323	I'm Gonna Sit Right Down	-
H2JB0324	Tell Me	-
H2JB0325	Exactly Like You	-
H2JB0326	Let a Smile Be Your Umbrella	-

February 20, 1957

H2JB0327	Mama Loves Papa	-
H2JB0328	Down Among the Sheltering Palms	-
H2JB0329	Last Night on the Back Porch	-
H2JB0330	Along the Way to Waikiki	-
H2JB0331	Whispering	-
H2JB0332	Mack the Knife	-

All titles also on RCA(E) RD27032.

TURK MURPHY December 2, 1958 San Francisco
Live at Easy Street

Bob Short (t), Turk Murphy (tb, vcl), Bob Helm (cl), Pete Clute (p), Dick Lammi (bj), Jack Crook (bas), Thad Vandon (d, vcl).

These sessions are air checks from Easy Street.

Down Home Rag	DC 12019
After You've Gone	-
Chimes Blues	
Hobson Street Blues (Ralph Sutton solo)	-
Cake Walkin' Babies from Home	-
Tishomingo Blues	
My Honey's Lovin' Arms	-

December 9, 1958

Ragtime Dance	-
St. James Infirmary	-
Milneburg Joys	-
In the Dark (Ralph Sutton solo)	-
Sadie Green, The Vamp of New Orleans	-
Memphis Blues	

RALPH SUTTON December 1959 Squaw Valley, California
Jazz at the Olympics

Ernie Figueroa (t), Ralph Sutton (p), Vernon Alley (b), Joe Dodge (d).

Winter Wonderland	Ome OML1051	OSL51
Button Up Your Overcoat	-	-
I've Got My Love to Keep Me Warm	-	-
I'll Follow You	-	-
Hot Buttered Rum	-	-
Let It Snow	-	-
I'm Shooting High	-	-
Winter Weather	-	-
I've Got a Feeling I'm Falling	-	-
Squaw Valley Blues	-	-

THOSE RAGTIME YEARS August 1960 New York

Ralph Sutton (p).

The Cascades

Eubie Blake, Hoagy Carmichael, Ralph Sutton, Dick Wellstood (p).

Maple Leaf Rag

An NBC television program, presented on November 22, 1960. The Wilbur de Paris band and the NBC studio band joined the four pianists on the last two choruses of "Maple Leaf Rag." The De Paris band consisted of Sidney de Paris (cnt), Wilbur de Paris (tb), Garvin Bushell (cl), Sonny White (p), John Smith (g), Hayes Alvis (b), and Wilbert Kirk (d).

Discography

EDDIE CONDON Late 1960 New York
Live at Eddie Condon's

Peanuts Hucko (cl, ts), Ralph Sutton (p), Dante Martucci* (b), Buzzy Drootin* (d).

I Found a New Baby	Chiar CR167
Slow Boat to China	-
Hobson Street Blues	-
Stealin' Apples	-
Lazy River	-
Alligator Crawl	-
Lazy Mood**	-
Running Wild	-

*Liner notes list Martucci as Montucci and George Wettling instead of Drootin.
**Labeled as I Guess I'll Have to Change My Plan.

RALPH SUTTON 1962-1963 New York
Ragtime U.S.A.

Ralph Sutton (p), Jack Lesberg (b), Buzzy Drootin (d).

Eye Opener	Rou R25232
Snowy Mornin' Blues	-
Alligator Crawl	-
Echo of Spring	-
Wolverine Blues	-
Honky Tonk Train	-
Hobson Street Blues	-
In a Mist	-
Checkin' with Chuck	-
Maple Leaf Rag	-
Through for the Day	-
Rosetta	-

CLANCY HAYES 1963 Los Angeles
Swingin' Minstrel

Bill Napier (cl), Ralph Sutton (p), Clancy Hayes (bj, g, d, vcl), Bob Short (tu).

Willie the Weeper	GTG M12050	S100500	Voc(E) LAG573
When You and I Were Young, Maggie	-	-	-
Honeysuckle Rose	-	-	-
Limehouse Blues	-	-	-
Wolverine Blues	-	-	-

RED ALLEN February 16, 1963 New York
Nice!

Red Allen (t), Cutty Cutshall (tb), Tony Parenti (cl), Ralph Sutton (p), Bennie Moten (b), Mickey Sheehan (d).

Memphis Blues	Phoe LP24
Yellow Dog Blues	-
Cherry	-
Fidgety Feet	-

Air check includes Honky Tonk Train and Algiers Bounce.

NINE GREATS OF JAZZ (JAZZ IN THE TROC) July 21, 1966 Denver

Yank Lawson (t), Cutty Cutshall, Lou McGarity (tb), Peanuts Hucko (cl), Bud Freeman (ts), Ralph Sutton (p), Clancy Hayes (bj, vcl), Bob Haggart (b), Morey Feld (d).

Fidgety Feet	Troc WCS-1769
Rose of Washington Square	-
Honky Tonk Train	-
Stealin' Apples	-
At the Jazz Band Ball	-
Three Little Words	-
Big Noise from Winnetka	-
Get Out and Get Under the Moon	-
I Found a New Baby	-

Loose Shoes

RALPH SUTTON   November 6, 1966   Charlotte, North Carolina
Suttonly

Ralph Sutton (p, vcl), Johnny Haynes (b), Jim Lackey (d).

Honeysuckle Rose	Solo S-103
I'm Gonna Sit Right Down	-
St. Louis Blues	-
'Tain't Nobody's Bizness	-
I Found a New Baby	-
Carolina in the Morning	-
Sunnie's Blues	-
On the Sunny Side of the Street	-

BOB CROSBY   November 18, 1966   New York
Live at the Rainbow Grill, Mardi Gras Parade, & Lou McGarity: In Celebration

Yank Lawson (t), Lou McGarity (tb), Matty Matlock (cl), Eddie Miller (ts), Ralph Sutton (p), Bob Haggart (b), Don Lamond (d), Bob Crosby (vcl).

Someday	MoEv MES6815	Emb(E) CJS827
Basin Street Blues	-	-
Battle Hymn of the Republic	-	-
Lazy Mood	-	-
Keepin' Out of Mischief Now	-	-
St. James Infirmary	-	-
Puzzy Cat	-	-
I Loves You, Porgy	-	-
Oh, Baby	-	-
Summertime	-	-
	MoEv MES7026	
Mardi Gras Parade	-	
Ballin' the Jack	-	
Lazy River	-	
South	-	
C Jam Blues	-	
Jelly Roll	-	
Smile	-	
Tin Roof Blues	-	
Mardi Gras Parade	-	
	November 1966	
Fidgety Feet	IAJRC36	

RALPH SUTTON & GEORGE BARNES   November 26, 1966   St. Louis

Ralph Sutton (p), George Barnes (g).

Fractious Fingering	Private Recording
Lonesome and Blue	-
Honeysuckle Rose	-
Shine	-
Stars Fell on Alabama	-
Echo of Spring	-
When My Sugar Walks Down the Street	-
I Found a New Baby	-

ODESSA JAZZ PARTY 1967   April 18-23, 1967   Odessa, Texas

Yank Lawson (t), Cutty Cutshall (tb), Peanuts Hucko (cl), Bob Wilber (cl, sop), Ralph Sutton (p), Jack Lesberg (b), Morey Feld, Ray McKinley (d).

Hindustan	Odessa Jazz Party LPS 1967
Echo of Spring	-
Jitterbug Waltz	-
Tishomingo Blues	-
Swing That Music*	-

*Labeled as Swingin' the Blues.

Discography

TEN GREATS OF JAZZ (JAZZ IN THE TROC)   July 21-22, 1967*   Denver

Yank Lawson, Billy Butterfield (t), Cutty Cutshall, Lou McGarity (tb), Peanuts Hucko (cl), Bud Freeman (ts), Ralph Sutton (p), Clancy Hayes (bj, vcl), Bob Haggart (b), Morey Feld (d).

That's a Plenty	Troc WCS-2831
Beale Street Blues	-
Viper's Drag	-
Dinah	-
Runnin' Wild	-
South Rampart Street Parade**	-
Summertime	-
Peoria	-
St. James Infirmary	-
Do You Know What It Means**	-
Jazz Me Blues	-

*Dates given as July 22-23 in liner notes.
**Matty Matlock (cl) replaces Hucko.

RALPH SUTTON   February 27-29, 1968   Aspen, Colorado
On Sunnie's Side of the Street

Ruby Braff (cnt), Ralph Sutton (p), Milt Hinton (b), Mousie Alexander (d).

Someday, Sweetheart	BA BAJC-501
A Hundred Years from Today	-
I Found a New Baby	-
Can't We Be Friends?	-
I'm Crazy 'bout My Baby	-
On the Sunny Side of the Street	-
St. Louis Blues	-

TEN GREATS OF JAZZ (JAZZ IN THE TROC)   July 19-20, 1968   Denver

Yank Lawson, Billy Butterfield (t), Cutty Cutshall, Lou McGarity (tb), Peanuts Hucko (cl), Bud Freeman (ts), Ralph Sutton (p), Clancy Hayes (bj, vcl), Bob Haggart (b), Morey Feld (d).

Hindustan	Troc WCS-3853	WGJB-1
New Orleans	-	-
Silver Dollar	-	-
Royal Garden Blues	-	-
Cherry	-	-
Just a Closer Walk with Thee	-	-
Wolverine Blues	-	-

WORLD'S GREATEST JAZZBAND   December 10, 1968   New York

Yank Lawson, Billy Butterfield (t), Carl Fontana, Lou McGarity (tb), Bob Wilber (cl, sop), Bud Freeman (ts), Ralph Sutton (p), Clancy Hayes (bj), Bob Haggart (b), Morey Feld (d).

Sunny	Proj PR5033SD	WRC ST1091
Panama	-	-
Baby, Won't You Please Come Home	-	-
Up, Up, and Away	-	-
Ode to Billy Joe	-	-
Honky Tonk Train	-	-
A Taste of Honey	-	-
Limehouse Blues	-	-
Big Noise from Winnetka	-	-
This Is All I Ask	-	-
Mrs. Robinson	-	-
Bugle Call Rag	-	-

Loose Shoes

WORLD'S GREATEST JAZZBAND December 1968 New York
Extra!

Yank Lawson (t), Billy Butterfield (t, flgh), Carl Fontana, Lou McGarity (tb), Bob Wilber (cl, sop), Bud Freeman (ts), Ralph Sutton (p), Bob Haggart (b), Gus Johnson (d).

Love Is Blue	Proj PR5039SD	Parl PCS7138
I'm Prayin' Humble	-	-
It Must Be Him	-	-
59th Street Bridge Song	-	-
Alfie	-	-
Wolverine Blues	-	-
What the World Needs Now Is Love	-	-
Savoy Blues	-	-
Wichita Lineman	-	-
Do You Know the Way to San Jose?	-	-
The Windmills of Your Mind	-	-
South Rampart Street Parade	-	-

RALPH SUTTON February 16-19, 1969 Aspen, Colorado
The Night They Raided Sunnie's

Bob Wilber (cl, sop), Ralph Sutton (p), Al Hall (b), Cliff Leeman (d).

Lulu's Back in Town	BA BAJC-504
Stumbling	-
Give Me a June Night	-
As Long As I Live	-
I'll Be a Friend with Pleasure	-
I Believe in Miracles	-
I'm Always in the Mood for You	-
Just Friends*	-

*Omit Wilber.

WORLD'S GREATEST JAZZBAND March 1969 New York

Yank Lawson, Billy Butterfield (t), Carl Fontana, Lou McGarity (tb), Bob Wilber (cl), Bud Freeman (ts), Ralph Sutton (p), Bob Haggart (b), Gus Johnson (d).

Panama	MIS 5 (Private Recording)
At Sundown	-

RALPH SUTTON May 8-9, 1969 New York
Knocked-Out Nocturne (Ralph Sutton Plays Great Jazz Piano)

Yank Lawson (t), Bob Wilber (sop), Ralph Sutton (p), Bob Haggart (b), Gus Johnson (d).

Honeysuckle Rose	Proj PR5040SD
I Got Rhythm	-
Snowy Mornin' Blues*	-
Echo of Spring*	-
In the Dark**	-
Viper's Drag*	-
Hobson Street Blues	-
Eye Opener	-
Ain't Misbehavin'*	-
Love Lies***	-
In a Mist**	-
Alligator Crawl*	-

*Omit Wilber.
**Omit Haggart and Johnson.
***Omit Lawson.

Discography

TEN GREATS OF JAZZ (JAZZ IN THE TROC) July 18-19, 1969 Denver

Yank Lawson, Billy Butterfield (t), Carl Fontana, Lou McGarity (tb), Bob Wilber (cl, sop), Bud Freeman (ts), Ralph Sutton (p), Clancy Hayes (bj, vcl), Bob Haggart (b), Gus Johnson (d).

Bugle Call Rag	Troc WCS-3330 (2 records)	WGJB4
Willie the Weeper	-	-
Savoy Blues	-	-
In a Mist	-	-
Limehouse Blues	-	-
Tiger Rag	-	-
It's a Lazy Afternoon*	-	-
Ace in the Hole	-	-
Mood Indigo	-	-
Original Dixieland One-Step	-	-
After You've Gone	-	-
Undecided	-	-
Viper's Drag	-	-
Tin Roof Blues	-	-
California, Here I Come	-	-
I Want to Be Happy	-	-
Lady Be Good	-	-
Jack Gurtler Blues**	-	-
Washboard Blues	-	-
Sheik of Araby	-	-

*Labeled as It's That Rainy Day.
**Labeled as Jack Gurther Blues.

TEN GREATS OF JAZZ (JAZZ IN THE MOUNTAINS)

This record consists of tunes from the group's 1967, 1968, and 1969 *Jazz in the Troc* recordings.

South Rampart Street Parade	WJ WJLP-S14
Viper's Drag	-
Tin Roof Blues	-
Wolverine Blues	-
Just a Closer Walk with Thee	-
Savoy Blues	-
Summertime	-
After You've Gone	-

BUD FREEMAN December 10-12, 1969 New York
The Compleat Bud Freeman

Bob Wilber (cl, sop), Bud Freeman (ts), Ralph Sutton (p), Bob Haggart (b), Gus Johnson (d).

Dinah	MoEv MES7022
Another Sunday	-
Exactly Like You	-
You Took Advantage of Me	-
What Is There to Say?	-
I Got Rhythm	-
Uncle Haggart's Blues	-
Out of My Road, Mr. Toad	-
Ain't Misbehavin'	-
Song of the Dove	-
That D Minor Thing	-
Just One of Those Things	-

Loose Shoes

WORLD'S GREATEST JAZZBAND April 17-18, 1970 New York
Live at the Roosevelt Grill

Yank Lawson (t), Billy Butterfield (t, flgh), Vic Dickenson, Lou McGarity (tb), Bob Wilber (cl, sop), Bud Freeman (ts), Ralph Sutton (p), Bob Haggart (b), Gus Johnson (d).

That's a Plenty	Atl SD1570	Atl 2402037	Atl 90982-2 [CD]
Five Point Blues	-	-	-
My Honey's Lovin' Arms	-	-	-
Black and Blue	-	-	-
That D Minor Thing	-	-	-
Royal Garden Blues	-	-	-
Come Back, Sweet Papa	-	-	-
Under the Moonlight Starlight Blue	-	-	-
Constantly	-	-	-
New Orleans	-	-	-
Jazz Me Blues	-	-	-
Just One of Those Things			-

WORLD'S GREATEST JAZZBAND January 22-23, 1971 Hollywood
What's New?

Yank Lawson (t), Billy Butterfield (t, flgh), Vic Dickenson, Lou McGarity (tb), Bob Wilber (cl, sop), Bud Freeman (ts), Ralph Sutton (p), Bob Haggart (b), Gus Johnson (d).

Bourbon Street Parade	Atl SD1582	Atl 2402038
Smile	-	-
The Eel	-	-
What's New?	-	-
Mercy Mercy Mercy	-	-
Root Dog	-	-
Walk Him Up the Stairs	-	-
Girl on the Beach	-	-
Dogtown Blues	-	-
Doodle Doo Doo	-	-
My Inspiration	-	-

WORLD'S GREATEST JAZZBAND January 17-19, 1972 Los Angeles
Century Plaza

Yank Lawson (t), Billy Butterfield (t, flgh), Vic Dickenson, Eddie Hubble (tb), Bob Wilber (cl, sop), Bud Freeman (ts), Ralph Sutton (p), Bob Haggart (b), Gus Johnson (d).

Century Plaza	WJ WJLP-S1
A Long Way from Home	-
At Sundown	-
Colonial Tavern	-
Out Back	-
Frog and Nightgown	-
Dreaming Butterfly	-
Heavy Hearted Blues	-
She's Funny That Way	-
Navarre	-

WORLD'S GREATEST JAZZBAND September 5-7, 1972 Hollywood
Hark, the Herald Angels Swing

Yank Lawson (t, vcl), Billy Butterfield (t, flgh), Vic Dickenson (tb, vcl), Eddie Hubble (tb), Bob Wilber (cl, sop), Bud Freeman (ts), Ralph Sutton (p, cel, vcl), Bob Haggart (b), Gus Johnson (d, vcl).

Hark, the Herald Angels Swing	WJ WJLP-S2	WGJB8
The Little Drummer Boy	-	-
Rudolph, the Red-Nosed Reindeer (GJ-VD-YL)	-	-
Silent Night	-	-
Joy to the World	-	-
Jingle Bells (VD)	-	-
White Christmas	-	-
I'll Be Home for Christmas (RS)	-	-
The Christmas Song	-	-
Winter Wonderland	-	-
Deck the Halls	-	-

Discography

WORLD'S GREATEST JAZZBAND December 4, 1972 Toronto
Massey Hall

Yank Lawson (t), Bobby Hackett (cnt), Vic Dickenson, Eddie Hubble (tb), Bob Wilber (cl, sop), Bud Freeman (ts), Ralph Sutton (p), Bob Haggart (b), Gus Johnson (d).

Original Dixieland One-Step	WJ WJLP-S3
Crawfish Shuffle	-
I Want to Be Happy	-
Do You Know What It Means	-
California, Here I Come	-
Fidgety Feet	-
South	-
Lover, Come Back to Me	-
If You Knew Susie	-
St. Louis Blues	-

WORLD'S GREATEST JAZZBAND January 17, 1973 New York
Carnegie Hall

Yank Lawson (t), Bobby Hackett (cnt), Vic Dickenson, Eddie Hubble (tb), Bob Wilber (cl, sop), Bud Freeman (ts), Ralph Sutton (p), Bob Haggart (b), Gus Johnson (d), Maxine Sullivan (vcl).

At the Jazz Band Ball	WJ WJLP-S4
Just a Closer Walk with Thee	-
I Found a New Baby	-
A Hundred Years from Today	-
The Lady Is a Tramp	-
Sweet Georgia Brown	-
Muskrat Ramble	-
When Your Lover Has Gone	-
I Got a Right to Sing the Blues	-
Keepin' Out of Mischief Now	-
Chicago	-
Swing That Music	-

HAPPY JAZZ BAND & WORLD'S GREATEST JAZZBAND April 8, 1973 San Antonio

Jim Cullum, Jr. (cnt), Yank Lawson (t), Gene McKinney (tb), Jim Cullum, Sr. (cl), Bud Freeman (ts), Ralph Sutton (p), Bob Haggart (b), Harvey Kindervater (d).

Introduction of WGJ by Jim Cullum, Sr.	Aud 119
Royal Garden Blues	-

TERESA BREWER & WORLD'S GREATEST JAZZBAND March 12-13, 1974 New York
Good News

Yank Lawson (t), Bobby Hackett (cnt), Vic Dickenson, Bennie Morton (tb), Bob Wilber (cl, sop), Bud Freeman (ts), Ralph Sutton (p), Bucky Pizzarelli (g), Bob Haggart (b), Gus Johnson (d), Teresa Brewer (vcl).

Good News	Sig BSL1-0577
I Want to Be Bad	-
Button Up Your Overcoat	-
Keep Your Sunny Side Up	-
Lucky in Love	-
Varsity Drag	-
Just Imagine	-
Together	-
You're the Cream in My Coffee	-
The Best Things in Life Are Free	-

Loose Shoes

WORLD'S GREATEST JAZZBAND July 16, 1974   Nice, France
Tribute to Louis Armstrong

Yank Lawson (t), Bennie Morton (tb), Bob Wilber (sop), Bud Freeman (ts), Ralph Sutton (p), Bob Haggart (b), Gus Johnson (d), Maxine Sullivan (vcl).

You're Driving Me Crazy   RCA(F) FXL1 7159

BUD FREEMAN   July 20, 1974   Vallauris, France

Bud Freeman (ts), Ralph Sutton (p), Bob Haggart (b), Gus Johnson (d).

The Eel	Mem ME 02
Dinah	-
Alligator Crawl	-
Big Noise from Winnetka	-
Sunday	-
What Is There to Say?	-
You Took Advantage of Me	-
Don't Blame Me	-
Three Little Words	-
Memories of You	-
Way Down Yonder in New Orleans	-
Lullaby of the Leaves	-

WORLD'S GREATEST JAZZBAND   1974   Hollywood
Jazz Me Blues

Yank Lawson (t), Vic Dickenson (tb, vcl), Bennie Morton (tb), Bob Wilber (cl, sop), Bud Freeman (ts), Ralph Sutton (p), Bob Haggart (b), Gus Johnson (d).

Beale Street Blues	WJ WJLP-S23
Crazy Rhythm	-
Sheik of Araby	-
A Smile Will Go a Long, Long Way	-
Tie a Yellow Ribbon	-
The Saints	-

WORLD'S GREATEST JAZZBAND   May 1975   Phoenix
Cole Porter

Yank Lawson, John Best (t), Carl Fontana, George Masso (tb), Peanuts Hucko (cl), Tommy Newsom (ts), Ralph Sutton (p), Bob Haggart (b), Gus Johnson (d).

Love for Sale	WJ WJLP-S6
All of You	-
It's All Right with Me	-
Let's Do It	-
I Concentrate on You	-
Just One of Those Things	-
Anything Goes	-
It's D'Lovely	-
Rosalie	-
So in Love	-
You'd Be So Nice to Come Home To	-
From This Moment On	-

WORLD'S GREATEST JAZZBAND August 4, 1975 Los Angeles
Rodgers & Hart

Yank Lawson, John Best (t), Carl Fontana, George Masso (tb), Peanuts Hucko (cl), Al Klink (ts), Ralph Sutton (p), Bob Haggart (b), Gus Johnson (d).

Mountain Greenery	WJ WJLP-S7
Have You Met Miss Jones?	-
Isn't It Romantic?	-
My Funny Valentine	-
Blue Room	-
You Took Advantage of Me	-
The Lady Is a Tramp	-
Dancing on the Ceiling	-
Where or When	-
Bewitched	-
Thou Swell	-
Lover	

WORLD'S GREATEST JAZZBAND October 21, 1975 Stockholm, Sweden
Live at the Atlantic Club (On Tour)

Yank Lawson, Billy Butterfield (t), George Masso, Sonny Russo (tb), Peanuts Hucko (cl), Al Klink (ts), Ralph Sutton (p), Bob Haggart (b), Bobby Rosengarden (d), Maxine Sullivan (vcl).

Sheik of Araby	WJ WJLP-8
Basin Street Blues	-
Wrap Your Troubles in Dreams	-
Just One of Those Things	-
Do You Know What It Means	-
St. Louis Blues	-
Mandy, Make Up Your Mind	-
Stardust	-
Limehouse Blues	-
Dear Old Southland	-
The Saints	-

On Tour II

Stumbling	WJ WJLP-10
Poor Butterfly	-
Caravan	-
Running Wild	-
Big Butter and Egg Man	-
I've Got the World on a String	-
Too Marvelous	-
Squeeze Me	-
Hindustan	-

RALPH SUTTON October 24, 1975 Scheveningen, the Netherlands
Piano Moods (Alligator Crawl)

Ralph Sutton (p), Koos van der Sluis (b), Ted Easton (d).

Alligator Crawl	Riff(Du) 659009*	Jazl JCE92
Blue Turning Grey Over You	-	-
Ain't Misbehavin'	-	-
The Curse of an Aching Heart	-	-
Can't We Be Friends?	-	-
Honky Tonk Train	-	-
Squeeze Me	-	-
Honeysuckle Rose	-	-
Rose Room	-	-
Handful of Keys	-	

*This LP was reissued under the title of *Alligator Crawl* by Jazzology, which did not include one of the original tunes, "Handful of Keys." Sutton had recorded this tune a day later. The record, except for "Blue Turning Grey Over You" and "The Curse of an Aching Heart," was reissued by Solo Art on a CD, also called *Alligator Crawl*. The CD contained Sutton's *Off the Cuff* album of April 17, 1976, as well, except for "Keepin' Out of Mischief Now."

Loose Shoes

RALPH SUTTON October 25, 1975 Scheveningen, the Netherlands
Piano Moods

Ralph Sutton (p).

Handful of Keys Riff(Du) 659009 190001

RALPH SUTTON October 25, 1975 Scheveningen, the Netherlands

Bob Wulffers (t), Hank van Muyen (tb), Frits Kaatee (cl), Ralph Sutton (p), Jacques Kingsma (b), Ted Easton (d).

South Rampart Street Parade Riff(Du) 190001

DICK CARY October 30, 1975 Scheveningen, the Netherlands

Dick Cary (t, ah), George Kaatee (tb), Frits Kaatee (cl), Ralph Sutton (p), Pim Hogervorst (bj), Jacques Kingma (b), Hans Eekhof (tu), Ted Easton (d).

Somebody Stole My Gal Riff 659014
It's a Sin to Tell a Lie -
Mandy, Make Up Your Mind -
You Brought a New Kind of Love to Me -
In the Dark Riff 659031

MILAN COLLEGE JAZZ SOCIETY November 1, 1975 Milan, Italy
25 Years After

Giorgio Alberti (t), Gianni Acocella (tb), Bruno Longhi (cl), Paolo Tomelleri (ts), Carlo Bagnoli (bs), Ralph Sutton (p), Lino Patruno (g), Marco Ratti (b), Remi Ettore (d).

Fidgety Feet Dur(I) 77381
After You've Gone -
Savoy Blues -

RALPH SUTTON November 13, 1975 Zurich, Switzerland
Suttonly It Jumped!

Ralph Sutton (p).

'Round My Old Deserted Farm/ 88UR-004
   Cottage for Sale/'Tain't So
   Honey, 'Tain't So
Echo of Spring -
Morning Air -
Eye Opener -
In the Dark -
Honky Tonk Train -
My Fate Is in Your Hands -
Viper's Drag -
Love Lies -

RALPH SUTTON November 16, 1975 Haywards Heath, England
Live!

Ralph Sutton (p).

Eye Opener Fly LP204 Fly CD911 [CD]
Echo of Spring - -
Morning Air - -
In the Dark - -
Viper's Drag - -
Cottage for Sale/Old Folks/'Tain't So, Honey, 'Tain't So - -
Honeysuckle Rose/Handful of Keys/ - -
   Somebody Stole My Gal
Ain't Misbehavin'/Keepin' Out of Mischief Now/ -
   My Fate Is in Your Hands/Alligator Crawl
I Found a New Baby - -

Loose Shoes

CHICAGO JAZZ GIANTS May 10-11, 1976 Villingen, West Germany
Live!

Wild Bill Davison (cnt), Eddie Hubble (tb), Bob Wilber (cl, sop), Ralph Sutton (p), Isla Eckinger (b), Cliff Leeman (d).

Ol' Miss	MPS 68172
When You're Smiling	-
New City Ditty	-
As Long as I Live	-
The Blues My Naughty Sweetie Gave to Me	-
Beale Street Blues	-
Blue Again	-
Thanks a Million	-
Ain't Misbehavin'	-

WILD BILL DAVISON & RALPH SUTTON May 23-24, 1977 Copenhagen, Denmark
Together Again!

Wild Bill Davison (cnt, vcl), Ole "Fessor" Lindgreen (tb), Jesper Thilo (cl, sop, ts), Ralph Sutton (p), Lars Blach (g), Hugo Rasmussen (b), Svend Erik Norregard (d).

Everybody Loves My Baby	Stv SLP4027
Blue Room	-
Time After Time	-
Old Cape Cod	-
Exactly Like You	-
Shine	-
After I Say I'm Sorry	-
Try a Little Tenderness	-
Cute	-
Squeeze Me	-
Running Wild	-

RALPH SUTTON May 24-25, 1977 Copenhagen, Denmark

Ralph Sutton (p), Lars Blach (g), Hugo Rasmussen (b), Svend Erik Norregard (d).

Thou Swell	Stv(Dan) SLP275	SLP4013
You're Driving Me Crazy	-	-
You Can Depend on Me	-	-
At Sundown	-	-
Undecided	-	-
In the Dark	-	-
Jeepers Creepers	-	-
Gone with the Wind	-	-
I Want to Be Happy	-	-
If I Could Be with You	-	-
St. Louis Blues	-	-
Worrying the Life Out of Me	-	-

RALPH SUTTON & CLASSIC JAZZ COLLEGIUM July 10-11, 1977 Prague, Czechoslovakia

Lubos Zajicek (cnt), Jiri Pechar (tp), Miloslav Havranek (tb), Josef Rejman (cl, as), Bohumil Vesely (ts), Ivor Kratky (bas), Ralph Sutton (p, vcl), Miroslav Klimes (bj), Zdenek Fibrich (tu), Alex Sladek (d).

Opus No. 1	Supra(Cz) 1152416 ZA
Honeysuckle Rose	-
Alligator Crawl	-
Them There Eyes	-
Gee, Baby, Ain't I Good to You	-
Stomp Off, Let's Go	-
Savoy Blues	-
Dream a Little Dream of Me	-
Open Ears	-
I'm Gonna Sit Right Down	-
Dark Blue World	-
You Don't Know What the Middle Ages Were Like	-

Discography

RALPH SUTTON　　　　　　　　　　c. November 20, 1975　　　London
Changes

Ralph Sutton (p).

I Want a Little Girl	77(E) 77S57
Everything Happens to Me	-
Coquette	-
Sweet and Lovely	-
Sweet Lorraine	-
I Found a New Baby	-
I Surrender, Dear	-
'Tain't So, Honey, 'Tain't So	-
Squeeze Me	-
Changes	-

PIANO SUMMIT　　　　　　　　　　November 24, 1975　　　London

Lennie Felix, Keith Ingham, Brian Lemon, Ralph Sutton (p).

Indiana (LF & RS)	77(E) 77S58
If I Had You (LF)	-
You Took Advantage of Me (LF)	-
Stars Fell on Alabama (LF)	-
Lotus Blossom (KI)	-
Day Dream (KI)	-
Just Friends (RS)	-
Truckin' (KI)	-
Yesterdays (BL)	-
Stella by Starlight (BL)	-
Exactly Like You (BL)	-
'S'Wonderful (LF & RS)	-

RALPH SUTTON　　　　　　　　　　December 6, 1975　　　Blandford Forum, England
Jazz at the Forum

Peter Gilmore (t), Tony Hurst (tb), Dave Challis (cl), Mike Snelling (sax), Ralph Sutton (p), Brian Mursell (b), Paul Brodie (d).

Love Lies	Geo 101
Shine	-
All the Things You Are/Taking a Chance on Love	-
I've Got My Love to Keep Me Warm/ You Took Advantage of Me	-

　　　　　　　　　　　　　　　　　　　June 19, 1976

Echo of Spring	-
Sheik of Araby	-
Eye Opener	-
Honky Tonk Train	-
C Jam Blues	-

RALPH SUTTON　　　　　　　　　　April 17, 1976　　　Scheveningen, the Netherlands
Off the Cuff

Ralph Sutton (p), Koos van der Sluis (b)*, Ted Easton (d)*.

Echo of Spring	Riff(Du) 659021	Solo Art SACD92 [CD]**
Love Lies	-	-
Eye Opener		
Two Sleepy People	-	-
Muskrat Ramble	-	-
I Found a New Baby*	-	-
Memories of You*	-	-
Viper's Drag*	-	-
Dinah	-	-
Keepin' Out of Mischief Now		
Handful of Keys	-	

**See note with recording of October 24, 1975.

365

Discography

RALPH SUTTON (Piano Rolls)	January 1979		Turlock, California
Sophisticated Lady	Play-Rite	396-A	
Brother, Can You Spare a Dime?	-	397-A	
Honeysuckle Rose	-	398-A	
Old Folks/Cottage for Sale	-	399-A	
Viper's Drag/ Alligator Crawl/ Handful of Keys	-	120-B	
Echo of Spring/Morning Air	-	400-B	

GENOVA DIXIELAND JAZZ BAND May 19, 1979 Genova, Italy

Fausto Rossi (t), Lucio Capobianco (tb), Carlo Casabona (sop), Ralph Sutton (p), Egidio Colombo (g), Luciano Milanese (b), Roberto Gargani (d).

At the Jazz Band Ball	FDC(I) 3002
Someday You'll Be Sorry	-
Echo of Spring	-

RALPH SUTTON & RUBY BRAFF October 29, 1979 New York

Ruby Braff (cnt), Ralph Sutton (p).

Get Out and Get Under the Moon	CJ 101
Think Well of Me	-
I'm Gonna Sit Right Down	-
Between the Devil and the Deep Blue Sea	-
'Tain't Nobody's Bizness	-
'Tain't So, Honey, 'Tain't So	-
Royal Garden Blues	-
Deep Summer Music	-
I Believe in Miracles	-
Keepin' Out of Mischief Now	-
Dinah	-
Ain't Misbehavin'	-

RALPH SUTTON & RUBY BRAFF October 30, 1979 New York

Ruby Braff (cnt), Ralph Sutton (p), Jack Lesberg (b), Gus Johnson (d).

Shoe Shine Boy	CJ 102
What Is There to Say?	-
Sweethearts on Parade	-
I Ain't Got Nobody	-
You Can Depend on Me	-
Big Butter and Egg Man	-
I Wished on the Moon	-
Sunday	-
I'm Crazy 'bout My Baby	-
Little Rock Getaway	-
I Would Do Anything for You	-

RALPH SUTTON December 10-11, 1979 North Hampton, New Hampshire
The Other Side of Ralph Sutton

Ralph Sutton (p).

Cattin' on the Keys	CJ 107
Lazy Mood	-
Stanley's Waltz	-
Say Yes	-
Brother, Can You Spare a Dime?	-
When Gabriel Blows His Horn	-
Keep Your Temper	-
Willow Tree	-
I'm Always in the Mood for You	-
Bond Street	-
If It Ain't Love	-
Honeysuckle Rose	-

Loose Shoes

RALPH SUTTON & KENNY DAVERN December 12-13, 1979 North Hampton, New Hampshire

Kenny Davern (cl, vcl), Ralph Sutton (p), Gus Johnson (d, vcl).

That's a Plenty	CJ 105
Jazz Me Blues	-
Gus Que Raf	-
Black and Blue	-
Take Me to the Land of Jazz (KD)	-
Sweet Lorraine (GJ)	-
My Honey's Lovin' Arms	-
Memphis Blues	-
I Would Do Anything for You	-
	CJ 106
St. Louis Blues	-
Am I Blue?	-
All by Myself	-
A Porter's Love Song to a Chambermaid	-
Old Fashioned Love	-
'Tain't Nobody's Bizness	-
My Daddy Rocks Me	-

RALPH SUTTON & JAY McSHANN December 15-16, 1979 New York
The Last of the Whorehouse Piano Players

Jay McShann, Ralph Sutton (p, vcl), Milt Hinton (b), Gus Johnson (d).

Little Rock Getaway	CJ 103	Chiar CR(D) 206 [CD]
Am I Blue?	-	-
All of Me (JM)	-	-
Honky Tonk Train	-	-
Rosetta	-	-
St. Louis Blues (JM)	-	-
Please Don't Talk About Me	-	-
Girl of My Dreams	-	-
	CJ 104	
I Got Rhythm	-	-
I'll Catch the Sun (JM)	-	-
Dog A Blues	-	-
Girl of My Dreams	-	-
Hootie's Ignorant Oil	-	-
Truckin' (RS)	-	-
Ain't Misbehavin'	-	-
After You've Gone	-	-
I Ain't Got Nobody	-	-
Variations on a Weeping Willow		-

RALPH SUTTON TRIO WITH THE REASONABLE BAND February 1981 Denver

Ralph Sutton (p, vcl), Charlie Burrell (b), Gus Johnson (d, vcl), Pat Browne III (g, vcl), Phil Esterbrook (man), David Harvey (man, fid, vcl), Doug Foulker (b).

I Ain't Got Nobody	Bare BR3322
The Object of My Affection	-
Confessin' (GJ)	-
Honeysuckle Rose	-
I'm Gonna Sit Right Down (RS)	-
Texas Blues	-
Honky Tonk Train	-
Stay All Night	-
Three Little Words	-
Stompin' at the Decca	-

Discography

RALPH SUTTON & THE JAZZBAND February 1981 Minneapolis

Ruby Braff (cnt), George Masso (tb), Kenny Davern (cl), Bud Freeman (ts), Ralph Sutton (p), Milt Hinton (b), Gus Johnson (d).

Struttin' with Some Barbecue	CJ 113
Keepin' Out of Mischief Now	-
Ain't Misbehavin'	-
Muskrat Ramble	-

RALPH SUTTON & JACK LESBERG March 3-28, 1981 New York
Live at Hanratty's

Ralph Sutton (p), Jack Lesberg (b).

Sophisticated Lady/In a Sentimental Mood/I Let a Song Go Out of My Heart	CJ 111
I'm Gonna Sit Right Down and Write Myself a Letter	-
All of Me	-
Honeysuckle Rose	-
I Ain't Got Nobody	-
Rosetta	-
I Found a New Baby	-

RALPH SUTTON March 3-28, 1981 New York
Live at Hanratty's

Ralph Sutton (p).

Morning Air	CJ CJC 201 [Cassette]
Rippling Waters	-
Everything Happens to Me	-
Slightly Less Than Wonderful	-
Give Me a June Night	-
Love Lies	-
Ain't Misbehavin'	-
I'm So Sorry for Myself	-
Eye Opener	-
This Is So Nice It Must Be Illegal	-
When I Grow Too Old to Dream	-
I've Got a Feelin' I'm Fallin'/ Keepin' Out of Mischief Now	-
Memories of You/On the Sunny Side of the Street	-
Sophisticated Lady/Ring Dem Bells	-
Indiana	-
St. Louis Blues	-
Confessin'	-

RALPH SUTTON & EDDIE MILLER March 17-21, 1981 New York
We've Got Rhythm

Eddie Miller (ts), Ralph Sutton (p).

I Got Rhythm	CJ 110
I've Got a Crush on You	-
Three Little Words	-
Sweet Lorraine	-
Lady, Be Good	-
Lazy Mood	-
Everybody Loves My Baby	-
Sugar	-

Loose Shoes

WOLVERINES JAZZ BAND   May 2, 1981   Bern, Switzerland
20 Years

Hans Zurbrügg (t), Rudolf Knöpfel (tb), Beat Uhlmann (cl, ts, sop), Ralph Sutton (p), Walter Sterchi (bj, g), Fredy Lüthi (b), Christian Ott (d).

Eccentric	PAN(Sw) PAN 132037
Yellow Dog Blues	-
Undecided	-
Royal Garden Blues	-
Honky Tonk Train*	-
I Got Rhythm	-
The Blues My Naughty Sweetie Gave to Me	-
Crazy Rhythm	-
In the Dark	-

*Add Heinz Geissbühler (p).

CHANGING TIMES JAZZ PARTY   July 8, 1981   Darien, Connecticut

Ruby Braff (cnt), Vic Dickenson (tb), Kenny Davern (cl), Al Klink (ts), Ralph Sutton (p), Marty Grosz (g), Jack Lesberg (b), Buzzy Drootin (d).

When You're Smiling	Private Recording [Cassette]
Mean to Me	-
Jeepers Creepers	-
Keepin' Out of Mischief Now	-
These Foolish Things	-
Somebody Stole My Gal	-

RALPH SUTTON & PEANUTS HUCKO   July 15, 1981   Wayzata, Minnesota
Big Noise from Wayzata

Peanuts Hucko (cl), Ralph Sutton (p), Jack Lesberg (b), Cliff Leeman (d).

Honeysuckle Rose	CJ 112
Memories of You	-
The World Is Waiting for the Sunrise	-
Ain't Misbehavin'	-
I Got Rhythm	-

FLAT FOOT STOMPERS & FRIENDS   November 9, 1981   Ludwigsburg, West Germany

Peter Bühr*, Peanuts Hucko (cl), Ralph Sutton (p), Jack Lesberg (b), Jake Hanna (d), Carrie Smith (vcl)**.

See You Again*	SP 8283
Keepin' Out of Mischief Now**	-

RALPH SUTTON & COSENZA JAZZ WORKSHOP   February 7-8, 1982   Cosenza, Italy
Great Piano Solos & Duets with Raffaele Borretti

Silvano Colloca (t), Gennaro Bruno (tb), Vincenzo Pace (cl, ts), Raffaele Borretti (p), Ralph Sutton (p, vcl), Franco Beltrano (g), Giuseppe Pallone (b), Ermanno del Trono (d).

On the Sunny Side of the Street	FDC 3003
Honeysuckle Rose	-
Echo of Spring	-
My Blue Heaven	-
Time on My Hands	-
I'm Gonna Sit Right Down/ It's a Sin to Tell a Lie/ Two Sleepy People	-
Nobody's Sweetheart/Ultime Foglie	-
Eye Opener*	-
O Sole Mio	-

*Labeled as Sneakaway.

Discography

RALPH SUTTON & VIC DICKENSON September 20, 1982 New York
Blowin' Bubbles

Vic Dickenson (tb, vcl), Ralph Sutton (p, vcl).

I'm Forever Blowing Bubbles	CJ 114
I'll Try	-
Constantly (VD)	-
I Ain't Got Nobody	-
Little Girl (VD)	-
If I Had You	-
Sweet Thing (RS)	-
A Good Man Is Hard to Find	-
My Baby Just Cares for Me (VD)	-
Exactly Like You	-

CHANGING TIMES JAZZ PARTY October 5, 1982 Boston

Bob Wilber (cl, sop), Nick Niles*, Ralph Sutton (p), Jack Lesberg (b), Buzzy Drootin (d).

There'll Be Some Changes Made	Private Recording [Cassette]
Keepin' Out of Mischief Now	-
I Guess I'll Have to Change My Plan	-
I Can't Give You Anything but Love*	-
Lady, Be Good	-
Limehouse Blues	-
Honeysuckle Rose	-
Indiana*	-
Jubilee	-
Jumpin' at the Woodside	-

CHANGING TIMES JAZZ PARTY October 7, 1982 New York

Joe Wilder (t), Vic Dickenson (tb), Bob Wilber (cl, sop), Nick Niles*, Ralph Sutton (p), Marty Grosz (g), Milt Hinton (b), Cliff Leeman (d).

Changes	Private Recording [Cassette]
Ain't Misbehavin'	-
Indiana*	-
Cherry	-
My Blue Heaven	-
I Got Rhythm	-
I Want a Little Girl	-
Sheik of Araby	-
Take the A Train	-

JACKIE MILLIET JAZZ BAND November 2, 1982 Schaffhausen, Switzerland

Roland Hug (t), Daniel Thomi (tb), Jackie Milliet (cl), Ralph Sutton (p, vcl), Jean-Yves Petiot (b), Georges Bernasconi (d).

Struttin' with Some Barbecue	Vogue VG 521001
I'm Gonna Sit Right Down and Write Myself a Letter	-
Muskrat Ramble	-
Basin Street Blues	-
Beale Street Blues	-
Clothesline Ballet	-
Clarinet Call Rag	-
That Dada Strain	-

Loose Shoes

RALPH SUTTON & BOB BARNARD August 25, 1983 New York
Partners in Crime

Bob Barnard (t), Ralph Sutton (p), Milt Hinton (b), Len Barnard (d).

Swing That Music	Dia SVL505	SK(Can) C1-2023 [Cassette]	C2-2023 [CD]
One Morning in May	-	-	-
Old Folks	-	-	-
Rain	-	-	-
I Never Knew	-	-	-
Slow Boat to China	-	-	-
It's Wonderful	-	-	-
How Can You Face Me?	-	-	-
West End Avenue Blues	-	-	-
Diga Diga Do	-	-	-

CHANGING TIMES JAZZ PARTY September 21, 1983 New York

Yank Lawson (t), Eddie Hubble (tb), Bob Wilber (cl, sop), Sam Margolis (ts), Nick Niles*, Ralph Sutton (p), Jack Lesberg (b), Buzzy Drootin (d).

After You've Gone	Private Recording [Cassette]
Wolverine Blues*	-
Wabash Blues	-
Exactly Like You	-
Struttin' with Some Barbecue	-
Honeysuckle Rose	-
St. Louis Blues	-
Keepin' Out of Mischief Now	-
There'll Be Some Changes Made*	-
I Found a New Baby	

CHANGING TIMES JAZZ PARTY October 20, 1983 Boston

Bob Wilber (cl, sop), Nick Niles*, Ralph Sutton (p), Jack Lesberg (b), Buzzy Drootin (d).

Tea for Two	Private Recording [Cassette]
Honeysuckle Rose	-
Ain't Misbehavin'	-
You Took Advantage of Me	-
Fine and Dandy	-
There'll Be Some Changes Made	-
St. Louis Blues*	-
Jubilee	-
Sweet Lorraine	-
When You're Smiling	-

RALPH SUTTON 1983-1987 Toronto
At Cafe des Copains

Ralph Sutton (p).

Laugh Clown Laugh (2-7-84)	SK(Can) C1-2019 [Cassette]	C2-2019 [CD]
You Can Depend on Me (2-7-84)	-	-
Poor Butterfly (1-28-87)	-	-
Snowy Morning Blues (2-7-84)	-	-
Russian Lullaby (2-8-85)	-	-
Sweet Sue (1-28-87)	-	-
This Is All I Ask (1-28-87)	-	-
Somebody Stole My Gal (1-28-87)	-	-
St. Louis Blues (2-7-84)	-	-
My Blue Heaven (2-7-84)	-	-
Exactly Like You (6-1-83)	-	-
Christopher Columbus (2-8-85)	-	-

Discography

LEGENDS OF JAZZ January 5 & 9, 1984 Taos Ski Valley, New Mexico
Jazz at Thunderbird Lodge

Kenny Davern (cl), Ralph Sutton (p), Milt Hinton (b), Gus Johnson (d).

Everybody Loves My Baby	Private Recording [Cassette]
I Got Rhythm	-
Joshua Fit the Battle of Jericho	-
Love Me or Leave Me	-
My Honey's Lovin' Arms	-
Please Don't Talk About Me	-
Echo of Spring	-
Lover, Come Back to Me	-
Keepin' Out of Mischief Now	-
New Orleans	-
After You've Gone	-
These Foolish Things	-
Exactly Like You	-

PENINSULA JAZZ PARTY '84 July 27-28, 1984 Menlo Park, California

Billy Butterfield (t), Trummy Young (tb, vcl), Kenny Davern (cl), Jim Galloway (sop), Eddie Miller (ts), Barbara Sutton Curtis, Jay McShann, Ralph Sutton (p), Red Callender, Jack Lesberg (b), Nick Fatool, Butch Miles (d), Phil Harris (vcl).

That's a Plenty	Private Recording [Cassette]
Lady, Be Good	-
Sophisticated Lady	-
I Ain't Got Nobody	-
I Never Knew What Love Could Do	-
Sometimes I'm Happy	-
Mack the Knife	-
She's Funny That Way	-
Old Fashioned Love	-
Basin Street Blues	-

CHANGING TIMES JAZZ PARTY September 25, 1984 New York

Ed Polcer (cnt), Dan Barrett (tb), Bob Wilber (cl, sop), Buddy Tate (ts), Nick Niles*, Ralph Sutton (p), Jack Lesberg (b), Butch Miles (d).

From Monday On	Private Recording [Cassette]
Someday	-
St. Louis Blues*	-
Somebody Stole My Gal	-
Ain't Misbehavin'	-
I Would Do Anything for You	-
Basin Street Blues	-
You're Driving Me Crazy	-
Hindustan	-

FLAT FOOT STOMPERS & FRIENDS October 21, 1984 Ludwigsburg, West Germany

Ernst Eckstein (cnt), Roland Muller (tb), Kenny Davern (cl), George Kelly (ts), Peter Bühr (sop, bs), Ralph Sutton (p), Wolfram Grotz (cel), Werner Neidhardt (bj), Milt Hinton (b), Uli Reichle (sous), Gus Johnson (d).

Eccentric	Ti TTD529
Wolverine Blues*	-

*Omit Grotz and Neidhardt.

October 23, 1984

Peter Bühr (sop), Ralph Sutton (p), Milt Hinton (b), Gus Johnson (d).

Indian Summer/My Inspiration	Ti TTD529

373

Loose Shoes

JAZZ LEGENDS (Vol. 1) January 2-18, 1985 Taos Ski Valley, New Mexico

Kenny Davern (cl), Flip Phillips (ts, bcl*), Buddy Tate (ts), Ralph Sutton (p), Herb Ellis, Bucky Pizzarelli (g), Milt Hinton (b), Gus Johnson (d).

Moonglow	Private Recording [Cassette]
Body and Soul	-
Tea for Two	-
Rosetta	-
Sheik of Araby	-
All of Me	-
Sweet and Lovely	-
Old Man Time	-
Jumpin' at the Woodside	-

(Vol. 2)

Viper's Drag	-
Just Friends	-
Fascinatin' Rhythm	-
'S Wonderful	-
Nature Boy*	-
Sweet Georgia Brown	-
Deep Purple	-
Broadway	-
I Surrender, Dear	-

CHANGING TIMES JAZZ PARTY June 15, 1985 Bloomfield Hills, Michigan

Joe Wilder (t), Dan Barrett (tb), Bob Wilber (cl, sop), Nick Niles*, Ralph Sutton (p), Jeff Halsey (b), J.C. Heard (d).

Lady, Be Good	Private Recording [Cassette]
Do You Know What It Means	-
All of Me*	-
Ain't Misbehavin'	-
I Got Rhythm	-
There'll Be Some Changes Made	-
St. Louis Blues*	-
It's All in Your Mind	-
Alligator Crawl	-
You Turned the Tables on Me	-
I Can't Give You Anything but Love	-

SACKVILLE ALL STARS March 29-30, 1986 Toronto
Christmas Record

Jim Galloway (sop), Ralph Sutton (p), Milt Hinton (b), Gus Johnson (d).

Santa Claus Is Coming to Town	SK(Can) 3038	C1-3038 [Cassette]	C2-3038 [CD]
We Three Kings	-	-	-
At the Christmas Ball	-	-	-
Winter Wonderland	-	-	-
Go Tell It on the Mountain	-	-	-
Good King Wenceslas	-	-	-
Santa Claus Came in the Spring	-	-	-
Silent Night	-	-	-
Let It Snow	-	-	-
Old Time Religion	-	-	-

Discography

CHANGING TIMES JAZZ PARTY　　　July 22, 1986　　　Los Angeles

Ed Polcer (cnt), Kenny Davern (cl), Nick Niles*, Ralph Sutton (p), Jack Lesberg (b), Jake Hanna (d).

There'll Be Some Changes Made	Private Recording [Cassette]
You Can Depend on Me	-
On the Sunny Side of the Street*	-
Dinah	-
Hindustan	-
Indiana	-
Rosetta	-
Ain't Misbehavin'	-
I Can't Give You Anything but Love*	-
I Got Rhythm	-

CHANGING TIMES JAZZ PARTY　　　September 23, 1986　　　Chicago

Ed Polcer (cnt), George Masso (tb), Bob Wilber (cl, sop), Nick Niles*, Ralph Sutton (p), Jack Lesberg (b), Bobby Rosengarden (d).

Chicago	Private Recording [Cassette]
Keepin' Out of Mischief Now	-
St. Louis Blues (NN & RS)	-
I Guess I'll Have to Change My Plan	-
Indiana*	-
There'll Be Some Changes Made (NN & RS)	-
Ain't Misbehavin (NN & RS)	-
Dinah	-
On the Sunny Side of the Street*	-
Struttin' with Some Barbecue	-

PIANO PLAYERS & SIGNIFICANT OTHERS*　　　July 28, 1987　　　New York

Ralph Sutton (p).

Eye Opener	MM 5042-2-C
Viper's Drag	-

July 20, 1988

Dick Hyman, Derek Smith, Ralph Sutton (p).

Nagasaki	MM 5042-2-C

*This recording also features pianists Roger Kellaway, Jay McShann, Marian McPartland, and Dick Wellstood.

RALPH SUTTON　　　June 1987　　　Tokyo
After You've Gone

Ralph Sutton (p).

You Took Advantage of Me	PC D28P6121 [CD]
Clothesline Ballet	-
Honeysuckle Rose	-
Love Lies	-
Honky Tonk Train	-
Don't Blame Me	-
Taking a Chance on Love	-
I Guess I'll Go Back Home/ Old Folks	-
Alligator Crawl	-
Ain't Misbehavin'	-
Viper's Drag	-
After You've Gone	-

Loose Shoes

SACKVILLE ALL STARS June 20-21, 1988 Toronto
A Tribute to Louis Armstrong

Jim Galloway (sop, bs), Ralph Sutton (p), Milt Hinton (b), Gus Johnson (d).

Song of the Islands	SK(Can) 3042	C1-3042 [Cassette]	C2-3042 [CD]
You Rascal You	-	-	-
Save It, Pretty Mama	-	-	-
On the Sunny Side of the Street	-	-	-
Willie the Weeper	-	-	-
I Got a Right to Sing the Blues			-
A Kiss to Build a Dream On	-	-	-
Big Butter and Egg Man	-	-	-
Pennies from Heaven	-	-	-
Keepin' Out of Mischief Now	-	-	-
Sweethearts on Parade			-

RALPH SUTTON & KENNY DAVERN August 1988 Adelaide, Australia
Revelations

Kenny Davern (cl), Ralph Sutton (p), Bill Polain (d).

Shine	JazHi A8801 [Cassette]
New Orleans	-
Three Little Words	-
Indiana	-
Ellington Medley	-
In a Sentimental Mood/Sophisticated Lady/Ring Dem Bells	
Sugar	-
Should I	-

RALPH SUTTON & JAY McSHANN March 27-28, 1989 Englewood Cliffs, New Jersey
Last of the Whorehouse Piano Players

Jay McShann (p, vcl), Ralph Sutton (p), Milt Hinton (b), Gus Johnson (d).

Honey	Chiar CR(D) 306
Old Fashioned Love	-
'Fore Day Rider	-
On the Sunny Side of the Street	-
Sweet Georgia Brown	-
Do Wah	-
Indiana	-
'Deed I Do	-
Crazy Rhythm	-
Cherry	-
Pretty Baby	-
I Found a New Baby	-
JazzSpeak	-

MILT HINTON March 28, 1989 Englewood Cliffs, New Jersey
Old Man Time

Ralph Sutton (p), Milt Hinton (b), Gus Johnson (d).

Time on My Hands	Chiar CR(D) 310

Discography

RALPH SUTTON   April 7, 1990   Woking, England
Eye Opener

Ralph Sutton (p).

Rippling Waters	J&M(E) CD500 [CD]
Viper's Drag	-
Memories of You/Taking a Chance on Love*	-
Gone with the Wind	-
I Found a New Baby	-
Clothesline Ballet	-
Honey Hush	-
When I Grow Too Old to Dream	-
Eye Opener	-
Give Me a June Night	-
Old Fashioned Love	-
Honeysuckle Rose	-
Old Folks/Sharecropper's Blues/Cottage for Sale/'Tain't So, Honey, 'Tain't So	-
Alligator Crawl	-

*Taking a Chance on Love not listed in liner notes.

STRIDE PIANO SUMMIT*   June 15, 1990   San Francisco

Ralph Sutton (p).

Eye Opener	Mile MCD 9189-2 [CD]
Clothesline Ballet	-
Old Fashioned Love**	-
Dinah***	-

*This recording also features pianists Dick Hyman, Mike Lipskin, and Jay McShann.
**Add Jay McShann (p), Red Callender (b), Harold Jones (d).
***Omit McShann.

1991 TRIANGLE JAZZ PARTY BOYS   September 29, 1991   Raleigh, North Carolina

Randy Sandke (t), Dan Barrett (tb), Chuck Hedges (cl), Rick Fay (ts, sop), Ralph Sutton (p), Jack Lesberg (b), Jake Hanna (d).

Indiana	FIN 101*	FINCD 101 [CD]*
Under the Moonlight Starlight Blue	-	-
I Can't Give You Anything but Love	-	-
I'm Gonna Sit Right Down	-	-
Triangle Jazz Blues	-	-
Ghost of a Chance	-	-
I'll Be a Friend with Pleasure	-	-
Just Friends**	-	-
Sweet Lorraine	-	-
Blues for Gus Johnson	-	-
I Found a New Baby	-	-

* Produced by Arbors Rexcords.
**Add George Broussard (tb).

BARBARA SUTTON CURTIS   November 2, 1988 & November 8, 1989   Toronto

Barbara Sutton Curtis (p).

Honey Hush	SK SKCD2-2027 [CD]
Oh Baby, Sweet Baby	-
Hootie Blues	-
Don't Let the Sun Catch You Crying	-
"A Flat" Dream	-
Davenport Blues	-

                                                 November 17, 1991   Baden, Switzerland

Why Am I Alone	-
Oriental Tones	-
Crazy Rhythm*	-
These Foolish Things**	-
Love Me or Leave Me*	-
Keepin' Out of Mischief Now**	-
St. Louis Blues*	-
Chicago*	-

*Add Ralph Sutton (p), Reggie Johnson (b), Jake Hanna (d).
**Add Ralph Sutton (p).

Loose Shoes

OSCAR KLEIN INTERNATIONAL CHICAGO JAZZ ORCHESTRA July 1992 Zurich, Switzerland

Oscar Klein (t, har), Bill Allred (tb, vcl), Heinz Bigler (cl), Bruno Longhi (ts), Ralph Sutton (p), Roman Dylag (b), Rolf Rebmann (d).

Struttin' with Some Barbecue	PA 82018 [CD]
As Time Goes By	-
St. Louis Blues	-
China Boy	-
On the Sunny Side of the Street	-
Who's Sorry Now	-
Just a Blues	-
There'll Be Some Changes Made	-
I'm Always in the Mood for You	-
Indiana	-
Some of These Days	-
Dinah	-
Make Believe	-
Ida	-
Jada	-

RALPH SUTTON August 8, 1993 Berkeley, California
At Maybeck

Ralph Sutton (p).

Honeysuckle Rose	Con CCD-4586 [CD]
In a Mist	-
Clothesline Ballet	-
In the Dark	-
Ain't Misbehavin'	-
Echo of Spring	-
Dinah	-
Love Lies	-
Russian Lullaby	-
St. Louis Blues	-
Viper's Drag	-
After You've Gone	-

Index

Adams, Armon 38-39, 40, 188-190
Ain't Misbehavin' (musical) 240
Al Capone Memorial Jazz Band 177
Albright, Gail 33-35, 38-39, 188-189
Alden, Howard (guitar) 259, 289, 292, 303, 319, 325, 339
Alderson, Barbara 77-78, 223, 300
Alexander, Monte (piano) 259
Alexander, Mousie (drums) 130, 143, 200
Allen, Red (trumpet) 68, 114
Alley, Vernon (bass) 104
Allred, Bill (trombone) 314
Altvater, Mary Ann 235-236
Altvater, Roger 235-236
American Jazz Hall of Fame 312
Anderson, Mr. 174-175
Anderson, Arthur 122, 247, 255
Anderson, Eleanor 335-336
Anderson, Ernest 80
Anderson, Irene 122, 247, 262, 308
Anderson, Sunnie (see Sutton, Sunnie)
Appleyard, Peter (vibes) 221, 247, 253
Archey, Jimmy (trombone) 58, 94
Armstrong, Louis (trumpet) 9, 57, 95, 128, 248-249, 254, 267, 312, 329, 338
Armstrong, Lucille (piano) 210
Ash, Marvin (piano) 176-177
Atlantic Club 217
Aurthur, Bob 75
Autobiography of Black Jazz, An 5

Bacin, Bill 179-180
Bacos, George 9-10
Bailey, Mildred (singer) 312

Bailey, O.J. 47-48
Baker, Bonnie (singer) 59
Ballenger, Bob 177
Barker, Danny (guitar) 58
Barman, Herb (drums) 107
Barnard, Bob (trumpet) 254, 256-258, 270, 304, 310, 338
Barnard, Len (drums) 257, 270, 304
Barnes, George (guitar) 133-134, 152, 246
Barnes, Russell 218-221
Barnet, Charlie (tenor sax) 9
Barney Gould's Gold Rush Steak House 147
Baron, Charlie 70-71, 86-92, 113, 114, 245-246, 252
Barrell Bar 61-63
Barrett, Andy 304
Barrett, Dan (trombone) 11, 269, 288-290, 292, 304, 306, 315, 324, 338, 339
Basie, Catherine 175-176
Basie, Count (piano) 97, 107, 174-176, 254, 312, 319, 325
Bastien, Bill (bass) 145-146
Bauduc, Ray (drums) 264
Baum, Lewis C. 40, 42
BBC 221-223, 225, 227
Bechet, Sidney (soprano sax) 58, 254, 261
Beiderbecke, Bix (cornet, composer) 64, 65, 70, 81, 82, 97, 109, 111, 184-185, 248, 272, 301, 312, 317, 339
Bell, Aaron (bass) 108
Beltrano, Franco (guitar) 299
Beneke, Tex (tenor sax) 217

Berigan, Bunny (trumpet) 249
Bettencourt, Frank (piano) 230
Big Horn Jazz Festival 178
Biggerstaff, John 42
Bigler, Heinz (clarinet) 314
Bill Muchnic's San Diego Jazz Party 295
Billings, Deane (bass) 126
Billings, Josh (suitcase) 74
Black, Dave (drums) 93
Blades, Dottie 288-290
Blades, Josh 289-290, 304
Blades, Mike 288-290
Blades, Steve 288-290, 304
Blake, Eubie (piano, composer) 108, 204, 210, 212
Blake, Marion 204
Blandford Jazz Circle 218-221
Blesh, Rudi 58, 74-75, 108
Blowers, Johnny (drums) 56, 58
Blue Angel 51
Blum, Lou 87, 89
Bob Cats 1, 132, 242, 264-265
Bodner, Phil (clarinet) 303
Bolger, Ray (dancer, singer) 235
Borretti, Raffaele (piano) 299-300
Boulevard Room 102
Bower, Roy (trumpet) 217
Bowman's, Roy 48
Boyd, Brian G. 311
Bradley, Will (trombone) 212
Braff, Ruby (cornet) 130, 143, 149, 246, 253, 257, 284
Braud, Wellman (bass) 107
Brewer, Teresa (singer) 206
Brooks, Harry (piano) 96
Broussard, George (trombone) 11, 290
Brown, Barbara 147
Brown, Lawrence (trombone) 108
Brown, Mitchell 147
Brown, Ray (bass) 259
Brown Palace 145, 150
Brownell, Elisabeth 258-260
Brownell, Tom 258-260
Bruehl, Marty 200

Brunis, Georg (trombone) 64, 67, 68
Bryant, Ray (piano) 254
Buchanan, Doris 156-158
Buchanan, John 156-158
Bühr, Peter (clarinet) 280
Burdick, Larry 234
Burns, Gene (drums) 113
Burns, Ralph (piano) 140
Burrell, Kenny (guitar) 254
Burtscher, Margrit (see Geiger, Margrit)
Bush, George 315
Bushkin, Joe (piano) 114
Butterfield, Billy (trumpet, flugelhorn) 2, 47, 64, 82, 151, 152, 200, 208, 264, 339
Byas, Don (tenor sax) 249

Cafe des Copains 10, 256, 272, 280-282, 311, 326
Cafe Kandahar 261-262
Calabrese, Anthony 174
Callender, Red (bass) 284, 324, 339
Calloway, Cab (singer) 258
Campanella, Roy 175
Candoli, Conte (trumpet) 259
Canterbury Hotel 95
Capp, Frank (drums) 338
Carlos I 284
Carmichael, Hoagy (composer, piano) 108
Carmichael, Judy (piano) 276
Carnegie Hall 266, 277
Carpenter, Lillian 27-28, 35
Carr, Ian 6
Carter, Benny (alto sax, trumpet) 254, 312
Carter, Betty (singer) 312
Cary, Dick (piano, trumpet, alto horn) 63, 69-70, 83, 94, 158
Casey, Al (guitar) 247
Casey, Bob (bass) 74, 114
Castle, Lee (trumpet) 64
Central Plaza 68
Chaix, Henri (piano) 254

Index

Chase Hotel 48-49, 51, 53
Cheatham, Doc (trumpet) 88, 254
Chester, Gary (drums) 59
Chung's Restaurant 328
Clayton, Buck (trumpet) 132, 254
Cless, Rod (clarinet) 114
Cleveland, Carter 280
Cleveland, Paul M. 278-280
Clifford, Peggy 2, 129-130, 133, 147-149, 154-155
Clinton, Bill 315
Coe, Barbara (see Alderson, Barbara)
Cohn, Al (tenor sax) 139, 339
Cole, Cozy (drums) 88
Cole, Florence 161, 238
Coleman, Bill (trumpet) 210, 254
Coller, Derek 169-170, 311-312
Colonel's Ranchwagon 113
Colonial Tavern 169
Combs, Betsy Fulkerson 33, 51
Commodore Music Shop 87, 89
Condon, Eddie (guitar) 56, 63, 64, 66, 68, 69, 71, 73, 74, 76, 78, 82, 83, 85, 91, 109-110, 132, 234, 327
Condon's, Eddie 1, 17, 55-56, 63-74, 76-78, 81-84, 87-91, 95-96, 99, 109-110, 118, 119, 124, 132, 153, 188, 200, 215-216, 221, 223, 227, 232, 235, 240, 242, 278-279, 300, 317, 319, 337
Conger, Al (bass) 96, 104
Conger, Larry (trumpet) 95-96, 104, 132-133, 170
Conger, Mary 132
Continental Denver Hotel 212-213
Cook, Eddie 253
Coon, Jackie (flugelhorn) 280
Corbalis, Laina 287
Cotton Club 277
Crazy Fingers 5
Cregg, Hugh A., Jr. 104, 113
Crosby, Bing (singer) 93-94, 105-106, 153, 267
Crosby, Bob (singer) 1, 132, 152, 264
Crump, Tiny (piano) 93

Crystal, Billy 87
Crystal, Jack 87, 89
Cullum, Jim, Jr. (cornet) 141, 266, 268, 277, 339
Cullum, Jim, Sr. (clarinet) 141, 266-267
Culter, Bill 42-43, 267
Curtis, Barbara Sutton (piano) 8, 17-18, 22-23, 25, 27, 28, 29, 38, 68-69, 96, 103-104, 113, 126, 133, 144, 211, 222, 225, 248, 256, 274-275, 280-282, 285, 307-308, 310-311, 313
Curtis, Hal 17-18, 67-69, 93, 103, 109, 113, 144, 167, 211, 248-249, 274-275, 281, 310, 313
Curtis, Terry (see Manning, Terry Curtis)
Cushing, Alex 101, 103-106
Cutshall, Cutty (trombone) 68, 88, 132, 149, 150, 152, 153

Dahlander, Bert (drums) 139
Dance, Stanley 107
Davern, Elsa 210, 259, 274-275, 285-287, 326
Davern, Kenny (clarinet) 210, 228, 230-231, 246-247, 255, 259, 274-275, 276, 279, 285-287, 289, 292, 300, 303, 310, 316, 319, 320, 325-326, 337, 338
Davies Symphony Hall 284
Davis, Charles 176
Davis, Eddie (Lockjaw) (tenor sax) 242, 339
Davis, Russ (bass, clarinet, sax) 228, 230
Davis, Wild Bill (organ) 254
Davison, Anne 69
Davison, Wild Bill (cornet) 55-56, 58, 67, 68, 69, 72, 82, 88, 100, 126-127, 149, 233-234, 249, 339
De Paris, Wilbur (trombone) 108
Decker, Duane 73
Denver Jazz Club 98-99, 141, 305, 315
Dickenson, Vic (trombone) 2, 88-89, 181, 208, 238, 247, 254, 339
Dinah's Shack 46

381

"Dixieland North" 231
Dodds, Baby (drums) 58
Dodge, Joe (drums) 104
Dorsey, Jimmy (alto sax, clarinet) 64, 214
Dorsey, Tommy (trombone) 64, 249
Dozier, J.C. 160
"Dr. Jazz" 76
Drew's Blues 53
Drootin, Buzzy (drums) 74, 83-84, 88-89, 109-110, 209
Duggan, Evelyn 123
Duncan, Hank (piano) 175
Duncan, Louise (piano) 124, 130, 138, 339
Duvivier, George (bass) 339
Dyne, Paul (bass) 279

Earthquake McGoon's 147
Eastwood, Clint 234
Easy Street 95-96
Ebert, Corinne 19, 20, 21, 25, 26, 27
Eckinger, Isla (bass) 243
Eddy, Jane 302
Edison, Harry (Sweets) (trumpet) 242
Eight Greats of Jazz 150-151
Eisenhower, Dwight D. 192
Eldridge, Roy (trumpet) 314
Elitch Gardens 7, 150, 155-156, 210, 304
Elkins, Howard (guitar, banjo) 306
Ellington, Duke (piano, composer) 9, 19, 93, 107, 108, 147, 175, 248-249, 270, 285, 312, 329, 331
Ellington, Mercer (trumpet, composer) 175
Ellis, Herb (guitar) 259
Emporium of Jazz 202, 204
Encore Lounge 83
Erstrand, Lars (vibes) 266
Erwin, Pee Wee (trumpet) 247
Evans, Bill (piano) 312
Executive Tower Inn 233, 240

Fairmont Hotel 107

Fairweather, Digby (cornet) 6, 233
Famous Door 56-57, 119
Fatool, Nick (drums) 94
"Fats" in Fact 196
Fats Waller 174
Fats Waller Memorial Jazz Festival 285, 313-314
Fay, Rick (tenor sax, soprano sax) 289
Feld, Morey (drums) 68, 124, 146, 149, 150-151
Felice, Dee (drums) 111
Figueroa, Ernie (trumpet, bass) 104, 111, 173
Fina, Jack (piano) 52-53
Fitzgerald, Ella (singer) 9, 107, 175, 249
Flamingo 93
Flanagan, Tommy (piano) 254
Flanigan, Phil (bass) 259, 339
Flat Foot Stompers 280
Flory, Chris (guitar) 339
Folly Theater 283
Fontana, Carl (trombone) 151, 259
For Listeners Only 88-89, 222
Ford, Betty 234
Ford, Gerald 234
Forrest, Jimmy (tenor sax) 62, 325
Foster, Pops (bass) 58, 94, 113-114
400 Club 55
Fox and Hounds 217
Francis, Panama (drums) 210
Freeman, Bud (tenor sax) 2, 7, 64, 81, 88, 151, 152, 156, 167, 184, 189, 210, 217, 241-242, 246, 304, 338-339
Fridley, Currier 20
Friends In Need 11, 289-290
Frog & Nightgown 176
Fuerman, Leonard 23-24, 36, 37, 44
Fulcher, O.A. (Jim) 124-125, 131
Funaro, Bill 66-67, 70

Gaiman, Hymie 62-63
Gallacher, Ken 152-153, 169
Galloway, Jim (soprano sax) 259, 265-266, 273, 280, 310, 326-327

Galloway, Rosemary (bass) 326
Garber, Jan 230
Garner, Erroll (piano) 100, 222, 254
Gauvin, Aime 76-77
Geiger, Margrit 242-245
Geiger, Mat 132, 242-245
Gibson, Dick 118-121, 124, 129, 131, 136, 142, 150-155, 157, 158, 179, 181, 193, 235, 245, 287, 290-291, 317-318, 320
Gibson, Don (piano) 177
Gibson, Maddie 118, 120, 136, 179
Gibson Girl Lounge 110-111
Gieg, Colin (bass) 212, 305, 315
Giese, Steve 197-198
Gillespie, Dizzy (trumpet) 312
Gleason, Jackie 70
Gleason, Ralph J. 95
Glenn Ranch Jazz Party 300
Godfrey, Bernie (drums) 218
Goepfert, Arthur 81
Goetze, John 42
Golden Belle 228, 233, 241, 256
Goodman, Benny (clarinet) 9, 206, 212, 214, 269-270, 312
Gordon, Helen 187-188
Gordon, James L. 187-188
Gowans, Brad (valve trombone) 64
Green, Dave (bass) 243-244
Greenspan, Al 71
Greenwood, Juanita 338
Grey, Al (trombone) 62, 107, 255, 292, 325
Gross, Charlie 21
Grossman, Alex 102, 117
Grosz, Marty (guitar) 289, 306, 309, 319
Gurtler, Jack 150-151, 154
Guy, Barbara 290-293
Guy, Peter 290-293

Hackett, Bobby (cornet) 64, 94, 139, 185, 206, 208, 214, 323, 339
Haggart, Bob (bass) 2, 150-153, 156, 167-168, 170-171, 176, 182, 189, 210, 215, 242, 259, 264, 276, 295, 303, 315, 316

Hall, Al (bass) 130, 141-142
Hall, Edmond (clarinet) 58, 68, 72, 73, 83, 84, 88, 124, 126, 149, 265, 302
Hall, Herb (clarinet) 132
Hall Brothers 202
Hamer, Bill 278, 309
Hamilton, Scott (tenor sax) 259, 292, 315, 327-328, 339
Hamlin, Jesse 284-285
Hampton, Lionel (vibes) 254, 302
Hangover Club 74, 84, 94, 96, 98, 101
Hanna, Denisa 274, 316
Hanna, Jake (drums) 138-140, 221, 253-254, 259, 271, 274, 280, 289, 292, 305, 309-310, 315, 316
Hanna, Roland (piano) 252
Hanratty's 248, 258, 276, 333
Happy Jazz Band 141, 267
Happy Medium 2, 177
Harbourfront Festival 273
"Harlem Rhythm" 19
Havens, Bob (trombone) 269
Havens, Dan (trumpet) 111-112
Hawes, Pat (piano) 312-313
Hawkins, Coleman (tenor sax) 254, 314
Hayes, Clancy (banjo, guitar, singer) 93, 126, 149, 150, 157-158
Haynes, Johnny (bass) 132
Hedges, Chuck (clarinet) 289
Heidbreder, Edward 32, 35-36, 156
Heidbreder, Marie 156
Heinz, John 98-99
Helleny, Joel (trombone) 339
Helms, Jesse 338
Henderson, Fletcher (piano, arranger) 19
Henrich, Tommy 112
Herby's Bar 233-235, 240-241
Herman, Woody (clarinet) 249
Herth, Milt (organ) 59-60, 132
Hewitt, Mark 241-242, 256-258
Heyn, James M. 178
Hickox, Barker 181

Higginbotham, J.C. (trombone) 55
Higgins, Eddie (piano) 259
Hines, Earl (piano) 94, 107, 113, 248, 254, 312
Hinton, Milt (bass) 6, 130, 139, 142-143, 174-176, 200, 230, 245-247, 250-252, 254, 255, 256, 257-258, 259, 264, 265-266, 271, 273, 275, 284, 292, 295-299, 300, 303, 304, 309, 316, 319, 320, 321, 338
Hinton, Mona 174-175, 274, 295, 297, 316
Hirsch, Bob (piano) 204-205, 285
Hodges, Johnny (alto sax) 108, 254
Hoeffler, Paul J. 256, 273
Hohengarten, Carl (conductor, arranger) 51
Holiday, Billie (singer) 254
Hollenbeck, C. Fred 23, 24, 31, 33
Holley, Major (bass) 124, 289, 303-304, 339
Homeyer, Eve 290-293
Hope, Bob 234
Hopkins, Claude (piano) 5
Hopper, J. Lee 176-177
Hopper, Kate 176
Hopper, Tex 176
Horne, Lena (singer) 175
Horowitz, Max 113
Horwitz, Victor 274
Hotel Innere Enge 316
Howard, Darnell (clarinet) 94
Howell, Francis 14
Hubble, Eddie (trombone) 2
Hucko, Peanuts (clarinet) 56, 95, 109, 145-146, 149, 150-151, 152, 153, 157, 162, 193, 208, 210, 212-214, 216, 221, 246, 247, 253-254, 305
Hudson, George 62
Huesemann, Warren (Red) 39, 40
Hughes, Dick 270
Hughes, Jody 203
Hughes, Rush 55
Hutton, Jack 282

Hyman, Dick (piano) 252, 268, 273, 275, 277, 284-285, 289, 292, 306, 314, 315, 317-318, 335

Inn of the Golden West 124

Jacquet, Illinois (tenor sax) 175, 254, 314
James, Harry (trumpet) 212
Janis, Conrad (trombone) 68
Janis, Harriet 58
Jarratt, Curt (bass) 229-232
Jarratt, Mildred 229
Jaylin's Club 265, 302
Jazz: The Essential Companion 6
Jazz Legends 259
Jazz Party, The 275, 287, 337
"Jazz Show, The" 248-249
Jeffrey, John 85
Jenkins, Gordon (arranger) 51
Jenson, Joya 304
Jerome, Hotel 120, 154, 290-293, 304, 305, 315
Jerome Jazz 290-293, 314-315
Jim Cullum Jazz Band 266-269, 277, 294, 306, 338
Johnson, Budd (tenor sax) 312
Johnson, Dennis 203-204
Johnson, Gus (drums) 2, 6, 107, 139, 167, 170, 181, 183, 189, 201, 208, 216, 228-233, 241, 242-244, 245-246, 247, 250-252, 253, 255, 256, 258, 259, 264, 265-266, 271, 273, 276, 284, 289-290, 292, 299, 300, 303, 305, 309, 315, 320, 321, 324, 329, 339
Johnson, James P. (piano) 57, 82, 95, 109, 113, 170, 175, 184-185, 212, 219, 241, 254, 262, 284, 295, 319, 326
Johnson, Leslie 202-204
Johnson, Mildred 244, 258, 290, 305
Johnson, Pete (piano) 186
Johnson, Reggie (bass) 310
Johnson, Renee 203

Index

Johnson, Tony 203
Jones, Jo (drums) 242
Jones, Jonah (trumpet) 74
Jones, Wayne (drums) 178
Joplin, Scott 82
Jordan, Louis (alto sax) 95
Jose, Amos E. 24, 32, 36
"Joy-A-Jazz, The" 304

Kambestad, Karen 269-270, 277, 306
Kaminsky, Max (trumpet) 56, 60
Kasinecz, Debbie 198
Kathan, Marge 198
Katz, Alex 261
Keillor, Garrison 202
Keller, Werner (clarinet) 243
Kennedy Center for the Performing Arts 167
Kennington, Alan (bass) 218
Kessel, Barney (guitar) 259
Kiely, John 272
Kienberger, Charles A. 31-32
Kilgallen, Dorothy 57
Kirk, Andy 19
Kirk, Todd 40
Kirkeby, Ed 79
Klein, Oscar (trumpet) 314
Kleinjan, Colleen 231
Kleinjan, Jasper 231-232
Klink, Al (tenor sax) 217
Korsunsky, Konrad R. 310-311
Krell, William H. 203
Kriegsman, Sig 274-275
Krupa, Gene (drums) 64, 242
Kyle, Billy (piano) 140

Lackey, Jim (drums) 132
Lafitte, Guy (tenor sax) 254
Lamare, Nappy (guitar, banjo, singer) 1, 186, 264, 339
Lambert, Eddie 170
Landers, Bob 114
Landing, The 268, 306
Lascelles, Gerald 79, 169

Last of the Whorehouse Piano Players 6, 245, 247, 250-253, 256, 261, 264, 266, 283-284, 299
Lawson, Yank (trumpet) 2, 150-153, 156, 167-168, 170, 181, 183, 189, 201, 206, 210, 217, 230, 264, 273, 280, 292, 303, 310
Lawson-Haggart Jazz Band 152
Ledbetter, George 51, 59-60
Lee, Chris (drums) 315
Leeman, Cliff (drums) 70, 72, 82, 130, 132, 140-142, 150-152, 157, 179, 212, 247, 326, 339
Lemmon, Jack 234
Leonhart, Jay (bass, singer) 295-299, 339
Lesberg, Jack (bass) 56, 68, 82, 109, 119-120, 138-139, 143, 149, 171, 186, 205, 221, 227, 233, 242, 247, 253-254, 266, 271, 275, 280, 289, 291-292, 309, 316, 319, 320
Lesberg, Linda 316
Levermore, Jim 270-271
Levin, Floyd 300-301
Levine, Ed 178-179
Lewis, Meade Lux (piano) 112, 186, 254, 339
Liepolt, Horst 257
Lindgreen, Ole (Fessor) (trombone) 254
Lipskin, Mike (piano) 284
Livesay, Bob 223-225, 313-314
Livesay, Hazel 223-225, 313
Lodice, Charlie (drums) 84
London House 6, 93, 98-99, 210, 320
Loney, Jim 281
Loney, Olive 281
Louis, Joe 175

Mackay, Bill 232
Mackay, Bill, Jr. 232
MacPherson, William A. 130-132, 161, 201
Mades, Theodore (Tot) 21
Mang, Herman J. 33
Manning, Terry Curtis 103, 126

Mark Hopkins Hotel 95, 113
Marshall, Eddie (drums) 284
Martin, Freddy 52-53
Martin, Pepper 21
Martin, Sara 196
Martucci, Dante (bass) 109
Masso, George (trombone) 214-215, 230, 243-244, 247, 264, 273, 280, 289, 292, 303
Matarese's Restaurant 84
Matlock, Matty (clarinet) 186
Maxted, Billy (piano) 186
Maybeck Recital Hall 335
Mayl, Gene (bass) 231
McBride, Doc 232
McCorriston, Dorothy 159-160
McCorriston, Dottie Gale 160
McCorriston, Hugh 159-160
McCorriston, Mary 160
McCorriston, Sheila 159-160
McGarity, Lou (trombone) 136, 149, 150, 152, 179, 339
McGhee, Howard (trumpet) 314
McGill, John 110-111
McKenna, Dave (piano) 140, 252, 254, 306, 318
McKenzie, Red (singer) 57, 74
McLeod, Norman 66
McPartland, Jimmy (trumpet) 64, 339
McRae, Barry 80
McShann, Jay (piano) 6, 245-247, 250-253, 256, 261, 263-264, 283-284, 308, 316
Meadowbrook ballroom 336
Medwick, Joe 21
Menees, Charlie 62-63
Merry-Go-Round Room 51-52
Mid-America Jazz Festival 8, 55, 264-265, 266-267, 270, 277, 307-308, 310
Midland Jazz Classic 280, 318, 319
Miles, Butch (drums) 259, 316, 321-322, 339
Miller, Eddie (tenor sax) 230, 246, 264, 339

Miller, Glenn (trombone) 64, 210, 217
Miller, Mark 272
Mince, Johnny (clarinet) 247, 264
Minton, Doodles 176
Mission Mountain Wood Band 197-198
Mississippi Rag, The 202-204, 287
Montaubon Jazz Festival 301-302
Monterey Jazz Festival 108
Montgomery, Buddy (piano) 113
Montreal Restaurant Bistro 282
Moody, James (tenor sax) 259
Mopsick, Don (bass) 306, 338
Morley, Jane 200
Morley, Thomas J. 200
Morning Air Ranch 8, 173, 213, 226, 237, 253, 262, 270, 285, 332, 335
Morrison, Barry 212
Morton, Bennie (trombone) 64, 167, 184, 189, 199
Morton, Jelly Roll (piano, composer) 77, 95, 249, 267, 312
Moss, Danny (tenor sax) 139
Mr. Kelly's 194-195, 197-198, 200
Muhm, Verna 23, 134
Müller, Peter (clarinet) 302
Murphy, Turk (trombone) 95, 104, 202, 203, 277
Music Was Not Enough 171
Muschany, Barbara 134
Muschany, Claude 16, 17, 30
Muschany, Don 26
Muschany, J.C. 22-23
Muschany, Morris 17
Muschany, Norman K. 15-16, 17, 21-22, 26-27, 29-30, 36, 71, 99-100, 134

Nance, Ray (trumpet, violin) 108
Navarre, The 145-146, 151, 157, 162-163, 173, 193, 205-206, 227
New Hampshire, University of 283
Newsom, Tommy (tenor sax) 214
Nicholas, Albert (clarinet) 58, 60-61, 63
Nichols, Catherine 302
Nichols, Madeleine 302-303

Nine Greats of Jazz 151
Nixon, Richard M. 167
Norris, John 256, 310-311, 326
Northern Hotel 228-233, 241, 253, 256
Norvo, Red (vibes) 95
Nygren, Shireen 269

O'Brian, Helen 73
Odessa Jazz Festival 124, 206, 213, 215, 253, 273, 283, 321, 322, 325, 326, 335
Ohms, Freddy, (trombone) 64
Oliver, Eddie 122
Oliver, King (cornet) 128, 267, 338
Oram, George 223
Oriental Theater 59
Ory, Kid (trombone) 254
Oscar Klein International Chicago Jazz Orchestra 314
Oxford Hotel 208

Page, Drew 53
Page, Lips (trumpet) 55, 64, 84, 88
Page, Walter (bass) 84, 88, 229
Palmer, Jack 57, 131
Palmer, Jimmy (Dancin' Shoes) (trumpet) 123
Paradise Valley Jazz Party 295
Parenti, Tony (clarinet) 75, 109
Park Plaza Hotel 49, 51-52
Parker, Charlie (alto sax) 312
Payne, Wilbur G. 63
Pearl, Mary (piano) 102-103
Peninsula Jazz Party 273
Pensacola Jazz Party 294
Peplowski, Ken (clarinet) 289, 325, 328-329, 339
Pesci, Pete 64, 67, 109
Peters, Helle (drums) 302
Peterson, Charles 73-74
Peterson, Debbie 203
Peterson, Don 73-74
Peterson, Harney 98-99
Philippi, Hans 81

Phillips, Flip (tenor sax) 255, 259, 263, 275, 292, 319
"Piano Playhouse" 65
Piano rolls 241
Pied Pipers 221, 247, 266
Pinkstaff, Marie 133
Pinkstaff, Virgil 133
Pittsley, Mike (trombone) 269
Pizza Express 312-313
Pizzarelli, Bucky (guitar) 206-207, 259, 338
Pizzarelli, John, Jr. (guitar) 207
Placer Inn 121
Plantation Club 62
Plattner, Christian (clarinet) 280
Podewell, Polly (singer) 289
Polain, Bill (drums) 285
Polcer, Ed (cornet) 215-216, 275, 289, 339
Pozzi, Giovanni 81
Previn, Andre (piano) 95
Priest, Rich 172-173, 179
Priest, Sylvia 172-173
Priestley, Bill 178
Priestley, Brian 6
Priestley, Crick 178
Prima, Louis (trumpet) 122
Profoundly Blue 265
Pruett, Hubert S. 54-55, 134-135
Pump and Derrick 173, 205

Race, Steve 80
Ragtime 43, 58, 90-91, 108-109
Railhead, The 267-268
Rainbow Grill 132-133
Razaf, Andy 339
Reasoner, Harry 250-251
Rebmann, Rolf (drums) 243
Redfield, Jan 315-316
Reich, Bill 45-46, 98
Reich, Marilyn 98
Reich, Tom 98
Reid, Dottie (singer) 43-44
Reinhart, Randy (trumpet, trombone) 306

Rey, Alvino (guitar) 49
Reynolds, Tommy (clarinet) 82
Reznikoff, Genevieve 71-72
Reznikoff, Mischa 71-72
Rich, Buddy (drums) 242
Rick's 250-251, 256
Riverboat Room 151, 154-155
Roberts, Luckey (piano) 241, 326
Robinson, Jackie 175
Robison, Willard 131, 158, 241, 243, 272, 311-312, 331
Roden, Tom 124
Rogers, Shorty (trumpet) 249
Rohloff, Kristy 238-240
Roosevelt, Franklin D. 32
Roosevelt Grill 176
Roscoe, Connie 179
Rose, Wally (piano) 58, 109
Rosengarden, Bobby (drums) 185, 247
Rowles, Jimmy (piano) 254
Royal, Marshall (alto sax) 292
Royal Festival Hall 79
Rubin, Charlotte 145, 160
Rubin, Harry 145, 160
Rushing, Jimmy (singer) 107-108, 113, 314, 331
Russell, Pee Wee (clarinet) 68, 74, 135
Ruth, Babe 175
Ryan's, Jimmy 57, 60, 65
Ryker, Virginia 35

Salas, Freddy (tenor sax, soprano sax) 306
Sample, Joe 227-230, 233, 287, 337
Sample, Miriam 227, 230, 287
Sande, Earl 175
Sandke, Randy (trumpet) 289, 292, 322, 325, 339
Santa Fe Jazz Party 302
Say When Club 74
Scher, Zeke 255
Schierbaum, Clifford 13
Schierbaum, Emmett 13, 15
Schirmer, Joe (guitar, banjo) 48-55, 133-134, 339

Schlegl, Emmy 260
Schmidli, Peter (guitar) 243
Schneider, David 15, 33
Schneider, Eric (tenor sax) 259
Schreiber, Carl 122
Schroeder, Gene (piano) 69, 74, 76, 82, 88, 140
Schweizerhof, Hotel 265
Schwimmer, Mike (washboard) 177-178
Scobey, Bob (trumpet) 93-94, 101, 105, 267
Second Line, The 10
Segovia, Andrés 331
Selchow, Manfred 265-266, 280, 302
Selchow, Renate 265-266, 280
Sellers, Roger (drums) 279
Shaffer, Sam (drums) 284
Shaughnessy, Eddie (drums) 56
Shearing, George (piano) 182, 248
Sheldon, Jack (trumpet) 315
Sheraton Denver Airport Hotel 213, 216
Sheraton-Gibson Hotel 110-112
Sheraton-Jefferson Hotel 102
Sheridan, John (piano, arranger) 267-270, 277, 294-295, 306, 338, 339
Silver, Horace (piano) 312
Simeon, Omer (clarinet) 84
Simkins, Benny (tenor sax) 217
Simkins, Geoff (alto sax) 217
Simkins, Pete (piano) 217-218
Simmen, Johnny 81, 186, 243, 254-255, 302, 316, 335, 337
Simmen, Liza 81, 243, 302
Sims, Zoot (tenor sax) 206, 339
Singleton, Zutty (drums) 242, 312
Singular, Stephen 263
"60 Minutes" 250-251
Slaughter, Enos 21
Smith, Carrie (singer) 280
Smith, Willie the Lion (piano) 64, 70, 74, 81, 82, 94, 102, 106, 109, 113, 165, 184-186, 212, 221, 226, 241, 254, 272, 317, 326, 339
Snyder, Curtis 29-30

Index

Snyder, Olive 29-30
Southern Oregon Traditional Jazz Society 283
Spanier, Muggsy (cornet) 94, 114, 117
Spargo, Tony (drums) 75
Squaw Valley Lodge 101-106, 112
Stacy, Jess (piano) 1, 95, 169, 183, 185, 241, 265
Statiras, Gus 294-295
Staub, August W. 10
Stein, Lou (piano) 140, 152, 222
Stern, Jack (bass) 49-53
Stewart, Anne (see Davison, Anne)
Stewart, Slam (bass) 312
Storyville 93
Strayhorn, Billy (arranger, composer) 312
Stride piano 9, 200
Stride Piano Summit 284
Sugar Hill 107
Sullivan, Joe (piano) 1, 52, 63, 140, 169, 183-184, 241, 319
Sullivan, Maxine (singer) 60-61, 184, 208, 217, 339
Summit Jazz 267, 338
Sunnie's Rendezvous 120, 123-124, 126-131, 133, 136-145, 147-149, 156-157, 164, 179, 235, 246, 290
Sutton, Alexander 332
Sutton, Amanda 330
Sutton, Barbara (see Curtis, Barbara Sutton)
Sutton, Beth 25
Sutton, Charline (Chuck) 54, 64, 71-72, 85, 89, 93, 96-97, 113, 124-127
Sutton, Clare 270, 332
Sutton, Doreen 330
Sutton, Earl S. 15-17, 19, 20-21, 25, 26, 27, 28-29, 30, 35, 37, 38, 133, 211
Sutton, Edna S. 15-16, 19, 22, 25-26, 29, 36, 133, 225
Sutton, Harold 15, 16-17, 25, 29, 37
Sutton, Janice 17, 18, 26, 29
Sutton, Jean 332-333
Sutton, Jeff 54, 64, 72, 85, 97, 126, 128-129, 211, 330-331, 333
Sutton, Laura 332
Sutton, Madeline 332
Sutton, Nathan 270, 331-332
Sutton, Nick 54, 65, 85, 89, 97, 101-102, 114, 126, 128, 211-212, 330, 332-333
Sutton, Nicole 332-333
Sutton, Pete 7, 54, 65, 85, 97, 113, 126, 128, 211, 270, 311, 330-333
Sutton, Ralph Lionel 309
Sutton, Spencer 332-333
Sutton, Sunnie 2-3, 5, 7-8, 120-131, 135-149, 154, 156, 157, 159-165, 170, 172, 173, 179, 191-194, 197, 205-206, 208-213, 221-222, 225-226, 230, 233, 237-240, 241, 243, 244, 246, 247-248, 250-251, 253, 256, 258-259, 262, 263, 265-266, 270, 271, 273, 274-275, 285-287, 290-293, 305, 308, 314-316, 317, 318, 325, 326, 330-333, 334-335, 337
Sutton, Tara 330
Swain, Bobby 51
Symphony Hall 88-89

"Talent Scouts, Arthur Godfrey's" 28
Tate, Buddy (tenor sax) 259
Tatum, Art (piano) 29, 46, 83, 87, 94, 97, 102, 148, 164, 219, 254, 295, 312, 329
Teagarden, Addie 43
Teagarden, Jack (trombone) 1, 41-42, 43-44, 47, 55-57, 62, 64, 94, 102, 117, 119, 141, 261, 269, 304, 320, 331
Teagarden, Norma (piano) 269
Ten Greats of Jazz 7, 151, 156, 304
Terbois, Catherine, 222
Terbois, Pierre 221-222
Terry, Clark (trumpet, flugelhorn) 62, 275, 314
Theobold, John 61, 66, 88, 197
They All Played Ragtime 58, 108
"This Is Jazz" 58-59, 108
Thomas, Dave 112
Thompson, Butch (piano) 202-204

389

Thompson, Sir Charles (piano) 314
Thomson, Virgil 75-76
Those Ragtime Years 108
Thunderbird Lodge 258-260, 303, 316
Thurber, James 72
Tobin, Louise (singer) 212
Tommy Loy's Upper Dallas Jazz Band 267
Tompkins, Ross (piano) 259
"Tonight Show, The" 132, 153
Torff, Brian (bass) 259, 304
Tough, Dave (drums) 312
Town Hall 88-89, 222, 295
Toyama, Yoshio (trumpet) 303
Traill, Mips 80, 169
Traill, Sinclair 79-80, 169, 253
Trappier, Arthur (drums) 60-61, 63, 267
Travis, Dempsey J. 5
Tremble Kids 243
Triangle Jazz Party 288-290, 304
Triangle Jazz Party Boys 290
Trocadero ballroom 150-152
Tune Town Ballroom 55-56
Turner, Joe (piano) 81, 254

Vaché, Allan (clarinet) 339
Vaché, Warren, Jr. (cornet) 259-260, 289, 300, 303, 316, 323, 339
Vaché, Warren, Sr. (bass) 5, 312, 323
Van Eps, George (guitar) 222
Van Vorst, Paige 203-204
Venuti, Joe (violin) 223, 339
Village Inn 48
Village Vanguard 51, 60-61
Vince Giordano's Nighthawks 277
Vine, Johnny (drums) 84

Waller, C.W. (Chili) 124
Waller, Fats (piano) 1, 10, 19-20, 25, 49, 57, 76, 77, 80, 82, 84, 94, 95, 97, 102, 105, 106, 109, 110-111, 113, 114, 133, 141, 148, 160, 164, 169, 170, 174-176, 181, 184-186, 196, 197, 205, 209, 210, 212, 215, 224, 234, 238, 240-241, 246, 247, 251-252, 254, 260, 261, 278, 280, 284, 287, 295, 301, 302, 304, 313, 314, 317, 319, 320, 322, 326, 336-337, 339
Waller, Maurice 174-175, 196
Waller, Ronald 174-175
Ware, Munn (trombone) 84
Waterloo Village Jazz Festival 266
Watkins, Earl (drums) 95
We Called It Music 56
Webb, Chick (drums) 249, 254
Webster, Ben (tenor sax) 108, 113, 157, 173, 331
Webster, Derek 171
Weems, Ted 122-123
Wellington Jazz Club 278, 309
Wells, Charlie 55-56
Wellstood, Dianne 274
Wellstood, Dick (piano) 108, 222, 245, 247, 252, 254, 273-277, 280, 295, 320, 339
Wettling, George (drums) 110, 242
Weyrauch, Elmer 28
Weyrauch, Marguerite 28
Weyrauch, Virginia 28
White, Al 276
White, Ann 276
Wickham, Wally (bass) 270
Widder Bar 265
Wideröe, Arild 309-310
Wiggins, Gerald (piano) 259
Wilber, Beth 173-174
Wilber, Bob (clarinet, soprano sax) 2, 64, 130, 141, 151, 153, 167-168, 170, 171-173, 182-183, 189, 194, 200, 210
Wilber, Rickie 172-173
Wiley, Lee (singer) 60
Willard Robison and His Piano: A Discography 311
Williams, Beatrice 278-279
Williams, Clarence (piano, composer, arranger) 175
Williams, Claude (Fiddler) (violin) 247
Williams, Jackie (drums) 289, 301
Williams, John 277-278

Index

Williams, Julie 277
Williams, Norman 278-280
Williams, Peter 278
Williams, Roy (trombone) 243-244
Wilmer, Pearl Rehmeier 32
Wilson, John S. 152, 284
Wilson, Teddy (piano) 87, 102, 140, 185, 254, 329
Windhurst, Johnny (trumpet) 56, 64, 72, 83
Winston, George (piano) 232-233
Winter, Bill 162
Winters, Jonathan 173
Wolfe, Bill 306-308
Wonder, Stevie (piano) 179-180
Woodyard, Sam (drums) 108
World's Greatest Jazzband 1-4, 6-7, 142, 147, 148, 151-156, 159, 162-163, 166-172, 174, 176, 177, 178, 179, 180, 181-186, 187-190, 194-195, 197-201, 206, 208-218, 235, 242, 294, 304, 311, 317, 338-339
Wright, Laurie 196, 301-302
Wrightsman, Stan (piano) 246
Wynn, Ken 87

"Yesterday Shop" 177-178
Young, Snookie (trumpet) 292
Young, Trummy (trombone) 275, 310, 339

Zettl, Herbert L. 97
Zeyen, Barbara 15
Zeyen, Nicholas 15, 25, 29
Zeyen, Pete 20
Zurke, Bob (piano) 1, 52, 95, 183-184, 241, 254